The Property Management Tool Kit

THE PROPERTY MANAGEMENT TOOL KIT

Mike Beirne

ΛMΛCOM

American Management Association

New York • Atlanta • Brussels • Chicago • Mexico City • San Francisco
Shanghai • Tokyo • Toronto • Washington, D.C.

Special discounts on bulk quantities of AMACOM books are
available to corporations, professional associations, and other
organizations. For details, contact Special Sales Department,
AMACOM, a division of American Management Association,
1601 Broadway, New York, NY 10019.
Tel.: 212-903-8316. Fax: 212-903-8083.
Website: www.amacombooks.org

This publication is designed to provide accurate and authoritative
information in regard to the subject matter covered. It is sold with the
understanding that the publisher is not engaged in rendering legal,
accounting, or other professional service. If legal advice or other expert
assistance is required, the services of a competent professional person
should be sought.

The stories and examples used in this book are general compilations of
events and stories that we have heard about or experienced in more than
25 years in the real estate profession. They are structured to illustrate
specific teaching points. Any resemblance to actual events or persons is
coincidental. In other words, if you think we are talking about you, we
aren't.

Library of Congress Cataloging-in-Publication Data

Beirne, Mike.
    The property management tool kit / Mike Beirne.
        p.   cm.
    Includes index.
    ISBN-13: 978-0-8144-7351-1
    ISBN-10: 0-8144-7351-2
    1. Real estate management—United States—Handbooks, manuals, etc. 2. Rental
housing—United States—Handbooks, manuals, etc.   3. Real estate investment—United
States—Handbooks, manuals, etc.   4. Real estate management.   I. Title.

    HD1394.5.U6B45   2006
    333.5068—dc22   2006015401

Printing number

10   9   8   7   6   5   4   3   2   1

To Nicole Huber-Vogl, who taught me the light is always there. . . .

To Sandra Johnson for showing me all the colors in that spectrum of light. . . .

To my daughters, Marisa and Meredith, that
they see always all those colors. . . .

To my mother, Virginia, whose light burned out
too soon to see this book come to fruition.

Contents

Acknowledgments

No effort in business or life is ever achieved without the support and encouragement of others who willingly give unselfishly of themselves. I've been fortunate to have many people assist me in putting over two decades of my experiences into a format where I could return the favor and share what I have learned with those embarking on their own journey into investment and management.

I want to thank first and foremost Sandra F. Johnson, my personal editor and most valued business adviser. Without her input and willingness to challenge me, I would not have been able to accomplish this project. She is a true professional and a true friend.

As someone who has been blessed with the opportunity and experience to excel in my field, I recognize that role models have everything to do with the future maturation of the professional. For this reason, I would like to thank my two business and life role models: Mr. Don Benson, who taught me how to communicate in a very personal way with others in my field and respect what they achieve; and Mr. Richard Kurtz, for helping me understand that continuing to trust and appreciate people can grow an organization and create a lifetime of friendships, even when most people in business do not think that is possible. He showed me that carrying yourself with class and integrity, no matter what the circumstances, is a lifestyle.

Let me extend thanks to my father, whose respect for team and integrity through his military experiences has everything to do with the way I choose to manage.

Many professionals served as technical advisers in this endeavor. My hat's off to Dr. Jeanne Gorman, David Legow, Jason Eifert, Rob Petersen, Steve Hervatic, and Debra Maron. To my acquisitions editor, Christina Parisi, who set the sails in the right direction and helped correct the rudder. To my wife, Shari, who kept the kids out of the house every weekend for months so I could finish this project.

Finally, a sincere thank-you to all those I have had the privilege of dealing with every day of my career, people like Rosemarie, Jean, Dave, Jeff, Adele, Steve, Deb, Carmella, and all those I haven't mentioned. At all levels of the property management experience I find common themes with those who do the work every day. They are unselfish, hardworking, and true in their personae, and I am very lucky to have had their assistance and friendships throughout my years in this business. This is an industry full of truly special people.

The Property Management Tool Kit

Introduction

In the more than 20 years I've been in the business, I have been struck continually at how investors in multifamily real estate often do not have a firm grasp of how property management can vastly improve the *value* of the real estate. In many instances, property management is treated as a "necessary evil." If the business and art of property management is truly married with the investment, it can have a tremendous effect on the bottom line, and it's equally true that when it is minimized or ignored, the negative effect can be just as immense.

In this book I show how property management is a fundamental part of a real estate investment strategy and how you can exploit the concept so that you can increase the value of your investments. To help you get started, I provide some of the "tools of the trade" and explain how to use them. I don't lay out *investment* strategies, but rather sound *management* strategies to protect and grow those investments by constantly searching out and adding value to the real estate.

Property management is not a difficult concept. At its core, it is about managing details and having the discipline to carry out and review the details. But more important, property management is people management. Whether you choose to only dabble in real estate or grow an investment portfolio, you will need to know how to communicate with and listen to the people you rely on in your physical absence and the people you rent to, because in the end they become your success or failure. People are your best asset. Whether you decide to allow someone else to manage or you end up stewarding a management team yourself, the key to success is understanding how to communicate and how to interpret information and delegate tasks.

It's incredibly satisfying to enter a community I have helped develop when I know that the people who reside there, and those who own and manage there, are proud to call this apartment community their home. You can succeed financially and leave a lasting, positive impression on people, and it doesn't have to be a difficult process. Most of all, as an investor, learn to understand and utilize the profession of property management to its fullest extent, because it is not a necessary evil; it is your vehicle to larger success.

CHAPTER 1

The Investment

Sizing Up the Possibilities and Probabilities

Property management is the practice of growing the intrinsic value of the asset while paying down the financing by operating the property on rental income. The goal should be that the property operates strictly from the *cash flow,* or income minus expenses, including any financing costs such as interest and principal. For this reason, you should consider whether a particular rental property makes sense in terms of achieving value and positive cash flow goals before you buy.

Another reason that investors are attracted to real estate as an investment is that the federal government has provided tax incentives that can add to the bottom line. As an owner of property, you are permitted to deduct operating expenses, thereby defraying the actual taxable income and your tax liability. The government also allows deductions for *depreciation*. Depreciation is an accounting practice whereby you are allowed to deduct a calculated proportion of your property's value over a period of time, since property and its main components suffer wear and tear over the years. While these two tax advantages make rental property investment attractive, they should not be the main reasons that you decide to invest. Although operating expenses are deductible, the goal is to operate any business at a profit, so counting on expenses to defray the bottom line means the business may not be operating efficiently. While the deduction for depreciation is a positive, it is minimal on a yearly basis when looking at the overall decision to make a long-term investment.

Rental real estate can be an enormously satisfying and financially rewarding endeavor. If you enter into the market knowing what you want to achieve and what it takes to operate an investment over time, there are very few long-term investments that appreciate in value and pay a consistent return on investment (ROI) like rental property.

Understand How the Characteristics of an Investment Affect Income

When evaluating rental investments, there are a number of property characteristics that you should keep in mind. Some of the most important factors affecting income are:

❑ *Layout.* Most apartment-unit layouts are predetermined, so if you buy a 100-unit apartment complex with 50 one-bedrooms and 50 two-bedrooms, that's the layout you are likely to be stuck with.

Commercial rentals are another matter. Often they can be partitioned any way the physical building structure will allow, so the number and type of renters can change over time. If you can change the layout, you can increase your income.

❑ *Rental Basis.* Rent rates in apartments are described as "per unit." You pay a specific rental fee for a specific type of unit.

Commercial rents are usually calculated as the number of square feet times a negotiated per-square-foot price. Because the size of the commercial rental space can change based on the tenant, often the interior can be redesigned and partitioned to accommodate different types of businesses and the same size space can be occupied by multiple renters.

❑ *Marketing.* Apartment units are marketed and rented through a very structured process. The marketing will state what the unit will possess, how it will be decorated, and who will be responsible for the utilities.

In commercial renting, much of what ends up being part of the lease is negotiated before a renter takes possession of the space. The renter is operating a unique business and therefore layout and financial concerns are part of the process of negotiating a fair deal. How you negotiate these terms will affect your income.

❑ *Ancillary Charges.* Apartment rental rates are predominantly all-inclusive. If there are extra charges, they are for ancillary services (such as a garage rental).

In commercial rental there may be "common area maintenance" (CAM) charges, which are proportionally charged to the renter in addition to rent.

❑ *Length of Lease.* Apartment lease terms can be extended for years but are usually short term, either month to month or for a single year.

Commercial space is usually rented with a multiyear lease because it involves capital investment up front for both the owner of the property and the business looking to rent. The return is realized with a long-term occupant.

❑ *Responsibilities.* Responsibilities in apartment renting should be clearly laid out and apply consistently to all who rent in the community. Responsibilities in commercial renting can vary among renters within the same building. Again, all responsibilities are negotiated.

❑ *Lease Enforcement.* Many local municipalities and states have separate rules for enforcing residential and commercial lease terms, such as rent not paid; others have identical rules. If the process is lengthy and requires legal fees, lease enforcement will cut into your profits.

❑ *Lease Liability.* Apartments are rented to individuals and their fellow occupants. The rental is solely for the possession of the leaseholder.

Commercial renting involves renting to a business entity, and businesses are commonly bought and sold. It is important for the owner of commercial space to factor this possibility into a lease and have provisions to keep the lease enforceable no matter who owns the business. This concept and lease provision is what is called *assignment.*

❑ *Utility Costs.* Apartments are structured such that utility costs are "common" among the different renters. Certain utilities are included with rent and others aren't, but each renter usually has the same deal.

In commercial space, each business has specific requirements unique to its operation. A restaurant, for instance, will use a lot more fuel and electricity than a card store. Even if there are multiple renters in the same property, each commercial rental's utility costs may be different.

Financing

In addition to operating considerations, there are other factors that will directly affect your bottom line. For example, how will the purchase be financed? Will you finance it through a conventional lending source (a bank), or will you negotiate with the present owners to have them finance the deal? Will you use secondary sources of capital to reduce the need for heavy financing? Obviously the more cash invested, the lower the mortgage payment, based on an equivalent interest rate. The lower the payment, the more flexibility you have with the term of the loan.

The shorter the term of the loan, the quicker your *equity* position, or the strength of your ownership piece, grows and the sooner the investment becomes free of debt. Often institutional lenders can and will require some say or control over how a property is being managed. There are often financial goals that have to be met and constraints on how some dollars will be spent, since some money has to be dedicated to capital improvements over the years.

Many institutional lenders also have requirements about environmental issues. As a condition of sale, they may require certain aspects of the property be changed immediately, such as removing oil tanks or removing all asbestos-based materials or lead-based paint from a property. They may also implement operations and maintenance (O&M) programs in order to monitor and manage sensitive environmental issues over and above what is required by local, state, and federal law.

There are also options for third-party purchases, such as forming a partnership. If, as an investor, you are the primary interest in a piece of real estate, forming partnerships and gaining partners defrays your up-front costs. The obvious concerns for this type of arrangement are that to gain the investment dollars, there has to be an obligation to pay these investors a return. This limits the size of the return to you, the primary investor. It is also important in this arrangement that you make sure the controlling interest in this investment remains with you. The other investors must be "limited" in their ability to operate the investment. Otherwise it is not your investment. What some investors do over time is promise a payback of the original investment plus a suitable return, after which the percentage of ownership and control becomes stronger for the primary investor.

Other third-party programs are available, too, such as Section 8 programs, which are federal- and state-subsidized housing. With these programs a portion of each occupant's rent is guaranteed by the governmental agency over the course of a lease. What is important to understand, though, is that these types of loans and programs permit the third party (the government) substantial say in how the properties are operated on a daily basis. There are rigorous reporting requirements and a specific set of renting guidelines, the most serious of which govern the ability to raise rents. In recent years, Section 8 funding has been drastically cut and therefore the governing bodies of these agencies have restricted rent increases on renewal. If you decide to make this kind of purchase, it may be difficult to project income because the rents over the years may turn out to be far less than expected.

■ Assess Management Needs, Self or Fee Managed

The best time to decide whether you will manage the investment yourself or contract a management company is before the purchase is actually made. Part of making a proper investment decision is being thorough in the process of reviewing the pluses and minuses of a potential purchase.

Ask yourself these key questions:

☐ Do you feel confident in your ability to understand what makes a successful investment decision with income-producing real estate?

☐ Do you understand how and what it takes to operate that investment on a daily basis?

If this is an initial investment in real estate, it's more than likely going to be smaller in scale and the investor is going to have (and remain in) a full-time job. Maybe you think the property isn't large enough to support staff. If you want to attempt to manage your new property independently, then make sure you are honest with yourself. As property manager, you'll need to understand many different disciplines. Remember, no matter how small the property, the manager is now running a community.

Just like any community, there are mechanical issues, financial issues, marketing concerns, and regulatory requirements. Most important, if we are talking about multifamily housing, then, as the manager, you will be dealing with people's homes. Whenever dealing with something so personal, emotions can run high. The manager has to be a very adept "people person" capable of communicating effectively all the time. You must understand that the residents are going to view their situations as personal, even though, as a manager, you are running a business.

If you are trying to decide whether to self-manage your new property, first ask yourself whether you possess the traits that are absolutely necessary for success:

☐ *Diplomacy.* A manager must be comfortable communicating with people on emotional issues; diplomacy becomes a very important skill.

☐ *Sales Skills.* Sales skills are a must. More often than not, the seller is what draws the prospective resident into consummating the deal.

☐ *Ability to Handle Details.* Property management requires attention to detail. The little things do matter. Remember, your investment is someone else's home.

☐ *Organizational Skills.* Property management involves review and follow-up on many issues, so organizational skills are absolutely essential.

☐ *Administrative Skills.* If paperwork bothers you, then property management probably will too, because careful documentation is required.

❏ *Resourcefulness.* Being analytical is helpful because there is an answer to virtually every problem that occurs in property management. Logically reviewing a problem often reveals a simple answer.

❏ *Ability to Be Proactive.* Situational awareness can be a very useful trait. Often a problem is brewing, but if a manager is proactive, then a much more serious problem can be avoided.

❏ *Mechanical Skills.* Basic mechanical skills are a plus. The manager may not be able to fix everything that breaks, but knowing what isn't working correctly and being able to understand what a contractor might do can save money.

❏ *Discipline.* Much of the manager's work is repetitive, and it must be timely. Creating a structured schedule of daily and monthly events simplifies the process and ensures necessary jobs are carried out regularly.

❏ *Self-Awareness.* Knowing your weaknesses is a key to success! Because managers must handle many different disciplines, the ability to understand what you don't know becomes critical. Sometimes a lawyer is needed, or a plumber, or a rental specialist. Many owners make the mistake of insisting on doing it all alone and end up paying financially for not understanding the depth of a problem. Even the most experienced managers in the business don't understand some concepts and bring in professionals.

If, as a would-be investor, you possess a substantial portion of these skills, then the decision may be to self-manage your property investment. But there are some other factors to take into consideration. Managing a property can be time-consuming. Preparing a newly vacated apartment for rental can take several days. A mechanical problem could take many hours or days to correct. Going to court for a resident problem may consume a whole day at the courthouse.

The two most mentally taxing issues a manager will deal with are 1) the uncertainty of events and 2) the psychological, stereotypical view many people have of property owners/managers. On the first issue, managing a community where people live is a twenty-four-hour-a-day, seven-day-a-week operation. Events can and do take place without regard to day and time. The police could be summoned to an altercation at two in the morning, a fire can occur on a holiday, and a mechanical failure can take place at the most inconvenient time.

A manager has to be prepared to deal with what happens, when it happens. A good example is a blizzard. Even when the authorities are telling everyone to stay inside their homes, a property manager needs to assume responsibility for a community. As bad as the weather is, the property manager and staff must be out there making the community safe for the residents in the bad weather.

In regard to the second issue, the term *landlord* often carries with it a negative stigma. Whether the stereotype is fair or not, many people view a manager or an owner as an authority figure who rarely has good news. The average renter hears from the manager either when he has done something wrong or when something is broken. The successful manager learns how to shoulder criticism and becomes proactive about communicating with residents in a diplomatic and positive light. A positive personal disposition can certainly be a useful trait for a manager.

Fee Management

If you've carefully considered all these issues and end up deciding that it may be better to have others manage your property, then the process of picking a management company becomes a very important one. Hiring a company to watch an investment is what is known as *fee management.* There are many different types of fee managers, so one of the first questions you need to ask is: Do the companies being considered specialize in what you are asking them to manage? There are fee managers who specialize in residential properties, others who specialize in commercial real estate, and yet others who specialize in association management.

If you are purchasing a multifamily residential apartment property, then you'll want to choose a company that predominantly operates in this realm. Real estate brokers often market management services, but remember they are predominantly in the business of selling real estate. Their motives for offering management services are often ancillary to their main business. The size of the property management firm is very important, too. If the initial investment is a simple duplex, a large firm may not be advisable. Property managers who are employed by a fee management firm are often assigned a *portfolio,* or group of properties, for which they are primarily responsible.

If your investment is relatively small compared to the other properties the fee-managed organization has responsibility for, then it may not get the attention it deserves. When deciding on a management company, visit the company offices and scrutinize the office operation—remember that property management is all about detail and organization. A management office should reflect that. Obtain a list of properties and clients the management company services; ask for a complete list, not its selected list. Visit the properties listed and talk to the owners of those properties. There are multiple questions you should be asking during this process:

❑ *Licenses.* Is the company properly licensed to be managing real estate? Many states require that real estate broker licenses be held by managers of rental property. Some locations require further certification and licensing. A prospective company should produce proof upon request.

❑ *Certifications.* Do the professionals involved with this organization possess any industry certifications, such as the Institute of Real Estate Management (IREM) certified property manager designation (CPM), or the National Apartment Association (NAA) certified apartment property supervisor (CAPS) designation? Do their employees additionally possess required and industry-accepted certification, such as real estate salesperson licenses or designations such as NAA's certified apartment manager (CAM) or IREM's accredited residential manager (ARM)? Do these professional organizations in fact recognize this management firm?

Additional questions that are equally important to ask are:

❑ How many properties does the company assign to each manager? A manager already watching twenty properties isn't going to watch any more than that effectively.

❑ How does the company collect and manage the money?

❑ Does the company designate individual bank accounts for each entity it manages? Money commingled is hard to account for; your money should be looked after separately.

❑ Is the company properly insured for liability and errors and omissions? The management company should be able to provide proof of insurance and should be willing to name your entity as additionally insured.

❑ How does the company screen employees? Remember, any firm that you hire will be handling your money and going into people's homes; therefore you will want to be comfortable with its security methods. Ask if the company's employees are bonded.

❑ Does the company operate, or has it ever operated, in or near the location and municipality where your investment is located? If not, and the management company doesn't know the area any better than the prospective owner, it may turn out to be the blind leading the blind.

If the answer to these very basic questions is satisfactory it is now time to ask the money questions. The first question to ask is about fee structure. As a property owner, you must decide whether hiring a fee management firm makes economic sense; if the investment is very small, it may not. If it seems to make sense on the surface, then make sure all fee questions are explored. Some companies charge a flat fee or charge by the unit, but the best arrangement is with a company that is willing to be paid a percentage of rent collected (not rent expected). This provides incentives to that company to work for its money. This is not the only fee-based concern. Many companies have fee schedules for certain administrative tasks such as copying and mailing. Another concern should be whether this company has its own maintenance division and if it collects additional charges and fees from a maintenance perspective. Also, some firms keep certain collectible fees such as late fees and mark-ups on credit check fees. These arrangements should be frowned upon. For example, in the instance of late fees, a company might not be as diligent in rent collection if it stands to make money off of late-paying renters.

Management Agreements

If the fee structure is acceptable and all other concerns are investigated, then a management agreement is entered into. There are many facets of a management agreement that should be considered before signing on the dotted line. Here are some considerations that should be part of any management agreement:

❑ The fee structure just discussed should be itemized clearly on any agreement.

❑ The term of this agreement should be comfortable to all parties and the terms under which each party can end the relationship should be clearly spelled out. Beware automatic renewal clauses. A clear end to the term of an agreement allows for clarification of what was expected as opposed to what has happened over the course of an agreement.

❑ How funds are collected and where funds are deposited should be definitive (remember, this firm is handling your money).

❑ The owner of the real estate should always be in charge, so establish spending guidelines for the management firm. Be clear on what and how much it can spend without ownership approval and under what circumstances the management firm needs ownership review before spending. Establish firm financial thresholds that the management company must follow.

❑ Establish firm procedures for rent collection and debt collection that include dates, fees, and who keeps those fees.

❑ Itemize the responsibilities that the management company is expected to under-take. If financial reporting is a concern, then be explicit as to how often you receive reports. If the property has, for example, garages for rent, make sure that responsibility is itemized as well.

Whatever you feel is necessary to make sure you maintain control of your in-vestment property you should require in this agreement. Be leery of "hold harm-less" clauses embedded in these agreements. A management company presumably is a hired, experienced professional organization, so it should take responsibility for all of its actions. Let the management company know that as an owner, you reserve the right to have its records independently audited should the need arise. This rela-tionship should last a long time, so this process should not be one the management firm objects to. If it does, it isn't the right company.

Once you have picked a management company, stay in constant contact with its representatives and visit your property regularly. Property owners make a dangerous mistake if they assume a management company will always handle the property the way they would wish. Like any business, management firms change personnel, and although some of them establish very good internal controls, the people who actu-ally do the work have a lot to do with a property's success or failure. As an owner, don't become removed or detached from what takes place at your investment prop-erty. Many property owners equate success with the money they receive today; however, bad management may satisfy short-term needs at the sacrifice of long-term potential liabilities. An owner who stays engaged will recognize that; those who don't will one day see more money going out of their pocket than into it.

Do Your Market Research

The general goal of any long-term investment is to grow value and get an expected ROI, which is the return based on the original cash investment. The amount of money invested, the amount of financing necessary to complete the deal, and the anticipated return are key factors in what piece of real estate is ultimately purchased. There are other factors that should be taken into account as well. If this is your first investment, it is advisable to buy in a location you are geographically close to and understand. Managing your investment from a distance is an art unto itself, and it can become burdensome and costly if you are a first-time investor. Knowing the town or municipality is also more desirable. While many multihousing regulations and codes are similar, there are nuances to each town and state. In addition, each market is unique. For instance, many New Jersey shore towns are very populated in the summer but empty out in the winter months. If someone thinks he is buying a supposedly year-round investment, this situation could prove disastrous. This is also a good reason to have established a relationship with a local property management firm that knows all those nuances.

When you find a property that seems to be a good bargain with the dollars you have to invest, do some homework on the area and on the property itself. First, identify what seem to be competitors in the local marketplace; a broker can supply a list of comparable properties. Once a list is procured, "shop" the competition—that is, physically go and review the competition and gain information about rents and amenities. Income is the most important variable in a positive rate of return; make sure the anticipated rents are realistic. If the best property in the area is charging $1,000 a month, do not fool yourself into believing $1,500 a month is realistic, even if your property is better. Also, make sure the realistic income supports your expenses. One important question to ask the competition about is vacancy rates, because this information will give you a general sense of the rental market. It is always advisable to factor a reasonable vacancy rate into your income picture. If the area seems to maintain a 5 percent vacancy rate, then it is unreasonable to expect that your investment will have a zero vacancy rate.

The property itself should be scrutinized. Visually there are things that should be reviewed. Are there obvious major defects that will affect the purchase price or that must be taken into account as costs? What does the roof look like, and the pavement? Do the structures look solid? What is the neighborhood like? The surrounding community very much can affect an owner's ability to transform a property or simply operate it. Do the present tenants appear to be responsible, or is it obvious that the insane run the asylum? Many owners believe that the present management can be improved upon, which in many cases is possible. However, sometimes a property or a neighborhood simply isn't going to get better anytime soon, and you shouldn't blind yourself to the fact that transforming the property will take a lot of energy and money. Is the property in a suitable location? People rent for many reasons, but if a property isn't accessible to the renting public or is not convenient to live in, it will be hard to rent.

In general, when first identifying a possible investment property, look at these factors:

❑ Cost to purchase
❑ Cost to maintain and upgrade
❑ Marketability (e.g., is the property rentable?)
❑ Manageability (e.g., will the property be too work intensive?)

If you have satisfied yourself that all of these factors seem realistic, it is time to get down to the facts.

■ Quantify the Value: The Due Diligence Process

When you make an offer, the contract should allow for what is known as *due diligence*. If you involve lenders, they will require many inspections and disclosures about the property and they will most likely have to scrutinize the numbers. But, regardless of whether a mortgagor does or doesn't investigate all aspects of a property, the prospective owner should. The due diligence process is a chance to be a detective of sorts and look at anything and everything you, as the potential buyer, think is pertinent. If a seller limits a buyer from reviewing certain aspects of a property and its operation, the buyer should be suspicious. It doesn't necessarily have to break the deal, but any would-be buyer should have both eyes wide open.

Due diligence has two key components: 1) review of the financial information and tenancy, which constitutes the paperwork stuff; and 2) review of the physical property in detail. If you are not an expert, it is money well spent to get professional help when it comes to either of these issues. It is not advisable to trust what a broker says about financial returns, and it is also not advisable just to trust past numbers, since they can always be manipulated. Proper due diligence looks at both sides of the equation and then the potential buyer can come to his own, much better educated conclusion.

On the paperwork side, past financial statements are a must. Take note of how the previous owner spent money. When were the most expensive aspects of property management last addressed? For example, when was the last time the roof was replaced? If the owner has schedules of replacements, ask for copies. Are the expenses that the previous owner undertook reasonable, and are there areas that a new owner can reasonably improve on? Does the income from the most recent year generally match the advertised rents? Examine the occupancy, note the units listed as vacant, and understand how current the present tenancy is in rent payment. The goal is to understand if the income you'll need is attainable, if the expenses related to this purchase will be reasonable, and if the present resident base is reliable. There is one other thing that a complete review of the paperwork will accomplish: It will allow you to verify what the documents say and compare them to what you see during a detailed site inspection.

Inspecting the property in person is the equivalent of kicking the tires when you purchase a used car. When doing the site inspection portion of the due diligence process, you need to pay special attention to the following:

❑ *Structural Problems*. For example, in the basement, newer reinforcements are noticed supporting the basement structure. It could be that serious foundation or settling problems once existed. This is the time to demand an explanation from the previous owner. The problem could be totally resolved, or maybe it's ongoing. This kind of structural problem can be very costly. Other structural components to inspect are roofs, porches, decks, stairways, and fascia and soffit material.

❑ *Specialized Inspections*. Lenders will almost always require inspections, by licensed professionals, to look for termites, lead-based paint, asbestos, radon, and mold. Oil tanks and septic or sewage treatment facilities, if present, also must be thoroughly inspected, and sometimes fire safety systems, too. Property owners must know their potential liability, and often a buyer can require some remediation or funds credited to take care of these problems since they are vitally important, costly, and could potentially expose the would-be purchaser to extreme liability. Ask the broker for recommended licensed contractors to review this information, or contact a local industry trade organization, such as the local affiliate of the NAA or IREM. Do not attempt to inspect these systems on your own, because they are highly technical and any oversights will cost you dearly.

❑ *Common Areas*. These include parking lots, playgrounds, landscaping, pools, garages, clubhouses, laundry rooms, and storage facilities. There are others, but the key here is that some of these common areas, such as the parking lot and pool, are quite expensive to maintain but they make the property more attractive to renters. Note their condition and factor in what will need to be done to make them marketable and usable.

❑ *Major Operational Systems*. Heating and cooling systems, water treatment and pumping facilities, storm water–pumping facilities, elevators (if present), garbage compactors, electrical mains, intercom systems, camera systems, and lighting should all have operating and maintenance logs. Check them and physically review the equipment against what the logs reflect. These systems may require up-front capital expenditure; they also are recurring costs, so they should be scrutinized in the potential purchase process. It's a good idea to have a property management professional in tow to review these major operational systems if you do not feel confident about your own understanding of the equipment.

❑ *Apartment and Tenancy Inspections*. Each apartment should be reviewed individually, and if the right documentation is available a prospective purchaser can figure out, to the dollar, what the anticipated fix-up costs will be. Bring to the inspection a premade form, such as the one shown in Figure 1-1, that highlights all apartment components. Mark each item that needs replacement or repair. By the time the inspection is finished you'll be able to tabulate anticipated costs. The other part of this inspection is to determine the resident base you'll be inheriting. Remember to take note of vacant units and resident records. Does the number of vacant units on paper match the number found during the on-site inspection? Take note of some of the residents' names and the number of occupants—does this information match the leases and listed occupants? These details will give the buyer a feel for the accuracy (and possibly the honesty) of the previous ownership. Ask the residents questions about how well the property has been maintained and whether there were any significant problems.

The due diligence process is designed to separate reality from the sales pitch so that as a buyer you more fully understand the nature of the purchase. It might also be useful to visit the local municipal building and talk to town officials because they may provide some very important history about the property and the present ownership. Not everything will be discovered in this process, but the more information that is reviewed and taken into account, the better the chances are that the excitement of the purchase will be tempered by the reality of the work ahead and the better you'll be able to forecast what the operating costs and income from your new multifamily property will be.

■ Effectuate the Takeover

The assessments have all gone well and you've made the decision to purchase. As a buyer, you'll want the seller to voluntarily produce several very important pieces of documentation. The following types of documentation are strongly suggested when closing on a property:

❑ *Certified Rent Roll and Security Deposit Reconciliation.* The seller should produce a current rent roll at the time of closing of all units and the location and amounts of each security deposit. The buyer and seller also need to agree on who will be responsible for collecting all delinquent rents and who will keep collected funds (only on delinquency owed at time of closing). The buyer should insist that no resident who paid a security deposit at the time of the move be left without one at the time of closing. Many of the suggested management practices in this book

Figure 1-1. Apartment condition report.

Apartment Condition Report

Complex Name: _____   Apt. #: _____

LIVING ROOM
Walls _____
Ceiling _____
Floor _____
Other _____

DINING ROOM
Walls _____
Ceiling _____
Floor _____
Other _____

KITCHEN
Walls _____
Ceiling _____
Floor _____
Cabinets _____
Formica—Tile _____
Range _____
Refrigerator _____
Dishwasher _____
Disposal—Sink _____
Vent Hood _____
Other _____

HALL
Walls _____
Ceiling _____
Floor _____
Other _____

BEDROOMS
Walls _____
Ceiling _____
Floor _____
Other _____

(continues)

Figure 1-1. Continued.

BATHS
Walls _____
Ceiling _____
Floor _____
Cabinets _____
Formica-Tile _____
Fixtures _____
Tub Enclosure _____
Other _____
CARPET _____
DRAPES _____
BLINDS _____
WINDOWS _____
DOORS _____
SCREENS _____
LIGHT FIXTURES _____
OTHER _____
_____
_____

COMMENTS _____
_____
_____

are not necessarily followed by property owners, but as a buyer, it is important that you insist on this information.

❑ *All Resident Files and Correspondence.* Leases, applications, renewals, maintenance records, and resident correspondence are all necessary. If the seller has a comprehensive renewal list that may be very helpful also.

❑ *Utility Reconciliation.* Make plans prior to closing to have all utilities switched and all meters read, with the assistance of the seller, if necessary. Make it very clear that as a new owner you aren't going to assume past utility liabilities. Make sure you ask for and receive a complete list with the location of all owner-paid utility services and meters. When residents vacate, you also need to know if the utilities are turned over to the ownership; otherwise, these costs can come as a surprise.

❑ *List of All Personal Property.* Many properties come equipped with items that are not fixtures—that is, not permanently affixed to the property. These items might include vehicles, lawn equipment, golf carts, large shop machinery, copy machines, and computers. A full inventory should be presented and a full check against this list should occur.

❑ *Contracts and Service Agreements.* Contracted services can include landscaping, power plant preventive maintenance, security services, porter services, elevator maintenance, garbage collection, telephone services, attorney retainer agreements, laundry facility contracts, utility commodity or transportation agreements, and office equipment leases and contracts. It is important to know which of these agreements are severable and which "run with the land" (i.e., are enforceable upon a change in ownership). You want to be aware of your costs, responsibilities, possible profit centers, and how much flexibility you have during the transition. One very important document to obtain is an insurance certificate. The seller's policy won't cover the new ownership, but it will provide you with all the pertinent information you need to make sure you are insured immediately at closing time.

❑ *Licenses and Permits.* Infrastructure such as boilers and elevators may need operating licenses. Some municipalities require licensing to operate a rental business; still others require that real estate brokers be licensed and that rental agents possess sales licenses. There may be work in progress that requires building permits. Make sure all current licenses and permits are produced at the closing.

❑ *Architectural or Mechanical Drawings.* Detailed drawings will help you understand the building's infrastructure and layout. For instance, in high-rise buildings the valve system for heat and water is vital to the safe and continuing operation of the building. There also may be a need for these drawings in the future and the cost of having them redrawn is very expensive.

In your enthusiasm to enter into a real estate deal, don't overlook these important details. They are key to successful ownership and understanding your property purchase.

Communication with Residents

You have successfully taken over a piece of real estate; now you need to notify your new residents about the turnover. Here are some things you can do:

❑ Pose a letter to residents explaining all pertinent information about the new ownership, rent payment, and goals for the property. (Figure 1-2 is a sample letter.) Do not commit, in writing, to anything you aren't sure you will accomplish.

Figure 1-2. Ownership change notification.

Ownership Change Notification

_____, 2005

Dear Resident:

Please be advised that effective _____, 2005, the new owner of _____
Apartments is _____, LLC.

       EFFECTIVE IMMEDIATELY CURRENT RENTS SHOULD BE
       MADE PAYABLE TO:

       _____ APARTMENTS

       AND MAILED TO:

       _____ Apartments
       _____
       _____

Beginning with the _____ 2005 rent billing, you will receive a monthly rent bill that will
include a coupon and return envelope. Please return the _LOWER SECTION_ of the coupon with your
check in the envelope that will be provided and keep the _UPPER_ section for your records.

Your rent is due on the 1st of each month. In accordance with your current lease, there will be a
twenty-five dollar ($25.00) late charge for rent received after the 5th of the month. Payments must be
received by the 5th of the month, not postmarked by the 5th.

_____ is the managing agent for _____, LLC.

I am the Property Manager, my name is _____, any and all questions can be brought to
my attention. Please feel free to contact me at _____. If am not in, you can speak
to _____, who is the Administrative Assistant, or _____ from the Accounting
Department.

Your anticipated cooperation is greatly appreciated.

Sincerely,

_____
PROPERTY MANAGER

LLC D/B/A   **Apartments**

APARTMENT # _____

CORRECT SPELLING OF ALL NAMES—PLEASE PRINT

NAME(S) ON LEASE

_____   SOCIAL SECURITY #_____

_____   SOCIAL SECURITY #_____

NAME(S) OF OTHER OCCUPANTS

_____   SOCIAL SECURITY #_____

_____   SOCIAL SECURITY #_____

RENT AMOUNT _____

MOVE-IN DATE _____ LEASE EXPIRATION DATE _____

SECURITY AMOUNT _____

     TENANT SIGNATURE _____

     HOME TELEPHONE # _____

     BUSINESS TELEPHONE # _____

     TENANT SIGNATURE _____

     BUSINESS TELEPHONE # _____

AUTO INFORMATION:
MAKE & MODEL _____

LICENSE PLATE NO. _____ YEAR _____

IN CASE OF EMERGENCY:

     CONTACT _____ TELEPHONE # _____

RETURN TO:

_____

_____

_____

❑ Send with this letter a new resident information sheet asking the residents for the names of all occupants, car tag numbers and the vehicle make and model, emergency phone numbers, and anything else that might aid in the understanding of the residents. From the day you take over, the occupants of the property should be called residents, not tenants, and the property should be referred to as a community, not apartments. Encouraging a sense of belonging to a community and demonstrating your respect for the residents will allow you, as the new owner, to gain more of their participation in making the community operate to your ownership expectation. It also starts fostering residents' belief in the community so that they'll recommend it to friends.

❑ Inspect each apartment at this time, too, with the goal of personally meeting the residents. Introducing yourself to your residents can break down misperceptions and teach you about the good and bad in your community.

❑ Prepare a new lease and new rules and regulations, if possible. Check the local regulations, though. With existing residents it may not be possible to immediately change the lease; instead, it may need to be done at renewal. Unless the previous ownership's lease paperwork was completely acceptable, it is advisable to effect this change as soon as possible.

Vendors should also be contacted right away so they can be told who is authorized to purchase and who is not. Where at all possible, make sure the vendors are put on notice that they will stay with a property by performing up to new ownership expectations.

Finally, if you inherit employees along with the property, make it clear on the date of possession what your intentions are in regard to their employment. If you intend to reduce staff, then tell them and possibly provide financial incentives to those you will let go to get their cooperation. If you intend to provide a probationary period, be clear on that, too. The worst thing a new owner can do is alienate the new staff before beginning to operate. Any new owner will need their input in starting operations, and even if their input becomes bad advice, it adds to a complete understanding of the property.

Effective management of a real estate investment starts with managing the purchase and the turnover and making sure investors know what they are buying. Fully educating yourself at purchase is essential. It is property management in action before an investment is owned!

◼ "From New Jersey to Topeka"

Any property can seem to be a bargain and might even have temporary financially redeeming qualities. However, if you "leap before you look," it may in fact be a liability in disguise. I once worked for an ownership that truly worked the "art of the deal." The owner perused auctions and talked to brokers and received specialized lists for sale, such as Department of Housing and Urban Development (HUD) auctions. This owner would often purchase on the basis of the purchase price and hard expenses, but what he didn't pay much attention to were all the ancillary costs and reasons the purchase may have warts.

The ownership was based out of New Jersey, but the owner had purchased property all over the United States. The properties were often stand-alone purchases, which meant they were not located in a market where the ownership had any other interests. This is one of the first concerns any owner should have: If you don't have any interests in a market, what do you know about that market and how are you going to manage it?

The owner looked for deals—properties in foreclosure or on auction blocks. One such property was found and purchased through these means. It was small compared to the rest of our portfolio, about 100 units. Smaller properties are always harder to operate because you have to rely on limited staff. It was a fully HUD-subsidized property, so all units were under a HUD subsidy contract, which meant that all occupants had to qualify and were renting with federal assistance. This is a more complicated property to run than a conventional rental property. The advantage of such a property is that the subsidized funds are guaranteed by the federal agency. The negative of these properties is the federal oversight on the property and the paperwork connected with that oversight. In essence, it's a much more management-intensive atmosphere for many reasons. My organization at the time only had managed one other HUD-subsidized property. The other factor in buying this property was its location in Topeka, Kansas, which is about a four-hour plane ride from New Jersey. The closest property the ownership had at the time was in Ohio. It would be absolutely necessary to hire reliable on-site management.

The property initially performed well financially, the funds were guaranteed, and the then-president of the organization was making it his responsibility to watch the property from purchase. Sooner or later the president had to tend to new acquisitions and handed the property over to what would be a series of corporate-based managers, none of whom were enthusiastic about managing the property and all of whom never could quite get an understanding of how to operate the property properly. The owner never visited the property and therefore wasn't engaged in what was starting to happen at this property. After a review of current financial statements, the owner understood in his own language that the property was starting to fail financially.

I had developed a knack for operating remote properties from a distance and was asked to take on this property. I was no more thrilled with the thought of flying to Kansas from New Jersey than any of the other managers were. Any time I would have to fly there it was certain I would have to stay several days. Kansas is a nice place, but it is difficult to commute that far just to keep an eye on one location. When I got there the first time, I was appalled. The property was in a state of disrepair, there were groups of people hanging out all over the place, and it appeared they were breaking the law. There were several clearly vacant units left wide open. When I walked into these units for the first time, they were completely destroyed.

I had met the site manager, who at first seemed nice, but it was apparent as time went on that he was complicit in the illegal activities, too. The office was in horrible shape and the residents had no confidence in anyone involved with the management. I visited the town hall and inquired with local officials. They were at once happy to see me (so they could hand me numerous violations) and incensed because they felt our property was a horrible influence in the town. The crime rate had put the neighborhood where our property was located at the top of the "danger zones" list. This was a property on the brink of total failure.

I made an attempt to correct what I could at this property. I went through an endless string of managers and personnel, but I could never establish a real bond because I could only stay so long. Once I'd leave, the on-site staff was again left to its own devices with a rough crowd. Worse, the managers often left while I was back in New Jersey and the insane ran the asylum. I hired off-duty police to correct the crime problem and moved aggressively on residents I thought were causing the problem, but I knew it would take an extended period of time to really turn things around. While I was attempting to clean up the property, several violent acts took place; needless to say, my ability to reshape the tenancy was not going well. Nobody wanted to live there except those who thrived on trouble. The end result was diminishing income. The infrastructure was destroyed. Try as I might, the owner either wouldn't or couldn't provide the necessary funds. At some point, even with my previous level of success, I came to truly believe this property would not see better days and I was burned out from trying. I went back to the owner after about a year and a half of traveling back and forth and told him that I believed it was time to divest this property and that I personally couldn't handle managing it anymore. The owner eventually agreed and sold the property.

Some people would argue that improper management practices caused this debacle and that continued inconsistent management aided the demise. But for purposes of this chapter, let's look very close at the baseline decision-making process in purchasing the property. I believe it was a purchase that never should have been made and was doomed from the closing date. Why? First, the ownership reviewed the numbers but did not correlate those numbers to absentee ownership. Second, the property was more than 1,000 miles away from the base of operation and hundreds of miles from any sister property. Third, the property was small, so the staff was too, which meant no one could watch the staff on a regular basis. Fourth, the property was of a unique type (subsidized Section 8) and needed a specialized manager, whereas the ownership had limited experience with how that type of investment worked. Finally, the ownership made a commitment to the purchase, but not a commitment to the time and energy it would take to run property so far away, in a market it didn't understand. The end result was a misunderstanding of the potential based on all pertinent circumstances.

When you invest in multifamily real estate, look at all the factors that will influence the operation and financial health of the property. Be realistic and be thorough. Start the management process when you are anticipating a possible investment, not after you already own the property.

CHAPTER 2

The Financials

Budgets and Financial Goals

The property has been purchased with care; it is almost time to start operating your new community. But before operations begin, it is very important to understand what the goals are in ownership and what the operating challenges are with this new community. Are you operating this real estate for short-term or long-term purposes? Are you seeking to take the property to another living environment level? Does the property require constant care? All these questions and many others need to be asked and answered in a general sense before the daily operations begin. Operating multifamily housing provides for many unforeseen events in a calendar year—storms, code or regulatory changes, mechanical failures, soft rental markets— that can force the hand of the ownership. It is important to know the aspects of a property that can be monitored and controlled. As an owner and manager, it is important to have performance expectations of certain aspects of the community operation and a way to monitor them.

Establish Your Financial Philosophy

To start, go back to the core question: What is the goal of this new investment? Property management is the practice, profession, and art of maintaining and creating value in an investment. Presumably, property owners are always looking to create value and maximize their return on investment (ROI), which is the amount over and above all expenses they receive relative to their original cash investment.

There are two common mistakes made relative to return that are important to understand when establishing a financial philosophy. First, new owners often overestimate what they can receive in rent initially and base their expectations on income numbers that just don't play out realistically. Second, many owners look at return while disregarding the upkeep and condition of the property they purchased. In combination, these two strategic and philosophical miscalculations mean that the property doesn't perform to expectations based on purchase price, or else the ownership pockets cash initially but the investment suffers over time because the investment's value is diminished and the cost to operate escalates exponentially.

The philosophy that all owners should have when investing in multifamily real estate is very simple: *Operate a property for the property's sake.* In other words, from the beginning, view this possible investment on its face value. What can you realistically hope to receive in rent? What are the specific operational and structural nuances of this investment that will cost you on a onetime basis and what will be recurring costs? Finally, after determining these factors, how do you manage them so that value is maintained and created and a return is paid on the investment consistently over time? An important concept to become comfortable with is that the goal of a consistent return does not always happen immediately. Any multifamily property owner must understand that patience is definitely a virtue. When making operational decisions, always look at the long-term cost and benefits.

Another common miscalculation is not realizing that things will break and structural elements of your investment only carry with them a finite *useful life.* A roof, for example, will only last so many years before it will have to be replaced, no matter how well it is cared for. If you own and manage multifamily housing, whatever breaks needs to be fixed immediately, whether or not you, as an owner, were prepared to make the repair. Maintenance of the investment will definitely increase the inherent value over time.

Obviously the personal benefit to the investor is paramount, but when it comes to multifamily real estate, personal goals will be achieved relative to the health of the property itself. Thus, while maintenance and improvements to a property carry intrinsic costs, they have a direct relationship to increased personal financial gain. The better the product you provide and the more you reinvest in the building, the more long-term residents you will have with a greater likelihood that rents will steadily increase. Your operating costs will be held to a minimum because you don't have resident turnover and the building systems are being properly maintained. The end result in the income and expense equation is that income rises, expenses stabilize, and the return steadily grows, thus satisfying the personal goals of the investor.

In the long run, your property not only derives rental income, but if it is properly maintained, its value for resale or refinancing steadily appreciates. These are all compelling reasons to establish a philosophy of operating a new real estate investment based on its realistic income potential, with a firm understanding of the expenses. Only then will your property become a satisfying investment in the long run.

Simple keys to remember:

❑ Establish the philosophical mind-set; run a property for the property's sake.
❑ Patience is definitely a virtue when owning multifamily real estate.
❑ Be realistic where income is concerned and in maintaining the building's infrastructure.

◼ Determine Accurate Benchmarks

Now it's time to establish the key elements of the property that should be continually monitored and measured against past performance. This is achieved by forming an *operating budget*. Budgets are created and exist to review and measure performance; however, you don't want to operate a property according to a budget. Instead, construct a budget based on the reality of your property. A budget should be a tool that an owner or a manager refers to, not lives by.

Operating multifamily real estate is dynamic; the residents live in this community twenty-four hours a day, seven days a week, so operations are constantly being readjusted depending on the circumstances at a given time period. An example would be snowstorms in the winter. For one recent past winter, the Northeast recorded thirty separate snowstorms. As an operator of multifamily housing, you are required to remove that snow; it is an expense you'll have to incur whether you like it or not. Another example is a broken underground heat line from a boiler. The boiler is still running, so do you incur the large expense to fix it now? The answer is yes, because if you don't the line may be further damaged, which will then be more expensive to fix. Furthermore, the operating costs for heating the building will escalate because the boiler with a leak is not operating to its maximum efficiency. Decisions like these have to be made in a practical sense, not through a strict set of numbers.

What a budget can do, though, is create for an owner or a manager a collective intellect about what constitutes a reasonable cost for maintaining a particular aspect of a building. It is time to create those financial benchmarks (as opposed to financial rules) that will help you manage. Let's use the example of the boiler again. Each month as more and more data about monthly fuel costs are compiled, you'll be able to make a more realistic forecast about what it should cost to heat the building. When your expectation doesn't meet reality, a budget and review of operating expenses might reveal an operational problem with the boiler. A budget is an empirical way to understand how the investment is performing.

When the building is first purchased a baseline budget should be created. This baseline will be difficult to produce because you have no collective experience with this investment. The best place to start is with the records of the previous ownership, which should be available to you. Review the income and expense information from the previous owner and begin to create a *line item budget*. Such a budget is basically a list of income and all common expenses a property has or may incur. Much of what goes into operating this property can be discovered from the records of the previous owner. There are, however, some cautions to take when interpreting data from another source. One is that the expenses may not be broken down well enough. An example would be if the previous owner reported heat, lighting, and water as "utility" costs. As the new owner, it is important for you to know what the fuel costs are, what the electric costs are, and what the water costs are. Even though the aggregate number for these costs would be the same, effective property management is achieved only by becoming very educated with each aspect of a building and making those distinct aspects operate as efficiently as possible. Another caution: The previous owners may not have spent on items they should have. Therefore, you'll need to understand the level or quality of spending by the previous ownership relative to the expectations you have set for this investment.

Before you bought the property, you should've conducted due diligence and done a thorough inspection of the property. Particular attention should have been paid to what costs would be necessary based on the physical condition of the property. If you take the information from the previous owners, plus the information gleaned through due diligence, you can now list all pertinent operating income and expenses. What are typical line items for a budget and what are some considerations to take into account on these line items?

Baseline Income Budget

Income is a function of rent expected as well as rent collected. It is a classic mistake of many who invest in real estate not to make that distinction. When forming the initial operating budget to establish what your annual income could potentially be, this is your *gross potential income*. The number of apartments in the community and each respective rent added together will produce your monthly income expectations—but be realistic. If market surveys show that a comparable-size unit, comparably equipped with similar amenities, rents for $900 a month in that market, don't set your expectations at $1,500; you won't achieve it. Local restraints or limitations on rental income may exist in the form of *rent control* or *rent stabilization*. Many municipalities have created a mechanism that in effect "limits" how much you can increase rent on renewal or creates a threshold you cannot exceed. Some towns go further and limit the increase on rents that can be applied to a newly vacated apartment; *vacancy decontrol* is not part of their rent control ordinance. Still other locations allow larger increases if significant improvements are undertaken to a vacated apartment. All of these possibilities limit to a certain extent the level to which income can be reasonably maximized. These factors have to be taken into account when forming an operating budget. The most important point to understand is this: Be realistic and know what the municipal as well as market limitations are.

The property may have ancillary sources of income as well (such as storage facility rents, garage rents, and laundry room income). If that's the case, create those line items under income, too. A property additionally may have fee structures for certain amenities that generate income. Some examples of this type of income stream are pool memberships, gym memberships, and pet fees. For purposes of a budget, these are hard items to predict, but the best way to start is to use the most recent history with that fee. Make sure such fees, whether charged to residents or charged to you, are taken into account on the expense side.

If your property has multiple units, you should expect some vacancy time. Previous records will likely confirm the property's vacancy factor. If the property has ten apartments and historically the property has at least one apartment vacant constantly, the vacancy rate would be 10 percent. If you create an operating line item to account for the income lost relative to that 10 percent vacancy (along with the sources of income), you can ascertain, fairly accurately, what the net income would be. Residents who do not pay rent can be factored in, too, but if residents are being financially qualified properly (as is discussed in a later chapter) this number should be minimal. Here is what a line-item baseline budget for that ten-unit property might look like:

Income	Monthly	× 12 Yearly
Rents $1,000 for each unit	$ 10,000	$120,000
Storage $50 for each of ten units	$ 500	$ 6,000

Laundry (subcontracted set fee)	$ 100	$ 1,200
Subtotal	$ 10,600	$127,200
Less		
Vacancy 10%	($ 1,000)	($ 12,000)
Net income (all income minus vacancy)	$ 9,600	$115,200

It is now very easy to understand what income should be derived from this investment in the following operating year and what is realistic. In future years, add a column for actual numbers from the previous year. If you do this each year, then estimating these numbers will become easier and your sense of how the property is performing will become more accurate. This process is repeated for expenses.

Operating Expenses

If a budget is to be an effective tool, then a comprehensive listing of all pertinent operating expenses is essential. For baseline purposes, most of the numbers related to expense items will have to be derived, once again, from past building experience and your own judgment about what wasn't expensed (or shouldn't have been expensed) by the previous owners.

Basic Expense Line Items
- ❑ Heating fuel
- ❑ Electricity
- ❑ Water and sewer
- ❑ Real estate taxes
- ❑ Payroll
- ❑ Office expense
- ❑ Supplies and equipment
- ❑ Subcontracted services such as landscaping
- ❑ Operating expenses (e.g., phone, copying, mailing)
- ❑ Repairs
- ❑ Vacancy expenses (e.g., painting, cleaning)
- ❑ Insurance
- ❑ Debt service (e.g., interest and principal)

❑ Advertising

❑ Trash removal

❑ Management fees

❑ Funding reserve accounts (technically not an "expensed" item, but an important consideration, as I'll explain below)

There are obviously other expense line items, and some of the listed line items can be further defined. For example, painting can be an expense line all by itself. The key is to be as comprehensive as you possibly can and to expand your list as your understanding of the property grows. The expenses should then be tabulated much the same way the income was.

Cash flow is income minus expenditures, including expenses such as interest and principal and depreciation (all items not considered by tax code to be income). Of course, the goal for any property owner is to realize a consistent positive cash flow, because that means you've made a healthy real estate investment. Many owners look to run the total property operation out of cash flow, including large capital expenditures, or those items that, when replaced, can be depreciated over time. The problem with this approach is that many such items, if not properly saved for, will very quickly erode the positive cash flow picture. The onetime cost for many capital items cannot possibly be paid for with all other regular operating expenses in a given period. For this reason, it is prudent to create a separate *capital reserve account* immediately upon purchasing the building. A safe rule of thumb is to fund this account with the equivalent of one month's mortgage and basic operating expenses. As you draw from this account, it is prudent to regularly contribute to this fund as well so that it remains liquid. In accounting terms, funding such an account is not an "expensed" item. Many owners simply don't factor the refund into their operating expenses each month, and often the reserve fund is neglected. I'm listing it as an operating expense to illustrate the need to keep this fund liquid.

Another important concept to understand is *net operating income* (NOI). This is calculated by taking only those line items defined as income and expenses, before debt service and without regard for cash invested. It is simply what is taken in and what is expensed to operate the buildings for a given period of time. Managers of real estate often use NOI as a guide or tool because these line items can be controlled. A manager of property cannot change how a property was financed or what the purchase price was, but a good manager has direct control over the operating expenses. If you purchase a community and hire an operating manager, establish with this manager how the budget process and review will be administered. If the cash flow view of the operation is confusing to the manager, try using NOI to simplify the process, showing the manager what he can do to affect the property in a positive way through prudent daily operating decisions.

The most important concept to remember is that however you organize a budget and however that information is reviewed, it is only a tool to verify and quantify the management decisions that are made every day when running a property for the property's sake.

Simple keys to remember:

❑ Create a baseline operating budget listing all income and known expenses.
❑ Use previous ownership records, and the due diligence process, to determine all expenses.
❑ Create consistent positive cash flow.
❑ Create a capital reserve fund account and continually fund it for large expenditures.

■ Seek Sound Financial Advice

Owning real estate carries with it some tax advantages such as *depreciation,* which is an allowable accounting practice whereby you offset taxable income based on aspects of your investment that have a useful life and deteriorate with wear and tear. The IRS allows what is called a straight line depreciation deduction over 27.5 years; or stated differently, each year you can deduct 1/27th of value from a depreciable item. In addition, if you own real estate for the purposes of operating a business you can deduct all operating expenses against income. If operating real estate as a business becomes more than a hobby, you can utilize *tax-deferred exchanges,* in essence "trading up" to larger properties without having to immediately pay a capital gains tax.

As a property owner, these advantages can alter the cash flow position of a property in a positive way. Depreciation laws can be complex, and it is worth hiring a professional financial adviser to review and audit how a property's monetary flow is operated.

◼ Manage the Residents' Money

Most all income derived from owning a rental property comes from the residents. Making sure the residents' rent is monitored properly is of paramount importance for the continued health of a property. This process should start when the property is being purchased. A certifiable rent roll, listing each resident and his or her current rent and security deposit, should have been obtained as a requirement of sale. You should also require a current list of *arrears,* meaning an accounting of any residents who are behind in their scheduled rental payments or owe ancillary fees or fines. In regard to the security deposits, it is important to discern whether the previous owner has deposited these funds in separate accounts for each resident or has commingled the deposits with operating funds. Before the sale is complete, come to a contractual understanding of how rents and security deposits as well as arrears are to be reconciled. For example, if the previous owner has a resident who owes a significant amount of rent, you need to determine who will seek to collect from that resident and who will receive any funds collected. Although the overall dollar amount may not be significant, in the long run what is significant is that you properly understand the financial position of each of the residents in the community from the first day of ownership. Make sure you know who is current, who is in arrears, and where the security deposits are. Be sure that all of the residents' funds are accounted for. As a rule of thumb, don't be responsible for what someone else has created; instead, negotiate in "credits" off a property's sale price for security deposits from the previous ownership that cannot be located or haven't been properly recorded.

It is time now to set up how rent is received and recorded and to inform residents about any new rules for paying rent. It is prudent to reiterate for residents what the payment policy is. It is equally important to adhere to the policy very tightly. This "trains" the residents to the idea that the policy will be enforced. For example, if the policy is that rent is due on the first of each month and is considered late after the fifth of each month (many rental policies do allow for such "grace periods"), after which a late fee is assessed, then that is the policy that should be followed at all times. Make sure your rent policies are well defined; if they aren't, they can become an "excuse" for late rent received. Here are some common policies:

❏ Indicate what forms of payment you will accept. Some operations do not believe in taking cash, since it cannot be accurately followed. If an unscrupulous or careless manager does not create a paper trail or receipt, then there is no proof of a transaction with cash. Personal checks are often acceptable, but you need to state whether you will accept postdated checks.

❑ Have policies in affect for third-party funds; for instance, parents paying for an adult child's apartment.

❑ Be clear about where and how rent is paid and provide all necessary means for the rent to be paid. For example, if rent is paid at an office location, indicate when that rent can be dropped off and whether there are after-hours depositories.

❑ Decide how rent received on weekends will be recorded. An example, if rent is late on the fifth of a month, which falls on a Sunday, make it clear whether rent picked up on Monday morning will be viewed as late or current.

❑ Establish policies and fees concerning late rent, as well as bounced or nonsufficient funds (NSF) checks.

❑ Indicate policies on receipts and on rent reminders. Many states do not require any sort of billing for rent if the rental policies were stated in the lease. Renters need to understand it is not the ownership's obligation to remind people when their rent is due.

All of these stated policies are designed to tell people *exactly* how rent is handled. The more structured your policies are and the more consistently they are carried out, the less they can be manipulated by people who simply don't manage their money well.

When it comes to charges for late rent, NSF checks, and legal fees should a resident remain in arrears, these fees should never be viewed as an income stream. All these fees are simply necessary tools to be utilized in maintaining good rent collection on a property. How should those fees be set? Most nonpayment of rent situations that go to the point of legal action will end up in a dedicated court for landlord/tenant matters. They may be called different names in different states and locales, but the important thing to understand is that each state has definitive rules for how nonpayment is to be handled, including fees. Check with the local courts regarding these rules and set fees that the courts would deem reasonable; however, make these fees substantial enough so that people think twice about incurring the expense. The idea is to discourage late payment.

Once the policies are constructed, it is time to follow the money. If the property is small enough, set up a ledger system to record rent received. Rent received should be recorded immediately upon receipt by amount and date, and it is advisable that funds received on a daily basis be deposited the same day. It is important that all funds recorded in a resident's account match the funds received and that they match whatever deposit is going to the bank. This is a very good reason why cash should be the payment method of last resort. By accepting only recorded funds such as checks and money orders, you'll have a verifiable paper trail for both the property and the resident to follow rental payments. As part of the recording process, you must also assign late fees and legal fees to resident's accounts consistently on the day that your policy designates. It is also advisable to create letters regarding late rent and possible legal action; these letters should be sent out to residents when the fees are incurred. Figure 2-1 is a sample letter. It is prudent to review with the local courts if there are notices the court requires when it becomes clear a resident is not paying rent. Once again, constructing a consistent policy—and enforcing that policy—will lead to more effective rent collection.

There are some options for how you can collect rent and record it. Many financial institutions have created services, known as a *lockbox system,* to accept rent and account for it on your behalf. Many owners utilize such a system because it cuts down on the number of staff necessary to properly follow funds and it reduces the amount of staff contact with residents' money. These services obviously carry a fee, and they have some inherent problems of their own. Because the individuals at the lockbox institution receiving the rent never see the residents, they are not familiar with them or their handwriting, or they aren't aware the rent is paid by a relative or friend. Funds can sometimes be temporarily misplaced in residents' accounts. Also, because "lockbox" funds are usually mailed, there can be discrepancies with the date the funds were actually received.

Many banks offer direct deposit over the Internet so that recording rent received is once again taken out of the hands of the owner. If you opt to use an online payment system you'll have to provide a portal for residents that "links" to the actual financial institution. There are also full-service property management and accounting software programs that will perform all of these rent-collection tasks. Obviously, the more real estate properties you have, the more these types of programs can benefit you. If you are thinking of expanding your property holdings in the future, then using management and accounting software such as Yardi, MRI, and Rent Roll is advisable. If you buy software and use other rent-collection means, such as a lockbox or direct deposit service, make sure the software the financial institution uses and the software you've purchased are compatible.

Nonpayment of rent should be mitigated by proper resident screening at application time, but it is inevitable when owning rental property. Handling nonpay-

Figure 2-1. Late rent letter.

NOTICE OF UNPAID BALANCE

DATE:

TO:

Dear Tenant:
APT. #

As you know, your rent is due on the FIRST DAY of every month. Our records indicate that your account has not been paid during the five-day grace period allowed.
Therefore, WE HAVE CHARGED YOUR ACCOUNT A LATE CHARGE OF $ _____

$ _____ Current Rent for _____
$ _____ Past Due Rent for _____
$ _____ Late Charges for _____
$ _____ Legal/Attorney fees _____
$ _____ Other _____
$ _____ Other _____

If you have already mailed your payment, please notify this office so it may be noted.

If you have not yet mailed your payment and rent bill in the envelope provided, YOU MUST BRING YOUR PAYMENT IN THE FORM OF MONEY ORDER OR CERTIFIED CHECK AND THIS LETTER TO THE RENTAL/MANAGEMENT OFFICE IMMEDIATELY.

If our payment is not received by the _____ of the month, your account will automatically be turned over to our attorney for eviction and collection proceedings. ONCE THIS ACTION HAS BEEN STARTED, WE CANNOT CANCEL IT UNTIL YOUR ACCOUNT HAS BEEN PAID IN FULL. You will also incur additional charges for court costs and attorney fees.

We urge your immediate attention to this very serious matter. If you have any questions, please contact the Rental/Management office or Resident Manager.

ment issues quickly and properly minimizes the rent loss and clearly should make a resident understand that the terms of the lease are enforced. Each locale has specific rules for filing nonpayment cases, adjudicating them, and rectifying them. The most effective method of settling a nonpayment issue is by the use of an eviction action. Either the resident settles the outstanding balance or the owner has the right to gain back possession of the apartment to again rent to a ready, willing, and able applicant. In some states, along with filing an eviction action, there is the simultaneous ability to file and obtain a money judgment should the resident not settle the debt; this can be determined by querying the local courts or an attorney who specializes locally in the landlord/tenancy field. There are some important steps to follow if you become involved in an eviction action:

❑ File a nonpayment action as close to the date in the lease indicated as the delinquent date. Again, promptly enforcing your rent payment policy trains your residents to be on time.

❑ Communicate constantly with any residents in arrears, so you'll be able to separate fact from fiction and the residents know they will be held responsible until the debt is collected.

❑ If the local courts require specific paperwork, follow it precisely. If this action reaches the courts, some courts will require that a lawyer be present. Regardless, the situation demands a professional, so be sure to use a lawyer. Remember, in most states, charging back the legal costs is permitted.

❑ Once a court has issued a ruling, there are further explicit steps that need to be taken to effectuate an eviction, so follow them very carefully. You'll only protract the process of getting an apartment back in ownership possession if you skip or ignore any steps. This means lost rent revenue. An example would be that some locations require a court officer to post a *warrant of removal* before evicting a resident at the unit in question.

❑ Once an eviction has taken place, follow all local laws requiring disposition of residents' belongings. Some states require the owner to store belongings; some locations allow the owner to place belongings outside an apartment, literally on the curb.

❑ When discussing arrears with a resident once a court hearing has been scheduled, don't agree to any deals for rent that haven't been agreed to before the court. You want to reserve your right to gain possession should the resident fail to abide by any agreement.

❑ Be prudent with back rent agreements. The resident should have a reasonable ability to pay both back rent and current rent, but don't extend an agreement past that so that the resident owes too much. It is more important to get possession of the apartment so the unit can generate income again.

Dealing with the possibility of evicting someone is never pleasant, but it is sometimes necessary in the business. What do you do when a resident withholds rent because of perceived poor maintenance? Most jurisdictions have specific conditions under which a resident can withhold rent under these circumstances, and it usually involves posting the rent with an official arm of the court or an attorney. The key to avoiding such situations is handling any perceived or real maintenance and safety situations properly and immediately. If a resident persists in maintaining that the situation has not been corrected, correspond with that resident in writing and document every action taken with that resident. Most of the time, if problems are taken care of and the property owner can produce complete documentation, a resident won't be able to use nonpayment of rent as recourse.

Collecting rent in arrears once a resident has been evicted varies from location to location, but each court has prescribed rules for placing collections on an individual. Several collection companies exist whose sole purpose is chasing bad debt. If a decision is made to use such companies, research them thoroughly, make sure they are licensed and insured, and review any agreement you enter into with them completely. Collection companies often take a percentage of back rent as their fee and they will charge for any legal costs. The best negotiating tactic with these companies is to insist that no fees be paid unless funds are collected and all fees be paid out of collected funds. This gives them incentive to actually chase the debt. If you choose to have the debt collected through such an independent source, it is important to understand that it is no longer your debt to collect; the collection company simply pays on bad debt minus its fee and expenses.

One other issue to be mindful of is bankruptcy filings. The federal bankruptcy laws were changed in 2005, but because of recent natural disasters the changes have been put on hold by the federal government. As a general rule, residents can enjoin the apartment they possess into a bankruptcy under certain circumstances. Because the laws are in such flux, it is highly advisable to seek the advice of a bankruptcy attorney and understand your rights before this happens.

Simple keys to remember:

❑ Establish a baseline understanding of each resident's rent payment history at purchase.

❑ Create firm rental policies immediately and adhere to them.

❑ Record residents' payments as soon as they are received.

❑ Follow any required local court procedures when initiating an eviction action.

Other Money Stuff to Consider

Insurance

Owning multifamily real estate carries with it risk. All of us would like to think we sincerely look after a property with care and make it as safe as possible. Accidents do happen and natural occurrences can adversely affect a property. If the property is financed, the mortgagor will probably require insurance. Yet, whether or not there is a requirement, insurance is a must. Coverage should be arranged to take effect from the moment a property is purchased. Ask for a *binder,* issued by the insurer, for proof of insurance. Your investment should be covered in two important ways: 1) for the actual structures should they be damaged or destroyed and 2) for matters of liability—for example, if someone visiting your property should slip and fall and become injured.

In the case of property coverage, there are some important concepts to understand. The first is that using an insurance broker is important. Insurance can be confusing, and missing something important could leave a particular loss uncovered. Although I include some general guidelines below, this information is no substitute for a good broker. Premiums are determined by basically three factors: the type of coverage and amount of coverage requested; the deductible; and the history or loss run of a particular property or properties (which is more pertinent to multiple property portfolios insuring under a single policy).

In regard to types of coverage, there are two sets of factors that contribute to cost. The first is the type of coverage. There are three types of coverage:

1. *Basic coverage* will cover most common loss situations, such as fire, vehicle theft, explosion, or vandalism, but generally it does not cover contents such as mechanical equipment (e.g., heating and cooling systems).

2. *Broad form coverage* includes additional occurrences that generally aren't picked up by a basic plan. One example is covering some plumbing malfunction occurrences.

3. *Special form coverage* is comprehensive except for incidents specifically excluded from the actual policy. And it is obviously the most expensive of the three types of insurance coverage.

The second factor that contributes to insurance cost is the level of coverage in relation to a loss. Most written policies cover a loss in *actual cash value,* which pays replacement cost minus depreciation. Other policies specify *replacement cost.* This type of coverage is more expensive.

Deductible amounts can affect the cost of insurance also: The higher the deductible, the lower the cost of the insurance. Remember, with any of these cost-benefit issues, increased cost today relates to better coverage tomorrow. If the goal is to limit cost today, then you are risking that when a loss occurs, some aspect of the loss won't be covered completely. Remember also that there are some losses that require special insurance such as flood and earthquake. There may be additional coverage for things such as rent loss. Take care to review all your options when deciding on what is proper for your investment.

Liability insurance is basically coverage to defend the property entity in the case of a lawsuit, which unfortunately is a common experience in owning multifamily real estate, so it is equally necessary. You can purchase what is called an umbrella policy that vastly increases overall coverage and is reasonable in cost. Insurance is a significant operating cost and should be reviewed very carefully when purchasing.

There are ways to mitigate insurance costs as time goes by. One additional way insurance premiums escalate is the number of claims reported against the policy over a given time period. Here are some things you can do:

❑ Establish a policy of how possible liability events are to be handled by staff. Always take an accident report and statements from all parties involved. Most liability cases don't get handled for months or years after they occur, so a proper recollection of events is necessary. Take photographs as well. Two sample incident reports are shown in Figure 2-2.

❑ Decide what kind of property losses you would be willing to cover yourself and what losses you will turn over to an insurance carrier. If the deductible is fairly low, the impulse is to turn over everything, but that will affect future premium rates.

❑ Identify possible safety hazards, such as lifted concrete, and repair them as soon as possible.

Figure 2-2. Sample incident reports.

General Liability Report

This report is to be completed when an incident is reported by tenant, visitor, etc., and is not to be completed in the presence of the claimant. This report is not for employee injuries.

Date of Incident _____ Approx. Time of Incident _____ AM/PM

Name of Property _____

Temperature and Weather Condition _____

Name of Claimant _____

Claimant's Address _____

City _____ State _____ Zip _____

Claimant's Phone # (____)_____ Date of Birth: _____

Location of Incident _____

Is the claimant a tenant?   Yes _____   No _____

Briefly, how did the claimant describe the incident? (Then write detailed report on page 2)
_____
_____

Did the claimant allege any injuries? _____

If yes, which part of the body was injured? (Please indicate left or right if applicable)
_____

Do you know if the injury resulted in medical treatment by a doctor or hospital?
Yes _____   No _____

If yes, name and address of doctor, hospital, or medical facility _____
_____

Name
& Phone # of Witness: _____

Name
& Phone # of Witness: _____

General Liability Report
Page 2

Has the claimant mentioned hiring an attorney or filing suit in connection with this claim?
_____

Were photographs taken? _____ Was a police report filed? _____
Who reported the incident to you? _____
How long after the incident occurred was it reported to you? _____

Please describe the incident in <u>detail</u> below and include any additional information or comments:
_____
_____
_____
_____
_____
_____
_____
_____
_____
_____
_____
_____
_____
_____
_____
_____
_____
_____
_____
_____
_____
_____
_____
_____

Attach police report, photographs, winter weather condition reports, or any other pertinent information.

DATE OF REPORT: _____ REPORTED BY: _____

(continues)

Figure 2-2. Continued.

Property Loss Report

All property damages must be reported to the Insurance Department immediately!

Date of Loss _____   Approx. Time of Loss _____ AM/PM

Name of Property _____

Location of Damage _____

Type of Damage _____

Was the local police department called?   Yes _____   No _____

If yes, when? _____

By whom? _____

Was the fire department called?   Yes _____   No _____

If yes, when? _____

By whom? _____

Which fire department responded to the call?
_____

Has the origin of the property damage been determined by the fire/police department?
Yes _____   No _____   If yes, what caused the damage? _____
_____

Were there any injuries?   Yes _____   No _____

If the property damage originated in an apartment, please provide the following information:
Tenant's Name _____
Apartment #_____
Telephone # (_____) _____-_____

Property Loss Report
Page 2

Did the tenant have renter's insurance?   Yes _____   No _____

If yes, please provide the following information:
Insurance agent's name _____
Address _____
City _____ State _____ Zip _____
Telephone # (_____) _____-_____
Name of tenant's insurance company _____
Policy # _____

Did the tenant need to be relocated?   Yes _____   No _____
If yes, where to? _____
_____

Were any other apartments affected by the property damage?   Yes _____   No _____
If yes, please list below (attach additional page if necessary):

Tenant's Name	Apartment #	Relocated
_____	_____	Yes _____ No _____
_____	_____	Yes _____ No _____
_____	_____	Yes _____ No _____
_____	_____	Yes _____ No _____
_____	_____	Yes _____ No _____
_____	_____	Yes _____ No _____
_____	_____	Yes _____ No _____
_____	_____	Yes _____ No _____
_____	_____	Yes _____ No _____
_____	_____	Yes _____ No _____
_____	_____	Yes _____ No _____

(continues)

Figure 2-2. Continued.

Property Loss Report
Page 3

Below, please describe the incident in detail and also include the names of any employees who responded to the scene of the incident:

_____
_____
_____
_____
_____
_____
_____
_____
_____
_____
_____
_____
_____
_____
_____
_____
_____
_____
_____
_____
_____
_____

Important: Please complete and attach a separate liability claim form for any bodily injury claim. Please attach any police reports, fire reports, and estimates of damages.

Date of Report: _____ Reported By: _____

❑ Develop training programs for staff to make sure the workplace and community remain as safe as possible.

❑ Follow all local safety codes as they relate to your buildings; if the insurance carrier provides recommendations based on a safety inspection, follow them as well.

❑ Always show concern for the resident when a resident reports an accident or a mechanical failure, and handle any such occurrence with care.

One way to mitigate some aspects of loss is recommending to all incoming residents that they purchase renter's insurance as a level of protection in regard to liability. In some locations, owners are now requiring that proof of insurance be produced at move-in. Be sure to check the legality of making such a request, but if it can be required it is advisable. The insurance is not expensive for minimum liability coverage (typically somewhere between $10,000 and $30,000) and personal protection for belongings; the premium cost is somewhere in the range of $150 to $300 a year. If local law does not permit requiring this insurance, then at least strongly suggest that it is in a resident's best interest to obtain a policy. Most fires that occur in apartments are the result of resident negligence, and although these policies will not cover an owner if there is any substantial loss, they can defray some of your costs.

Be aggressive in your efforts to convince residents to obtain this insurance. Most renters aren't well informed about insurance and therefore don't consider its purchase will be cost-effective. In fact, most renters believe any mishap will be the responsibility of the ownership and are stunned to find out that isn't always the case. If a resident obtains renter's insurance, it leaves her with an option in the event of a loss that does not immediately fall back to the owner. Having the insurance coverage does, to a certain extent, help to reduce resident/management tension in the event of unforeseen losses that result in residents losing personal belongings.

Payroll

If the property purchased requires staff, it will have payroll as part of the operating expenses. It is important to understand the total makeup of payroll. If you are assuming a staff from a purchased property, one question to ask is whether the previous ownership was providing benefits such as healthcare to its employees. The cost of these services is typically in addition to the "pay rates" of the individual employees. Often payroll and payroll taxes constitute distinct line items. The combination of these two factors can blind a new owner to the real cost of payroll. Make sure you know the total payroll picture—wages, taxes, and benefits, including workers compensation. In some states disability insurance may be included, too. The key is to recognize the total cost of payroll, not just the amount the employee is being paid. Mention when hiring someone that all pertinent forms of identification must be produced. Individuals have to be legal to work in this country; therefore, they have to produce Social Security cards and work papers that clearly indicate they can legally work in this country, according to the federal government. As an owner you'll have an obligation to pay all required taxes and Social Security benefits, but you cannot fulfill that obligation for someone who isn't legally eligible to work in this country. If you violate immigration and work-related laws, the fines to an owner are substantial.

Property Taxes

Property taxes are an unavoidable cost to owning real estate and doing business, and they are a significant line-item operating expense. Property taxes are known as an *ad valorem* tax. Typically the local tax assessor's office or municipal appraiser is the official responsible for assigning a "value" to property. The most often used method is by appraising the property or assessing its value as compared to what comparable properties in that market sell for—what appraisers call the sales/market approach. Several factors are taken into account, such as equivalent square footage, acreage, and amenities. Each municipality establishes a "tax rate" and applies the value of a property mathematically to that tax rate to establish what the property taxes will be.

Land and building assessments are often done separately, and some municipalities have local requirements to periodically reassess the property value. The value of your property could be increased in any given fiscal year and the tax rate could change, which obviously affects the tax bill for a particular property. More often than not, the tax adjustment is adverse to the property owner. For purposes of operating strategy, it is important to understand that if the tax bill increases due to a reassessment of value, an owner has the right to challenge the assessment. You do not have to automatically accept such valuations. It is advisable to first informally challenge the assessment with the tax assessor's office in the municipality where the property is located. Sometimes there is a need to bring a tax issue to a court to decide. This is what is known as a tax appeal.

When an appeal is undertaken, one of the essentials to success is proving that in some fashion the property is overvalued. You might hire an independent appraiser to refute or challenge the municipal assessment of the property. There is more than one way to appraise a property; in fact, there are three basic appraisal methods:

1. The *sales or market approach* is the most often used approach. Again, it is accomplished by comparing similar properties with similar amenities and their sale value in the same economic market.

2. The *cost approach* calculates what the replacement cost of a property would be minus accrued depreciation. The terms "economic life" and "effective age" are often used when calculating certain aspects of a property. This method is often used in assessing a special-use property where structural improvements have a direct influence on value.

3. The *income approach* has significance to the rental business because it looks at income derived from owning real estate for purposes of profit. It assesses value in terms of income derived.

When, as a property owner, you make the decision to undertake an appeal, you should retain an attorney who specializes in appeals. The attorney will most likely know what method primarily suits the particular property and the particular appeal.

It is important to remember that you do not have to accept the value assigned to your property as it relates to taxes, because taxes are a significant cost. Challenge it!

Fees

There are numerous fees associated with many aspects of operating real estate. It's a simple fact of life. Municipalities derive income from charging fees, and although most of the fees are "reasonable" in cost, the trend in recent years has been toward new fees created for a multitude of activities that are part of operating and maintaining multifamily investments. The cumulative effect of fees, and the administration of the activity related to them, can become financially and logistically cumbersome. Each municipality is different, of course. Some towns require operating licenses or business licenses to operate multifamily real estate. Many towns require a *certificate of occupancy* (CO) for the property as a whole or for each apartment before it is occupied. Obviously, when a town requires such a certificate there is a fee attached to it.

If you want to save time and money, make an effort to clearly understand how your town and municipality view fees and their administration. If we use the example of the CO fee, it is usually connected to a site inspection of a rental unit just before a new resident moves in. If the apartment fails the inspection, you'll need to spend more money to correct the violated problem and there could be a reinspection fee. The failure could also postpone a projected move-in date and that could discourage a prospective renter from following through on occupying the apartment. Some municipalities allow for the cost of these fees to be *passed through*—in essence charged to the resident—but make sure that's permissible before actually charging these fees.

Fees such as these may seem a nuisance at best and, at worst, a chip in the bottom line; however, there is another significant side effect. Once a municipality creates a policy for occupancy, although the motivation may have been revenue, it also becomes a standard that will be held against an owner in the case of a mishap. For instance, a property has a fire and a unit burns, injuring a resident. The fire is determined to have been accidental in nature, started by the resident, but the property owners never applied for or received the CO. The owners, in this case, have exposed themselves to extreme liability.

Many states additionally have created fee-generating mechanisms; for instance, New Jersey has a five-year required state inspection. This inspection is comprehensive and costly. If there are violations left uncured after a "cure period" expires, there are reinspection fees and possibly fines. An additional fee has been assessed strictly to inspect apartments that do not possess a federal lead-based paint-free certificate. It is easy to see how the myriad of fees and their administration can add up.

There may also be fees to license certain classes of employees. Some municipalities look to license maintenance personnel, for example, and some states require leasing agents to possess real estate licenses. Some pieces of equipment such as boilers may also require certificates, permits, or licensing.

When you purchase a building, make sure you ask for verification of all required licensure and are satisfied with the currency of that licensure. Take the time to fully educate yourself about all fees and practices. Much of this information can be derived from financial records and by inquiring with the local municipality and specific state.

■ "The Bubbling Courtyard"

Running a building for the building's sake may sound like a very logical concept, yet in my time, I have seen even long-term property owners take their "eye off the ball." I have managed many properties over the years, usually directly employed by or partnered with the owner, though on occasion I was put into the role as the fee manager—that is, managing in a third-party capacity. In one particular situation, our firm took over the responsibility of multiple buildings in multiple locations. None of these buildings were small. The owners had contracted our firm because they said they were unhappy with the previous fee management company and the buildings were not performing well.

On our first visit, it was apparent that these buildings had been neglected. There were clear infrastructure problems and the residents were beginning to match the shape of the buildings. The owners had been what some in the business call "absentee," meaning they always left the buildings in the care of a fee manager and sometimes disregarded the quality of the fee management they hired. The buildings were located in an urban setting very convenient to highways, mass transit, and urban centers of business. The locations had some basic selling points and, in their prime, they were once sought-after properties. Upon reviewing the ownership history, we realized that the present owners had held these buildings for a long time and therefore were involved when the market and the properties were desirable and profitable.

We decided to meet the owners' representative for the first time at the largest and worst of the properties, in terms of the conditions. The representative was the "front man" for a syndicated ownership of many partners. Because the partners rarely saw the property and the conditions, they were looking for return on investment and financial statements as proof that it was being run well. This meant they didn't understand what was necessary to maintain the value of the property.

During the first tour of the property it became clear that this representative was walking past obvious defects in the building and was constantly referring to what we "couldn't do" monetarily on the property because funds had to be doled out in a measured way. He believed all expenses should come from cash flow and that cash flow had to remain positive. If you have a large expense that usually means something gets deferred. The representative explained that we had to concentrate on the basics of renting and we had to use good old-fashioned "elbow grease" and we would soon clean up the property and all would be well. I suggested some upgrades to at least give a better feel for the buildings or enhance the curb appeal. He again short-circuited the conversation and repeated his claim that basics would do the job.

What he failed to grasp was that the philosophy of "pay as you go" and not "saving for a rainy day" had in fact diminished the property's intrinsic value. There are two things that begin to occur when these methods are practiced for extended periods of time. First, the residents feel the effect of the diminished services and environment and you lose them, creating vacancy and turnover costs. Then the residents replacing the move-outs tend to have a lower threshold for the quality of living, and slowly but surely they become part of the problem. The second circumstance that becomes more obvious is that major infrastructure components start failing and the Band-Aid approaches to maintenance at some point don't work. The equipment fails totally or runs so inefficiently that the cost to replace or operate it grows exponentially. Then the two factors feed on each other: Vacancy and bad tenancy together don't allow for steady income, then the major breakdowns occur, and when they can't be fixed the next level of resident moves out of the building. These buildings were in that "death spiral" you see a plane do at an air show. Unfortunately, soon they weren't going to be able to pull out of the dive.

The owners' representative visited several times, and the back-and-forth was always the same: In his view we weren't improving the properties and we hadn't put any elbow grease into the property. Our view was that some capital investment and fiscal discipline would have to take place. In his mind, however, spending the money demonstrated lack of discipline! I was struggling to show this man how he had the picture so wrong.

One day we had a meeting on the tenth floor of this building in a model apartment. It was cold outside and snow covered the courtyard. The conversation was going in circles, just as it had in previous meetings. I was getting restless and walked to the window—and I saw an illustrative way to get my point across. I asked the representative to join me at the window. There was a courtyard that was rather large between these buildings and the heating system for these very large structures was located in the other building approximately 200 yards away. I asked him if he knew why there was snow all over except this large spot of green grass (in the winter) in the middle of the courtyard, and why there was water "bubbling up" in that grass with steam. He thought it odd, and then body language let me know it finally registered with him what was going on. The heating lines for this building were broken underground, and judging from the green grass, the warm water had been surfacing for quite some time.

I asked him if he knew how much more he was paying in fuel costs and water costs because of this problem. I then asked him if he was willing to let that continue—he wasn't. I quizzed him on what he thought repairing something like this might cost, factoring in that it was the middle of winter. Finally, I asked him to think about how many residents he may have lost because service hadn't been adequately provided for quite some time.

The pipe couldn't be repaired because it was in deplorable shape. Several hundred feet had to be totally replaced, disturbing the sidewalks, which then also had to be replaced. There were several more major problems on these properties. They finally were getting addressed, but slowly, because the money wasn't there and the tenancy wasn't stable enough to sustain better income.

The point to take out of this story is that the owners had fooled themselves into establishing financial benchmarks that ignored the condition of the property itself. Sooner or later this results in a property in need of a lot more than elbow grease. The goal of any investment is to a certain extent self-serving, but if multifamily real estate is the investment, and you're in it for the long term, run the property for its own sake and the return will follow, and follow consistently.

CHAPTER 3

The Human Ingredient:

The People You Hire

You've secured your investment; you have put your financial game on the drawing board. Now comes the most significant decision you will have to make if your multifamily property is of any appreciable size or is any great distance from your home base. It comes down to picking the right people to manage your investment. A good rental property can sell itself, but having the right people manage it is what makes a good property a great investment. The human aspect of property management can raise the level of a marginal property significantly, and it can absolutely destroy a property virtually overnight.

▓ Hire for the Future

Picking the right people, and fostering their understanding of your goals, carries more significance in the multifamily atmosphere than any other investment. Why? Typically, there are very few employees in the average rental property. If your property is less than 100 units, you may have only one full-time person. Although you may expect to spend less on payroll, this one person's skill set is critical to the maintenance of the property.

For a 100-unit property with common hallways, an adequate staff would include one or two maintenance professionals and a full- or part-time rental professional. In addition to marketing your property, collecting rent, delivering customer service, and addressing expected and unexpected maintenance issues, someone will have to regularly:

❏ Perform common area housekeeping.

❏ Maintain landscaping (including upkeep for visual appeal and snow removal).

❏ Execute apartment turns (re-prepping apartments for new residence).

This is a very small staff, with diverse responsibilities, running a very expensive and valuable asset. Without proper hiring or direction, these few people could cause irreversible damage to the future value of the asset. Your choices, and the way you deal with those you hire, become either an extension of a profitable investment or a real blunder. For these reasons, it is important that you start thinking right away about the type of property you own and who fits there best.

One mistake owners make all the time is allowing the staffing decision to become strictly financially driven. Understaffing or improper staffing will cost you more than you are saving. In the case of the 100-unit complex, the exterior will have to be maintained by somebody, the halls will have to be cleaned by somebody, and the turns will have to be done by somebody. Whether you decide to do it in-house or use subcontract services, it is an expense that can't be avoided. If done incorrectly, basic maintenance becomes a much larger capital expense. Too many owners do not factor in the cost of hiring the *wrong people.*

How do you start? Profile your property, determine your needs, and hire to fit those needs.

Profile Your Property and Determine Needs

In the first two chapters of this book, you had an opportunity to learn a lot about your new investment. When drawing up your business plan, you may have made simple, cursory decisions about staffing. But did you ask all the right questions as it relates strictly to staffing?

The physical makeup of your property should greatly influence your staffing decisions. For example:

❏ *Age.* Older buildings have a higher maintenance component in general and therefore are more work intensive on a maintenance staff. Often equipment is obsolete and parts are no longer available. In this case, a maintenance engineer who is resourceful can be more beneficial than one who is technically trained.

❑ *HVAC Units.* Your power plants may be an issue. Does the property have sophisticated heating and cooling systems that need constant care and attention? For
instance, a high-rise typically has larger heating units and intricate cooling systems that are "central" to the building and require a well-trained individual to
operate and monitor. A "garden" apartment complex usually has simpler systems,
so with regard to staffing, you may need to hire a "technician" for your heating
and cooling and a less skilled person to balance the workload.

Too many owners and managers try to hire the quintessential "jack of all
trades." The result in the high-rise scenario, for example, is somebody not qualified
to run the sophisticated equipment, or one very overworked individual. In the pure
operating budget mind-set, the payroll line item may look good, but check down a
little farther on the expense side of the ledger and, over time, you may find you're
spending more than the cost of one additional employee or one higher-paid, better-
trained individual who could have avoided a big-ticket repair.

Bad hiring decisions can affect the income side of the ledger also. When evaluating staff for your property, take into account the historical apartment turnover
rate (i.e., the percentage of total units that you turn over in a prescribed period of
time, best averaged over a year or more). If you have too few individuals performing your vacant unit "make readies," you effectively increase your vacancy rate
because you cannot keep up with demand, quality suffers, and new resident referrals
decline. If you know how many turnovers, on average, you have a month, you can
figure out how many hours it takes for a technician to do an average turnover. That
will give you a good guess on how many labor hours will be needed on a monthly
basis.

Build sales and marketing into your staffing needs as well. This way you will
avoid a classic mistake commonly made in this business, which is delegating your
marketing function to whoever is there. This affliction occurs more on smaller
properties where there is a perceived need to keep staffing to a minimum. "Mom-
and-pop" or "husband-and-wife" teams have been used for years because it affords
the owner the use of a couple and because compensation usually involves housing,
which limits the bottom-line cost to the owner. Often one or both of these individuals are not qualified to perform the role for which they are hired, so these arrangements can produce disastrous results in the end. The person who rents or "markets"
your apartments must be a professional who represents your investment in the correct manner. Unless the property is too small and you have discovered that there is
literally no room to afford a sales presence, "profile" your property to always have
a sales and marketing component.

There are several other property profile issues that should be taken into account to ensure you will have the right staff. Here is a quick list, with an explanation of why each consideration is important:

❑ *Equipment.* Heating, cooling, and other major building systems are sophisticated and may need to be looked after by highly qualified or even certified personnel.

❑ *Structure.* Buildings that possess "common areas" such as hallways require daily cleaning and upkeep.

❑ *Grounds.* The amount of grounds and the layout on your property, plus the sophistication of your landscaping, will determine whether you subcontract or hire staff to do groundskeeping.

❑ *Apartment Turnover.* You need to make time for your staple task. If your property turns a significant number of units in a given time period consistently, you'll need to staff for it.

❑ *Local Codes.* Some states and municipalities have requirements for minimum staff or specially licensed staff, which will affect your staffing choices.

❑ *Amenities.* If your property has a pool or other amenities, you may need additional staffing to provide services.

❑ *Administrative Functions.* Depending on how much maintenance and services-related work you expect your on-premises staff to do, you may need someone else to handle rents and paperwork, which also take time.

❑ *Size.* The property will need a more sophisticated staff the larger it is. Tasks grow exponentially, and at some point you cannot expect multitasking and quality to coexist.

Simple keys to remember:

❑ Profile your property and determine your needs.
❑ Hire to fit those needs.
❑ Include a sales marketing component.
❑ Staff for talent, not for budget.

■ Hire to Fit Your Property Needs

The property profile is only one-half of the hiring equation. The other is knowing the skill set and personalities that each of your new employees will need to optimally carry out the responsibilities in front of them. You should develop and use a check-list when hiring for each position.

This checklist should take into account all perceived tasks you feel an individual will perform. List them all and add to them as time goes on. The checklist should also include any necessary certifications. For example, some states require individuals working on boilers to have a "black seal" license, which signifies basic boiler knowledge. The National Apartment Association (NAA) has an "available and industry-recognized" program for certifying National Apartment Leasing Profes-sionals. NALP certification signifies that the individual certificate holder has been trained in a professionally sanctioned program that teaches proficiency skills to leas-ing professionals. Details of such training and certification programs can be found on the NAA website at www.naahq.org.

Your checklist should also include the personality and behavioral traits you are looking for when filling each property position. This part of your checklist is the one that is ignored or minimized too often and can come back and bite you. While each position has particular needs in terms of experience or training, it is best to understand the overall traits necessary for any property professional first. My advice is simple: *Hire for attitude first and experience second.*

All property professionals must share the following traits:

❏ *Enthusiasm.* All property professionals should be thrilled with your property. You purchased a property with high expectations, so when you interview people, make sure they exhibit and can articulate that they have high expectations, too. Have you ever attempted to purchase anything from a sales representative who was less than sold on the product himself? If so, it's a product you probably had second thoughts about buying. Everyone who works at an apartment complex will, at some point, have to be a salesperson. If they believe in the product, so will the prospective renter.

❏ *Independence.* These representatives of your investment are often left to their own devices on a daily basis. Although it is obvious to look for self-sufficiency in a manager, even individuals who report to a supervisor often work independently as well. Apartments are mutually exclusive entities; therefore, subordinates on a site spend much of their working day on their own. As the owner, you may have your office in a separate location and the staff members minding your property may operate in separate locations on that site. They must be able to operate on their own productively for extended periods of time. Independence is an important per-sonality makeup in any property professional.

❏ *Patience.* As in any service business, patience is definitely a virtue. Apartments are home to the people who live in your community, and that home is probably the most important and most costly aspect of their lives. Often people have an emotional connection to where they and their families live. A property professional must therefore have the ability to understand and deal with other people's stress and personal situations when discussing or solving an apartment or community issue. Take, as an example, the frequently occurring event of an apartment with a plumbing backup that damages a resident's personal belongings. The office personnel have to be understanding when discussing this issue, and the maintenance professional has to be delicate when dealing with the issue at the person's apartment. A good response on the part of each individual can reduce tension and help turn an "angry" resident into an "understanding" one.

❑ *Resilience.* No matter how small, an apartment community is just that—a community. A community by its nature has no opening and closing times, and much of what happens there is spontaneous. The popular phrase "stuff happens" certainly applies to the apartment business. Those who work in a community have to be willing to deal with events no matter when they occur. Remember that apartment staffing is usually minimal, with barely enough people to cover "daily shifts." Often the staff that went home at five o'clock is the same staff that gets called at 11:00 P.M. that same night, as well as weekends. Over the years, it's become clear to me that it takes a special human being, someone with stamina, who does not wilt under periodic barrages of unforeseen circumstances, to work in the apartment community business.

❑ *Organization.* Organizational skills are essential for performing any task in property management, whether it is following up on delinquent rent payers, maintaining a power plant system, or developing a follow-up system to capture possible renters who have inquired about renting but did not fill out a rental application.

❑ *Sense of Humor.* One intangible that appears in the best of property professionals is a good sense of humor, which complements many of the other traits previously mentioned. The very nature of the housing business is unpredictable and at times pressure packed. People who stay in this industry understand this and learn to perform and make light of their circumstances.

Here is a short list of the most common property positions and the specific traits each individual should possess:

Site Manager

❑ *Skill Set.* Communication skills, situational awareness, organizational skills, an eye for detail, conflict resolution abilities.

❑ *Training* (helpful but not required). Institute of Real Estate Management (IREM) Accredited Resident Manager (ARM), National Apartment Association (NAA) Certified Apartment Manager (CAM), or core real estate courses available through some universities.

Leasing Professional

❑ *Skill Set.* Enthusiasm, attentive listening, marketing, follow-up skills, creativity.

❑ *Training.* NAA-certified NALP program and State Real Estate Salesperson's license.

Maintenance Professional

❑ *Skill Set.* Organizational skills, attention to detail, analytical abilities, broad knowledge base, ability to take direction well, problem solving.

❑ *Training*: NAA-certified apartment maintenance technician (CAMT) or systems maintenance technician (SMT) as designated by the Building Owners and Managers Institute (BOMI).

Depending on the state and municipality, there may be specific licensing, certification, or other requirements for all of these positions, so it is always best to check your local codes. There are many other private training programs that provide similar programs and material, but be sure to verify the content to see if they apply.

Simple keys to remember:

❑ Hire for attitude first and experience second.
❑ Develop a "checklist" for hiring. The best tip is to hire professionals who are enthusiastic, independent, patient, resilient, organized, and humorous.

■ Teach Instead of Manage

People, you will begin to realize, are your best asset to manage and grow your investment! The multifamily environment is a difficult one to operate in every day. If you decide to assume a direct role in managing your own property, more than likely at some point you will still need to bring on additional staff to perform some of your needed functions. For that reason, there are some multifamily-specific management skills that are essential to ensure your investment is receiving the optimum tender-loving care.

The personality profiling traits mentioned previously carry a greater significance when we're talking about managing employees. When you work in an industry where all employees are on a manufacturing floor or always in the same office, the interplay is immediate and the results are obvious. But if you own multifamily housing, you are likely hiring individuals who will have to work independently for long periods of time and you cannot always "be there" because you may be managing your property from afar or with long time intervals between visits to the property. It becomes essential that you develop a very personal, interactive, mentoring managerial style and that you develop tracking methods to verify what you see and hear. There are three principles to follow when managing your property professionals: Become personal; don't delegate, proactively negotiate; and at all times, keep plenty of data, data, data.

Become Personal

Once you create a profile for each position you are filling, it can be used in the interview process to match the individual to the position and to open up a dialogue in which you begin to know that individual personally. Why is that more important in this industry? Unless you intend on purchasing only one piece of investment real estate and you intend on being there every day, your communication will be virtual—by phone or e-mail—much of the time. Human beings provide a lot of information through their language, syntax, and patterned responses. There has to be a trust and a real connection between you and your staff. The staff has to paint a picture over the phone, for example, and the picture they paint may cause you to make financial decisions on the spot, based on their word. The better you know who your employees are, the better you can understand what they are trying to relay to you.

You undoubtedly should visit each one of your sites regularly, but as a practical matter, you just aren't going to be there to witness everything that happens. Take, for example, the often-occurring resident dispute. You are very rarely going to be present when these occurrences take place. Often you will be asked to broker or mediate a situation from a distance or long after a situation occurs, even if you have the best of staff on premises. Residents know that on-site staffs are usually representatives of an owner and many states require owner contact information to be printed in apartment leases, so even if you are rarely on site you will get calls. If you do not have a firm understanding of your staff, trying to discern fact from fiction is going to be very difficult. In the case of on-site management, supporting your staff and understanding their view of an event is extremely important. Remember they too are often on their own for long periods of time, but if you've hired right, they have the property's best interest in mind as well.

The National Multi Housing Council (NMHC) released a study in October 2001 putting the turnover rate among industry professionals at 55 percent, of which 38 percent was voluntary. There is a high burnout rate in this industry. If you are going to invest in real estate that requires any type of staff, you have to know these people, communicate with them, and motivate them. They are the front line of contact with your income stream, your residents, and bad customer service from them costs you in turnover.

Don't Delegate, Proactively Negotiate

There is a method of communication that takes into account that each party is not in the same place at the same time, but each needs to understand the same issue the same way simultaneously. It has existed in another industry for decades—the air travel industry—where the stakes are much higher. If you have ever been in a cockpit of a plane or in a control tower, you can hear banter that usually involves a directive, a questioning of the reasoning, and a response. The pilot cannot see what the air traffic controller can see on his screens and the controller most likely doesn't know how to fly the plane, yet even in the worst of weather, the plane almost always lands safely. This is proactive negotiation, and it is custom built for the apartment industry. You, as the owner of the real estate, should always put yourself in the position of being that air traffic controller because you have a view of the entire picture, and you should always treat your apartment professionals as that pilot. You need them to land the plane.

Learn to give direction based on your goal, but then be a good listener. Encourage your people to ask you why you want them to do what you asked. This methodology provides you a level of comfort with their comprehension; it also is a way to "culture" your professional staff over time and teach them your way of doing business. More important, it builds trust. *Trust* is a word that will be repeated often, as will the reminder that apartment staffs are usually very small and left to their own devices. Thus, the working relationship between staff and ownership is necessary and needs to be close.

Your ability to understand and cultivate that relationship will translate into the creation of value on your property. If you don't have that trust and you don't have that instant sense of what is happening on your property, you will be amazed at how quickly your property can become a war zone. "Absentee landlord" is an often-used phrase that should just mean not living on premises; but it is often applied to communities in disarray, where the impression is that the landlord has a total disconnect with the property. If you, as an owner, become disconnected, the economic fallout can be enormous. There is an analogy that describes the effect of poor on-site management. Ask yourself this rhetorical question: "How long does it take me to break my leg and how long does it take to heal?" You obviously can break your leg very quickly. Disconnecting from your property and your staff will have the same net effect—it will cause instant damage that takes a long time to heal.

Two of the best ways to attract residents are resident referral (i.e., word of mouth) and drive-by traffic. They are both largely perception-based ways that people learn of your community. If you destroy positive perception, you destroy your income stream—and perception is harder to change than reality (i.e., the leg healing). For these reasons, picking the right people, becoming personal with them, and then developing a proper communication structure is of the utmost importance.

Communication alone cannot always paint a proper picture. You must also ensure that what you're hearing about is happening.

Keep Plenty of Data, Data, Data

Information *is* everything. Several other chapters discuss the reporting and data requirements for specific aspects of property management, but the point I want to make here is that all reporting is directly related to developing trust and understanding clearly the business problem. If information is communicated in some reporting form on a consistent basis and used as a tool to verify verbal communication, it becomes a highly reliable way of understanding your staff and how they comprehend and operate a property.

Let's use the example of a simple report to track occupancy from day to day or week to week. It's called a *vacancy report*. There are many variations of such a report and you have to decide what level of information is necessary. The more information provided, the more you can visualize the situation. Trying to figure out what is happening on a site when you are not physically there is like being in that air traffic control tower. The report is your radar screen. More important, by querying your on-site staff and matching up what your consistent weekly report is saying, you begin to develop the ability to judge your staff's strengths and weaknesses. Let's review the vacancy report shown in Figure 3-1.

As you can see, the report includes an apartment number, a resident's name, the

Figure 3-1. Weekly vacancy report.

ATTENTION: _____   TOTAL # OF VACANT APARTMENTS: _____
NUMBER OF PAGES: _____   TOTAL # OF APTS. RE-RENTED: _____
     TOTAL # OF TRANSFERS: _____
DATE: _____   TOTAL # OF UPCOMING MOVE OUTS: _____

WEEKLY VACANCY REPORT

COMPLEX: _____

VACANT APT #	ACTUAL MOVE-OUT DATE OR EVICTION	DATE RE-RENTED OR DATE OF TRANSFER	AMOUNT OF NEW RENT & RENT SPECIAL	ACTUAL MOVE-IN DATE OR ACTUAL DATE OF TRANSFER	NAME(S)	APT # & DATE OF UPCOMING MOVE-OUT OR TRANSFER

move-out date, a date when the apartment is re-rented, a name of the new renter, and a column for upcoming move notices for the near future. There are also cumulative totals for the number of vacancies and number of notices. If you follow this reporting format week by week, you'll have a pretty good picture of what is occurring in your units *and* how your staff is doing. You can, for instance, tell how long an apartment is staying vacant, so over time you can track if units are staying vacant for too long. If you know apartments are renting in the market fairly quickly but they are occupying much slower at your property, you can gain an insight into the efficiency of your staff in getting apartments ready for rent. They may not be efficient enough, and that can cost you money. This is only one example, but it is imperative to create and utilize reports to verify what you hear. Many other such reports are included throughout this book.

Another very important form of data gathering happens during the *site visit*. You should plan on visiting your locations at regular intervals. Make the intervals consistent so that not too much time lapses between visits; however, stagger the actual day and time. When you make the site visit, bring your reports with you and always verify that what your eyes see matches what you have heard in discussions with your staff. It is advisable when making a site visit that you develop a pattern of inspecting your property so that you are consciously reviewing all aspects of your property.

Simple keys to remember:

❑ Become personal.

❑ Don't delegate, proactively negotiate.

❑ Keep plenty of data, data, data.

▨ Mentor Like a Partner

The importance of picking the right people, knowing their personalities, and creating a communication system that builds trust and understanding results in an owner/employee relationship that operates much more like a partnership than a boss/subordinate arrangement. There are only a few people operating your property, so it is essential that they feel emotionally attached to your property just as a partner would. Ask them every day when they drive onto the property to "wear two hats" when they look at your real estate. First, ask them to view it as a prospective resident. Then ask them to put on another hat and look at the property as if they were owners. Indicate to them that if they see anything wrong while wearing either hat, then rest assured those individuals see it, too.

There is a small segment of the working population that is well suited for the apartment business, and because the turnover rate among employees is so high, you have a vested interest in fostering the talent of those individuals who chose to stay with this business for any length of time. Often those who remain for an extended period of time end up making a career out of it, and by emotionally investing in them, you are planting the seeds for more responsibility down the road as you grow. People are your biggest asset in the apartment business, so you must invest as much time and planning in this aspect of property management as any mechanical or administrative aspect. If you don't, rest assured you will have trouble. Remember, a little slipup and you can break your leg very quickly, but it takes a long time for it to heal.

Simple keys to remember:

❑ People are your biggest asset.

❑ Give your staff emotional ownership.

■ "Look, Listen, and Learn"

Here is a story to illustrate the property management principles discussed in this chapter and how they can bring value to your real estate.

We had recently taken ownership of a rather large property with a large staff. When performing our due diligence (the physical process of determining the value of the proposed real estate deal), it was very clear we would have to capitally invest on a large scale for infrastructure and marketability purposes. There was a significant upside in doing this: The property had tremendous visibility and was dynamic from the standpoint that it had seventeen different styles of apartments to market. But a lot of money was going to have to be spent and it needed to be spent where it made the most sense and with minimal waste. The management and staff needed to be very focused, very tight and intense, and all on the same page.

While assessing the possible purchase, the property profiling and the staff assessment had already begun. This process continued as we made the decision to go ahead with the deal. The most glaring concern I had was that the manager of the property did not possess team skills. The communication between staff and manager was demeaning, threatening, and overbearing. It was very clear to me that getting a staff to rally behind this type of management would be next to impossible and therefore getting a staff to really watch the huge financial process we were about to embark on was a real concern. These facts were compounded by the fact that this manager had been involved with employee litigation with some of the principals involved in the deal; she wasn't necessarily untouchable, but simply removing the manager wasn't an immediate option.

The staff was afraid of the manager and was ineffective. When you terrorize, you paralyze. Given the mitigating factors, my strategy was to quickly start installing on this staff individuals who did not have a predetermined fear of this manager, and then to take more direct control of the everyday management of this property. I started developing a "profile" of the type of people I needed at this site. They needed to be independent and they needed to be much more proficient than the present staff was in doing what we hired them to do. One of the problems was we had marginal people reporting to a headstrong manager. I needed people who could operate in their discipline at a higher level than the manager could. Finally, I needed people who weren't easily flustered by the manager's antics.

My goal was to build a strong staff and then either have this manager realize the value of having competent independent people or make this manager's modus operandi insignificant, with the idea of moving somebody else into that position. We received a resume from a young woman who had accounting skills, but what struck me more than her obvious skills was her almost stoic yet respectful confidence. I hired her, and I told the present manager that this person would be reporting to me, under the guise that I would get a chance to understand the economic ins and outs of this property on the fast track.

Throughout the next month or two, I made an effort to speak strategically to this individual directly, as well as a few other people on staff, to gain a trust and an understanding of the individual and the business problem. This exercise did not please the current manager, but it did start to change the staff perception of this manager's capability to disrupt and terrorize. Through these personal conversations I learned what did not come out in the interview process. First, this new accounting person owned approximately thirty-two duplexes with her husband; she knew the business from an ownership perspective and all facets of it. Second, she was extremely thorough with her reporting. Everything she said on the phone was backed up with data that were not only accurate, but added her insight.

This woman also had no problem with the manager. Although she didn't care for the manager, she wasn't at all intimidated because she knew this person's weaknesses and limitations. I also noticed the rest of the staff got along with this woman very well. The profile I had in my mind for the eventual manager was right under my nose. And through personal conversations, this woman made it clear she was ready for a challenge.

I decided to start giving her more and more responsibility. I knew that would force an eventual showdown with the present manager, but I had a confident feeling about which direction that showdown would take. There was one event that solidified this plan and carried the property into the future correctly. I had been looking for some financial data on utility usage and expenditure from the manager since taking ownership. The manager had been stalling because it was a large project and the manager did not have the acumen for this exercise. I gave the new accounting expert the task of carrying this project through, and I did it right in front of the manager. I believe I was talking to the manager for fifteen minutes when the accounting person knocked on the door and handed me a computer disk. She said that she didn't know if I used Excel or Lotus, so she copied the files on both.

This woman had been compiling this data all along. She intrinsically knew it was important and had independently decided to take up this task. The look on the current manager's face was priceless, and the end result was that the manager realized that her tenure was just about over. I had found my new manager. The present manager left the company on her own accord and I installed the accounting person in this position, where she stayed for three years, spearheading an economic success. We completed all the capital work efficiently and the property has been an economic winner ever since.

The accounting person turned manager now manages over $100 million worth of real estate for our organization. Two real estate entities she has taken leadership of have been named by regional industry trade organizations as the best in their class. More important, both properties have financially flourished and gone through a massive successful refinance. The value was inherent in the property, but the manager and her staff brought that value to the surface.

People are the single most important piece of the property management puzzle; spend as much time as necessary to get to know what your property needs and what each position requires. Once you have determined that, invest in these people, communicate with them, and understand them personally. Finally, encourage them to emotionally invest in your real estate as if they were partners. Your people will help you create value. Conversely, if you neglect to go through this exercise, your people can destroy value. Invest in finding and growing good people.

CHAPTER 4

The Strategy:

Create Value

Undoubtedly you have heard the phrase "one man's junk is another man's treasure." This is not to say that a goal of property investment is to purchase a substandard product. Rather, what should be gleaned from that statement is that every piece of real estate has an intrinsic value and most properties have yet-untapped value. If the goal is to buy the real estate and position it to be a long-term income-producing investment, then it is important to view this new investment in a futuristic way.

What can be done to create value? To start, it is important that this mind-set be established from the day the investment is anticipated; otherwise it becomes too easy not to reinvest in the property and simply count returns based on present income. The problem with settling into a habit such as this is that eventually the property will suffer and the funds won't be available if not planned for. The end result is that you start "sucking" value away from the property.

It is also important to understand that renting consumers are demanding of how their money is spent. Smart investors will understand that if they don't look to create value and maintain a property, it is more than likely that the competition will. Consumers today look at apartment living not as a necessary evil but rather the best "lifestyle" they can achieve for their money. In essence, simply providing four walls just doesn't cut it anymore. If investors want to maximize their return, they have to constantly review the property with a keen eye to how the investment is positioned in the marketplace and have a firm understanding of what will create additional value. Value can be realized through two main aspects of a property. The first is the community lifestyle and living accommodations; the second is the reliability of the services that are connected with the community.

In terms of community lifestyle and living accommodations, an apartment is a "home" to would-be renters. Therefore, value is created when all community and living arrangement aspects are maximized. This is why particular attention has to be put into the property as well as the individual apartment. Not unlike home owners, renters look to return to their neighborhood after a hard day's work and they want no less of an aesthetic experience than someone who manicures their own lawn. The apartment itself is important also. The reasons vary as much as there are different types of renters, but something about each apartment stands out to an applicant for an apartment.

The services connected with the community and their reliability can become a real factor in maintaining value. As discussed many times through this book, proper maintenance and customer service can make or break an occupant's desire to renew and stay at the community longer. As a property owner, you have to make sure that the "brick and mortar" is well maintained and that the staff responds promptly to breakdowns of equipment. Certain aspects of a property will inevitably break, but the savvy owner plans for and minimizes the possibilities. If a property is maintained properly, residents intrinsically rely on the service and therefore feel they are receiving value for their rent.

This chapter is meant to help you develop the philosophical mind-set to position your property as a successful long-term investment. It is important when making a real estate investment that a strategy and ownership philosophy be cultivated. Simply owning real estate does not in and of itself "create value." What does create value is a disciplined and consistent plan.

There are four aspects of long-term thinking that will put you on a path to creating and continually growing your investment's worth:

1. Identify the uniqueness of the investment.
2. Create value-added ancillary services and income.
3. Save for the future (i.e., capital investment is a must).
4. Utilize curb appeal, the greatest creator of value.

These four philosophies and strategies, in combination, are designed to reveal what the property intrinsically has to offer and then how you, as an owner, can augment and maintain that value over the course of years. It is critical that the renting public continually sees the value in the product. The remainder of this chapter examines each one of these aspects.

◼ Identify the Uniqueness of the Investment

What makes a consumer pick one similar product over another? The answer is probably as varied as the number of individual human beings who review the product. What manufacturers do over time is understand what key features of their product seem to attract attention. Multifamily housing is no different. Every community has selling points, and the challenge is to understand them and then use them to your benefit. This process can start while you anticipate the purchase. Start making a list of what attracted you to this investment over other properties. Break your list down into categories such as location, setting, amenities, and apartments.

❑ *Location.* What are the neighborhood-related selling points? Take a look around where a property is located. Is there something about the location that would entice people to rent? Is the property situated close to highways for commuting ease? What are the school systems like in the area? Are there local stores that are in close proximity and easy to travel to? These are all issues that individuals searching for a new home will take into consideration. It doesn't matter what the location is, because there are positive aspects to almost any location, and the goal of ownership is to determine what specific advantages can be derived from this unique location. Be creative when viewing a property. For example, maybe a property is situated in what area residents might call a "tough" neighborhood. Whether it is truth or perception, you can offset any doubts associated with that label if the property sits in a very desirable school district, because the selling point becomes the education system. The property could be in a hustling, bustling part of town that's certainly not a peaceful location but an active one. The selling point here is the proximity to shops and restaurants and the nightlife. A property could be right next to a major highway. To some people it might be a noisy place to live, but to others the adjacent highway may be the answer to their commuting worries. Knowing what aspects of a property's location are unique is something that will most likely stay constant throughout the time you own the property and therefore always has to be factored into the value the property has and can create.

❑ *Setting.* The property's setting and ambience become a value to many prospective renters. If, for example, a property sits in an urban area but is well landscaped and has large courtyards, the property has created for itself a rustic setting within the urban landscape. A segment of the renting population may view it as having a dual advantage. It is conveniently located yet it doesn't feel like the city. Another example could be a property with large courtyards conducive to families, so that the children have ample room to play on the property. In the case of a high-rise, maybe the views of the surrounding area are spectacular. It is important to mention again that these "setting"-type issues can be augmented over the years, but they rarely are removed from the property and therefore should always be considered value-adding aspects of a community. They should be part of the marketing and should always carry significance with an owner and a staff through the years when discussing the property with applicants.

❑ *Amenities.* Property amenities are part of a community lifestyle. Existing amenities or new ones created over time are aspects that any renter will review. Apartments, by their nature, are generally limited in space and the capacity to provide services that a home owner may expect. Apartment communities today have recognized that adding lifestyle-enhancing dynamics to the community enhances that intrinsic value. And, unlike location and setting (as discussed previously), a property doesn't always come with amenities included. Here an owner should review what exists that is a value presently and assess what might be a value-enhancing amenity in the future. The interesting thing is that the renters do not always utilize these features, but the fact that they exist does factor into the decision to rent.

There are two types of amenities that an owner should look at: those that a property offers simply by the way it was constructed, and those that provide added value by augmenting the property with additional features. In the first category would be something like ample parking spaces. In the twenty-first century, the average family owns more than one car, and one of the most contentious issues of a property is a lack of parking. So you might augment your property by providing assigned parking on the property, thereby ensuring that when an individual moves onto a property, that person will have adequate parking facilities. Some other amenities that can be utilized to sell the value of the property are:

❑ Pools
❑ Playgrounds
❑ Laundry facilities
❑ Storage facilities
❑ Clubhouses
❑ Business centers
❑ Exercise facilities

❑ Balconies or decks

❑ Picnic and barbeque facilities

There are many others. The point here is that each property has its own intrinsic amenities and additional amenities can be created. As an owner, you can stay competitive in the marketplace simply by knowing your property and what it possesses and having a keen eye for future possibilities. Some of the amenities listed previously may appear to apply only to larger properties, but even in a small community with four apartments, any of them can be achieved.

❑ *Apartments*. Apartment size and configuration often sell a community. The apartment or living space itself does matter in the "value" a property possesses. A property with loft apartments usually has more success in an urban setting, whereas larger units tend to have more success in a suburban atmosphere. The configuration of an apartment can make a difference, and square footage is always a selling point. The size of a kitchen can be critical to a rental, and the amount of storage or closet space is something almost every would-be renter reviews. Know what works in the community. Apartments by their structure can also provide convenience and value; an example is an apartment that has its own heating and cooling unit as opposed to having to rely on a central heating and cooling system common to all residents. Individual residents can then control the flow of heat or air-conditioning to their particular apartment. Or, if an apartment has enough room to accept laundry equipment, the individual does not have to venture outside to find a launderette.

As an owner, it is essential to become aware of what your investment's potential is and what makes it special. Once you've established that, then you already have the ability to market the value of your community to the renting public. If you maintain the condition of the property and its inherent advantages over the years, then a portion of worth or value will always be there, no matter how old the property. Identify the uniqueness of the investment and always pay particular attention to factoring that uniqueness into managing, maintaining, and marketing the property.

Simple keys to remember:

❑ Recognize the intrinsic value of each property.

❑ Look at location, setting, community amenities, and the apartment value itself when reviewing an investment's uniqueness.

❏ Focus on the value the uniqueness adds to the long-term success of a property—and protect it.

Create Value-Added Ancillary Services and Income

After reviewing the unique qualities that a property possesses, the conclusion may be that there are amenities that are not available that could make a difference to a renter who is comparing several properties. These additional amenities may change over time as the renting public continually redefines what is valuable to it. The multifamily business now provides a host of products and services that enhance the value of a property both in a tangible and in a less obvious, collective way. Services and products can be added to a property at an additional cost, thereby creating another income stream. Even if the income stream is not substantial, the perception the renter can get is that a community with many amenities and services is a more complete community, which therefore justifies the cost.

There are several income-producing amenities that can be added to a property in terms of both products and services. One typical example is laundry facilities. There are many national companies that will come onto a property and contract with an owner splitting revenue in an agreed-upon fashion to set up a full-service laundry room. The advantage to the property is that the laundry company does all the hard work, such as servicing the equipment; the resident gets the use of the amenity; and the ownership derives income at the same time. Laundry contracts tend to be long term over several years, so it is advisable to negotiate graduated income levels over the course of the contract. It is also advisable to insist that the laundry company keep the room in respectable shape by constantly upgrading and maintaining the facilities throughout the contract. Some other typical examples of income-producing amenities are:

❏ *Storage Facilities.* Companies can come in and build prefabricated storage facilities, again under contract. Facilities can literally be erected where it didn't appear the possibility existed. Income is divided, however.

❏ *High-Speed Internet Capability.* Broadband service can be provided by a cable company, the phone company, satellite providers, or wireless providers. These services again typically require long-term contracts with either guaranteed returns or graduated returns based on a percentage of residents buying services. One important note: Refrain from entering "exclusive" arrangements with such providers. Technology moves fast, and entering into an exclusive precludes a property from staying competitive.

❏ *Alarm Systems for Individual Apartments.* Providers can market directly to residents or offer discounted rates by arranging service through a community.

❏ *Exercise and Pool Facilities.* Creating an exercise area and charging minimally may not produce much income for you, but it can pay for itself and becomes a significant selling point for incoming residents.

❏ *Additional Apartment Services.* An example is providing laundry equipment in an actual apartment. The unit that has such equipment possesses a higher intrinsic value and therefore can be marketed and rented as such.

The key is to know what services will make a difference over and above the inherent value of the real estate as it relates to the market surrounding it. If, for example, the property's apartments are townhouses with basements and garages, building storage may not make sense. Yet offering "tiered" rental packages, with certain units, for example, having laundry equipment included, presents a prospective resident with a choice and lets an owner charge a premium, accordingly.

In addition, there are services that may initially cost the owner but can return value or perceived value because renters put a premium on such services. The two best examples are doorman services in a high-rise or mid-rise building and patrol services in a garden-style apartment community. Quantitatively, there is no clear answer as to whether such services actually make a property safer, but the perception is that they give the renter peace of mind. Video surveillance services have the same effect, as do gated communities. The owner could choose to build in a price structure that accounts for this "added value." This issue relates directly to knowing the value a property possesses on its own and being able to determine what value is derived by adding to the existing property.

Save for the Future; Capital Investment Is a Must

There is something to be said for the adage that to make money you need to spend money. Properties have an infrastructure, and like anything else manufactured, all aspects of a property have an expected or useful life span. If an owner plans on the investment being long term, then the investment has to be properly cared for. Many renters "drive by" a property before they make the decision to rent, so they can see and understand how the owners value their own property and residents. It is essential to factor structural or other property improvements into your long-term strategy for economic stability and growth.

As explained in previous chapters, this process starts with identifying, through the due diligence process, what aspects of the property have immediate needs. Then it is important to establish a reserve fund that is continually funded, a comprehensive plan for the future as to the cycle of property upkeep, and a careful review of the property on a continual basis. Inevitably, you will have to put money back into a property, and some of those investments can impact value in a positive way and can make economic sense. As an owner, you need to look at the net value derived from this strategy of investing capital over time in a consistent and predetermined way as opposed to expending cash when the physical plant wears out.

The prudent owner realizes if capital is invested back into a property, it is usually on the owner's timetable and the value is at the very least maintained. If an owner is forced into expenditure because an aspect of the property has fallen into neglect, the owner has little control over when that happens and how much it is going to ultimately cost. When parts of your property are allowed to fall into a state of disrepair, this also affects the bottom line on what the renting public perceives as an apartment and the community's true worth. If the renter doesn't believe the property has worth, then the intrinsic value of the property suffers as well in terms of potential income. It is obvious why upkeep is a true determiner of value; yet, oddly enough, there are owners who simply wait for the proverbial rainy day when the roof starts to leak for real.

When creating a long-term strategy, owners need to determine what aspects of a new investment will deteriorate and thus cost over time. Then they must make certain to have reserve funds available to take care of these larger issues on a property. An owner has to also have a relatively informed idea as to when things may need to be taken care of, so they can be planned. Roofs, siding, gutters and leaders, sidewalks, paving, doors, windows, and power plants all need constant replacement. In the interior carpet, appliances, cabinets, sinks, and tile floors are some of the issues that eventually have to be dealt with. Knowing the useful life of these items and then caring for them on a continual basis will help you decide what needs to be done next and how often such replacements will be necessary. Subsequent chapters discuss how best to achieve this, but what is important for now is that you understand how important putting money back into a property can be to maintaining and enhancing the value of your investment.

Some investors may want more tangible proof. So let's use the example of a roof that's allowed to deteriorate long past its useful life. The economics alone explain why it is essential to save, plan, and review a property and reinvest in the capital infrastructure. If a 100-foot by 50-foot roof needs to be reshingled with simple asphalt roofing tiles and it is done when the roof is reaching the end of its useful life but before its deterioration is structurally apparent, it might cost an owner $100 a square foot to reshingle. If, however, that same roof is let go until the deterioration is apparent with several leaks, further investigation may reveal that the plywood decking is also now deteriorated. So not only do the shingles need to be replaced but all the plywood needs replacement as well. Quite possibly the water could have permeated into the support beams of the structure, too. If this has occurred, this job may now cost $200 or $300 a square foot, substantially raising the cost. If the roof replacement simply was not planned for, then it probably wasn't saved for, either. This means the out-of-pocket expense to the owner affects all other expenses and distribution of income.

Finally, current residents may have experienced one leak too many and have decided that this community is not providing the best value for them. Residents who move out tell others not to rent there, and individuals who drive by the property can watch the roof slowly deteriorate. The result is that an owner who waits for the rainy day diminishes the value a property possesses, which in turn affects the potential for additional future income and value.

You can achieve positive economic results by choosing to improve specific aspects of a property or an apartment—not because they need to be improved, but because improving them increases the value a renter will be willing to pay for the improvements. An example is upgrading a kitchen with new cabinets, new floor tile, new appliances, new countertops and fixtures, and new lighting. This could potentially cost an owner a significant amount of money. If we use the base figure of $3,000 for those costs but charge an extra $75 a month in rent for the upgrades, an incremental $900 in annual income is derived. The $900 in additional income constitutes a 30 percent return on the original money invested in one year. The expenditure pays for itself in slightly over three years, and the value of the apartment basically remains at the higher rate. In an average year, there are very few investments (even the stock market) that will pay a 30 percent return on investment.

Part of the strategy for long-term investment in rental property should include saving for and putting money back into the property itself. The infrastructure of a property will eventually require repairs and replacements, but if planned for and implemented over time, value is maintained. If intentional improvements are added to a property, value can be created.

Simple keys to remember:

❑ Plan for deterioration. Property infrastructures will deteriorate over time, so plan for repair and replacement costs.

❑ Put money back into the property. Reinvesting brings tangible returns.

❑ Save, plan, implement, and review. Remember that property and its infrastructure have to be cared for, so regularly look for ways to make improvements.

Utilize Curb Appeal, the Greatest Creator of Value

When someone chooses to rent at one community instead of another, what are the factors that draw that individual to the apartment that eventually becomes his or her home? Most people are exposed to a property through two main sensory sources: what they hear and what they see. A property receives most of its rental inquiries through referrals, as does any good business. Referrals, though, only give some sense, from a distance, as to whether a community is adequate for a person's living needs. The primary way a property sells itself is by its presentation—or what's commonly called its *curb appeal,* referring to what people see as they drive by or pull onto the grounds. The importance of curb appeal to the entire renting process cannot be understated. Remember that the actual apartment to be rented is the last thing an applicant will see. Everything leading up to that apartment—the sidewalks, the entranceway, the hallways, the landscaping, etc.—must provide positive reinforcement to prospective residents so that they want to see the apartment. If a property lets down its guard, the process of showing the apartment may be thwarted before you've even had a chance to verbally engage an applicant. In other words, many individuals who otherwise would stop in instead turn away when they see something they don't like, and that ends the process.

Likewise, if the visual appearance of a property and everything leading up to the eventual apartment showing is very appealing, a property will attract many more prospects. Most people wouldn't think of an apartment as an impulse item, but it is like any other anticipated financial decision; part of the decision is affordability and part of the decision is personal taste. How many people go out to buy a reasonable car and end up buying just a little bit more than they thought they would? Curb appeal builds value through the volume of applicants that it can attract, the number of renters it can turn serious, and the perception it provides to everyone who drives by the property every single day and finally to those who live there.

It is essential to your investment/ownership strategy to emphasize every day, to anyone who watches that investment and manages that community, that curb appeal matters immensely. Sound management practices require that on a daily or routine basis, key curb appeal aspects be reviewed and adjusted. People don't rent the flower bed out in front of the property, but they most definitely notice and may choose to rent because of what a well-manicured flower bed represents. There are a number of curb appeal essentials that can make a difference. Remember, if you don't attract people, they certainly won't rent. Here is a list of typical eye pleasers:

- ❑ *Well-Maintained Flower Beds.* These beds should be weeded and trimmed, and because most flowers do not bloom all year, constant attention should be put into changing out certain flowers with seasonal flowers that are always in bloom. The term used all the time when referring to the seasonal flower replacement is *seasonal color.* These flower beds should be strategically placed near main en- trances on public streets and also near rental offices and anywhere else groups of people will frequent in a community.

- ❑ *Signage.* Clean, attractive, readable signs should exemplify and communicate what a property is. These signs often can be situated among the "color." If there are multiple signs for a community, they should all be similar.

- ❑ *Monuments.* The combination of signs, color, rocks, fountains, and any other ornamental object constitutes what is called a monument. Often these features are situated at a main entrance and, simply put, they are there to attract curiosity.

- ❑ *Well-Groomed Landscaping and Entrance Roads.* Roads should be clean, curbs and lines bright, the grass edged and cut. The entire sensory perception is that the place is cared for.

- ❑ *Clean and Enclosed Refuse Areas.* There is nothing more offensive to the eye than garbage everywhere.

- ❑ *Fresh Paint on Railings, Doors, and Signposts.* A fence post that stays broken for weeks on end gets noticed by passersby, and it will breed the perception someone doesn't care.

- ❑ *Fresh Balloons and Flags at Main Entrance.* This signifies that the community staff is actively seeking people's business. It exudes enthusiasm and because it's fresh every day, people recognize the effort being put into the presentation.

❏ *Continuous Holiday Decorations*. Be careful not to exclude or offend, but constantly changing up with the seasons makes people turn their head instead of just drive by the property.

The curb appeal concept does not stop with physical monuments, either. The way a property is managed is reflected in the curb appeal. For instance, allowing cars to be worked on in a parking lot will affect how a property is viewed by a passerby. The rules and regulations that are established for a community and the diligence to which the management staff enforces those rules directly affects the curb appeal of the property. The presentation at the rental office or where a manager meets a visitor is equally important. The entire marketing effort is discussed in another chapter, but what is important to understand is that an individual coming to rent has, for some reason, decided that this community is worth looking into further. A well-trained management staff that understands this concept will be mindful that the show never stops. Curb appeal applies to the way the staff is dressed, as well as the way materials for rental are packaged and disseminated.

In the twenty-first century, curb appeal has gone virtual and high tech, also. With the advent of Internet advertising, renters can virtually and instantly "drive by" a property anywhere in the world simply by going online. The Internet allows an almost unlimited number of pictorial resources to be viewed by a prospective resident; especially popular is 360-degree photography, where the viewer can get a panoramic view of the subject property. When you put photographs of your property online, remember that they may look different on-screen than they do in person. The advantage of the digital medium, though, is that it allows you to update pictures in real time, so if your property has notable features in the summer or fall, in a second's time the curb appeal that is advertised can be changed to fit the season.

One might try to argue that curb appeal is just a show and doesn't accurately reflect what a property is about, but if the owner continually stresses how important curb appeal is, then the staff gradually becomes conditioned to knowing that's what the ownership expects and that's what the renting public requires. Focusing on curb appeal means focusing on what everyone is looking at. Therefore, the community is being cared for. Obviously, if prospective renters are sold on everything that has been presented to them and then they view an apartment that appears contrary to all they have seen, the staff has failed. How staff take care of the outside of a community is exactly the way they should be taking care of the entire property. The key to curb appeal, though, is that if you can't get people to come through the front gate or front door, there is no way they will rent an apartment that a staff never gets the opportunity to present.

Curb appeal is essential to all facets of owning multifamily real estate. Think of how anyone would purchase his or her own property. The property has to carry some appeal. If a used car had a dent, wouldn't it be discounted for sale? Property obtains some value from how it is perceived. Value can be appreciated by confirming and augmenting a property's visual appeal. People do pay more for the living environment and for the perception the property carries in the market. Code enforcement individuals often come away with a perception that if a place is well taken care of from an appearance standpoint, then most likely there's responsible ownership. Responsible owners often get the benefit of the doubt when something doesn't go quite right. Lenders often have reasons to assess the value of a property, and though their biggest interest is the financial statements, if they arrive on the property and are exposed to positive visual feedback, they will more likely look at the economic glass as half full, not half empty.

In the chapters before and the chapters after, you are given many specific ways of handling the myriad issues that owners and managers deal with every day. Every single bit of the information presented will have a positive effect if you apply it correctly. If the goal of real estate investment is to create value, then achieving that goal requires knowing what makes a property special, keeping a property functionally operating, saving for a rainy day, and finally understanding that value is something that has to be worked at and fostered every day through effective community presentation. These principles have to be communicated to everyone who works to keep a community running. What you, as the owner, philosophically reinforce should be carried through in everything a staff does. Strategy and concepts such as curb appeal do create real value. Speak of their importance every single operating day.

■ "The $17 Million Yellow Paint"

The creation of "value" can do many things for an owner of real estate. It can provide a basis for increasing what each apartment is valued at in the open market, thereby increasing income. It can position a property in regard to total value should the owner choose to sell the property at a significant return. Value can allow ownership to use an investment and its appreciated worth for whatever purpose the ownership deems appropriate through refinancing. Refinancing is a common practice in the industry; it can recapitalize a tired investment by restructuring debt. "Cashing out" provides a capital stream for other future investments. Building value over time and using the *equity,* or the value an investment has attained to borrow against, is a common real estate practice.

Value becomes a key facet of this practice because without a substantially appreciated investment, refinancing simply does not make sense. When financial institutions look at refinancing a property, they have internal thresholds of how much they will allow a borrower to refinance. It's known as *loan to value*—that is, how much money can be borrowed in regard to what a property's value is at the time the loan is being considered. Loan to value is a negotiable item, but most institutions have a high end limit. Generally speaking, a benchmark ratio is about 80 percent loan to value. What this means is that if a property is valued at $100,000 the most a lending institution will allow you to borrow is $80,000.

An owner has to view the refinancing process in terms of what debt is left on the original mortgage (if there is an original mortgage) and what the additional funds will be used for, because obviously while refinancing is establishing another source of capital, it is also creating a source of new debt. If the value of a property has not appreciated substantially enough over the primary mortgage period, then refinancing achieves little more than creating an overburdened property in terms of loan commitments. Properties are "valued" through what is called an appraisal process. The appraiser is usually a subcontracted individual or a hired lender representative who views the subject property and measures its worth and performance in relationship to competition and operating efficiency. While the appraiser has no final say on whether a loan is made to an investor/owner, the appraiser sets the "bar" for how the lender calculates the loan deal based on the "value" the appraiser assigns to the subject property. It is quite obvious, then, to see that value and how it is arrived at is a very important concept.

It is also important to recognize that when such a deal is being structured, the lender and the appraiser are in essence speculating somewhat because the decisions they make are made in a very short period of time, yet the loans that end up being consummated through this process are usually large in terms of dollars and can be long-term commitments. If you anticipate refinancing, remember that the appraiser and the lender are at best getting a "snapshot" of a property and its performance, and although they may not like to admit it, there is some subjectivity to that process. If an owner realizes that, then steps can be taken to level the playing field in regard to value. Make no mistake about it—sound financial performance is the most assured way to maximize value, but you may be surprised by some other things that can enhance the perception of those involved. This story goes to the heart of why creating value and being very attentive to curb appeal and property perception can positively influence the renting public or a lender trying to decide if a proposed refinance makes financial sense.

I once worked with a property owner who had been trying to refinance a large holding for years. He was as successful in the financing game as any individual I had ever had the privilege to work with. He had attempted to refinance this property several times but never seemed to be able get a structured deal that worked for him and the lender. The subject property had incredible value, in my estimation. It was unique in the marketplace and very desirable to the average renter. The property had everything—it was close to highways, and stores and restaurants were in walking distance. The property was large enough that one could live in a quiet, removed area or be in the thick of things. The amenities were as competitive as those of any surrounding property. The units were desirable and modern and the price was very competitive. I was perplexed as to why he couldn't seem to refinance this project.

We had several financial institutions that went through the application process with us and were very impressed, but the deals never went through. When I sat down with the ownership, it became very clear that the problem was the appraised value reached by each of these financial lenders wasn't ever high enough for the deal to make financial sense to this principal. He could get a refinance deal, but it wouldn't justify the expense and commitment the ownership would then have to the new debt. The highest appraised value the principal had been able to obtain through this process was approximately $88 million, and as he best calculated it, he needed an appraised value of at least $100 million for it to make financial sense. Some others may have stopped trying altogether, but as I said, this individual was one of the best financial managers of multifamily real estate I had ever encountered, so he knew very well the "value" of the real estate he bought and managed. He believed very firmly that the lenders who had reviewed the property to this point weren't seeing its true value and he decided to press on. This owner and I had a similar philosophy about how properties were perceived in the marketplace, so he asked me to think very seriously about what we could do to sensitize the lenders and their appraisers to the intrinsic worth of the real estate.

I considered what the owner could do, and then something struck me. When appraisers look at an investment, they review it by several standard appraisal approaches. They look at your income and expense, they look at your market potential, and they look at your history relative to those points. It's all standard. How could we move the financial bar by $12 million if those things are relatively constant? An owner not in tune with *property management principles* would suggest that it couldn't be done and move on, but this owner knew better and so did I. In my experience, appraisals are in part subjective and therefore can be changed. The strategy was to focus on the next appraisal. Even though the income and expense numbers wouldn't change dramatically in that time, changing the perception of the property and its "value potential" was the goal.

One of the most important concepts in multifamily real estate, as I have mentioned, is "curb appeal." The actual apartment itself is the last thing potential renters will see. They won't entertain living at your property if they don't feel comfortable with the "show" you provide leading up to the apartment. How does this concept translate to the appraiser? If you can't change the financials or the market, what you can change is the perception that the appraisers have when they perform their site inspection for the appraisal report. Not unlike potential renters, they too form their first impression as soon as they approach the property. That was my solution: We needed to use curb appeal to our advantage! This is not to say that curb appeal wasn't always important, because it was. In fact, it had always been a philosophical necessity with this ownership and my management. But we had to go out of our way to make sure that the property was viewed as better in every way than what the competition was showing. This should always be your goal as an owner, but sometimes when you look harder you see more, especially if you are looking through the eyes of an appraiser, whose job is to look very hard for a very short period of time.

I instructed my staff to pay particular attention to all curb appeal details leading up to the next financier's appraisal site inspection. The entire staff paid particular attention to visuals that would leave these very temporary visitors with a lasting positive impression. I had learned over the years that a simple and inexpensive way to indicate a responsible, sincere ownership was on the job every day was making sure all curbed areas were freshly painted yellow. The yellow paint is extremely eye-catching, and it can become the focus of all that is being taken care of on a property and all that is not. If the curbs are allowed over the years to get dull and scarred by tires, the yellow paint is still very noticeable, but for the wrong reasons. There were many other curb appeal issues that we paid attention to, but because eyes focus on color and cleanliness, I put a lot of focus on the yellow curbs. I instructed my staff to pay extra special attention to the curbs in preparing for the inspection. This became somewhat comical because the appraisers had to cancel several times in a row and we painted the curbs each time a new appointment was scheduled. By the way, this has become a source of pride with the staff, and the curbs are always freshly painted!

Although the property always looked good, it was looking rather immaculate when the appraisal team finally visited the property. The site inspectors were effusive in their comments about the condition of the property and the detail that they believed the site staff constantly paid attention to. In fact, they visited on two separate occasions. And they specifically mentioned the yellow curbs in relation to the detail!

They were highly impressed with the property and the operation of the property, and I firmly believe they reasoned that if any property could maximize the market potential, our property could. In the four months since the last and best $88 million appraisal, the occupancy of the property remained constant and our collections were maintained at the same level (this staff had always been good at controlling expenses). Not much had changed in that four months except the impression left on the people valuing the property. The end result of this most recent attempt to refinance was an appraised value of $105 million! That is not a typo.

It needs to be emphasized that the idea here isn't to "fool" people; rather, you just want to constantly pay attention to the detail that people see every day when they pass your property. The first impressions left do have an intrinsic and direct impact on the value of the real estate. A luxury car may not perform any better on the road than a good, reasonably priced vehicle, but people perceive it does and will pay much more for the luxury automobile. This basic management principle of utilizing curb appeal helped increase the value of the asset by $17 million in a short period of time.

This may be an exceptional example of what property management does to create value, but it's a good example to amplify what effect management can have on a property. Though a property may not be refinanced every day, it does receive looks from potential residents each day. Collectively, fully occupied buildings that can constantly raise rents build long-term real value. There is nothing wrong in making sure that people's perception of your property draws them to you over the competition first.

The owner consummated that refinance deal and had the property appraised for $5 million more than his target!

CHAPTER 5

The Operations

KISS (Keep It Super Simple)

The four keys to an effective property management operation are:

1. Establish simple procedures.
3. Detail and standardize.
4. Communicate on all levels.
5. Follow up consistently.

Relatively speaking, no matter how expensive the investment is, managing multifamily real estate can and should be a very logical exercise with surprisingly very few essential components. You don't have to be a rocket scientist to operate this kind of business, as long as your operation is structured and management enforces repetitive, almost religious performance of structured tasks, as well as verifies the accuracy of reporting relative to those tasks.

The premise is simple: The more time that an apartment stays occupied by a resident who pays for the right to possess that space, the more income you'll derive and the less money you'll spend having to prepare that apartment for future residents. This premise is maximized by "controlling" several distinct aspects of this process.

■ Establish Simple Procedures

When purchasing any property, ask the previous owner for all records related to the current occupant of each unit and the current value of each unit (i.e., the rent). A good owner will provide much more information than that, but all previous owners are not necessarily efficient in their own right. Take whatever information that has been provided and create a baseline database about the property. Additionally, there should be rental records for each unit. Those records should include the lease for each rented unit as well as any application information about each occupant in each apartment.

Very early into your ownership, make a comparison of the inherited occupant listing with the lease records. Go a step further and inspect each apartment more thoroughly and interview each resident. Verify that all three independent sets of information are accurate and complete. If any information is incorrect or incomplete, this is the time to correct it. This process is vitally important because it establishes the current condition of the tenancy and ensures that any information going forward is based on actual fact. Construct a basic information-reporting system or what is called a *rent roll*. The rent roll will list the total number of apartments in the community individually but may include other information, too. Put some thought into creating such a list because it can become a comprehensive reference guide from this point forward. An example of what typically appears on a rent roll is shown here:

Sample Rent Roll

Apt #	Occupant	Unit Type	Rent	Renewal Date	Security Deposit	Square Feet
1	Smith, John	1bd1ba★	$750.00	8/31/05	$1,125.00	800
2	Vacant	2bd2ba	$1,000.00	—	$1,500.00	1,100

★bd = bedroom, ba = bathroom

Most simple rent rolls will have totals in each of these categories to provide you a clear picture of the key aspects of a property. These few bits of information become the central themes in the daily communication with staff and residents and can also be used to review the progress and success of the investment. Tracking methods can now establish a true set of information. It is absolutely essential that this information remain current.

This would also be an appropriate time to decide whether to keep records in manual form or to computerize. As part of the purchase, accounting or property management software and accompanying hardware may have been inherited from the previous ownership. The smaller the initial investment the less likelihood records will have already been computerized. Manual records will suffice, but if the intention is to invest for the long term and expand, then software is a valuable tool. Rather than create record-keeping and tracking methods from scratch, there are several good software products on the market already. Some examples are Yardi, MRI, and Rent Roll (this product is often used by owners who buy and operate HUD-assisted properties through the Section 8 program). All software providers have websites. The links for these three in particular are: www.yardi.com, www. mrisystem.com, and www.realpage.com/products/software.asp. There are obviously many other providers for property management software; these are just a small sample of the products available.

There are some considerations to think about when purchasing property management software. First, there are products that solely concentrate on the accounting aspects of managing multifamily real estate, yet there are others that manage the money and the operations. If you decide to purchase a software program, then assess what features you need today but also project out what you think you will need five years from now, and buy for the future. Test the product personally. If you find the software is difficult to navigate, then more than likely your employees will not be able to use or understand it. In the constantly evolving computer market, make sure the software package will be providing constant product upgrades and continuous support.

Finally, consider the product's ability to be accessed via the Web. That is, instead of buying disks to install and having the program exist only on the computer it was installed on, you want to be able to go online and access the information virtually from anywhere. More important, your computer support group will be able to maintain the Web-based program from anywhere. Neither you nor anyone on your staff has to become a computer expert. Many computer programs provide comprehensive reporting, too, so if you decide at the outset to use such a program and your operations expand, the staff will understand and use that software to its fullest extent.

Suppose the closing has just occurred in the purchase of a ten-unit, garden-style apartment complex. There are five one-bedroom apartments and five two-bedroom apartments that make up the community. You've asked for certain financial and historical benchmarks through the contract period. There is a record of what the apartments have rented for in the past, and the previous ownership records should also indicate how many apartments have turned over on a yearly basis. A cursory physical inspection of the property and each apartment is also completed or will be shortly after purchasing. You've done a comparison of the complex and the surrounding competition. Finally, by this time you have also made a decision about what you will spend to improve this investment to try to maximize value. It is now time to create methods to tightly follow the progress of this investment. There are three very essential areas of review and control that should be established:

1. Occupancy
3. Delinquency and rent collection
4. Maintenance and physical plant

Occupancy

While each of the aforementioned control areas is discussed at greater length in other chapters, the general rule of thumb is to create simple ways of tracking the business. Occupancy records will become more critical as an organization grows and expands. But right from the outset, no matter how small the property is, you should be keeping a running record, from day to day and week to week, so that you and the staff are always aware of the status of each apartment. This can be accomplished with a simple vacancy report, such as the one given in Chapter 3, Figure 3-1.

Collectively, what does the number of vacant units indicate? It tells you what needs to be rented. If you are constantly reviewing the local competition and what they are doing, it is also a way to keep abreast of where your investment stands in the marketplace. For instance, if you have a ten-unit complex and there are two vacant units, the occupancy rate is 80 percent of the total units. With that information you can ask, "Is the occupancy rate of surrounding communities similar to this community's?" Based on the answer to that question you can determine your position in the marketplace.

To discern the competition's occupancy rate, consider doing a *market survey* periodically. A market survey is a quick snapshot of what the local competition possesses as amenities, what they are charging in rent, and what their occupancy rates are. For a sample, see Figure 5-1. By performing a market survey, owners can better understand where their property sits relative to competition.

Another way of establishing occupancy is to know when each lease expires. This is important so that you can contact renters before their lease expires and attempt to get them to renew their lease. Equally significant, with this information you'll be able to make a fairly accurate monthly prediction about when possible vacancies may be created by residents who aren't renewing.

Figure 5-1. Market survey.

MARKET SURVEY

Property	Clinton St. Lofts	Forest Hill Towers 1 & 2	Abington	Parkwood Place	Parkwood	Audubon Place	Forest Creek	Inverness	Lakeview	Hyde Park	Clinton Towers	Gaslight Commons
Phone #	000-0000	000-0000	000-0000	000-0000	000-0000	000-0000	000-0000	000-0000	000-0000	000-0000	000-0000	000-0000
Units	63	401	220	290	290	161	656	368	699	332	500	200
1 Br.	$1,005–1,600	$1,025	$900	$750	$750	$825	$600	$600	$800	$700	$1,025	$1,575
SQ. FT.	516–827	800	900	850	700	750	687–706	700	660–1000	647	700	676
2 BR.	$1,542.00	$1,325	$1,200	$0	$950.00	$1,250–1,300	$700	$750	$950	$785	$1,555	$1,920
SQ. FT.	910/1107	1,200	1,250	0	850	779	800	930	964	900	850	896
3 BR.	0	0	$1,500	0	0	0	0	0	$1,600	0	$1,625	$2,175
SQ. FT.	0	0	1,100	0	0	0	0	0	1,100	0	900	1,033
Utilities	H/HW	H/HW/G	E/H/HW	H/HW	H/HW	H/HW	W/S	HW/S	H/HW/CG	H/HW/CG	H/HW	H/HW/CG
Laundry	YES	YES	YES	YES	YES	YES	YES	YES	YES	YES	YES	YES
Pool	NO	NO	NO	NO	NO	NO	YES	YES	YES	YES	YES	YES
Club House	NO	NO	YES	NO	NO	NO	YES	NO	NO	NO	YES	YES
Patio	NO	NO	NO	YES	NO	NO	YES	YES	YES	YES	YES	YES
Play Area	N/A	NO	N/A	YES	NO	NO	YES	YES	NO	YES	YES	YES
Pets	NO	NO	NO	NO	NO	NO	YES	YES	YES	YES	YES	YES
Lease Term	12	12	12	12	12	12	12	12	6 & 1 YEAR	6 & 1 YEAR	12	12
Sec. Deposit	One Month	$785–1,325	One Month	One Month	One Month	One Month	One Month	One Month	One Month	One Month	One Month	One Month
Specials	Lofts	NONE	Spacious	NONE	NONE	NONE	NONE	NONE	NONE	NONE	NONE	One Month Free Rent

Simple keys to remember:

Occupancy can be forecasted if you do the following:
- ❑ Track vacancies from week to week.
- ❑ Review the surrounding market.
- ❑ Track lease renewals.

Delinquency and Rent Collection

You also need to develop simple systems to track delinquency and rent collection. Residents will pay their rent the way you let them. If the methods for rent collection are not clear and concise, it will be hard to track. Residents respond to regimentation, or the lack thereof. Training the residents that rent is due on a specific day, after which it is considered late, normalizes the rent-paying process for the resident and for an operational understanding of the collectibles on a monthly basis.

Establish a date when the rent is due and a date the rent is considered late, with a late fee, so that the late date has some significance. Finally, establish a date at which legal action will be taken to evict or return possession of the apartment to the ownership should the resident not pay the rent on any of the set thresholds. Check local and state regulations concerning late fees and legal fees because there can be limits and restrictions. Where and how the rent is to be paid is equally significant. Residents need a roadmap of sorts that clearly indicates what is expected of them. The forms of payment a management office will accept are important also. It is not advisable to take cash when it can be avoided. Likewise, you should have rules in place should individuals pass bad checks, for instance. If you receive a check that bounces, make sure the resident covers any fees. After that, it may be prudent not to accept personal checks from any individual who has passed a bad check.

Office personnel often get fooled into making exceptions when confronted by a renter's explanation of why rent cannot be paid on time. There will be those times when the resident's tale is legitimate; experience will lead you to understand when that is the case. But in the vast majority of situations, rent is late because the owner/manager has given the renter the idea that it is okay to pay late. Once that's been allowed to happen, it becomes much harder to "reel in" delinquent renters and discipline them. The most important thing to remember about the process established for delinquency and rent collection is that once the policy is established *stick to it consistently.*

Maintenance and the Physical Plant

Maintenance is the third area where systems should be established—first, because maintenance is a cost center and, second, because poor systems will create vacancy for the investment. We explore maintenance in much greater detail in Chapter 7. However, simply put, make sure there's a mechanism to follow for how vacancies are readied for rent, how maintenance requests are handled, and how the property and its common areas are reviewed. Establish systems for how supplies are purchased and how work is awarded to contractors. Each of these areas, when given some basic controls, saves money and makes money.

Finally, there is an aspect of maintenance that concerns itself with major systems. These are typically the power plants, boilers, hot water vessels, air-conditioning, water-pumping and sewer-pumping systems, or large capital items such as roofing and pavement. When these systems are not regularly cared for in a structured way, they can be extremely expensive to repair or replace. They can run so inefficiently that the operating costs escalate and no one is aware until the big money has to be spent to repair these systems. Establish continuous review of these systems to ensure a reasonable useful life and, in the case of power plant systems, efficient operation.

Simple keys to remember:

Establish procedures in three important areas:
- ❑ Occupancy tracing
- ❑ Delinquency/rent collection
- ❑ Maintenance and the physical plant

Detail and Standardize

When establishing those repetitive procedures for reviewing the occupancy, collecting rent, and maintaining the physical plant, it is very important to detail and standardize how operational issues are discussed and performed. Doing so will create very logical solutions to everyday apartment issues. If paperwork isn't something you relate to well, then property management is not for you.

The apartment industry is cyclical in terms of what has to be done every day. Unlike in many other industries, once a property is purchased, the location cannot be changed. The property can be altered, but the basic apartment remains the basic apartment. Actually, very few things change, so the work that has to be performed and reviewed daily in multifamily real estate is minimal. Yet, if there are no standardized methods of handling those few functions daily, it is amazing how confusing things will look and how poorly an apartment community will be managed.

The importance of standardization becomes evident when tracking vacant units and whether they are rented. If a weekly vacancy report is maintained showing vacant units and move-out dates and projected move-in dates, then you start to understand the turnover patterns and the staff's ability to get units rented in a timely fashion. That information in turn reveals monthly and yearly patterns for the property and the market. If the vacancy report isn't consistently maintained, updated, and reviewed, then owners and managers start to guess and don't proactively see when a vacancy problem starts to occur.

When establishing a rental policy, you need a consistent and clear benchmark as to when an apartment is actually rented. A typical rental process starts with an application and any necessary personal information that goes with an application, and usually you'll charge a fee to review the prospective renter's credit. Once that process is completed, you review the information received from the credit and/or background check. From that, you decide whether the applicant is financially qualified to rent an apartment. At this point, although the prospective resident has been approved, there is nothing holding that individual or "obligating" him or her to an apartment. It is appropriate to secure the apartment with some sort of deposit (also known as *earnest money* or a *reservation fee*; depending on the state, it is important to use the correct term). The apartment is then assigned a date in which it will be occupied.

At what point is that apartment considered rented? In this case, the apartment should be considered rented when the applicant is accepted for rental and has placed some funds to secure it. To follow that logic out, the date at which the resident moves in would be considered the date at which the apartment is occupied. Sounds simple enough, but if these principles are not standardized, then an owner may believe an apartment is occupied or rented when in fact it may not be even close to either. As an owner acquires more units, it becomes even more important to use standardized terminology in order to avoid future confusion about when an apartment is rented.

Create "staff syntax"—but make sure all involved are using the same comparable terms for the same functions. Misinterpreted information can affect the managing of a community and can even lead to confusion in how rental agents or managers think they should be compensated for the number of rentals produced. Here's an example: An ambitious rental agent may tell the owner that she has produced five rentals this week. If the owner simply trusts that number without really understanding what it means, the owner may decide to pull some advertising, thinking it is not necessary. The rental agent may think she produced five rentals when in fact she produced five applications for rentals. What the rental agent may have failed to relay to the owner was that those applications had not yet gone through credit and background checks. Once they did, three of those applications were denied for bad credit history. They were never rentals. This critical information would become very evident if a detailed procedure is established and standardized. Only then will you, as an owner, have the information necessary to make baseline decisions.

Determining when someone is considered "moved out" of an apartment is another important concept to standardize, and it is tied very directly to the lease, so it should be in concert with the legal documents. Even so, it is still important that the owner and staff view vacant units the same way. Is the unit vacant if rent hasn't been paid for a while and no one has heard from the resident? Not necessarily. In this case it may be prudent to initiate legal action to regain possession of the apartment. In most states, without some form of court sanction, an owner could jeopardize the property's legal position by viewing this unit as vacant, independent of a court decision.

Is a unit vacant if the residents indicated, in writing or verbally, they were going to move out on a predetermined date and it appears that they may have moved a good portion of their belongings out of the unit? Again, it's dangerous simply to assume that the residents might be moved out. Although different states and different municipalities view vacancy somewhat differently, a standard regarding vacancy should be established for all involved in the property. The standard should conform to local code and the lease but also should be understood the same way by all staff members.

Typically an apartment is considered vacant when residents have physically handed the keys to a recognized staff member and have indicated they have vacated. Staff should encourage residents through lease preparation or otherwise to give a written notice to vacate as a matter of confirmation. In the case of nonpayment of rent or continued absence from the property, always have a court or local governing authority determine when it is legally viable to regain possession of an apartment. Whenever standard policy is established, the policy should be viewed the same way by any employees as well as by the residents. There should only be one set of rules governing a property. These standard rules should always be explained at move-in time to residents and should be part of the lease process so there is no misunderstanding.

Here are some other important concepts to standardize:

❑ *"Rent Ready" Status.* How is rent-readiness determined? Establish a point at which a unit is completely suitable for occupancy and to show for rental purposes. Some locations require a certificate of occupancy, which is literally a certificate permitting a landowner to physically allow someone to occupy a particular apartment. This certificate is usually fee driven and is accompanied by an inspection. This certificate is issued by the local governing authority. It can become a clear indicator that an apartment is rent ready.

❑ *Rental Due/Late Dates.* When is rent due and when is it late? When deciding this procedural concept, you must make additional decisions as well related to how rent is handled when the late date falls on a weekend, what the late fees are, and when eviction actions are started for nonpayment. Also consider the cost of legal fees. Establishing a consistent recording policy for rents is an absolute.

❑ *Violations.* How are rules and regulation violations dealt with? Are there clear procedures to address a problem and bring a problem to a conclusion? Is the administration of these rules clearly spelled out? (Remember, in regard to violations, local ordinance or code may clearly dictate how matters are to be handled.)

❑ *Application Process.* Is the rental and application process, including the credit and background checks, clearly spelled out for both applicants and staff?

❑ *Subcontracting.* How does staff decide whether an item will be handled in-house or subcontracted, and how does that subcontractor bidding process get carried out?

❑ *Maintenance Issues.* What is normal procedure when a maintenance issue is reported? How is the problem corrected and how is the fix then reported and recorded, both to the resident and to management?

❑ *Operations Issues.* How are building operations issues (e.g., boiler operations) reviewed and maintained? Are logs kept on their daily operation and a regular maintenance procedure followed?

❑ *Emergency Issues.* What is "emergency maintenance" as it relates to normal operating business hours? There will be exceptions, but you should clearly define
what will be called an emergency and what kind of work will (and will not) be
permitted outside of normal business hours.

It is equally important to use as much detail as possible to make your property
procedures as accurate as possible. For instance, to determine whether an apartment
is ready to rent, it is helpful to establish a "progress report" showing incrementally
the status of any given apartment from its vacate date to its new occupancy date. If
this procedure is kept up on a daily basis, the apartment status will be always visible.
Terms that might be useful in understanding how close an apartment is to being
"rent ready" are illustrated in this short sample report:

Apt #	Date Vacated	Prepped	Painted	Carpeted	Final Cleaned	Move-in Date
1	8/13/05	8/17	8/21			9/1

In this example, the apartment is to be occupied on the first of September, but what
else can be gleaned from this simple report about the apartment's readiness to rent
at this time?

In the case of a delinquency policy, if you have established very clearly when
rent is considered late and when late fees are assessed, and that information is reviewed on a consistent, preset date every month, you'll be able to see the pattern
the community has developed and, from there, you may be able to deduce what
may be causing a problem to persist. Look for the average number of delinquent
rents this property experiences on a monthly basis. If the property is experiencing a
larger-than-normal vacancy rate, try to determine why by reviewing these two
functions: the turnover rate and the number of delinquencies. For example, if the
time it takes to prepare an apartment has spiked during this vacancy period or has
grown in any substantial way, the staff may be taking too long to prepare apartments
and schedule move-ins. Therefore, by the time the apartment is ready, the community has had more move-outs and effectively the vacancy remains or grows. If,
however, the turnover of the apartments seems consistent, but the delinquent rent
has grown noticeably, it might be an indication that the staff has become lenient on
applicant screening and several residents who cannot financially afford the apartments may have been errantly moved in. They will eventually fail, causing a spike
in the vacancy.

By establishing standard ways of looking at procedures and providing as much detail as possible, many of the processes in the apartment business become fairly simple to follow.

Simple keys to remember:

❑ Standardize daily operating procedures.

❑ Provide as much detail as possible when reporting on those procedures.

❑ Learn to use this structured, detailed information to understand the property.

Communicate on All Levels

Communication and listening skills are essential to any business, but uniquely so for the apartment business. Most likely, as an owner of a community, you don't live where you own. Therefore, much of what takes place in this business takes place over a phone or in the form of correspondence. The more property an owner accumulates, the harder it becomes to conduct business strictly on premises, and more likely than not, an owner will be relying on staff to operate the investments. It becomes essential, then, to create communication methods that allow an owner to "visualize" what is taking place on a particular property. This can be achieved by establishing standard methods of looking at the property and then consistently talking about them.

So, for example, you need a vacancy report and a discussion at a regularly scheduled time with staff about that vacancy report. The vacancy report should include a list of each vacant apartment and when it was vacated. Additionally, the report should include when each vacant unit has been rented and a projected move-in date. The report should be broken down by unit size. It should include notices to vacate or upcoming known move-outs, and it is also helpful to have the rental office traffic numbers for the following week. This review should be with an owner on a scheduled day each week. The report becomes a conversation tool, helping everyone to understand how a property is performing without an owner having to be present daily. Suppose the vacancy report reveals that there is one size unit with a larger percentage of vacancy than any other size unit. During weekly review, the owner can start asking the staff questions. For example, ask the staff what a comparable size unit in the surrounding market is renting for, or try to find out what amenities the competition is offering that you may not be offering in that type of unit. Perhaps you're charging too much for the area. By establishing a report that clearly breaks down these vacancy aspects, reviewing this report on the same day every week, and verbally going over this report with staff, it becomes very easy to detect where a possible problem or inconsistency exists.

Because you, as the owner, will end up relying on others to watch your investment, whether they are employees or subcontractors, effective communication is absolutely critical if you want to clearly understand what is going on at a property. If you want to be an effective communicator in the apartment business, first recognize that unlike in many other businesses, staff sizes are traditionally small relative to the size and/or value of the property. As an owner, a tremendous amount of trust has to be present in your staff relationships. Therefore, knowing these people well is a key to success in this industry. For this reason, the first rule in regard to communication is to *become personal*. The individuals who work a property have to feel as invested in the property as the owners themselves do. Make sure you ask staff about themselves and their lives.

How does this help the business of business? If an individual's personality traits are clearly understood, then fact follows form and how your people describe and discuss themselves will translate into how they are speaking about the property. As an owner, you'll begin to detect a pattern of response that becomes consistent across conversations, from personal to business. Once you are comfortable with the individual, then the fact that business frequently takes place over a phone and not in person becomes less important.

The second key to effective communication in the apartment business is to *be willing to communicate whenever your staff requests the need*. In this industry staffs are often left to their own devices for extended periods of time. They often need to communicate for reasons that may seem simple to the average owner but are not at all simple to them. If you are not readily available, a staff member may choose not to confront an issue. In a sense, he may ignore something that could be very detrimental to the property ownership, simply because in his mind he isn't receiving support. What you don't know can definitely hurt the investment. Although training is available for many of the professionals who need to be hired in the apartment industry, there are few who completely comprehend how a mistake or an omission can expose you, the property owner, to financial or legal trouble. If you are not communicating with and guiding your staff enough, they could just "allow things to happen" on a property that can become a real problem at a later date.

That brings me to the third key to effective communication: *Create structured times to communicate with your staff each day.* On top of that, each week spend time getting the staff to expect to discuss the issues of the day. If managers or leasing agents know that every Monday morning a phone call will come at 10:00 in which they will be asked to discuss vacancies, traffic, and advertising related to these vacancies, over time they will become prepared for those conversations, and whether they know it or not, they will also become sensitive to the issues that the ownership considers important. This is "culturing" a staff to think like the ownership and act instead of react.

A fourth effective measure of communication in this industry is to *use a regularly scheduled site visit to confirm everything that has been talked about since the last visit.* Some would argue that it is better to make "surprise" visits. Although an unscheduled visit is sometimes necessary, done too often it erodes trust. Trust is a two-way street, not a one-way street. During regularly scheduled conversations, take notes on what is talked about. Use those notes to guide certain aspects of a site visit. For example, let's say the focus of a conversation revolves around the amount of time particular units are remaining vacant. The staff indicates that the kitchen cabinetry is not showing well. So, go to those apartments on a site visit and look at the cabinetry with the staff. From this visit, establish a way for the staff to be proactive in this case. Discuss, as an owner, what you do and how you would decide which set of cabinets should be replaced; the next time the staff may replace them as a rule because their quality is less than the threshold you, as an owner, have set.

In the twenty-first century, there is no excuse not to get and receive constant information. To an owner not located on a site, information is everything. Therefore, *use all the modern methods of communication.* Use cell phones and the Internet. Make the operating of your investment virtual. Remember that the more your staff members feel they have the ability and the right to access ownership when confronted with a difficult problem, the more confident over time they become in making the tough decisions and the more vested they are emotionally in the property's success. The Internet is especially suited for the apartment business. A manager may be confronting a problem on a property but isn't adept at explaining the problem on the phone. The owner could be miles and hours away from the site when this problem occurs. A digital camera and an e-mail address may be all that you need. The manager can take a picture of the problem and have it instantaneously in the hands of the owner, potentially minutes after a problem has occurred. The ability to review the problem and discuss a solution with the aid of digital technology is very apparent. Use all technological means possible to support effective interpersonal communication when you, as the owner, will not be on-site.

Simple keys to remember:

☐ Become personal.

☐ Be willing to communicate whenever a staff needs to—in other words, be accessible.

☐ Structure consistent, regular discussion times.

☐ Follow up communication with site visits; use your notes to verify what you see.

☐ Use modern methods of communication, such as the cell phone and the Internet.

■ Follow Up Consistently

At this point, structure and standards have been set and they are detailed, but all these reporting methods alone mean nothing if the items in question don't have an effective follow-up procedure. The apartment business is all about detail, and that means there is a plethora of information and events that needs to be reviewed constantly. It has been touched upon already in this chapter, but scheduling regular days and times of review of significant information such as vacancies and delinquencies is very important. It is also advisable to create a simple follow-up system.

Create a folder by month and then file important information by day chronologically. This simple method ensures that on a prescheduled day, you will be looking at issues that are sensitive to that day. For example, you send a legal "cease" order to a resident who is violating a clause in the lease indicating a thirty-day cure period. This notice is required by that state's landlord tenancy law. If it looks like the matter might culminate in court, this state also requires that the next step might be a "quit" order, and it requires that that order be sent registered mail exactly on the thirtieth day according to the cease. If you place a copy of the cease order in the follow-up file for review in twenty-seven or twenty-eight days, you are ensuring that this notice is timely and the issue doesn't become extended because of a missed deadline. This follow-up file can also be used to track scheduled events, such as the delinquent review or the turn-on date for the heating systems every year.

■ "Driving Home with Rose"

The interpersonal connection that any owner or manager gains and grows with an important staff member has a direct relationship to improved, consistent operations.

If you learn to understand how your on-site manager thinks and listen to the way he discusses matters with you, and relate that to the information you see on paper in formal reports, you'll be able to "connect" with your property without having to be there constantly. If you regiment what is talked about and how in these conversations, it will become very easy to diagnose and understand most of what is happening systemically or temporarily on a property.

Rose was a longtime employee in our organization who had grown through the ranks to eventually manage a fairly large community for us. I had been made to understand upon taking her property into my portfolio that working was a matter of survival for this single mother. There was no doubt she had a work ethic; she had at one time run her own food service business on the streets of a major northeastern U.S. city even in the dead of winter. My understanding was she came to this business to get out of the city and provide a stable home for her daughter. She had worked for our organization for nine years at this point.

If you are the new buyer of a property and you are inheriting an existing staff, this information, by the way, is as valuable as any information you can glean about a property. Owners or managers who don't do some detective work before working with such an employee are doing themselves an injustice. This information establishes a "baseline" understanding of the personality and perspective your employee is coming from; it is the first step in the process of making her or his thought process and your goals mesh.

I had further learned that Rose's forte while growing through the ranks seemed to be leasing and customer service. She had, at one time, worked at our largest property, so her leasing training was developed there. Our training and regimentation at this property was as complete as it was anywhere in our organization, so it was clear to me that I had a hardworking, dedicated, and experienced manager. I had asked my administrative staff before my first visit to provide me with the most recent market survey and a one-year history of occupancy. The market survey indicated to me that we were competitive pricewise, if a little cheaper than we should be. We were very competitive in regard to amenities with our competition. I also asked to see the most recent advertising the property had done, and it was some of the best I'd seen. But one thing bothered me: For all our competitive equality, and despite having a strong leasing manager, we seemed to be perpetually in a renting rut and we were lagging behind the market-average occupancy rate. I hadn't seen the property yet, and that would be important, but it just didn't match with what I had heard. It was time for a site visit.

Unfortunately, the ownership at the time had not informed Rose that she was getting a new manager. When I met her, she was shocked and apprehensive. She was very guarded and didn't seem willing to talk much, but she indicated that if the organization wished the situation to change then she would come to speed with it. Rather than go full bore into the business of the day, I decided to do what any manager should do in a new situation: I let the manager teach me what she would and could do about the property. I used my five senses. In property management, it is what I call the *look, listen, and learn period*. Many managers launch right into taking charge, but when you do that too soon, you don't allow much pertinent material to surface and you start creating a wall or barriers with your people. You can take the approach of being Sherlock Holmes if you wish, but if you do that you must be an expert in forensics. If you start engaging your manager and form the foundation of trust, there will never be a need to be a sleuth.

I asked Rose if we could take a walk around the property. First of all, her rental office was a one-bedroom model; there was no stand-alone rental office, which often is the case. Her marketing sense was terrific; she had kept the model/office very clean. Her management desk was out of public view and her rental area was designed to be friendly and welcoming. She had all the marketing materials and brochures and a property picture book displayed for all to access. She even had freshly baked cookies in the oven—always—to give the office a homey aroma. Four or five people came in while I was there on my first trip, and it was very obvious that Rose connected with people, both residents and prospective renters, extremely well. I saw a side of her she wasn't giving me when we talked, but it was an obvious bright side to how she operated.

We then proceeded on our site visit. The property was for the most part clean, but it had some "curb appeal" warts. The strange thing was the marketing aspects of the curb appeal were excellent. There was ample signage. Welcome banners and flowers were situated near the rental office. Yet the rest of the property was tired looking. I walked in a few empties and met the maintenance staff. Maintenance crews in the apartment industry are often a challenge; they need to be constantly reminded they are in the public view as far as dress and demeanor, and this crew was true to the stereotype. The units they were preparing were not anywhere near completed, so I really couldn't judge what the quality of the work was. On the way back to the office I started to query Rose on her staff, and although she wasn't being descriptive and overtly verbal, I sensed there was a story to be told. I left that first day confused as to how a manager with such people skills wasn't renting, but I had some theories.

I reviewed the traffic, occupancy market surveys, and flow of work for several weeks; then I constantly tried to engage Rose in discussing these matters, but I couldn't get her to open up. From the flow of work I started tracking the move-out and move-in dates, and I realized that the crew was not turning over vacated units to make-ready very quickly. When you allow this to continue in a thirty-day cycle of move-ins and move-outs, you don't occupy apartments in an efficient manner; your new move-outs occur before your move-ins do, so even if you receive more rental applications in a month than you vacate, your occupancy will never gain positive ground. I also felt that, although Rose had provided all the marketing touches in her rental office and in her presentation, the curb appeal on many parts of the property had to be improved.

When I went over these issues with Rose, she was still very guarded. She seemed to agree with my perception but wasn't very proactive or quick to come to a solution, yet when you watched her with the renting public she was much more aggressive. I could have just forced some management directives on the situation and corrected the short-term problem, but I decided for the long-term health of the property it was more important to get Rose to engage more with me and to start rounding out what I believed was a very talented manager, and a loyal one. As an owner you can cut to the quick, but over the years you will discover that replacing people and retraining is far more difficult than establishing a trustworthy work relationship with the existing staff, as long as they have some desire and acumen.

I asked a little more about Rose and her career with our organization, including whom she had answered to before working with me. It seemed that over the years she had worked with very strong personalities who looked for Rose to do and not necessarily think. She had been groomed and regimented in her specific tasks, and at those she was good, but she wasn't translating the experience to problem solving. Her own paperwork even indicated a less-than-stellar maintenance crew, so she might very well see that was the problem, but she wasn't moving her staff more effectively and she wasn't finding a way to use my experience to help her.

I concluded the only way I was going to get her to understand that was by "connecting" with her as a human being more. I cannot understate how important it is to develop that trust with staff in this industry. Rose's office could get rather busy, and sometimes you could see that reduced her focus, but I also knew because it was so busy she often stayed after the rental office closed for some time to complete her work for the day. I also knew she left one "backline" phone number open in case an emergency occurred or her daughter was trying to reach her. I realized that I had an hour and a half commute home and I had a hands-free cell phone, so I decided I would use my drive time home to try to connect with her.

One very important key to establishing trust is to become personal. For this reason, the first phone call I made would have nothing to do with business. I called after hours and Rose was at first startled that I was calling. She wasn't letting her guard down. It was obvious she was nervous I was calling. Then I explained that I called about a nonwork issue that I believed she could relate to. This ended up being a way to get her to communicate while dropping her guard somewhat.

Over time, we continued such conversations, and the "wall" fell rather quickly from that point. What became very clear through our nightly conversations was that Rose knew what was wrong, but she hadn't been cultured in a managerial sense to make decisions. Rose and I created a game plan to regiment the maintenance staff both with their make-ready apartments and with the way they viewed the community's curb appeal. From that day forward Rose got stronger and stronger and the property occupancy rate climbed to where the market and the property should have been all along. Rose got to the point where she suggested a change in maintenance staffing and created some of those same trust and communication techniques with her new maintenance supervisor. The result went direct to the bottom line: She earned recognition in the industry for good work, her property was twice voted by the regional industry trade organization as the best in the market, and the maintenance supervisor she hired and trained was twice named the best in the field also. Rose has gone on to become a corporate director of all marketing, leasing, and resident retention issues in the organization, and her analytical skills are among the best I have seen in the business.

I have at least four or five of these conversations throughout the week at regularly scheduled times on my way home. Each one of them is designed to take the information I receive about a property every week and manage it from a distance through the on-site management. But you can't work this way if you don't have a relationship with individuals who manage your property that allows both you and them to be candid. Trust is absolutely essential in that relationship. When you combine the structured tools you have at your disposal (as long as they are applied in a consistent and timely way) and you establish a clear-cut way of communicating with all involved, the answers to a property problem are rarely very complicated. If you will remember my first site visit, I wasn't impressed with the maintenance staff yet I felt I had a good manager. The review of the occupancy numbers over time clarified my thoughts, and establishing a connection with my manager ensured that in my absence the property would move in the right direction on a daily basis. When you keep it super simple, property management is simply taking the clues you are provided with and following through on the observations you make.

CHAPTER 6

Leasing:

The Marketing of a Community

Apartment structures are brick and mortar so you are selling a product, right?

Wrong. *You are selling a community, its services, and a lifestyle.* The customer service that your leasing and management staff exhibit, the professional maintenance capability and response, the environment a community offers are all the value you are selling to the resident. More often than not, customers are sold not only "by" the leasing agent, but also "on" the leasing agent before they even see the units. How the property is marketed has a direct impact on what type of community evolves.

Whom you qualify to rent in the community (within the parameters of the law, which is discussed in this chapter within the context of fair housing guidelines), and the care taken to market to that population, over time "creates" the community. These factors in and of themselves can build or destroy "value" in the investment. For example, when you qualify residents legally you often find the responsibility they exhibit in their financial matters; their honesty in relaying information to you also reflects overall responsibility traits. If you don't clearly pay attention to those structured qualifying standards, as a manager or owner you end up chasing people for rent. Furthermore, as we will see, resident referrals are a main source of rental. The end result of improper screening is often a community that falls short of cash because renters don't respect the lease they signed; thus, a community cannot be maintained properly.

It's important in rental housing to occupy the vacant space as soon as possible, but occupying the vacant space with no thought process as to who is the target occupant can have a disastrous effect. One of the most predominant ways apartment communities acquire residents is through current or past resident referrals. If care has been put into identifying the ideal residents and developing a selection process, you can determine the difference between a good and bad referral.

Shortly after purchasing the property, one of the first tasks for you to initiate is the construction of a rental policy, also known as *rental criteria*. These criteria must be within the parameters of the federal fair housing guidelines. Once the rental criteria have been established, the second task will be the creation of the presentation process. In this regard, be aware of not only your personal presentation (both verbal and visual), but also the physical presentation of the property, including the location of the leasing office. Often by the time the leasing agent actually shows an apartment to a prospective renter, the prospect has already made a decision. Therefore, everything that leads up to presenting that apartment must be as important as the singular apartment itself.

Regardless of whether the investment is small or large, remember this: Always consider your "office" a leasing or rental office first and a management office second. Create a welcoming environment, and let the office be a statement as to what type of community you operate. If you start with this operational mind-set, you will have already gone a long way in determining the personality the community will carry. Now it is time to structure to whom and how you will market.

■ Construct Rental Criteria

The significance of constructing consistent rental guidelines is often not appreciated until the community has significant social and/or financial problems. Before you open the leasing office door for the first time, it is essential that the guidelines for qualifying to rent at the community be constructed. There are two very important reasons to construct criteria. The first is federal fair housing laws under Title VIII of the Civil Rights Act of 1968 and the Fair Housing Act of 1968. All rental housing practices are scrutinized and governed by the provisions of this act and the amendments made in 1974, 1988, 1998, and 2000. These federal policies were enacted in response to widespread discriminatory practices that were pervasive in the housing industry to prohibit or limit certain segments of the population or individuals from residing in a given rental property.

The second reason to construct consistent rental criteria is that the federal government prohibits someone from eliminating certain "protected classes" of individuals simply because they fall into that "class." Currently, the protected classes under federal fair housing are:

❏ Race

❏ Color

❏ Religion

❏ Sex

❏ Handicap

❏ Familial status

❏ National origin

The familial status provision prevents owners from not renting to pregnant women and families with children. One might wonder, then, how adult communities for people age 55 and older are allowed to exist. The 1988 amendments to the Fair Housing Act exempted these communities, and the Housing for Older Persons Act of 1995 (HOPA) clarified the parameters regarding senior housing.

It is important for you and the staff to know these classes and understand that under no circumstances are you to engage in rental practices that seek to eliminate an individual from renting based on him or her being a member of one or more of these classes. The rental requirements should reflect that you are aware of these regulations and that the property abides by its edicts. The fair housing regulations also prohibit practices relative to these classes when a person has occupied an apartment, as well as in the advertising of apartments. Post in the rental office both a copy of the rental criteria your property requires for a qualified rental and a public statement explaining fair housing (for sample statements, in English and Spanish, see Figure 6–1a and Figure 6–1b). Fair housing exists every day in a rental operation, and all who operate in the rental environment need to be aware that what they say and do could be deemed discriminatory.

Here are some examples of actions or statements that might be considered discriminatory in nature. Remember, too, that any direction given to the staff by the owner can be considered a violation of fair housing as well, even if the staff refuses to follow the directives.

Actions/Statements to Avoid

❏ A leasing representative discouraging a prospective renter by indicating the drawbacks of a community relative to that renter's physical condition (e.g., dis-

Figure 6-1a. Fair housing statement (English).

**EQUAL HOUSING
OPPORTUNITY**

We Do Business in Accordance with
the Federal Fair Housing Law.
(The Fair Housing Amendments Act of 1988)

It Is Illegal to Discriminate Against
Any Person Because of Race, Color,
Religion, Sex, Handicap, Family
Status, or National Origin.

In the sale or rental of housing or residential lots
●
In advertising the sale or rental or housing
●
In the financing of housing
●
In the provision of real estate brokerage services
●
In the appraisal of housing
●
Blockbusting is also illegal.

Anyone who feels he or she has been
discriminated against may file a complaint of
housing discrimination:
1-800-669-6777 (Toll free)
1-800-927-9275 (TDD)

U.S. Department of Housing and Urban
Development Assistant Secretary for Fair
Housing and Equal Opportunity
Washington, D.C. 20410

Figure 6-1b.   Fair housing statement (Spanish).

IGUALDAD DE OPORTUNIDAD EN LA VIVIENDA

Conducimos nuestros negocios de acuerdo a la ley
Federal de Vivienda Justa
(Acta de enmiemdas de 1988 de la Ley Federal de Vivienda Justa)

Es ilegal discriminar contra cualquier persona por
razon de raza, color, religion,
sexo, incapacidad fisica o mental, la presencia de
ninos menores de 18 anos o de mujer embarazada
en su familia o su origen nacional.

En la venta de vivienda y terrenos residenciales

En los anuncios de venta o renta de vivienda

En el financiamiento de la vivienda

Amenazar o interferir con la persona para que no registre su queja

En los servicios de corretaje que prestan vendedores de vivienda

En la valoracion de vivienda

Tambien es ilegal forzarle a vendor
o rentar su vivienda diciendole que gente de
otra raza, religion o grupo etnico
se estan mudando en su vecindario.

Cualquier persona que sienta que fue discriminada debe enviar su queja de discriminacion: 1-800-669-6777 (llamada gratis) 1-800-927-9275 (TTY llamada gratis)

U.S. Department of Housing and Urban Development Assistant Secretary for Fair Housing and Equal Opportunity Washington, D.C. 20410 couraging a handicapped prospect by showing only areas of the community that are clearly inaccessible). Don't steer individuals in their decision-making process.

❑ Using different rental criteria, standards, or procedures for different protected classes.

❑ Advertising in such a way as to suggest that certain protected classes would not be comfortable residing in a community (e.g., picturing only one race in a series of community photographs).

❑ Intentionally slowing down or limiting the maintenance repair process of an apartment dweller within a protected class in the hope that that person will move out.

❑ Instructing staff to use codes on rental applications to identify classes to segregate or to reject applications simply on the basis of their class.

❑ Disciplining staff members for accepting an applicant that you, as the owner, indicated you wished to be denied simply on the basis of their protected class.

The number of opportunities to inadvertently discriminate during the rental process, during a resident's occupancy, in the advertising process, and with the employees is voluminous. Common sense should prevail when dealing with this issue. If anything you market, say, or do in regard to any of these protected classes seems to exclude or treat any one of them differently, there is probably a better way to say it, write it, or do it.

Some additional and important advice: Once you construct the rental criteria, have an attorney review it for adherence to the fair housing guidelines. You should, as part of the hiring process, have each employee who works for you, regardless of position, review the rental criteria. In addition, you should include an overview of fair housing. Have employees acknowledge, in writing, that they understand these guidelines and will follow them. It is also prudent to verify that each and every advertiser with whom you place marketing material understands and follows fair housing guidelines. Advertisers often will correct copy in an ad they deem to be a possible unintentional violation of fair housing, and they won't publish an intentional fair housing violation.

Attracting conscientious individuals—that is to say those who are financially qualified to rent in the community—is a very good reason to construct rental guidelines. Cumulatively, the eventual makeup of the community population has everything to do with the financial well-being and "value" the investment creates and maintains. Given the discussion of fair housing, you may be asking yourself at this point: How can I, as the owner, possibly create a set of renting standards without violating the law?

There are several prudent and legal qualifying standards that should be included as rental criteria—and they must be adhered to consistently. This again is a legal requirement, but in practice it also attracts the best possible resident to the community. Here is a list of some acceptable criteria that should be considered when constructing rental guidelines:

Acceptable Rental Criteria

❑ *Employment and Wage Requirements.* Requiring proof of current employment and verification of current income or wages; establishing a minimum income standard (e.g., the cost of the apartment cannot exceed 30 percent of the applicant's gross monthly income).

❑ *Documentation.* Requiring verifiable government-issued identification in picture form for each rental applicant.

❑ *Credit and Criminal Checks.* Requiring each applicant to undergo credit and criminal background checks from an independent credit reporting agency.

❑ *Application.* Requiring each applicant to fill out a comprehensive rental application and charging a fee to apply. (A sample rental application is shown in Figure 6-2.)

❑ *Previous Residence.* Requiring as part of the application previous residence information and contacts to verify the residency.

You can also establish up-front community requirements, such as:

❑ Indicating that certain vehicles (such as boats) are not permitted on the property
❑ Listing all prohibited pets from the community
❑ Listing all rental payment policies, such as payment date, late date, and applicable fees

When these individual criteria are placed next to each other, it should become apparent that although you cannot eliminate or be deliberate about choosing a tenancy arbitrarily, you can obtain a financial picture of the potential tenant's ability to afford living in the community and you should know whether the individual applying is a potential credit or safety risk.

Figure 6-2. Rental application.

Rental Application for Residents and Occupants

Each co-applicant and each occupant over 18 years old must submit a separate applications.
Spouses may submit a single application.

Date when filled out: _____

NAA
NATIONAL APARTMENT ASSOCIATION

ABOUT YOU   Full name *(exactly as on driver's license or govt. ID card)*
_____

Your street address *(as shown on your driver's license or government ID card)*:
_____

Driver's license # and state: _____
   OR govt. photo ID card #: _____
Former last names (maiden and married): _____
Your Social Security #: _____
Birthdate: _____ Height: _____ Weight: _____
Sex: _____ Eye color: _____ Hair color: _____
Marital Status: ☐ single ☐ married ☐ divorced ☐ widowed ☐ separated
Are you a U.S. citizen? ☐ Yes ☐ No Do you or any occupant smoke?
                                              ☐ yes ☐ no
Will you or any occupant have an animal? ☐ yes ☐ no
Kind, weight, breed, age: _____

Current home address (where you now live): _____

City/State/Zip: _____
Home/cell phone: (____) _____ Current rent: $_____
Email address: _____
Name of apartment where you now live: _____
Current owner or manager's name: _____
Their phone: _____ Date moved in: _____
Why are you leaving your current residence? _____

Your previous home address: _____

City/State/Zip: _____
Apartment name: _____
Name of above owner or manager: _____
Their phone: _____ Previous monthly rent: $_____
Date you moved in: _____ Date you moved out: _____

YOUR WORK   Present employer: _____
Address: _____
City/State/Zip: _____
Work phone: (____) _____
Position: _____
Your gross monthly income is over: $_____
Date you began this job: _____
Supervisor's name and phone: _____

Previous employer: _____
Address: _____
City/State/Zip: _____
Work phone: (____) _____
Position: _____
Gross monthly income was over: $_____
Dates you began and ended this job: _____
Previous supervisor's name and phone: _____

YOUR CREDIT HISTORY   Your bank's name, city, state: _____

List major credit cards: _____
Other non-work income you want considered. Please explain: _____
Past credit problems you want to explain. *(Use separate page.)*

YOUR RENTAL/CRIMINAL HISTORY   *Check only if applicable.* Have you, your spouse, or any occupant listed in this Application ever: ☐ been evicted or asked to move out? ☐ moved out of a dwelling before the end of the lease term without the owner's consent? ☐ declared bankruptcy? ☐ been sued for rent? ☐ been sued for property damage? ☐ been charged, detained, or arrested for a felony or sex crime that was resolved by conviction, probation, deferred adjudication, court-ordered community supervision, or pretrial diversion? ☐ been charged, detained, or arrested for a felony or sex-related crime that has not been resolved by any method? Please indicate below the year, location and type of each felony and sex crime other than those resolved by dismissal or acquittal. We may need to discuss more facts before making a decision. *You represent the answer is "no" to any item not checked above.*
_____

YOUR SPOUSE   Full name: _____
Former last names (maiden and married): _____
Spouse's Social Security #: _____
Driver's license # and state: _____
   OR govt. photo ID card #: _____
Birthdate: _____ Height: _____ Weight: _____
Sex: _____ Eye color: _____ Hair color: _____
Are you a U.S. citizen? ☐ Yes ☐ No
Present employer: _____
Address: _____
City/State/Zip: _____
Work phone: (____) _____
Position: _____
Date began job: _____ Gross monthly income is over: $_____
Supervisor's name and phone: _____

OTHER OCCUPANTS   *Names of all persons under 18 and other adults who will occupy the unit without signing the lease. Continue on separate page if more than three.*
Name: _____ Relationship: _____
   Sex: _____ DL or govt. ID card # and state: _____
   Birthdate: _____ Social Security #: _____
Name: _____ Relationship: _____
   Sex: _____ DL or govt. ID card # and state: _____
   Birthdate: _____ Social Security #: _____
Name: _____ Relationship: _____
   Sex: _____ DL or govt. ID card # and state: _____
   Birthdate: _____ Social Security #: _____

YOUR VEHICLES   *List all vehicles owned or operated by you, your spouse, or any occupants (including cars, trucks, motorcycles, trailers, etc.). Continue on separate page if more than three.*
Make and color of vehicle: _____
Year: _____ License #: _____ State: _____
Make and color of vehicle: _____
Year: _____ License #: _____ State: _____
Make and color of vehicle: _____
Year: _____ License #: _____ State: _____

WHY YOU RENTED HERE   Were you referred? ☐ Yes ☐ No. *If yes, by whom:*
Name of locator or rental agency: _____
Name of individual locator or agent: _____
Name of friend or other person: _____
Did you find us on your own? ☐ Yes ☐ No *If yes, fill in information below:*
☐ On the Internet ☐ Stopped by ☐ Newspaper (name): _____
☐ Rental publication: _____
☐ Other: _____

EMERGENCY   *Emergency contact person over 18, who will not be living with you:*
Name: _____
Address: _____
City/State/Zip: _____
Work phone: (____) _____ Home phone: (____) _____
Relationship: _____
If you die or are seriously ill, missing, or in a jail or penitentiary according to an affidavit of *[check one or more]* ☐ the above person, ☐ your spouse, or ☐ your parent or child, we may allow such person(s) to enter your dwelling to remove all contents, as well as your property in the mailbox, storerooms, and common areas. If no box is checked, any of the above are authorized at our option. If you are seriously ill or injured, you authorize us to call EMS or send for an ambulance at your expense. We're not legally obligated to do so.

AUTHORIZATION   I or we authorize *(owner's name)* _____
_____
to obtain reports from consumer reporting agencies before, during, and after tenancy on matters relating to a lease by the above owner to me and to verify, by all available means, the information in this application, including income history and other information reported by employer(s) to any state employment security agency. Work history information may be used only for this Rental Application. Authority to obtain work history information expires 365 days from the date of this Application.
Applicant's signature _____
Spouse's signature _____

© 2004, National Apartment Association, Inc. *Applicant must also sign on the next page of this Application.*   10122004026800   Page 1 of 2

Simple keys to remember:

☐ Construct rental guidelines and policies (criteria).
☐ Follow fair housing guidelines.
☐ Establish prudent financial principles.
☐ Execute rental criteria consistently.

Establish the Marketing Environment

Two predominant ways to attract new rentals are *resident referrals* and *drive-by and walk-by traffic* (individuals who see the community from the car or while walking by). In either case, the community has the potential to market itself and that should be exploited. Curb appeal is the best way to market. Curb appeal does not end at the front door. Both the rental office and apartment must reflect the same curb appeal as the exterior of the property. Perception becomes reality in the rental business, and if prospective renters don't like what they see, they won't rent.

Remember, no matter how small the property is, there should always be some sort of established rental or leasing office. If the property is extremely small, for example, only three units, then when an apartment vacates, *it* becomes the leasing office.

From a marketing standpoint, let's revisit the curb appeal issue. Once you have purchased the property, make a visual inspection of the property on foot and in a car. Approach the property from all possible directions by all means of transportation and ask a few other people to do the same. Ask yourself and others some basic questions:

☐ Was the signage identifying the property easily recognized and attractive, and did it contain all pertinent information needed for the prospective renter?

☐ Is the signage directional in nature so it is very clear where an applicant goes to apply? (Even if the property is a duplex, the house number and a phone contact number should be very accessible and legible.)

☐ What were the first impressions of the property when approaching? For example, did you notice garbage cans? Are residents' personal belongings lying around the common area? Is the landscaping taken care of?

If something bothers you as the owner, it will most likely bother possible rental applicants as well. It should be a number-one goal to fix anything you observed during that ride or walk leading to the rental office that is unacceptable (unless it is financially impossible) and review it each time you visit the property.

What do you do if an adjoining property isn't well taken care of? Try to form a relationship with neighbors and at the appropriate moment request some help in correcting what could affect the property. Be proactive. Time is money, so if the individual balks, consider volunteering to perform the task yourself if the neighbor agrees. A good example is a local convenience store that is riddled with graffiti. If the owner won't remove it, then offer to do so. Although you'll incur a cost up front, the cost of leaving the graffiti may be the inability to rent. If the neighbor is uncooperative, then turn to local code officials for help. It may be a matter of economic survival, so do what you have to do to ensure the property shows well to passersby.

Before you enter the actual renting or leasing area, consider making a few customer service additions to the exterior that will indicate to an applicant that you and the staff care. As examples:

❑ Dedicate a number of parking spots for applicants, if you have the space. Label them "Future Resident Parking."

❑ Display signage that indicates this is, in fact, the rental office and include the operating hours. The sign should be pleasing to the eye and the word "Welcome" should appear somewhere.

❑ Install a weatherproof box that encloses rental marketing material in case you are not in the office.

❑ Strategically place an attractive ash urn and garbage can near the entrance.

❑ Display the universal fair housing symbol to indicate that you are aware of and comply with fair housing laws. There are no restrictions on using this symbol (see Figure 6-3), and it can be copied at will; most of your advertising sources will make it available.

These seem like small items, but making a statement to visitors that the property owner cares creates a sense of "home" to the prospective renter. The presentation has already begun.

The inside of the leasing office should be impeccable and spotless. It should be smartly decorated. The lighting should be bright and the office should smell good (an often-used trick of the trade, many rental offices bake cookies throughout the

Figure 6-3. Fair housing logo.

day for that "homey" aroma). The apartment business by its nature is awash with paper, but the area seen by the public should be pristine. The presentation desk or table area should be clean, and any necessary paper such as rental applications should be organized. Supply adequate seating for several possible applicants. Remember to display the rental criteria and fair housing statement.

If the property has more than one style of apartment, it is advisable to display floor plans and a site map somewhere in the office. Have handouts accessible for all who enter. No matter how small the property, always have even the simplest of descriptive handouts and basic welcome items such as coffee and water.

The curb appeal process never stops and should be on the staff's daily checklist. Review all of the previously mentioned items for ensuring exterior curb appeal; take that walk and drive every morning past the property, and clean the rental office daily. If you know what units in the complex are ready to show, take a daily walk by those units to ensure that they have received the same attention that you gave to the entrance and leasing office.

It is very important to try to follow the rule that you don't show an undone unit. Some people have trouble visualizing what a unit will look like completed. If shown an incomplete unit, the applicant gets a distorted picture. The possibility that this prospective renter will have second thoughts is higher when the apartment isn't complete. As with the exterior curb appeal checklist, interior considerations should also be part of the staff's daily regimen. Here are several things to keep in mind when finishing a unit from a marketing perspective:

❑ Paint the unit in a neutral bright color, usually a white or an off-white.
❑ Keep lighting on in bathrooms and the kitchen during the operating hours; keep all blinds open. Bright makes big.

❑ Completely clean the unit, including all countertops, sinks, and the interior of appliances. Rinse all sinks and flush all toilets daily.

❑ Test all appliances to ensure proper operation.

❑ Moderate the temperature. If there are heating or cooling systems, make sure the unit you will show is comfortable given the weather of the day.

❑ Test all keys before you actually have to show the unit for the day.

❑ Make small signs and place them strategically in the apartment to highlight unique features. For instance, if the refrigerator is large, put a sign on it that says "Large 20-cubic-foot refrigerator."

❑ Place air fresheners in the apartment.

These are just a few examples of how to make the renting experience not only a positive one but also a suggestive one. You are indicating to the applicant that this is a quality home for the individual to live in, and the management and ownership care for their residents. The attention and care given to the renting environment will be manifested in the type of resident who wishes to rent at the property.

Simple keys to remember:

❑ Visually inspect the property as if you were a prospective renter.

❑ Instruct your staff to inspect curb appeal daily.

❑ Maintain a clean and pleasant rental office.

■ Understand the Community's Place in the Market

Rental rates are a function of the market you are located in, combined with the uniqueness of the community. Now that you've made the community as nice as it can be, you want to know how much the local competition is charging for comparable units and what amenities they possess in comparison. This information helps to determine competitive pricing as well as what selling points should be used in the leasing presentation. It can easily be collated and updated by the use of a market survey.

The market survey is a simple listing of all surrounding apartment complexes and pertinent information on each of these complexes. A sample market survey was introduced in Chapter 5 in Figure 5-1. There are several important pieces of information that should be included on this survey:

❑ Apartment name, location, and phone number

❑ List of all types of units (e.g., one bedroom/one bath, two bedrooms/two baths) and square footage

❑ Rent rates for all sizes of units and security deposits required for all units

❑ List of all amenities the complex possesses (e.g., pool, garage, laundry facilities)

❑ List of whether the complex accepts pets and any associated fees

❑ Utilities (i.e., which are owner paid and which are renter paid)

❑ Rent specials given, such as free rent or discounted rent

❑ A comment section to note anything unusual or extraordinary about the competition

List your property on the market survey as well so the comparisons are immediate and complete; then update the market survey regularly. Shop the competition by phone and in person posed as a renter. Ask all the same questions as an applicant, and make all the same visual observations. The goal of consistently engaging and updating this process is to understand your community's place in the market, set competitive rental rates, and market the community to prospective renters. As an example, you might want to highlight "Heat Included" in winter advertising, especially if the competition has the renter pay for the same services. The market survey is an essential tool in the marketing process.

Simple keys to remember:

❑ Shop the competition.
❑ Complete a market survey.
❑ Compare your property to the market.

Begin the Selling Show

It is time to open the rental office for business. The leasing process had already begun with the attention to curb appeal and the care in preparing the leasing space.

You have also prepared yourself by knowing the competition and knowing how to sell your community. Although most rental traffic will come from referrals and walk-ins, there's a third opportunity at your disposal as well: Internet traffic.

Regardless of the source, some common principles apply to all forms of traffic:

❑ *Secure complete information upon first contact with potential renters.* You need to know who they are, what they are looking for, and a potential move-in date. Answering all questions begins the process of understanding if a prospective resident and the apartment are a fit.

❑ *Document the potential renter's needs.* Many prospective renters start the process but don't end the process on first contact. This information should be used to follow up with a lead should the first contact end without a rental commitment. Prompt and timely follow-up in leasing is essential.

❑ *Answer all inquiries.* Courteously reply to all questions, whether verbally or in writing and whether the answer you are giving is positive news or not.

❑ *Teach your leasing agents to answer questions honestly.* If they don't know an answer, they shouldn't make one up; and if the answer is no, then that is the correct answer. If a fair housing issue comes up—for example, if a prospective resident asks if you rent to a certain kind of people—the answer is simply that properties rent to financially qualified people, no other type.

Several principles are unique to specific sources, however, depending on whether the prospects are making phone inquiries, in-person visits, or coming to you via Internet traffic.

Phone Traffic

The phone is one of the most often used tools of the rental business. When used correctly, it can serve as the primary vehicle to attract renters to visit the community.

Three tools you should always have next to the phone are a pen, a traffic log, and a "cheat sheet" that charts the sales process over the phone. The traffic log (an example of which is shown in Figure 6-4) serves two purposes: First, it is a way to memorialize immediately all information discussed on the phone with a potential renter, such as name, phone number, basic needs, and how he or she found out about the community. Second, a traffic log allows you to track your lead sources. If

Figure 6-4. Weekly traffic log.

WEEKLY TRAFFIC LOG

PROPERTY: _____

WEEK OF _____ to _____

CALL OR WALK-IN	DATE	NAME	ADDRESS	PHONE #	APT SIZE & WHEN NEEDED	HOW DID YOU HEAR OF US?	FOLLOW-UP ACTION

you keep constant records of where people found out about the community, over time you'll be able to easily discern the best advertising or marketing source.

The goal of any good phone presentation should be to determine whether the prospects are qualified and, if so, to entice them to come in and see one of the apartments. The actual community often sells itself at that point. Renting an apartment sight unseen should be avoided. It is advisable to set an appointment for a tour, and if the prospect is unable to commit, verify where the person can be reached for future follow-up.

Make a habit of at least once a week contacting individuals who called and reconfirm whether they have an interest in the community. It also leaves a positive impression if you mail a thank-you card to acknowledge their inquiry. Follow-up is essential, and often on the second or third contact you secure a rental application.

Drive-By and Walk-Through Traffic

Some prospects will make an actual visit to the rental office or community. At this point, it is obvious that this is a serious renter. This individual took the time to stop at the community in person. Engage these prospects in the application process as soon as their qualifying status has been determined and the availability of the type of unit they are requesting has been verified. A good way to "prescreen" is to have a guest card available, such as the one shown in Figure 6-5. A guest card is an effective way to quickly assess whether they meet the basic rental requirements and what their specific needs are. Provide the same marketing information on this card as you would have asked over the phone so that the information can again be collated and used to determine the best advertising and marketing venues. You can also use this card to further the discussion. After it is filled out, it should be kept throughout the sales presentation and referred to while in conversation with the prospect.

Always have printed materials available to explain all aspects of the community. Even if you have a small location, have at least a simple handout or brochure listing all pertinent information about the community and individual apartments. Attach a professional business card to this handout or brochure. One piece of material that is essential and should be included is a copy of the rental criteria.

If the prospect is qualified, the primary goal is to convince her to fill out an application before she leaves; if she leaves without doing so, there is a good chance she will not return. If someone wants to fill out an application but you've determined that she is most likely not qualified, do not under any circumstances tell her

Figure 6-5. Guest card.

Day _____ Date _____ Time _____

Telephone ❑   Walk-in ❑

How soon do you need an apartment? _____

How many people will this be for? _____

Name _____

Mailing address _____

City _____ State _____ Zip _____

Phone _____ Cell phone _____

E-mail address _____

Size of Apt   Studio ❑ 1 ❑ 2 ❑ 3 ❑ Townhome ❑

Why are you moving? _____

What are you looking for in your new apartment home? ___

_____

_____

What is most important to you in your new apartment

home? _____

_____

Pet? Kind _____ Size _____

Are you currently renting?   Yes ❑ No ❑

If yes, where? _____

_____

Appointment date _____ *Time* _____ *am* ❑ *pm* ❑

What price range are you looking for? _____

If you are shown an apartment you like, are

you prepared to put a reservation fee on it today?

Yes ❑   No ❑

How did you hear about us?

❑ Apartments.com   ❑ Rentals.com

❑ Rent.com   ❑ Rentnet.com

❑ Apartment Finder   ❑ Apartment Guide

❑ Renters Guide Weekly   ❑ Yellow Pages

❑ Referral   ❑ Newspaper Type _____

❑ Walk-in

❑ Other Please list _____

EQUAL HOUSING OPPORTUNITY

FOR OFFICIAL USE ONLY

Rental agent _____

Size _____

Apartment shown Yes ❑ No ❑

Leased Apt ❑   Apt#_____

Hold on Apt ❑   Apt#_____

Follow-up:

Thank-you sent ❑   Date_____

Phone call ❑   Date_____

Notes _____

_____

If not shown, specify reason _____

1st follow-up date _____ By _____ Comments _____

2nd follow-up date _____ By _____ Comments _____

3rd follow-up date _____ By _____ Comments _____

Additional notes

_____

_____

_____

_____

she cannot fill out an application. If she has the information and funds you require for initiating the application process, allow her to continue.

If an individual leaves before filling out an application, make sure to ask him how and when he can be contacted. As in the case of the phone lead, follow up until the prospect declines renting, and again, a thank-you card goes a long way.

Internet Traffic

A relatively new form of advertising that leads direct traffic to the rental office is the Internet. Internet advertising has the advantage of bringing the community to prospects without them actually seeing the property firsthand. It is becoming an ever more important way to market and rent apartments and is widening the potential market. It is also one of the most cost-effective ways to advertise and lease. There are many companies that provide venues to market property online, such as Rent.com and Apartments.com.

Because the Internet is a technology-based form of advertising, there are some differences. Be prepared to ask potential online marketers some baseline questions. For example:

❑ How accessible is the site to the average Internet user? When browsing online, how prevalent is the site?

❑ Is the site easy to navigate—that is, can you find a particular location and complex easily in a relatively short period of time?

❑ Does the Internet provider allow you to edit the site? Do you have input in the information being put on that site?

❑ Is the site automated enough to allow a leasing agent to respond to inquiries as if the leads were going strictly to the rental office? An example would be that the provider has an automatic response "thank-you card" that can be designed to let individuals know their information was received.

❑ Does the site collate information through an online "guest card or information card" similar to how you log other forms of traffic?

❑ Does the provider offer you and your staff technical assistance and training for its site?

If the provider has answered all of the above questions satisfactorily, then you are ready to establish procedures to handle Internet advertising in much the same way as any other form of lead referral, with the exception that the process will be managed through a computer. It is important to follow all the same communication and follow-up guidelines previously discussed. Just as if the inquiry was a phone call, the idea is to convince the prospective renter to visit the community personally.

Internet advertising is less expensive than many conventional methods of apartment advertising, and there are the advantages of ancillary services such as an automated traffic log and the ability to "track" an applicant from first inquiry. Internet traffic, however, has created one dilemma in the leasing process. Individuals can now look at the property from across the country; therefore, they may not get to the actual property until the day they wish to rent. This situation forces you to be flexible during the renting process, on the one hand; yet, on the other hand, you do not want to, and should not, change the rental criteria. Be as accommodating as possible but do not create two standards.

Internet rental search will become more prevalent in the future, so if you own apartments for rent, you should make this form of advertising and traffic a part of the leasing function.

Simple keys to remember:

❑ Use the same inquiry format for all lead sources: phone calls, in-person visits, or Internet inquiries.
❑ Follow up on *all* inquiries.
❑ Log all communication, including how applicants found the property, their personal qualifying data, and their specific needs.
❑ Send thank-you cards.

▦ Decide Where to Advertise

Where should you advertise the apartments for rent?

If curb appeal has been maximized and the signage has been sharpened up, the property is in some ways advertising itself. Sometimes, however, the location or other factors require that you advertise in other venues. Before making a selection, make sure all advertisers follow fair housing guidelines, and make sure you know their cost relative to their benefit to the renting process—better known as the *cost per lease*. Some of the most predominant forms of advertising are:

❑ *Local Newspapers.* This form of advertising can be expensive (i.e., high cost per lease), but a large newspaper display ad is especially useful to draw phone traffic in a hurry—for instance, when there have been unexpected move-outs.

❑ *Rental Guides.* These periodical publications are strictly designed for rentals. They often appear in grocery stores or convenience stores and are usually free to the consumer. They can be very attractive, but they aren't cheap and they usually require contracted terms that commit the community to advertising whether you have vacancies or not. If you decide to advertise in a guide, make sure the book is actually distributed.

❑ *Internet.* Although relatively inexpensive, make sure you understand how the online advertiser's site works and ensure prospective renters do, too. Equally important is to make sure you regularly answer your Internet inquiries. You can create a property-specific Internet site, too, but keep in mind it has to be maintained.

❑ *Third-Party Internal Advertising.* Resident incentives, banners, and self-produced flyers are all effective in marketing your property; remember, drive-by traffic and resident referrals are a staple of the renting business.

❑ *Television and Radio.* This is the most expensive form of advertising and the least common in our industry.

It is important to remember that advertising is only as good as the product. Use traffic logs to determine the most frequently referenced sources of advertising. It is common to see competitors offer specials and giveaways such as one month's "free rent." However, the effectiveness of discount marketing is market driven. It is always preferred to provide something to the resident rather than give something away. For example, offer a complimentary microwave when it is not part of a regular rental rather than give free rent for a period of time. However, be flexible because the market may at times dictate otherwise.

Simple keys to remember:

❑ Curb appeal and resident referrals are the best forms of advertising.
❑ Study the traffic logs and know the strengths and weaknesses of each advertising medium.

Initiate the Application-Qualifying Process

Once the prospect and the leasing agent have both completed the initial inquiry process and the prospect is interested in renting, it is time for the application. By now the written rental criteria should have been explained to the prospect. Make sure the rental application is comprehensive and has been reviewed by an attorney so that it does not violate fair housing laws. There are several organizations that sell rental application forms. If you purchase a preprinted application it is advisable to ask the provider for proof that it stands up to fair housing muster as well. Next, it is critical to make sure the application is filled out completely and that all accompanying identification and proof required by the rental criteria is attached.

An often-made mistake is accepting an incomplete application for rental. Information not provided is often the first sign of some problem or deception. If an incomplete application is received, return it and request the missing information. If there is a reason the information is not provided, require the applicant to explain and to be prepared to verify the reasoning. The application process and the credit and background check are the only ways of ensuring a proper, qualified rental, so don't be squeamish about insisting on accuracy.

The credit and criminal background check is an essential part of the application process. These checks are facilitated through independent credit check organizations that get their information from the three major credit reporting organizations: Trans Union, Equifax, and Experian. The credit check organizations also gather civil and criminal information from local and state reporting functions. It is important to relay to the applicant that these reporting organizations are independent of the community or company. In most jurisdictions, a fee can be charged for this information gathering and the cost of the credit check can be passed on to the applicant. The credit check and background check in combination with all other verifiable documentation becomes the basis for an acceptance or a denial.

Credit check organizations in general provide either a recommendation for rental (based on all the evidence provided) or a credit score of "pass or fail" (based on a preset acceptance score). No matter what company and system you use, be consistent with the "accept" and "deny" thresholds. These thresholds don't allow one applicant to "win" over another by scoring higher; all residents who score accept should be accepted and those scored as denied should in fact be denied. You also need to be consistent about the level of check you do; for example, if you perform criminal background checks for one applicant, you must perform them for all.

How do you handle a denial for rental? If you are performing any form of background or credit check, the decision may fall under the Equal Credit Opportunity Act. Essentially, if someone is denied for rental, the person must be given an adverse action letter explaining why. This act also requires a letter should an exception be made, such as allowing the rental with a cosigner. It is acceptable to make an exception as long as the exception is carried out consistently from renter to renter. As part of their service, credit-reporting companies will usually have the ability to send out these letters.

Accepting cosigners is an independent business decision. The obvious advantage is having more than one income source to guarantee rent. However, the drawback is that the cosigner is not always located in the jurisdiction of the property and if access to that cosigner is needed, the person isn't always easy to locate.

Simple keys to remember:

❑ Hire an attorney to review your rental application.

❑ Ensure that the application stands up to the fair housing standards.

❑ Require all applications to be filled out completely, including all accompanying documentation.

❑ Consider using a third party to conduct credit and background checks.

❑ Follow the Equal Credit Opportunity Act consistently when denying an applicant.

Prepare for Move-In Day

Once the application has been approved, it is time to secure the rental, set a move-in date, and welcome the new resident. Up to this point, there is no commitment by the applicant to ensure that she will choose your community, other than the money she spent on the application, which is usually nominal. Most states and municipalities allow properties to "secure a rental" with some sort of deposit, earnest money, or reservation fee. Usually these fees are applied to the full *security deposit* upon move-in but are nonrefundable if an applicant should cancel. Securing an apartment is important, so check with your local and state governing bodies on what the parameters are.

The marketing efforts should not stop after an applicant has been approved and you've secured the rental. Move-in day is the single most important marketing day in a resident's stay in the community. A positive move-in day often results in a lengthier tenancy with the community; by the same token, a negative experience results in a tenuous tenancy often punctuated by an early exit from the community. One of the worst things a property can do is not be ready for the move-in when the excited resident walks through the door. For that reason, prepare for a move-in thoroughly. Start the process by preparing a checklist for the new resident indicating everything he will need and want to know for move-in. This document, as shown in Figure 6-6, will tell him what monies he will need for move-in day (both rent and security deposit). It will also list his new full address, phone numbers to utility companies and other service providers, as well as any further documentation required. All the legal documents for move-in such as the lease, rules and regulations, any riders and addendums to the lease, and any other informational documents (e.g., an information card for quick reference on the resident) should also be included. For purposes of good customer service, this package should be complete by move-in day and ready for review and execution. The lease and attached documents are reviewed in more detail in Chapter 8.

The day before or morning of a move-in, the actual apartment should be inspected and every moving part tested. The lease package should include a move-in inspection checklist that reviews the condition of the apartment with the new resident. A sample National Apartment Association (NAA) approved checklist is shown in Figure 6-7. Use this same checklist before a resident's arrival to check everything. If there is something that needs replacement or repair, it should be done before the resident arrives.

On move-in day, sit down and go through all documentation with the resident. Make sure to point out any portions of the lease and/or rules and regulations that are a concern. An example might be explaining the operation of smoke alarms. Make sure the rent-paying procedure is explained fully and the process to contact maintenance in the event of an emergency is clearly outlined. Also, allow the new resident to share his or her own questions and concerns, and make sure the resident signs everywhere indicated. (It is advisable, too, to have separate initial points on the lease for important clauses.)

After all the paperwork has been finalized, collect any monies owed by the resident; these funds should be of a guaranteed nature (e.g., certified check, money order). A resident may ask to look at the apartment before signing all documents; this is a judgment call on the part of the leasing agent. Most jurisdictions have a "buyer's remorse law," meaning the execution of the lease wouldn't prohibit a

Figure 6-6. Resident move-in checklist.

Move-In Resident Checklist

We would like to welcome you to _____. Please remember that on moving day, the keys to your apartment may not be picked up before 2:00 p.m. and they may only be picked up by the Leaseholder. Any balance due as stated below must be paid in the form of a CERTIFIED CHECK OR MONEY ORDER ONLY.

Your New Address Will Be

Any town, N.J. xxxxx

BALANCES DUE:
Your Account Number
Must Appear on All Checks &
Correspondence Is # _____

SECURITY $_____ Due upon approval of application _____
CERTIFIED CHECK OR MONEY ORDER ONLY.

Pro-Rate $ _____
Rent $ _____
Other $ _____
BALANCE: $ _____ Due on Move-In Day _____
CERTIFIED CHECK OR MONEY ORDER ONLY.

Please make arrangements as soon as possible for the installation of the following services. There may be a deposit due on these utilities if you have no prior credit with these companies, so please call immediately to make the proper arrangements:
  Public Service Electric & Gas (PSE&G):
  Comcast Cable:

Let me take this opportunity to welcome you to _____ Apartments. We're looking forward to you joining the _____ family!

Sincerely,

---

renter from opting away from the deal because of dissatisfaction with the apartment. Decide in advance how this issue should be handled. However, if the resident is allowed to inspect the apartment before moving in, make it a policy to do the inspection jointly so that any objections can be handled immediately, unless they are unreasonable or complicated.

Make sure this inspection checklist is signed, because you will use the identical

Figure 6-7. Move-in inspection checklist.

Inventory and Condition Form

Resident's Name: _____ Home Phone: (_____)_____ Work Phone: (_____)_____
Resident's Name: _____ Home Phone: (_____)_____ Work Phone: (_____)_____
Resident's Name: _____ Home Phone: (_____)_____ Work Phone: (_____)_____
Resident's Name: _____ Home Phone: (_____)_____ Work Phone: (_____)_____
Apartment Community Name: _____

or Street Address (if house, duplex, etc.): _____ Apt. # _____

Within 48 hours after move-in, you must note on this form all defects or damage and return it to our representative. Otherwise, everything will be considered to be in a clean, safe, and good working condition. Please mark through items listed below if they don't exist. This form protects both you (the resident) and us (the owner). We'll use it in determining what should and should not be considered your responsibility upon move-out. You are entitled to a copy of this form after it is filled out and signed by you and us.

☐ Move-In or ☐ Move-Out Condition *(Check one)*

Living Room
Walls _____
_____
Wallpaper _____
Plugs, Switches, A/C Vents _____
Woodwork/Baseboards _____
Ceiling _____
Light Fixtures, Bulbs _____
Floor/Carpet _____

Doors, Stops, Locks _____
Windows, Latches, Screens _____
Window Coverings _____
Closets, Rods, Shelves _____
Closet Lights, Fixtures _____
Lamps, Bulbs _____
Water Stains on Walls or Ceilings _____
Other _____

Kitchen
Walls _____
_____
Wallpaper _____
Plugs, Switches, A/C Vents _____
Woodwork/Baseboards _____
Ceiling _____
Light Fixtures, Bulbs _____
Floor/Carpet _____

Doors, Stops, Locks _____
Windows, Latches, Screens _____
Window Coverings _____
Cabinets, Drawers, Handles _____
Countertops _____
Stove/Oven, Trays, Pans, Shelves _____
Vent Hood _____
Refrigerator, Trays, Shelves _____
Refrigerator Light, Crisper _____
Dishwasher, Dispensers, Racks _____
Sink/Disposal _____
Microwave _____
Plumbing Leaks or Water Stains on Walls or Ceilings _____

Other _____
_____

General Items
Thermostat _____
Cable TV or Master Antenna _____
A/C Filter _____
Washer/Dryer _____
Garage Door _____
Ceiling Fans _____
Exterior Doors, Screens/Screen Doors, Doorbell _____

Fireplace _____
Other _____

Dining Room
Walls _____
_____
Wallpaper _____
Plugs, Switches, A/C Vents _____
Woodwork/Baseboards _____
Ceiling _____
Light Fixtures, Bulbs _____
Floor/Carpet _____

Doors, Stops, Locks _____
Windows, Latches, Screens _____
Window Coverings _____
Closets, Rods, Shelves _____
Closet Lights, Fixtures _____
Water Stains on Walls or Ceilings _____
Other _____

Halls
Walls _____
_____
Wallpaper _____
Plugs, Switches, A/C Vents _____
Woodwork/Baseboards _____
Ceiling _____
Light Fixtures, Bulbs _____
Floor/Carpet _____

Doors, Stops, Locks _____
Closets, Rods, Shelves _____
Closet Lights, Fixtures _____
Water Stains on Walls or Ceilings _____
Other _____

Exterior (if applicable)
Patio/Yard _____
Fences/Gates _____
Faucets _____
Balconies _____
Other _____

Bedroom *(describe which one):* _____
Walls _____
_____
Wallpaper _____
Plugs, Switches, A/C Vents _____
Woodwork/Baseboards _____
Ceiling _____
Light Fixtures, Bulbs _____
Floor/Carpet _____

Doors, Stops, Locks _____
Windows, Latches, Screens _____
Window Coverings _____
Closets, Rods, Shelves _____
Closet Lights, Fixtures _____
Water Stains on Walls or Ceilings _____
Other _____

06222004030006

Figure 6-7. Continued.

Bedroom *(describe which one):* _____
   Walls _____

Wallpaper _____
Plugs, Switches, A/C Vents _____
Woodwork/Baseboards _____
Ceiling _____
Light Fixtures, Bulbs _____
Floor/Carpet _____

Doors, Stops, Locks _____
Windows, Latches, Screens _____
Window Coverings _____
Closets, Rods, Shelves _____
Closet Lights, Fixtures _____
Water Stains on Walls or Ceilings _____
Other _____

Bath *(describe which one):* _____
   Walls _____

Wallpaper _____
Plugs, Switches, A/C Vents _____
Woodwork/Baseboards _____
Ceiling _____
Light Fixtures, Bulbs _____
Exhaust Fan/Heater _____
Floor/Carpet _____

Doors, Stops, Locks _____
Windows, Latches, Screens _____
Window Coverings _____
Sink, Faucet, Handles, Stopper _____
Countertops _____
Mirror _____
Cabinets, Drawers, Handles _____
Toilet, Paper Holder _____
Bathtub, Enclosure, Stopper _____
Shower, Doors, Rods _____
Tile _____
Plumbing Leaks or Water Stains on Walls or Ceilings _____

Other _____

Half Bath
   Walls _____

Wallpaper _____
Plugs, Switches, A/C Vents _____
Woodwork/Baseboards _____
Ceiling _____
Light Fixtures, Bulbs _____
Exhaust Fan/Heater _____
Floor/Carpet _____

Doors, Stops, Locks _____
Windows, Latches, Screens _____
Window Coverings _____
Sink, Faucet, Handles, Stopper _____
Countertops _____
Mirror _____
Cabinets, Drawers, Handles _____
Toilet, Paper Holder _____
Tile _____
Plumbing Leaks or Water Stains on Walls or Ceilings _____

Other _____

Bedroom *(describe which one):* _____
   Walls _____

Wallpaper _____
Plugs, Switches, A/C Vents _____
Woodwork/Baseboards _____
Ceiling _____
Light Fixtures, Bulbs _____
Floor/Carpet _____

Doors, Stops, Locks _____
Windows, Latches, Screens _____
Window Coverings _____
Closets, Rods, Shelves _____
Closet Lights, Fixtures _____
Water Stains on Walls or Ceilings _____
Other _____

Bath *(describe which one):* _____
   Walls _____

Wallpaper _____
Plugs, Switches, A/C Vents _____
Woodwork/Baseboards _____
Ceiling _____
Light Fixtures, Bulbs _____
Exhaust Fan/Heater _____
Floor/Carpet _____

Doors, Stops, Locks _____
Windows, Latches, Screens _____
Window Coverings _____
Sink, Faucet, Handles, Stopper _____
Countertops _____
Mirror _____
Cabinets, Drawers, Handles _____
Toilet, Paper Holder _____
Bathtub, Enclosure, Stopper _____
Shower, Doors, Rods _____
Tile _____
Plumbing Leaks or Water Stains on Walls or Ceilings _____

Other _____

Safety–Related Items *(Put "none" if item does not exist)*
Door Knob Locks _____
Keyed Deadbolt Locks _____
Keyless Deadbolts _____
Keyless Bolting Devices _____
Sliding Door Latches _____
Sliding Door Security Bars _____
Sliding Door Pin Locks _____
Doorviewers _____
Window Latches _____
Porch and Patio Lights _____
Smoke Detectors (push button to test) _____
Alarm System _____
Fire Extinguishers (look at charge level—BUT DON'T TEST!) _____
Garage Door Opener _____
Gate Access Card(s) _____
Other _____

Date of Move–In: _____
or Date of Move–Out: _____

Acknowledgment. You acknowledge that you have inspected and tested all of the safety-related items (if in the dwelling) and that they are working, except as noted above. All items will be assumed to be in good condition unless otherwise noted on this form. You acknowledge receiving written operating instructions on the alarm system and gate access entry systems (if there are any). You acknowledge testing the smoke detector(s) and verify they are operating correctly.
   In signing below, you accept this inventory as part of the Lease Contract and agree that it accurately reflects the condition of the premises for purposes of determining any refund due to you when you move out.

Resident or Resident's Agent: _____   **Date of Signing:** _____

Owner or Owner's Representative: _____   **Date of Signing:** _____

form for move-out and it is advisable to allow the resident to keep an identical copy.

A nice customer service touch is some sort of "welcome gift" for new residents. An example would be toiletries that can be promptly used for the first few days in the apartment (while they are still unpacking their own things). If the move-in process has gone well, this last offer usually is the icing on the cake to complete a positive move-in experience.

Simple keys to remember:

❑ Move-in day is the most important marketing day in a resident's stay.

❑ Prepare all paperwork in advance and have it ready for move-in day.

❑ Inspect the apartment jointly with the new resident and handle all objections promptly.

❑ Follow up with a welcome gift.

Follow Through with Aftermarketing

Apartment management is a customer service business. The marketing process starts on day one and never ends. Here are some effective ongoing marketing techniques to ensure that resident referrals will continue to be an excellent source of future rentals:

❑ Send a card the day after move-in, welcoming residents again and asking if they are satisfied.

❑ Send residents birthday cards.

❑ Schedule designated coffee and doughnut days in the office so residents can come down and casually discuss things.

❑ Follow up with customer service calls after maintenance is performed.

❑ Contact residents personally about their lease renewal.

❑ Create a community newsletter, even if it is small.

❑ Host "resident appreciation" gatherings throughout the year.

"Raise the Rents, Then We'll Lease Up"

Consistent review and a firm understanding of your market will pay off, and it can sometimes tell you a story and create value for the community on its own right.

That's a lesson I learned years ago when I was a regional manager over a large, sprawling, garden apartment complex that was a very desirable place to live. There was an even mix of one- and two-bedroom apartments, and for a long time the property stayed fully occupied. One summer we started slipping on occupancy. It wasn't that we had an inordinate number of new move-outs, but rather that our inquiry traffic had slowed to a trickle. Our traffic numbers, which we consistently had kept over the years, indicated that our *closing rate,* or ratio of possible applicants to actual rentals, was about the same for this property as it had always been. This is an important concept, because from a management point of view if the closing rate had gone down, there would probably be an obvious negative reason why. We had the same personnel, so our front-line marketers hadn't changed.

After watching this pattern for a few weeks, I decided to do what any good regional manager should: I inspected the entire property and all the empty apartments. I additionally reviewed our rental office and performed a set of diagnostics, so to speak, to hone in on the problem.

From my eye, I could see no obvious deficiencies or radical changes in the property's curb appeal, in the rental office, in the finished vacancies, or in the common property area. I took the investigation a step further. An often-used technique to determine if the curb appeal or rental presentation (or personnel) are lacking is to have a professional but independent source "shop" the property. I had three separate individuals shop the property. The shops all came back good.

We were closing at the same rate, our property showed well, and our personnel met the test. The one thing that wasn't the same was the traffic, the number of people who visited the office or inquired by phone or Internet about our apartments in a given time period. To properly assess traffic numbers, I asked for the most recent market survey. When we reviewed it, we had all the same amenities as our competitors, we were marketing the same way our competition was, and we seemed reasonably priced. We then checked all our advertising, reviewing for accuracy to make sure all the proper phone numbers were listed and the quality of the message was consistent.

The property manager at the time was in the habit of saving every single ad she had ever placed; she also kept a copy of the competition's advertising. After reviewing the competition's, we decided to change our ads slightly and provide a marketing incentive or rent special. We allowed this change to take its course for a few weeks, but to no avail.

Unbeknownst to me, at this point the property manager had gone out and "shopped" all our competition on her own, posing as a renter. Her observation at first amused me, but upon closer look it caught my attention. She told me she thought our apartments were underpriced. She said that after shopping all the competitors, she became aware that there was a definite line between one tier of rentals and the next higher tier of rentals in terms of quality of community. If you looked again at our market survey, we were moderately priced, very close to the lower tier, and our quality was definitely better than that. If you then revisited our ads, we were "giving away" as opposed to offering something.

My manager surmised that the average apartment hunter was grouping us with a totally different set of properties and then eliminating us as a possible visit even before inquiring. I took a chance, raised the rents just enough to meet that upper tier, eliminated the rent specials, and highlighted other aspects of our property.

Within two weeks, our traffic numbers had rebounded and our short-term problem dissipated. The moral to this story is that if you make an effort to know the market and then review market indicators consistently, your property's intrinsic value can be increased.

CHAPTER 7

Maintenance

Save Money, Make Money

Your community is a living, breathing entity, and as such you have to care for it just as you would any other living, breathing being. Similar to how you set up and market your apartments, it is imperative to set up a plan for how you'll maintain your community, both for the purposes of presenting the best product to the public and for the sustained well-being of your investment. Maintenance done haphazardly will cost you financially in two important ways:

1. *Needless Expense.* Improper care and improper planning means you'll be fixing neglect and poor work, which is often much more expensive than ordinary repair.

2. *Lost Revenue.* People move out because of poor maintenance or lack of maintenance; then not only do you incur costs to prepare an apartment again for rental, but during this time period you aren't making revenue on the unit.

There are six areas to concentrate on when it comes to forming an effective maintenance operation and game plan for your apartment community:

1. Capital and structural components (e.g., roofs, paving, power plants)
2. Curb appeal
3. Routine daily maintenance

4. Emergency maintenance

5. Vacant "make-readies"

6. Inventory and equipment control

When discussing the maintenance function, each of these areas plays a definitive role in the success of a property. When all of these functions are organized and coordinated, it is amazing how smooth an apartment operation can be. If they are not, you, as the owner of this investment, will wake up to a problem a day and, maybe worse, tremendous liability.

Although the customer service aspect is incredibly important, the safety and well-being of your residents should be a far greater priority. People come and make their home in your investment, and with that, ownership bears tremendous responsibility to provide a safe living environment. The volume of laws, regulations, and ordinances, and the governmental oversight that comes with that responsibility, can be intimidating and overwhelming. If you manage your property with particular attention to the maintenance component, chances are you'll be aware of the issues within your community that need to be addressed sooner and you'll be able to correct or maintain them quickly at minimal cost. An efficient, well-thought-out maintenance game plan will provide that safe environment while satisfying your bottom line.

■ Be Routine and Repetitive (Organize and Categorize)

Did you ever wonder why flying is such a safe mode of transportation? There is a routine and procedure for everything the plane mechanic and the pilot do. When a pilot "preflights" his plane, he walks around that aircraft in the exact same pattern each and every time he performs this practice. Consequently, very little is left to chance and very little is assumed. The very structured procedures in the aviation industry result in thousands of aircraft taking off all around the world every day, and with rare exception, they land at their scheduled destination.

In many apartment complexes, poor property maintenance procedures could result in a catastrophic event, given the power plants that exist on premises. Hopefully, though, the very least that will happen is that poor practices will only deter you from your scheduled destination.

The first step to an effective maintenance function is to create a routine and be repetitive and consistent with that routine. For the remainder of this chapter, we will assume that you have purchased a garden apartment complex with 100 units and 10 separate buildings; however, these principles apply to any size community and any size staff.

Capital and Structural Components

When closing on this complex, there should have been a lot of information handed to you, such as documentation concerning the age, condition, and history of all major facets of your buildings. You should have additionally undertaken a site inspection where you, as the purchaser, reviewed the same items physically. If you are financing a portion of this investment through a lender, many of them will have conducted some of their own inspections for appraisal purposes, capital reserve requirements, or environmental regulatory reasons. The combination of all these sources means that you should have a very good baseline of information to create an understanding of the condition of your property as well as an inventory of how your property is structured.

Knowing this information is vital to the large capital expenditures you will have to make over the life of your investment. As soon as you take over your new investment, review this information and institute ways to routinely reassess the components of your buildings that have a *useful life*. Let's use the example of the 100-unit complex. You know you have ten buildings and each building has a roof. What type of roofs are they—flat roofs, pitched asphalt tile, etc.? What is the useful life of that roofing surface and when was the present roof installed? What shape is it in now? If you finance, you may be required to escrow funds to take care of immediate issues; therefore, baseline information probably exists. From this information, create a chart of all your roofs. Place any answers you discerned from your questions on that chart. Then create a master calendar. On this calendar, create a schedule of when each roof is to be inspected on a routine basis. A sample schedule is shown in Figure 7-1. Repeat this process with all major elements of your buildings, property, and units. Whether you are the one inspecting or you hire someone to maintain your property, insist that all elements of your building be inspected in accordance with this schedule.

Someone might argue there is very little to "inspect" on a roof. There are, however, telltale signs to every major capital item of your building, including deterioration and hazards that hasten a system's demise. If regularly checked, you can slow the aging process down and eliminate the hazards.

In the example of the roof, two elements will accelerate a roof's life expectancy: the sun and water. Water is the number-one destruction agent to any building. But how can you stop the damage from the sun? Constant roof inspections will reveal

Figure 7-1. Yearly property inspection calendar.

YEARLY PROPERTY CALENDER AND INSPECTION

January
Winter-service cooling systems
Inspect roofs and attics
Obtain landscaping contracts
Obtain pool maintenance contracts
Inspect pool equipment
Review heating equipment operation
Inspect gutters and leaders
Inspect all safety equipment (smoke alarms, fire sprinklers, etc.)

February
Review buildings for paint; obtain bids
Review concrete; obtain bids
Inspect heating equipment
Award landscaping and pool contracts
Inspect all safety equipment (smoke alarms, fire sprinklers, etc.)

March
Review pavement condition; obtain bids
Do spring color planting (pansies)
Do spring cleanup; review landscaping condition
Review heating equipment
Inspect grounds equipment and service
Inspect all safety equipment (smoke alarms, fire sprinklers, etc.)

April
Review property for winter damage; obtain bids
Inspect gutters and leaders
Review signage
Review common hallway condition; schedule work
Adjust light timers
Inspect all safety equipment (smoke alarms, fire sprinklers, etc.)

May
Shut down heating equipment
Inspect and start up pool equipment
Start up and test cooling equipment
Award paving/roofing repair/concrete contracts
Award other winter damage contracts
Start up sprinkler systems

(continues)

Figure 7-1. Continued.

Adjust light timers
Add summer color
Review all landscaping replacement issues
Inspect all safety equipment (smoke alarms, fire sprinklers, etc.)

June
Open pools
Summer-service heating equipment
Perform all contract work
Inspect windows and doors
Review roofs and gutters
Adjust light timers
Inspect cooling equipment
Install landscaping replacement issues
Inspect all safety equipment (smoke alarms, fire sprinklers, etc.)

July
Review all contract work
Inspect cooling equipment
Inspect all safety equipment (smoke alarms, fire sprinklers, etc.)
Review heating service

August
Inspect all safety equipment (smoke alarms, fire sprinklers, etc.)
Obtain all snow removal bids
Service snow equipment

September
Adjust light timers
Inspect all safety equipment (smoke alarms, fire sprinklers, etc.)
Shut down pool equipment; winterize
Award snow contracts
Test heating equipment
Shut down cooling equipment

October
Install fall color
Inspect all safety equipment (smoke alarms, fire sprinklers, etc.)
Inspect gutters and leaders
Start up heating equipment
Inspect basements and crawl spaces
Adjust light timers

November
Inspect all safety equipment (smoke alarms, fire sprinklers, etc.)
Clean leaves; clear gutters
Inspect heating equipment
Obtain winter-service bids, cooling equipment

December
Inspect all safety equipment (smoke alarms, fire sprinklers, etc.)
Inspect heating equipment

articles either left on or thrown on the roof, such as nails. When the sun heats up the nail, it eventually "burns" through certain roof surfaces, allowing water to penetrate the roofing surface. Roofing systems also have components that warp or disfigure over time because of the sun, and then water and ice fill the voids left by the deformed component. Water will eventually rot and destroy almost anything with which it has constant contact. If you don't constantly review the roofing system, a small deformity goes unchecked and the decking and support structure not visible to the naked eye slowly but surely rots. It is far cheaper to replace a $10 roofing component such as flashing than it is to strip off otherwise-good roof tiles and replace support beams and wood decking. This could cost you thousands of dollars. Every time you repair or replace, update your records.

Make an extensive list of items that you know will cost you if they need replacement or major repair over the years. The list that follows will help you get started:

Capital Components of a Building/Property That Should Be Routinely Inspected

- ❑ Roofs
- ❑ Windows and doors
- ❑ Power plants (e.g., boilers, furnaces, hot water heaters)
- ❑ Plumbing systems and sewer systems
- ❑ Drainage and storm systems
- ❑ Parking lots
- ❑ Sidewalks and steps
- ❑ Safety systems (e.g., fire sprinkler and alarm components)
- ❑ Main electrical systems

❏ Amenity facilities such as laundry rooms

❏ Storage facilities such as oil tanks

Some items, such as the fire systems, might require inspection for compliance with local or state code. Stick to these requirements to the letter of the law. Require your staff to document these inspections, but also verify for yourself that the information they are giving you is correct. One way to reinforce this policy is to place charts in and around certain capital items such as your power plants. Check these charts when visiting the property. Verify the last time the staff or you reviewed the system and verify its present condition against that last documentation.

Simple keys to remember:

❏ Create a baseline list of all major capital items and their history.
❏ Create a calendar for scheduling consistent, periodic inspections of these items.
❏ Document what you find and what you correct with these inspections.
❏ Safety should always be the first priority, and water infiltration is the biggest daily enemy of your buildings.

Curb Appeal

Imagine yourself in the following scenario. You drive the same way to work every day and you pass an apartment complex that has a big monument sign decorated with flowers. It is very noticeable and attractive. One morning you drive by and an ornamental light fixture on top of the sign has been knocked over. The sign is so prominent you notice right away that the light is out of place. For the next two weeks you drive by that sign and nothing has been done to fix that light. Would you live at that complex, no matter how nice that sign is? That apartment complex just did its utmost to broadcast negative publicity about how it operates from a maintenance standpoint. Curb appeal is the best way to present an enticing picture of your community, or it can have just the opposite effect. You should instruct your staff to review curb appeal items on a daily basis for their aesthetics and operation.

Once you have taken that drive-by and approached your property from every angle, create a *daily curb appeal checklist*. Some items on this checklist may overlap with your routine maintenance schedule and checklist; nonetheless, make a separate list for curb appeal. If you want to combine the lists, make sure you create a separate subsection for curb appeal. You want the "curb appeal" mentality to become pervasive in every staff member because that curb appeal is what rents apartments, and you want staff to be sensitive to that fact on a daily basis. A broken light on your sign may seem like small potatoes when compared to the major plumbing repair you have scheduled today, but it can cost you just as much (or more) in lost revenue.

Maintenance Curb Appeal Concerns

❑ Signage and all aspects related to the signs (e.g., flags, lights, water fountains, plants)

❑ Common lighting

❑ Building complements (e.g., shutters, door kick plates, shrubbery)

❑ Clean parking lots, sidewalks, garbage areas

❑ Amenities (e.g., playground equipment, pools, community benches, laundry rooms)

❑ Leasing facilities and clubhouses

❑ Company vehicles

All these items, which prospective renters see each day, speak volumes about how well a community is taken care of. You or your staff should walk by them every single day, noting anything that will catch every person's eyes and correcting any defects immediately.

If you have a 100-unit complex, your staff may be large enough to have separate maintenance and leasing functions. In this case, someone from each staff should review curb appeal items daily. If you are not physically present at this site daily, on each visit you should review this list the same way your staff does. A big curb appeal item that often goes unchecked for long periods of time is graffiti. Leaving graffiti for any length of time on your property is an indicator to the public that the insane run the asylum; it will lose you many a prospective renter.

Simple keys to remember:

❑ Create a list of curb appeal items; make sure it is a stand-alone list (i.e., separate from your routine maintenance checklist).

❑ Inspect curb appeal items daily.

❑ Repair any defect immediately.

Routine Daily Maintenance

The bulk of what a maintenance staff does in apartments is preparing apartments for rental and routine daily maintenance. Apartments are like living organisms, and as such, they have functions that break and have to be maintained. Organizing work flow creates order and minimizes the chance that something will go unrepaired and upset a resident. Most residents understand it is nobody's fault that a sink trap wears out, but having to live with a leak for several days at a time is not understandable.

When organizing the maintenance function, start by setting the right tone. All your maintenance professionals will wear uniforms and recognizable name identification. (Some states require it.) Your entire maintenance staff will carry a pad and pencil at all times. All shop areas are to be cleaned at the end of each day, and all inventory areas are to remain structured and organized. The tone you set and the routine you are establishing will become part of the maintenance mantra. Make sure, additionally, that your professionals possess any required licenses or certifications. For example, if a building has a power plant or boiler vessel of a certain size, many states require that at least one custodian possess a "black seal boiler license."

Your maintenance systems must be able to handle 1) the structural demands of an apartment community and 2) customer concerns. Let's start with the structural demands. We have already discussed how constant review of capital items and curb appeal items can both save and make you money. From a maintenance standpoint you should also create standard operating procedures (SOPs)—the first of which should be the undertaking of a daily property inspection. Just like the airplane pilot, you should walk around your property the same way every day. Each maintenance professional should carry a "checklist" of both capital and curb appeal items (such as the one shown in Figure 7-2). That checklist should be reviewed daily. If you check the same areas on a daily basis, you are more likely to catch a problem when it is small and more easily corrected.

Setting the tone and routinely inspecting the work matters. As an example, consider a clean boiler room that's reviewed for temperature and pressure settings daily. If your boiler room is well lit, with the floor clean and painted (paint it gray, because that color reveals leaks at their smallest), and you know what your temperature and pressure settings should be on a daily basis, you'll recognize an abnormality

Figure 7-2. Daily property inspection report.

Daily Property Inspection Report

Date _____

Bldg. 1 (Repeat for Multiple Bldgs.)

Exterior lights _____
Gutters & leaders _____
Walkways & steps _____
Entrances _____
Shutters & windows _____
Common hallways _____
Safety systems _____
    a. Smoke alarms _____
    b. Fire exit lights _____
    c. Emergency lighting _____
    d. Sprinkler systems _____
Roofs _____
Heating systems _____
Garages _____
Sump pumps _____
Landscaping issues _____

Resident issues: _____

_____

_____

Other: _____

_____

_____

right away. A small spot of oil below a water pump may be an indication that a seal is going bad on that pump. The seal costs much less than a whole new pump. Make sure abnormalities are documented and, if the issue cannot be fixed on the spot, that this information is transferred into the future repair request queue. Safety items should be handled with priority, then curb appeal and then capital items. This routine should not be broken for any reason. It is too easy to think it can wait one more day, because that one day will lead to several days.

During this inspection walk-through you should also routinely *police your property,* meaning walk around the property for the sole purpose of picking up garbage and debris. Never let a piece of garbage sit.

The majority of your maintenance function will be handling the residents and their daily concerns. If customer concerns are handled well, you'll save untold dollars over the years. More important, you will keep or lose residents in a heartbeat depending on the effectiveness and consistency of your maintenance function.

When establishing your maintenance policy, ask three key questions: How is maintenance work generated? How is it delegated? How is it tracked? The most common way is through a "work order" system. You can create your own work order or (more likely) purchase one of many preprinted forms, such as the one shown in Figure 7-3. Preprinted systems consist of a book of work orders, usually in duplicate or triplicate, one page of which permanently stays in the book. One copy usually is assigned to a maintenance professional, and if there is a third copy, it will usually end up in a resident's file. If you use a management software package, most of them have a work order function. Obviously, if the work order is computer-generated, the ability for the program to cross-reference a work order with an apartment or a resident occurs instantly.

One very important part of the work order process is scheduling an appointment or securing permission from residents to enter their apartment without them having to be home. It is also advisable to designate one centralized place for all work orders to be picked up on a daily basis so that you can avoid missed or lost orders. If your maintenance professionals get a request out in the field or end up correcting an unrelated problem while in a resident's apartment, it should be documented on a work order, even if the work was simple and completed. This work order should be filled out completely, and whoever gets the initial request should be as specific as possible regarding the problem that exists.

Prioritize your work orders. Safety first, costly repairs second, but always keep in mind the level of resident discomfort when deciding which work orders to accomplish each day. If you have a work order that you know is complicated or time-consuming, it is best to plan that job at the start of the day and have all materials lined up beforehand. If residents will be without a major service in their apartment for any length of time, it is best to discuss scheduling the requested work. If possible, wait until a mutually beneficial time can be agreed upon. When the work is completed, the work order should be completed and signed off and returned to a predetermined "finished work drop-off," again to centralize the work flow. The work order book should be matched each day to the orders handed out. By routinely

Figure 7-3. Work order.

MAINTENANCE REQUEST AND WORK ORDER

Apartment #: _____ Name: _____ Time: _____ Date: _____

PERMISSION TO ENTER UNIT:

( ) ANYTIME
( ) BY APPOINTMENT, OCCUPANT PRESENT

_____ (DATE) _____ (TIME) _____

TELEPHONE NO.: _____

UNIT ENTRY NOTICE:
WE WERE IN YOUR APARTMENT TODAY
TO PERFORM THE NECESSARY REPAIRS OR
INSPECTIONS:

_____ (DATE) _____ (TIME ENTERED) _____
(TIME DEPARTED) _____

JOB STATUS:
( ) COMPLETE
( ) INCOMPLETE BECAUSE OF _____

( ) WILL RETURN TO COMPLETE
_____ (DATE) (TIME) _____
( ) OUTSIDE PROFESSIONAL ASSISTANCE

MAINTENANCE PERFORMED BY: _____

REQUEST: _____

WORK DONE AND MATERIALS USED: _____

doing so, you will note what jobs were accomplished and what is still outstanding, and that will determine the work flow for the next day.

Always make sure your routine maintenance policy includes instructions on proper conduct by the staff when in a resident's apartment, which includes proper cleanup and protection of resident's belongings. Maintenance can be a messy business, and sometimes you can fix a resident's problem and create a new one by ruining a personal belonging.

One way to mitigate future work is to do a cursory inspection of each apartment whenever you are doing any kind of maintenance, routine or emergency, and noting anything that may need attention. You can achieve a lot in five minutes. If you have battery-operated smoke detectors or carbon monoxide testers in your apartments (many jurisdictions require one or both), check them each time you or your staff go into a unit, and always have spare batteries on hand. You should check the equipment and then log that you checked it. Do the same with faucets and toilets to make sure they aren't leaking or running. If you make this part of every maintenance call, you will find potential problems before they become serious.

Simple keys to remember:

❑ To create an organized maintenance function, start off by setting a tone.

❑ Require your personnel to be personally organized; work areas should also be structured and clean.

❑ Establish systems to handle customer concerns and the structural demands of an apartment community.

❑ Develop daily inspections for your common areas, and use checklists.

❑ Prioritize safety items.

❑ Establish a maintenance policy by defining how work is generated, how it is delegated, and how it is tracked. The most common way is through a work order system.

❑ Follow the work order system consistently.

❑ Encourage customer care when working in a resident's apartment.

Emergency Maintenance

People only go to the video store when it is open; in most places you can't get your car washed at two in the morning. Yet in the apartment business, people live at your business and operate twenty-four hours a day. Through effective inspection, you can reduce the incidence of failure of equipment, but you cannot eliminate it, and mechanical items don't break only during normal business hours. When creating your maintenance function, be sure to have your after-hours policy clearly laid out to both staff and residents. Here's a five-step approach to success when dealing with emergency maintenance:

1. Define clearly the way to contact a representative of your community in case mechanical problems occur after hours.

2. Delineate at move-in which issues are handled after normal business hours and which are not. For instance, a backed-up toilet is clearly something to be taken care of whenever it happens, but a loose cabinet door is not. Itemize in writing the issues that are and aren't "emergencies."

3. Train your staff to "query" a resident over the phone about a perceived emergency. Oftentimes, with a little coaching over the phone, you can help a resident resolve a simple problem. For instance, a resident calls and says the refrigerator isn't running. Ask him if he knows where the circuit breakers are; if he does, ask him to try the breaker. If the refrigerator comes on, ask him to unplug or turn off other nonessential items in the apartment. Often, especially in older communities, there is a limit on how much power is going to a unit. The resident may have overloaded the circuit unintentionally. Always make a point to visit that unit the next day to verify the severity of the problem.

4. Store contingency items on hand for major failures. For instance, if you have central air in your units, have at least one spare window air-conditioner available; it may be critical to an individual who has health problems should their central unit fail. Have a generator to run critical items such as sump pumps in case of a major outage in a rainstorm.

5. Create a ready list of any critical contractors whose services may be needed for the bigger items that are beyond your scope. Make sure they know you expect prompt response in regard to after-hours issues.

Depending on the size of your investment, you may want to require that at least one individual in your employ lives on-site. For properties that reach a certain size, most states require on-site staffing. If it is required by your state, or if you can afford it, typically an apartment is used as a bartering chip in salary negotiations for such a person. Having an on-site presence twenty-four hours a day is desirable. If you have this arrangement, be very mindful of labor laws relative to overtime and other forms of compensation for additional time spent on the job after the traditional workweek.

On occasion, you or an employee will be asked to intercede in an after-hours issue other than maintenance. An example is an argument or dispute between residents when one is having a party. Although each one of your residents should know the community rules and regulations (reviewed during the move-in process), it doesn't mean that they will always follow them. You should use discretion when handling such issues. You have no idea what transpired before you were called, and if one of the residents is hosting a party, you have no idea what "condition" the person might be in. More than likely, if your rules and regulations are being violated, there is a chance local code is, too. Involve the proper authorities and remain neutral in events such as this. If punitive action has to be taken, that should be done in the proper venue at the proper time. Trying to referee an emotional and volatile situation at the moment can be very dangerous.

Major emergencies occur from time to time, such as fires and floods. Just like all other maintenance procedures, you should have a clearly defined strategy in place to handle such events. The most common major emergency is a fire. Know beforehand what you would do should a fire occur. Using a fire as an example, here are some simple procedures to have in place should this unfortunate situation occur:

Fire Procedures

❑ Create a phone list for each member of the staff that includes critical personnel and/or emergency management individuals to be contacted immediately upon discovering such an event. The fire department, police department, and the Red Cross are essential individuals to contact immediately. The Red Cross often provides emergency food, housing, and clothing to individuals made homeless in a tragedy. The sooner you can ease a resident's shock, the better for all involved.

❑ Clearly mark an egress path for all residents should they hear a fire or smoke alarm. Inspect these egress paths continually.

❑ Inspect all fire safety equipment regularly, not just to regulation but as often as possible.

❑ Design a clear diagram of all utility shutoffs, especially electricity and gas.

❑ Assign responsibilities to staff members in the event of such an incident. For example, who will direct emergency officials to the emergency shutoffs? Assign a point person to be the only individual to communicate with emergency personnel unless they request otherwise.

❑ Have a procedure in place to be implemented after the fire is extinguished. How do you make the affected area safe? Who needs to be called in to handle the loss and the eventual rebuild? How can you assist residents in relocation? How do you communicate to other residents properly to avoid disinformation? Having a plan for these events controls a situation much more efficiently.

❑ Role-play with yourself and staff members on how to handle press inquiries. Perception can do more damage than reality, and choosing your words carefully must be an integral part of this process.

If you find that a catastrophe was possibly caused by a systemic part of your building infrastructure, require inspections throughout your community right away; however, remember that during an emergency, your property becomes the jurisdiction of whoever is in charge of the emergency situation. Don't get in their way without their knowledge and permission.

Major emergencies are never pleasant experiences, but if some forethought goes into the eventuality of their occurrence, they can be managed.

Simple keys to remember:

❑ Create an after-hours policy and clearly lay it out to both staff and residents.

❑ Follow the five-step approach to being prepared for these occurrences.

❑ Use discretion when being asked to intercede in a nonmaintenance issue after hours; these situations, such as disputes between residents, can be volatile.

❑ Involve the proper authorities.

❑ Establish major emergency procedures and prepare for their eventuality, regardless of how rare they may be.

Vacant "Make-Readies": The Perfect Apartment Becomes the Perfect Home

Move-in day, as discussed in Chapter 6 on marketing, is possibly the most important day in a person's residency with you. It can also, from the maintenance standpoint, be a way to control and reduce your incidents of maintenance requests on a daily basis. Reduced maintenance calls minimize labor and material costs, so this is a bottom-line issue. More important, if you move in happy residents, they will most likely remain with you for a longer period of time, and that translates into an apartment that isn't vacant and is therefore gaining revenue. When an apartment does become vacant, there is always an urgency to get it prepared quickly and get it re-rented as soon as possible.

An often-made mistake is sacrificing quality for speed. It is a mistake that will come back to haunt you. You may think the apartment is adequate for a new rental, but adequate and acceptable are two different terms. Imagine the prospective resident who has scheduled a move-in, showed up to sign on the dotted line, and given you his or her hard-earned cash only to find the apartment is not ready or it is finished in poor condition. Many people at that point have no choice but to move in, but it probably won't be a pleasant stay. You can, as in all other aspects of maintenance, construct a procedure to ensure your apartment is done completely, on time, and not only to your satisfaction but to the resident's as well.

The process of getting a vacant apartment ready for rent starts with the previous move-out inspection. From the moment an apartment goes back into your possession, you should be inspecting it to assess what you will need to do to make this apartment marketable and comfortably livable. You should use the same inspection report that you use for move-in inspections (see Chapter 6, Figure 6-7). Itemize everything in the apartment that needs to be addressed; for instance, is the carpet in the apartment something you can keep or is it destroyed or past its useful life? Are the appliances operational and in good condition? Decide at this point what major work has to be undertaken and what amenities will need to be repaired or replaced. Now is the time to coordinate with the rental or leasing function.

If the community you manage has separate functions, it is advisable at this point to mutually determine how long it will take to prepare that apartment, and a move-in date should not be scheduled before this date. If you have contractors such as painters and carpet installers, they should be coordinated and scheduled at this point. Any large-item orders, such as carpet and appliances, should be executed at this time also. Use the same procedure for every single empty unit every single time, and if you have multiple units, have a system to track the progress. Make that system public to all involved. An example is to post a board somewhere in your leasing and/or management office. On that board, split up all regimented functions of a *make-ready*—that is, a vacant apartment that needs to prepared for an upcoming rental. Each time one of the functions is complete, mark it on the make-ready list on this board. (For a sample list, see Figure 7-4.) The board should include the move-in date so you and all can see how far from the goal each vacant unit has

Figure 7-4. Vacant make-ready list.

VACANT MAKE-READY LIST

UNIT #	UNIT TYPE	DATE VACANT	PREP	PAINT	FINAL CLEAN	MOVE-IN DATE	OTHER
100	2BD2BA	10-1	X	X		11-1	NEW CARPET
101	1BD1BA	10-15	X				APPLIANCES AND CARPET

progressed. When the painting of the unit is complete, for example, mark the date it was completed. Predetermine with your staff what the benchmark is on each of these items to be considered complete. The last item that should be undertaken in any apartment make-ready is the finish flooring. If improperly coordinated, the new flooring may be damaged before the resident ever gets to move in.

Once an apartment appears to have been through all make-ready stages, you should perform a *walk-through inspection* using the same move-out inspection form used with the actual resident. It is best to perform this inspection before the actual move-in day, and if you have a leasing function, the inspection should be carried out in tandem. Make sure the littlest of items are taken into account, such as the ease of door movement, cleanliness of counters and mailbox apertures. Make sure the apartment smells good and looks good. Pay particular attention to bathrooms and kitchens. They are the most heavily scrutinized aspects of apartment living on move-in day. It is helpful if at all possible on the actual move-in day for a member of the maintenance staff to accompany the resident and leasing personnel. Then if any minor issues come up during the new move-in inspection, maintenance can take care of them right away.

In the event that something major holds up an anticipated move-in day, it is always best to communicate with the renter as soon as you are aware of the delay. If she can rearrange plans prior to move-in day, the disappointment will be mitigated. The goal is to make the renting experience live up to the expectations of somebody who will view the apartment as her home for the foreseeable future. Your care in coordinating this day can make her feel at home, or it can make her start counting the days to when she can leave this bad experience—and remember, vacant apartments cost you money.

Inventory and Equipment Control

Whether you have a small community or one composed of multiple units and multiple buildings, you will need basic stock of certain items and basic tools. This aspect of maintenance management can be costly, especially if no thought is given to its organization. Each component in an apartment has parts. It is far cheaper to replace parts than it is to replace whole systems. For instance, a traditional sink faucet may cost you between $40 and $50 if it is of quality, yet most faucets fail because of smaller parts such as stems, seats, and O-rings. These parts are worth a fraction of what the whole faucet costs; therefore, always stock these items.

Tips for Stocking Maintenance Items

❑ Catalog all pertinent items included in your apartments.

❑ Separate them into categories: electrical, plumbing, windows and doors, cabinetry, appliances, wood, finish items (e.g., paint and Sheetrock), and common area items (e.g., mailboxes). Identify the brand and model of each. Go to your suppliers and identify all necessary parts associated with the major item.

❑ Create one central area where all stock is stored, and partition this area by the same categories.

❑ Create specific locations for each specific part and make that their permanent location. Create a "tag" with all important information about that part.

❑ Keep this area behind lock and key, and note parts coming in and going out.

❑ Order material at specific intervals and be consistent, unless an emergency arises.

❑ Develop an understanding of how many of an item you will use between intervals, and don't buy more than you need.

If you take this approach to inventory, you have broken down each item so that you can easily review what you use and how much you use. Over time you'll be able to minimize the type and volume of purchases. Whenever possible, try your best to buy the same make or brand. This is particularly important when speaking about plumbing material. If you have too many different plumbing setups in an apartment community, you will never be able to adequately keep stock or ensure you'll have the right part when you need it. If you track the cost from multiple suppliers along with usage of these items, it will be easier to review what is on hand. By working with one supplier, you can ensure you are always getting the right product, for the right price, for the right reason.

Many property management software programs can handle inventory control, and many suppliers today, as part of their customer care component, will provide you periodic reports of all purchased material. If you have the ability, use these reports to cross-verify all transactions you make.

If you anticipate multiple purchases in an operating week, then it is important you create some type of *purchase order* system and policy so that purchases aren't made by personnel without your knowledge or approval. Create thresholds not to be exceeded without your verbal or written permission. Create policies in regard to receiving material, such as who can purchase and who can accept deliveries and sign for them. And, create a system to match up what was ordered and delivered, and what the cost was, before paying an invoice for material.

Finally, with regard to equipment, many maintenance professionals have their own basic tools, but you will have to make the decision about what new or additional items you will purchase. Once you decide, control and care of these tools of the trade is essential.

Tips for Equipment Care and Control

❑ Centralize all equipment in one location. Make sure it is a secure location and in compliance with all Occupational Safety and Health Administration (OSHA) regulations and any local codes, such as fire. (Often gasoline-powered equipment cannot be stored below actual living space.)

❑ Create an inventory list of all pertinent equipment. Because this equipment is used on a daily basis, have the equipment "signed in and out" for each use.

❑ Review all operating manuals and follow all maintenance, care, and operating procedures.

❑ Keep a log of routine maintenance of these items.

❑ Require employees who may operate this equipment to read the manuals and sign off on the fact that they understand the procedures necessary in the operation and care of it.

By creating and adhering to these inventory and equipment procedures, you are minimizing loss and damage, and increasing the likelihood of proper use of equipment that most certainly is expensive to replace and repair.

■ Reduce Turnover with Good Customer Service

One thing you should be in the habit of doing is asking individuals who do not renew their leases why they aren't. Why have they chosen to leave your community? If they weren't forced to leave by job or the purchase of a home or some other unforeseen circumstance, they will most likely tell you they left because of poor customer service. The professionals that most renters will come in contact with the most are your maintenance staff. It is reasonable to deduce that if a resident leaves because of customer service, poor maintenance may have a lot to do with his or her dissatisfaction. Therefore, put care into this aspect of your ownership. Again, think of the bottom-line impact. If people don't move, you won't have to spend money attracting new residents, so you ensure a steady income stream with minimal expense.

There are some incidentals to mention as well. It is imperative to familiarize yourself with local regulation and code and to know what licenses and certifications your maintenance professionals must possess. It is highly unlikely your maintenance staff is qualified and certified to perform all facets of the job. However, don't hire anyone who doesn't minimally meet the base requirements, and never let employees perform tasks for which they are not qualified. You increase your liability and you might end up spending a lot more than you think you are saving. Be aware of sensitive environmental concerns endemic to the apartment business and make sure, from a maintenance standpoint, you are prepared and qualified to deal with them. Some examples are lead paint, asbestos, mold, and fossil fuel management. We explore these issues in more detail in the next chapter, but your maintenance people need to know procedure and follow it. The oversight on these issues on a federal and state level is noteworthy.

Finally, there are plenty of training programs available throughout the industry and in trade schools. If some aspect of maintenance will be a constant on a property, such as air-conditioning repair, afford your personnel the opportunity for training. Organizations such as the National Apartment Association and their local affiliates offer such training, and many of your supplier vendors also offer training. Take advantage of it. When you are not sure of the skill level of your staff, involve licensed and certified professionals. Remember, safety always comes first when providing people a home.

Here is a quick story to illustrate how proper maintenance procedures can radically transform a property, in appearance, expense, and quality of resident:

"The Tale of Two Managers"

I was given the assignment to take over a property that was labeled "trouble" by other managers who had worked it and a "challenge" by my ownership. It had been this owner's holding for quite some time, but recently the bottom line started deteriorating and the ownership was looking to make a management change. The property was almost 300 units and located in one of the most affluent counties in the state (and in the country, for that matter). It was a property situated on the edge of a good neighborhood/bad neighborhood. It was located on a beautiful riverbank with beautiful homes surrounding it on three sides. The other side was the beginning of an urban zone in some decay. This property was located only a mile from the ocean, and about the same from a major shopping mall and all major highways. There was nothing extraordinary about the schools, positive or negative. The property's brick and mortar was solid. The units were large and many of them had balconies overlooking the river.

At first blush, this would seem to be a building and a location full of potential. Upon closer inspection, I first went to the storage area near a bulkhead on the river. What a picturesque place this should have been, but it was littered with old appliances and furniture, piled in no organized fashion. When clearing past the debris, I could see a tractor, rusty and broken, leaking fluids all over the storage garage. I do not believe I saw one useful tool intact in the shed. Here I was introduced to the maintenance "super," as this position is sometimes called. I asked this man how long had he been here and he said about a year and a half. I asked him why all this furniture was lying here. He told me it was convenient, and he had it removed once or twice a year. I asked him an unrelated question that he obviously didn't relate to the furniture. I asked if he had a rodent problem on the property, which he answered in amazement that he did. He asked me how I knew. I didn't answer him, but I did ask to take a tour of the rest of the community.

I found out there wasn't any area within the complex that had showed an ounce of care for an extended period of time. The maintenance shop was a wreck. You couldn't find a tool or a part without throwing things around a bit. But there was a lot of stock. It seems this man couldn't find anything so he just kept ordering. I asked to see his records on resident calls; he could produce no more than a few scraps of paper. I asked to look at all his empty apartments—the growing number of empties is what drew the ownership's concern in the first place. I did not find one unit that was on its way to being substantially completed. I then visited the common laundry rooms and found them a mess. I wouldn't bring my own clothes into these facilities to wash. When I asked this man why he thought we weren't renting, he said, "Well, we are on the wrong side of the tracks."

Do you remember that "broken leg" theory? This property had broken its leg and it happened fast (this man was only here a year and a half). But it was going to take a longer time to heal. We had a property with decreased revenue in the form of empties, we were overstocked because of inventory mismanagement, we had no salvageable equipment, and we had started drawing the wrong crowd. The community was getting tough to handle. This property would be one of the first challenges of my career, and although its present status was bleak and intimidating, I knew the man we had left at the controls had crashed the bus. I let this man go.

I interviewed for his replacement for a long time. One day a gentleman in his fifties showed up at my door in a suit and tie with a folder in his hand. He came in and told me he took pride in what he did and proceeded to open the folder. Inside there were pictures of the community he had most recently worked at. It was immaculate. He had been in the business for almost thirty years and talked incessantly about the care you have to put into all you do in maintenance. I hired him and decided to trust his years in the business.

I met him at the site on his first day. We walked the same route I had walked with his predecessor. He had his notepad out and the only thing negative he had to say referred to the former keeper of the guard. I told him what my vision was, but I said I'd give him a week or two on his own and then we would reconnect and develop a game plan. I expected to hear at least one or two phone calls requesting a truckload of new supplies or a tool order. I heard none of that.

The two weeks had come and gone, so I visited again. I met this gentleman in the shop. What I saw flabbergasted me. The office was spotless, the desk clean, the floor washed and waxed. On the desk were an organized work order book, an in/out box, and a notebook. He walked me around the corner and the supplies were on shelves, organized by category and labeled. It was a fully stocked room. He then asked me to take a walk to the shed down by the river. The old appliances and furniture were gone. He opened the garage door (which now was in plain view) and then, to my amazement, he started the tractor. This room too was spotless.

He proceeded to show me how he would clear the brush that had been neglected so that the river view was better. He showed me one more thing: his two-page make-ready checklist, which included things such as "leveling closet doors." I asked him if that was a lot to do considering all the empty apartments, and his answer was that *if you do a perfect make-ready, you don't do daily maintenance.* I was sold. This man understood the potential of this property.

Through the next year all the vacant apartments were rented and all common areas were cleaned to the point where this man pruned every single bush on a 300-unit property himself. He completely cleaned all central heating units and marked them for proper operation. The list is endless; the result was incredible. Our supplies orders shrank to a quarter of what they were and we were not hiring any subcontractors to do anything. Our income jumped tremendously because we cured our vacancy issue, allowing us to raise the rent. With a full community we could test the high end of the rental market with little risk. Because of the added efficiencies, our fuel costs dropped by 40 percent and our electricity bill by 35 percent.

I did not change much advertising at all. In fact, I was able to eliminate much of it. I never dealt with an element from the "wrong side of the tracks." The people who lived in this community lived to expectations. By raising the expectations we raised the community. This was all done because an organized, experienced maintenance professional took his talent and married it with care and an eye for the property. Two different people, two very different results. And that's what a good maintenance component can do for a community.

CHAPTER 8

The Administration:

Tool Up

The business of renting apartments carries with it an occupational fact of life: paper and plenty of it. The lease is an instrument. It is an instrument to structure a residency for your protection as well as the resident's, and it indicates to the prospective renter that you abide by the regulatory system that exists where your investment is located. Anybody who would rent an apartment without this instrument, or with an unreviewed, nonsanctioned lease, is just asking for trouble.

Sanctioned refers to industry organizations that have pooled their vast resources and professional experience to build a "model" to utilize. If this is your first foray into multifamily housing, using a sanctioned lease will ensure that much of what the novice or first-time owner may not know is covered. If the "canned" lease is not desirable, the alternative is to seek the advice of an attorney to help construct a lease tailored to the investment.

For purposes of understanding what a lease might contain, Appendix A includes a version of the National Apartment Association (NAA) lease from the State of Louisiana. The NAA has created a nationwide lease program that is presently available in thirty-six states. Because the NAA has a network of state affiliates, including property professionals and lawyers who specialize in landlord-tenant laws, it tailors leases to each jurisdiction. (You can contact the NAA through its website, www .naahq.org, or by e-mail at information@naahq.org.) Other industry organizations have similar programs, and private organizations additionally carry out the same function. On turnover from one owner to another, many times the present lease is just accepted as the instrument to be utilized. That's a mistake you want to avoid. A new owner should have a different set of priorities; therefore, an old lease, although it may seem functional, may not suffice for new ownership.

Utilize the Lease

There are many issues to consider when deciding what will appear in a lease, and there are several things that absolutely must appear in a lease. The remainder of this chapter concerns itself with those aspects that should be considered and how they are carried out in the administrative process. These principles apply no matter how small or large the investment is. The areas to be discussed are:

❑ Setting the table (i.e., knowing what the investment requires before you start the lease process)

❑ Names, occupants, and identification

❑ Lease terms (short term as opposed to long term)

❑ Rent, security deposits, and keys

❑ Utilities

❑ Rules and regulations

❑ Owner's and renter's rights and obligations

❑ Addenda
  • Government required
  • Owner's discretion

❑ Move-out policies

Setting the Table

When an apartment complex is turned over for sale, there should be existing leases and tenant information. Review these against a verified rent roll for accuracy of tenancy. Then read the existing lease and all attached documents. A site inspection will give you an idea of how effective the previous ownership and management was (or wasn't) in controlling its community, both physically and financially.

You may notice that the property is overcrowded. If this is related to the lease, then it's possible that occupancy requirements and remedies were not clearly spelled out or enforced. Or you might notice that the parking lot is full of commercial vehicles taking up multiple spots, so there is a shortage of parking. Check to make sure that parking was clearly spelled out as a cohesive policy. On the financial side, perhaps rent comes into the office in no consistent pattern. The conclusion here might be that the payment policy of rent is not clear or was not followed. It is not possible to discern all a community's ills through this process, but it can clearly mitigate a lot of what may have not been done correctly.

Make sure you use a sanctioned lease for your jurisdiction. There may be local, state, and federal requirements regarding lease inserts. These requirements sometimes come with penalties for noncompliance. New owners who are not familiar with these requirements may innocently go into the future not realizing they may suffer the consequences of the last ownership. These requirements are discussed at greater length later in this chapter.

As a new owner, you can decide whether the documentation handed over at close of sale is adequate. Often it is not. As the new owner, think about what your vision for the investment is today and what that investment might look like down the road. If at all possible, and where local or state regulations do not prohibit, it is advisable to cycle every existing resident onto a new lease that has been constructed and reviewed by proper professionals, with present ownership goals in mind. If the process seems arduous to complete en masse, then the changeover can be achieved at lease renewal time for each resident.

Important note: There are local, state, and federal inserts that may be required in the lease documentation. Make sure that proper advice or research is done to ensure the new documents are in compliance.

Simple keys to remember:

❏ Use data from the previous owners and then create a vision for the future.
❏ Construct a new set of legal documents that take into account all jurisdictional requirements, using a sanctioned set of documents or professional counsel.
❏ Distribute these new documents as soon as possible to all residents.

Names, Occupants, and Identification

Now let's go through the particular areas of the lease that should receive maximum attention—starting with the names on a lease.

It seems rather elementary that names should be on a lease, but a commonly made mistake is not putting *all* names of *all* leaseholders and occupants on the lease and matching up all names with proper identification on move-in day. The lease is a contract, legally binding on both parties, and for that reason, it is imperative to know who is occupying a unit. It makes sense from an operational standpoint as well. You should know the number of people living there from move-in day, as well as who will occupy a particular apartment and the identity of these individuals. This deters and/or prevents several things from occurring:

❑ *Overcrowding of an apartment.*

❑ *Subletting of an apartment.* There should be an additional clause prohibiting subletting in the lease. If it is not known who is there on move-in day, there is nothing to compare to.

❑ *Proper subsidization.* If it is publicly assisted housing where the resident gets a subsidy from a government agency such as the Department of Housing and Urban Development (HUD), family composition has everything to do with eligibility for receiving the subsidy, so a change in occupants could jeopardize subsidy funds.

❑ *Minimum age compliance.* It is important to match age in regard to signers on a lease. Individuals under the age of 18 cannot legally sign a legal document with the exception of court-ordered circumstances. Not verifying that an individual is of legal age leaves an owner with no recourse. The lease is considered null and void and unenforceable.

Any one of these scenarios takes the control out of the ownership's hands. An example would be an unregistered occupant who did not go through the screening process. Imagine if this unregistered occupant has a felony criminal record. If a prescreening would have been done, it is highly likely that this person would *not* be accepted as a resident. If this person is now occupying a unit, and as the owner you are aware of it, legal action can be taken to remove the occupant as an illegal resident.

The bottom line is that the safety of the existing legal residents is important, and from a financial standpoint, knowledge of such an illegal resident might cause existing legal residents to choose not to remain in the community. Because you do not know the background of residents you did not have the opportunity to screen, there is an inherent liability to what they may do while on your property.

Simple keys to remember:

❑ Require all names of leaseholders and occupants be on the lease.
❑ Match these individuals with proper identification.
❑ Know the residents.

Lease Terms

The concept of lease terms is often hotly debated. The two biggest reasons for or against lease terms are 1) marketability and 2) flexibility, both for the renter and for the ownership. Some areas of the country traditionally offer structured lease terms such as a year as the norm. There are other areas of the country where month-to-month terms prevail. If a market survey is undertaken, then the prevailing market conditions will be evident. The ability to offer choices obviously increases the ability of the owner to rent, but there are pros and cons to each philosophy.

The concept of leasing on a definitive term such as a year is obviously stability in regard to total occupancy. Residents move in and there is an expectation they will be there for the year. If this policy is undertaken across the board at a community, you'll have a better handle on predicting when vacates may occur. As an owner, you'll be able to prepare in advance for this eventuality, either by marketing a unit when it has been noticed as a *nonrenewal* for an additional term or by contacting the current resident with enough time to convince the person to renew. In the latter case you'll contact the resident in writing with an offer to renew far in advance of the expiration date and require the resident to respond before that expiration date. If renewal dates are cataloged in one place, a schedule to follow up with residents can be constructed, again with the aim of achieving a stable residency.

The drawback to setting firm yearly dates is that it limits marketing choices. Our society has become ever more mobile and transient. Human beings like to have options, and if the decision is not to provide them, a segment of the renting population may choose to look past that community.

Shorter terms have been prevalent in some markets; they too have distinct advantages and disadvantages. The advantages are that not everyone moving into a market is planning on staying, so by offering shorter terms, the community becomes more "marketable." The drawback is obvious: By allowing residents options, the ability to stay ahead of the "occupancy curve" becomes more difficult to predict. There are also costs associated with a more transient population as well. Each time an apartment vacates, it has to be readied for a new resident. There are, however, some things that can be done to "straddle" this lease term dilemma:

❑ *Offer a year lease with a "buy out or lease break" clause.* This is to say people can break their lease with sufficient notice, at a cost and with certain restrictions. Check with state and local laws because there may be restrictions on such fees.

❑ *Offer tier pricing for shorter-term leases.* That way the option is available for a premium. Although this option may not eliminate the transient nature of such lease terms, it will mitigate some turnover costs.

There are some other considerations in regard to terms on a lease:

❑ *Flexible Move-In Days.* Don't restrict move-ins to a day that's convenient by the "numbers." Many owners move people in only on scheduled days, such as the first of a month. This may make it hard for a prospective resident to coordinate and it removes another choice. Instead, *prorate* a lease. That is, divide the rent by the number of days in a month, and then multiply that number by the remaining days left in a month. Make the terms of the lease start on whatever day the resident wants to move in and make the lease the original term plus the prorated days. For example, if the lease would have started January 1, 2007, and ended on December 31, 2007, but the individual wants to move in on December 20 of the previous year, the lease terms become December 20, 2006, to December 31, 2007, and the eleven days' rent is prorated.

❑ *Military Exceptions.* If a percentage of the community population is military, familiarize yourself with the U.S. Servicemembers Civil Relief Act (SCRA). This act basically gives relief in regard to lease obligations to servicemen who are being deployed out of area—although there are some interpretive issues with regard to dependants. The NAA lease example in Appendix A includes further details about this act, should it become an issue.

Simple keys to remember:

❑ Create lease terms that are marketable and flexible for both the renter and the ownership.

❑ Undertake a market survey so that prevailing market conditions will be evident.

- ❏ Stabilize occupancy by leasing on a definitive term—but remember, the drawback to setting firm yearly dates is that you are not marketing choices.
- ❏ Provide shorter-term leases if you want to open up to a wider renting population—but remember, this option will take away from stability and can cost in turnover dollars.
- ❏ Balance the short-term/long-term considerations by offering lease buyouts and tiered fee structures for shorter terms, since more flexibility with a renter can balance term considerations.

Rent, Security Deposits, and Keys

Rent seems like a fairly simple subject, but if not spelled out correctly on a lease it could cause problems for the rest of that lease term. The amount of monthly rent should be clearly stated on a lease on the per-month basis and on an aggregate basis for the entire lease term; for instance, $700 a month and for the twelve-month term, total rent due is $8,400. The reason to do this is to clearly identify what the resident's obligation is during the term of that lease. Obviously, if the lease terms are month to month, then one month's rent will suffice. Any prorated rent should also be clearly calculated and listed.

The conditions under which rent is paid and how it is paid should be clearly identified also. For instance, if rent is due on the first of the month and considered late after the fifth of the month, this should be indicated on the lease. If there are to be late charges for late rent, the exact dollar amount of the late fee should be addressed on the lease as well. There should be a clause in the lease that speaks to the procedure for unpaid rent and the remedies and legal fees under the law. If there are restrictions on forms of payment, such as not accepting cash, these specifics, too, must be clearly stated. This portion of a lease should be reviewed in detail at the lease signing time to avoid any confusion about what is expected from a resident when it comes to rent. Rent is the most basic of lease terms and can become one of the most contentious items in a residency.

Another essential issue to address on the lease is the security deposit. A security deposit is traditionally taken at move-in time as a "safety net" for damage done in an apartment during the term of a lease or for unpaid rent when a resident does not fulfill a lease term. The amount of the security deposit should have been discussed during the application process. It's possible that a portion of the security deposit was already secured as a *reservation fee* to confirm a future rental. This fee is then credited to the total security deposit upon move-in.

There is no rule of thumb for the amount of a security deposit. Security deposits often become a function of market forces. It is often a dilemma for ownership to decide on an adequate security deposit. If the deposit is set high—one to one and half months of the monthly rent, for example—most damages or unpaid rent should be covered. The drawback, however, is that many individuals simply do not have that much cash on hand to move into an apartment. If the monthly rent is $700 and the security deposit requirement is one and a half month's rent ($1,050), the new resident has to show up on move-in day with $1,750. In many instances, even if the move-in funds are not a problem, the local competition may in fact be affording individuals the opportunity to move in with fewer funds, thus forcing an owner to make a decision. If you decide to require a more affordable security deposit, the risk is that if the resident moves out prematurely or damages the apartment, those circumstances will not be covered by the funds.

One way to comfortably make a decision regarding security deposits is to review the qualifying process for renting the apartment in the first place. The qualifying standards and background check should tell any owner with reasonable certainty whether a rental candidate can afford the rent. It will also confirm whether there is a history in the past of nonpayment or collections. The security deposit then can be set with market forces in mind, where the ownership feels the balance of adequate funds and marketability meet.

When handling a security deposit there are some other, very important issues that should be considered as well:

❑ *Dedicated Accounts.* Security deposits should always be placed in a dedicated account for the resident, and these accounts are usually interest bearing. Most financial institutions are set up to administer this function and many states require these deposits be put into such accounts in a timely manner. Whether or not it is required, it is advisable to handle deposits this way. Never commingle security money with any other funds coming in, and don't ever look at security deposits as operating funds!

❑ *Location of Funds.* In the lease or in separate move-in documentation, residents should know where these funds are to be located (i.e., the name of the financial institution). If the account is interest bearing and the interest is to be credited to the resident, this information should be spelled out at the lease signing. If administrative fees are permissible for these accounts, this detail should also be highlighted clearly at this time.

❏ *Definition of Damage.* On the subject of damage to the apartment at the end of a lease, most leases will make the distinction between "normal wear and tear" and significant damage. Security deposits should never be used for normal wear-and-tear items, unless the local or state codes allow for the taking of basic turnover fees (e.g., carpet cleaning, painting). These fees, if permitted, should be discussed thoroughly with the resident at move-in time.

❏ *Repairs.* You should also issue at move-in a *schedule of estimated repairs* for all major repair items, with fees itemized. If these figures are updated they should be included in any renewal paperwork. For an example, see Figure 8-1. This information will mitigate much of the possible controversy that could occur when discussing charges upon move-out.

❏ *Inspection Checklists.* As discussed previously in Chapter 6, a move-in and move-out checklist should be used to mutually inspect the apartment at the beginning and end of tenancy. Reference these checklists within the move-in lease information.

Owners sometimes feel they have to collect deposits or fees in addition to security deposits. An example is a pet deposit or a pet fee. If you are thinking of charging these types of fees or deposits, make sure they are permissible under local and state code. If they are, understand the administrative requirements in handling such funds and make sure the lease documentation clearly states all parameters related to such taking of fees and deposits. The sample NAA lease package in Appendix A includes an "animal addendum." When taking additional deposits or fees, these addendums serve the purpose of clearly laying out all required parameters.

Keys are an item that must be handled with care. New residents expect that the keys they receive and the locks on their doors are exclusive to the apartment they will possess and of the individuals residing at that apartment. Yet ownership needs to inform new residents that those keys are not to be proliferated, and that all keys that a resident was given on move-in must be returned at the end of a lease term or residency. Some owners charge a key deposit to ensure return. Whatever the policy is, it should be spelled out in the lease. Keys can obviously be copied, but by spelling out expectations there should be a mutual understanding that the apartment is for the exclusive possession of the leaseholders.

Simple keys to remember:

❏ State the amount of monthly rent on the lease on a per-month basis and, unless not permitted by law in a given jurisdiction, on an aggregated basis for the entire lease term.

Figure 8-1. Estimated liquidated damages and repair fee schedule.

ESTIMATED LIQUIDATED DAMAGES AND REPAIR FEE SCHEDULE

KITCHEN:

REFRIGERATOR:
Badly damaged—replacement cost plus $45.00 installation
Cleaning—$35.00
Racks missing—$30.00
Crisper glass—$30.00
Crisper missing—$25.00

DISHWASHER:
Badly damaged—replacement cost plus $75.00 installation
Cleaning—$20.00
Basket missing—$15.00
Rack missing—$35.00

RANGE:
Badly damaged—replacement cost plus $50.00 installation
Cleaning—$50.00
Broiler pan missing—$40.00
Oven rack missing—$25.00

RANGE HOOD:
Badly damaged—replacement cost plus $20.00 installation
Cleaning—$15.00

COUNTERTOPS:
Badly damaged—replacement cost plus $100.00 installation
Cleaning—$20.00

FLOORING:
Badly damaged—replacement cost
Cleaning—$25.00
Linoleum—$125.00
Tile—$150.00

CABINETS:
Badly damaged door—$60.00
Badly damaged drawer—$45.00
Cleaning—$35.00
Removal of contact paper—$50.00

SINK:
Badly damaged—replacement cost plus $125.00 installation
Cleaning—$15.00
Drain cover missing—$5.00

(continues)

Figure 8-1. Continued.

BATHROOM:
Damaged vanity—$150.00
Damaged vanity door—$50.00
Cleaning—$50.00
Damaged sink—$100.00
Chip in porcelain—$5.00 each
Complete resurface—$400.00
Damaged curtain rod—$20.00
Replace tile wall—$125.00 per wall
Replace tile floor—$300.00
Damaged towel rack—$25.00
Damaged medicine cabinet—$95.00
Damaged toilet tissue dispenser—$15.00
Damaged mirror—$30.00
Damaged soap dish—$20.00
Missing shower head—$20.00
Replace toilet tank—$50.00
Replace complete toilet and tank—$160.00

CARPETING:
Not vacuumed—$15.00
Burn mark—small—$25.00
              large—$50.00
Tear—small—$25.00
         large—$50.00
Stained—cost to restore
Shampoo and deodorize (pet odor)—$100.00
Extermination (pet)—$35.00
Badly damaged carpet—current replacement cost plus installation fee

WALLS:
Extensive damage—replacement cost
Spackling small holes—$15.00
Remove wallpaper and repaint (1) wall—$90.00
Repaint (1) room—$100.00
Repaint (1) wall—$50.00
Repaint total apartment—$250.00
Extra cost of paint to cover dark color or smoke stains—$75.00 per room

DOORS:
Damaged exterior—$215.00
Damaged exterior trim—$50.00

Damaged exterior lock set—$45.00
Damaged exterior dead bolt—$45.00
Damaged interior—$120.00
Damaged interior trim—$50.00
Damaged interior lock set—$25.00
Damaged interior dead bolt—$25.00

KEYS:

Apartment entry door keys not returned at move-out—$50.00
Mailbox keys not returned at move-out—$20.00
Storage key, where applicable, not returned when surrendered or at move-out—$20.00
Garage key, where applicable, not returned when surrendered or at move-out—$20.00
Laundry room key, where applicable, not returned at move-out—$20.00
If Residents lock themselves out of their apartment, the fee to open their door is $25.00 each time

WINDOWS & SCREENS:

Broken window—$40.00
Damaged window—replacement cost plus labor
Damaged screen—$30.00
Screen replacement—$20.00
Miniblinds—$15.00

LIGHT FIXTURES:

Damaged light fixtures—replacement cost plus labor

GENERAL CLEANING:

Apartment not cleaned—$75.00
Special extermination treatment—$50.00

REMOVAL/DISPOSAL FEES:

If Landlord must remove and dispose of any trash or debris left in Resident's apartment at move-out, there will be a charge of $100.00
If Landlord must remove and dispose of any furniture left in Resident's apartment at move-out, there will be a charge of $50.00 for each piece of furniture.

RESIDENT AGREES THAT IN THE EVENT ANY OF THE ABOVE ITEMS ARE NECESSARY TO BE CLEANED OR REPAIRED AT THE END OF THE LEASE, THE PRICES SET OUT FOR EACH ITEM SHALL BE A PROPER CHARGE BY THE LANDLORD TO THE RESIDENT AND MAY BE DEDUCTED FROM THE SECURITY DEPOSIT OR RECOVERED FROM THE RESIDENT.

*Prices may be slightly higher or lower, depending on the extent of the condition.

❑ Identify clearly the conditions under which rent is paid and how it is paid, such as late dates and accepted forms of payment.

❑ Set the security deposit based on market forces and the qualifying standards, such as background checks, that have been created to approve prospective residents. Although there is no set standard for security deposits, there may be local "ceilings" on deposit amounts.

❑ *Never* commingle security money with any other funds coming in. Don't ever look at security deposits as operating funds!

Utilities

During the application process, and part of the marketing for any apartment, let prospective renters know what utility responsibilities they will have and which responsibilities (e.g., gas/oil, electricity, phone, and cable) the property will cover. When an applicant is accepted in the rental process, information relative to the leaseholder's responsibilities with utilities should be disseminated to the renter, who can then start the process of contacting the utility providers.

In regard to the lease process, the utility responsibilities should be marked appropriately so that there is no mistaking who will connect and pay for what service. It is also advisable to verify at lease-signing time if the utilities the resident is responsible for have been turned over in the renter's name. Some utility providers turn apartments back in the name of the owner upon the vacancy of an apartment and some just take it out of the previous renter's name. Without verification, the owner may not always know if the utilities have been switched.

Rules and Regulations

Although the lease itself has many rules and stipulations in it, many owners choose to use a separate addendum for more specific rules and regulations. Through the process of getting to understand the community you've just purchased and reviewing the set of documents received on turn of sale, there may be a need for specific rules that apply to that community in particular. For instance, the apartments may be two stories and all floors are hardwood. Hardwood is very noisy when walking on it. A rule may be that all second-floor apartments must install throw rugs or carpet.

A town ordinance may facilitate an additional rule. Many fire codes prohibit barbecues unless they are a safe distance from the buildings and that distance is usually spelled out. Installing this requirement in a separate document ensures the renter reviews and understands it. Because it is a stand–alone addendum, it makes it much easier to amend as time goes on. Many new owners are not immediately aware of some of the inherent situations that take place and cause problems in their apartments until they have built up a body of experience, therefore the rules evolve over time.

Rules and regulations are a way for property owners to shape and control a community with the vision they have for that community. Owners may not choose to use addenda as much as possible for fear of too much paperwork, but I recommend you use separate rules and regulations. A separate addendum for rules and regulations allows ownership to be more specific about how its community will operate and can be easily amended over time.

Owner's and Renter's Rights and Obligations

There are clauses in the lease that should be discussed with the renter at the lease signing because they will undoubtedly surface during the lease term. Some of these are:

- ❏ Owner's right to enter in the case of an emergency and with proper notice.
- ❏ Owner's obligations to repair and maintain the apartment—for example, to verify that all amenities such as running water remain operable.
- ❏ Renter's obligations to maintain the apartment—for example, to ensure the smoke alarm battery remains in the smoke alarm.
- ❏ Renter's right to *quiet* enjoyment or to occupy a unit without interference.
- ❏ Owner's right to possess a proper set of keys for each unit.
- ❏ Owner's obligation that all personal information regarding resident remains confidential. (Don't release a resident's address to anyone unless it is an emergency or of an official legal nature.)

There are a host of such clauses. The important thing to remember is that ambiguity regarding any rights or obligations could spell trouble; therefore, having it all spelled out in your lease is essential.

Addenda

Government Required. There are environmental and safety issues that over the years have become "higher case" issues to regulators and legislators. The result has been government-mandated addenda and policies. These issues aren't necessarily unique to the apartment business, but because apartments are where people live, the scrutiny of several issues has become intense.

During the purchase process, if a mortgagor was involved, myriad of environmental tests were already performed on the building for lead-based paint, asbestos, mold, and oil tanks. The lender, based on those tests, may have required operations and maintenance (O&M) programs for such environmental conditions. Therefore, the sensitivity to the issues already exists. However, sometimes the government, whether it be local, state, or federal, believes that there has to be a higher awareness to the renting public about existing conditions in a building and what or how the staff is prepared to handle such environmental conditions. An example of a federally mandated addendum, which is included in the sample NAA lease in Appendix A, is lead hazard information. Because lead-based paint can exist in housing built before 1978, owners are required, under federal law, to understand the condition of their property relative to lead, explain their understanding to residents in the form of a disclosure, and educate them in the form of a handout.

An example of a state-mandated addendum or disclosure would be the State of New Jersey's requirements to offer window guards for any family with small children living on the second floor or higher of a building. This requirement includes a signoff from residents acknowledging that they have been asked if they wish to have window guards installed and either have accepted or declined.

Using a sanctioned lease again ensures that if the state laws and regulations change, there is a better chance that the present documents being used are timely and conform.

Owner's Discretion. There are other reasons to install addenda at the owner's discretion. These addenda may relate to 1) environmentally sensitive issues or 2) issues that need more specificity or are unique to that individual community.

In the case of an environmentally sensitive addendum, it may be added to the lease because of the mortgage-required O&M plans described earlier, or because an owner simply feels that by adding these specifics the renting public has been educated to this issue and understands the "rules of the road." An example is a mold or asbestos addendum. It is not required by the state, but the owner nonetheless may wish to state the policy. (Examples of both are included in the NAA lease in Appendix A.) Environmental subjects such as mold, asbestos, lead-based paint, and others can be intimidating to a building owner, to say the least. The NAA and the National Multi Housing Council (NMHC) have excellent informative websites and links to downloadable material to educate property owners or managers to such hazards and how they should be addressed in regard to multifamily housing. These two websites are: www.naahq.org/govern_affairs/Issues/ and http://www.nmhc.org/Content/BrowseIssues.cfm?IssueID = 5.

An addendum can also be used to address issues specific to a particular property. Such an addendum might, for instance, explain the policy concerning the use of and installation of direct-to-home satellite dishes. This example is also included in the sample lease in Appendix A. Whenever the ownership sees the need to explain a community policy in detail, the addendum has the advantage of being added onto a lease, so it is much easier to implement than having to "rewrite" the lease.

Simple keys to remember:

❑ Use approved addenda relative to state and local requirements; sanctioned lease programs can accomplish this very easily.

❑ Perform attorney review if you decide to write a unique addendum. Don't attempt to write it on your own, if you are not legally trained.

Move-Out Policies

It almost seems to go against good sense to talk about move-out policies in the lease at move-in, but it is necessary. Most states have rules regarding "buyer's remorse"—that is, the eventuality that an individual commits to a transaction such as a rental and then regrets it shortly thereafter. If state law where the property resides has such a rule, then as an owner that occurrence cannot be avoided. Once the remorse window has expired, then the resident must be informed of his obligation to the lease. The resident also has to know how an owner considers an apartment vacated. It may be permissible to leave the hotel key on the desk in the room, but in apartments, this practice would leave an owner with no idea that the resident moved out. The move-out policy should cover all these facets in detail, including charges for early termination of the lease and inspection requirements upon vacating the apartment.

It is advisable to have additional notices to reiterate these policies should the owner receive a notice to vacate during the lease term. However, if explained in the lease in detail, no resident can claim he hasn't been properly advised and instructed.

■ Understand Your Legal Boundaries (Notices)

All the clauses and addendums installed or added to a lease now have practical use in the daily managing of an apartment complex. Depending on the location, each state and local governing authority requires proper notice as it relates to any lease violation. Some of these notice requirements are vague and some are quite specific. The important concept to glean from this is that if the owner has a problem with a resident or residents, there are structured procedures to remedy and document situations. In any case, always provide backup proving that ownership has followed up.

Some of these procedures require more than one piece of correspondence before exhausting all remedies and having an issue decided by a local court that handles landlord-tenant issues. The owner needs to become familiar with the procedural requirements governing the community and take action in accordance with them. Two terms often used when referring to such notices are *cease* and *quit,* and they mean just as they sound. A cease notice is usually a primary warning to cease the activity prohibited in the lease or else further action will be undertaken. A quit notice usually indicates that warning has been given. The action is continuing and the ownership is prepared to carry this issue to a higher authority. Obviously, the nomenclature the verbiage or legalese may vary when speaking of notices on a national scale, but basically they all are used for the same purpose. Where a jurisdiction specifies a written notice or a very distinct time frame to remedy periods, the owner should realize any deviation from procedure, no matter how small, can affect the end result.

Some notices may be required in some states, but it is just prudent practice to send a notice. An example is notice of late rent and the charging of a late fee. By lease terms, residents should know when the rent is late and what the fee is, but if you remind them, they may have a change of heart or not repeat the behavior. Some examples of often-used notices are:

- ❑ Late rent (for a sample notice, see Figure 8-2)
- ❑ Excessive noise
- ❑ Overcrowding
- ❑ Illegally parked car
- ❑ Refuse left in hallways
- ❑ Broken apartment features due to the resident's neglect or misuse
- ❑ Occupant or visitor behavior (for which the leaseholder is almost always responsible)

Figure 8.2. Unpaid rent.

NOTICE OF UNPAID BALANCE

DATE:

TO:

Dear Tenant:

APT. #

As you know, your rent is due on the FIRST DAY of every month. Our records indicate that your account has not been paid during the five-day grace period allowed.

Therefore, WE HAVE CHARGED YOUR ACCOUNT A LATE CHARGE OF $ _____

$ _____ Current Rent for _____

$ _____ Past Due Rent for _____

$ _____ Late Charges for _____

$ _____ Legal/Attorney fees _____

$ _____ Other _____

$ _____ Other _____

If you have already mailed your payment, please notify this office so it may be noted.

If you have not yet mailed your payment and rent bill in the envelope provided, YOU MUST BRING YOUR PAYMENT IN THE FORM OF MONEY ORDER OR CERTIFIED CHECK AND THIS LETTER TO THE RENTAL/MANAGEMENT OFFICE IMMEDIATELY.

If our payment is not received by the _____ of the month, your account will automatically be turned over to our attorney for eviction and collection proceedings. ONCE THIS ACTION HAS BEEN STARTED, WE CANNOT CANCEL IT UNTIL YOUR ACCOUNT HAS BEEN PAID IN FULL. You will also incur additional charges for court costs and attorney fees.

We urge your immediate attention to this very serious matter. If you have any questions, please contact the Rental/Management office or Resident Manager.

❏ Renewal notices (sent out beforehand to discern renewal status; for a sample notice, see Figure 8-3)

If any of these issues cannot be solved after sending notices, most states require some review by a governing judicial authority. This authority will most likely have the final say. The documentation leading up to an eventual eviction for lease violations increases the owner's chances of prevailing. When issues occur that appear to involve two or more residents, don't take sides unless the culprit is very clear. Issue fair notice to all involved that the prohibited activity "cease." If the issue becomes immediate and out of control, involve the local authorities. Don't become personally involved.

If an issue goes past the notice stage and ends up in a court, where a judgment of some sort is rendered and it appears there may be an eviction, then additional notice will most likely be required. Owners must additionally educate themselves to such notices. Eviction shouldn't be the goal in many of these issues, but it sometimes is the only suitable remedy. Proper notice throughout this process is essential.

■ Create a Review or Follow-Up System

Common themes within the apartment business are review and follow-up. Whether it is a system to indicate renewals on a monthly basis, or a designated day to review past-due rents, or a "tickler" (i.e., reminder) system regarding notices that have been issued, create such a system. A simple yearly calendar can be used for recording significant monthly dates to remember, such as when to review delinquent rent and when to send out renewals. Then create folders for the twelve months of the year and use them for follow-up. For example, send a notice to cease with a thirty-day remedy that has to be followed up. Put the notice in the monthly folder dated twenty-nine days from its inception. Then, at the appropriate time, you will be reminded in regard to the status of that notice and can readdress the issue.

Computer or Virtual Management

There are many computer-based products that can help you administer leases and handle property-related review and follow-up. The NAA lease package is, for example, also sold as a complete software package. The advantage here is when forms are updated, immediate updates are issued for the software. There is also a trend toward Web-based products, which means information can be accessed online from

Figure 8-3. Renewal notice.

MODIFICATION AND RENEWAL OF LEASE

DATE:

BLDG: APT #:

TO:

This notice is to advise you that your current lease expires on _____ and may be renewed automatically. We will be happy to renew your Lease beginning _____ and ending _____ at an annual rent of $_____, payable in equal monthly payments of $_____ each month on the first day of each and every month.

This Renewal and the attached Notice of Lease Expiration and Rent Increase shall constitute the only changes. All other terms, conditions, covenants, agreements, rules, and regulations as contained in the Original Lease and any Rider(s) heretofore made shall remain in effect.

Either party shall give written notice by registered or certified mail no less than forty-five (45) days prior to the expiration of the Lease, of their intent to renew or not renew said Lease.

SECURITY

You, the Tenant, currently have $_____ in your security account. With this rent increase, your new security required is $_____. Therefore, an additional security payment of $_____ MUST BE RECEIVED WITH YOUR SIGNED RENEWAL. When additional securities are received, Landlord will acknowledge such payment by signing here:

(Landlord's Signature when Additional Securities are received)

Enclosed are three (3) copies of the Notice of Lease Expiration and Rent Increase, Modification and Renewal of Lease and/or Riders or Addendums if attached. Please sign ALL copies on the appropriate line and return them with your security payment to _____ **APARTMENTS RENTAL OFFICE** BEFORE _____.

After Tenant has signed all copies, Landlord will execute same and return one copy to Tenant. **SHOULD YOU NEGLECT TO RETURN YOUR SIGNED RENEWAL BEFORE THE DATE SHOWN ABOVE, YOU WILL AUTOMATICALLY BECOME A MONTH-TO-MONTH TENANT AT THE NEW MONTHLY RENT PLUS $.00 MONTH-TO-MONTH FEE, WHERE APPLICABLE. YOUR REMAINING IN POSSESSION AND PAYING RENT SHALL BE DEEMED AN ACCEPTANCE OF THIS RENEWAL IN ACCORDANCE WITH THE TERMS OFFERED.**

(continues)

Figure 8-3. Continued.

1)   I agree to renew my Lease according to the Modification and Renewal of Lease.

_____
(Tenant Signature)   (Tenant Signature)   (Date)

or

2)   I plan to vacate my apartment when my Lease expires.

_____
(Tenant Signature)   (Tenant Signature)   (Date)

or

3)   I plan to stay on a Month-to-Month basis at a monthly rent of
      $_____. I will give thirty (30) days' (full calendar month) written
      notice if I plan to vacate during the term of this lease renewal.

_____
(Tenant Signature)   (Tenant Signature)   (Date)

Landlord:

By: _____
        (Landlord Signature)

virtually anywhere. Many common e-mail and communications programs such as Microsoft Outlook also have basic review and follow-up tools. If using a technology-based solution, make sure it is applicable to the community it is being purchased for and make sure the "total" cost (hardware, software, training, and support) is understood.

"Every Office Needs a Mary"

Whether the first apartment complex is run by one person or is expanded to many complexes, organization and follow-up are needed to fill in gaps that occur. I have worked with an office manager whose attention to detail is second to none; what she accomplished for the organization is astounding. We will call her Mary. For Mary, there is a checklist for everything, and the amazing thing is that no matter how tedious her methodology may seem at the time, over and over her attention to detail proves invaluable. As your organization grows, the number of things an owner or a manager has to review will be varied. It becomes hard to concentrate strictly on one thing. If, at the genesis of an organization, systems are set up and kept current (obviously evolving), then issues tend to work to their natural course.

Several years ago the federal government strengthened its regulations and requirements concerning the reporting and administration of lead-based paint issues in multifamily housing. The rules were very specific. The language you had to use was very distinct, and the penalties for not administering these policies were severe. The federal government distributed "boilerplate" documents to create this policy. These documents had to be distributed to all existing residents and new residents. Residents had to sign a disclosure form indicating they had been given the information and had been advised of the condition of the property they were renting in regard to lead-based paint.

The "rolling out" of this program was massive, and because it was federally mandated it had to be constantly administered. Mary devised a system of distribution and follow-up. She assured herself every property in our portfolio had done as it should, and she devised a system to know when new residents moved in that they had been given all needed paperwork and executed all disclosures. Mary would come to me almost weekly to give me an update on compliance and where she thought there were weaknesses. It almost became haunting to have Mary call because you knew you were going to get every detail, and as it turns out that was a very good thing.

The federal government had said it would randomly check apartment complexes for compliance without warning or cause. In my twenty years being involved in this business, I had heard of such practices, but as big as this country is, I had never actually had one of those inspections. Then the phone call came: "The federal government is down here at X property and they want all resident records now," said an excited site manager. I instructed the manager to cooperate and call me when it was over. Then I sat back in my chair as if I sat on a bed of nails.

Later that afternoon the manager called me back, completely calm if not giddy. "They left and said everything was just the way it was supposed to be," was the report. I knew immediately why that was: We had a system of detail and follow-up, and we had Mary to make sure that system was administered consistently and continuously.

It's a rather benign story, yet in property management, this is a happy ending. That mountain of paper is a must. It should be organized and filed. All pertinent information has a purpose when managing a community.

CHAPTER 9

The Vendors

Partner with Others

Owning and managing a property is a business that requires the ability to "switch gears" often. It is a diverse field. One day you're dealing with the legal aspects of owning and managing real estate, the next you're dealing with the rental market and how it affects your property, and by the end of the week you're tackling a new roofing system. There are so many facets of the infrastructure and managing of a building that it is not possible to be an expert at all of them. The natural question arises as to whether money is being saved by attempting to do something in-house as opposed to bringing in an expert in that area. Often, if the expertise does not lie within a community's staff, it might well be cheaper in the long run to enlist the help of someone who concentrates solely on the subject at hand.

This is a difficult decision for many because it means that there is a measure of blind faith that has to guide a manager at first, but the really good managers eventually turn that blind faith into trust. There are methods and a thought process that can give the manager/owner a level of comfort when having to make the choice to use outside vendors or subcontractors. Over time these vendors can become another arm of the community management team. The remainder of this chapter concentrates on how an owner knows when outside help is needed and how to pick the right help, minimize expense, and get the job done right.

■ Acknowledge Your Weaknesses

There are very few places that provide total and comprehensive training for people who want to enter the property management field. It is unlikely that many first-time owners have a full breadth of knowledge about all facets of their new real estate purchase. The due diligence undertaken during the purchase process will provide you with a baseline understanding of the condition and quirks in any given property. The information gleaned from the due diligence process should be very carefully analyzed and reviewed. For instance, knowing the age, model, and repair history of a building's boiler is a great starting place for an owner. None of that information in and of itself makes the owner an expert, but it may be enough information for you to ask a lot of other questions and educate yourself enough to make intelligent decisions.

If the purchase includes existing staff members, the first thing to do is determine their level of expertise. The site inspection will be a great indicator of how the inherited staff views and handles the real estate. If it appears on face value that the staff cares and has made a good attempt to maintain the property, you still want to spend time questioning it on specific systems that the building possesses. If the building owner and staff are one and the same (which might be the case if the purchase is small enough), then the owner has to ask these same questions of himself. The biggest reason to undertake this exercise is to determine what your weaknesses are. These questions aren't limited to physical plant activities such as roofs, boilers, and masonry; they also apply to office computer materials, legal matters, and advertising.

What type of questions should an owner ask? To start, it is best to allow staff members to give an overview of what they know on a given subject; they too are very rarely going to be experts in everything. Create a list of the most important subjects, where you break the list into operating expenses and capital expenses. If you go back to Chapter 7, you'll see that five of the six key areas on your list will cover expenses related to maintenance:

1. Capital and structural components (e.g., roofs, paving, power plants)
2. Curb appeal
3. Routine daily maintenance
4. Vacant "make-readies"
5. Inventory and equipment control

With this list in hand, break it down even further. For instance, in regard to capital structural components, list the items that are the most costly and need to be maintained over the years. An example might be paving, roofs, power plants, concrete and masonry (e.g., sidewalks and porches), wood decks, garages, and a pool.

Next to each of these list items write all the factual information obtained during sale of these items, and then go about the process of quizzing those responsible for maintaining these components on their knowledge of each one. Concern yourself with three major issues while going through this process:

❑ Which of these items, in order of priority, will need attention sooner rather than later?

❑ What is the staff's knowledge on that subject, and what is my personal knowledge on same?

❑ What are the legal requirements for operating and maintaining such equipment? (The exercise can obviously stop if licensed individuals are required to work on certain equipment and your staff members don't possess the licensure. Then, vendor help will be needed.)

If this exercise is repeated for all major functions in a building, you'll be able to ask the final question: "What are the staff's weaknesses?" Once this has been determined, it becomes easier for you to understand what work you can trust to be done internally, what the immediate priorities are, and what additional (outside) help is going to be needed.

This process can be repeated in the administration and marketing of a property also. These issues are just as important as the physical plant items, because they too can cost or make money. Here, the key areas of concern to ask about are:

❑ Rent collection and debt collection

❑ Marketing and advertising

❑ Legal issues

An important final point to make regarding knowing weaknesses: If it becomes obvious through this process that the inherited staff does not possess an appropriate level of expertise or acumen, it is best to replace that staff before making any further decisions. The fact is that sometimes the biggest weakness is overall staff incompetence. It has to take priority over any other concern and has to be the first thing addressed.

Simple keys to remember:

❑ Review all information passed onto you in the sale, focusing on the property's major operating and capital expense items. Review these items physically and by questioning staff in order to form an overall picture of strengths and weaknesses.

❑ Create a methodology to review all cost centers within a community, both physical and operational.

❑ Seek the help of a vendor if a license is required to work on certain critical equipment and your staff doesn't possess such a license.

◼ Enlist the Talent of Vendors

There will obviously have been some vendors used by the previous ownership for certain aspects of building maintenance. As a new owner, you don't want to simply trust that those past vendors or subcontractors are the right fit. What can people new to a property and new to the area do to ensure they are getting sound advice they can trust?

For purposes of this subject, let's suppose that the power plant or boilers in a building are large and have very technical or specialized components. Power plants cost money in two very important ways: 1) They have to be operated and maintained and 2) they require a fuel expenditure (where the fuel cost can increase or be reduced depending on the level of efficiency of the equipment). Both "cost centers" can, for any property, become a very large portion of the operating budget. If the power plant has a catastrophic failure and needs to be replaced, it can take a large chunk out of any yearly projection. Because these power plants operate mostly on fossil fuels, in most locations local or state laws govern who can operate them and who can repair and maintain them. Picking a vendor to service and advise on this equipment becomes a matter of utmost importance.

There are several things an owner can do to obtain a respectable service vendor:

❑ Question the current vendor (the one used by the previous ownership) on specific aspects of a subject.

❑ Visit competitors' properties and ask them which vendors they use.

❑ Contact these vendors and ask them to review the same issue as the present contractor.

❑ Ask the same questions.

❑ Ask each vendor for references in the business and outside the business of apartment management. Visit these references in person.

❏ When equipment is the issue, contact the manufacturer of the equipment and ask the same questions.

This methodology will not immediately satisfy all economic questions about cost or affordability of a particular vendor, but what it will do is clear up who is providing a comprehensive and honest assessment of the present condition of your power plant system and what problems might be on the horizon. More important, it will connect you, as the owner, with someone you can trust and understand well enough to make intelligent decisions.

The questions that you ask a vendor are very important. Don't limit the questions to what's "wrong" with a system, but make sure a major part of the discussion revolves around maintaining a system to extend its useful life and maximize its efficiency. Any vendor can say the system in a building is antiquated and inefficient, but if again we use the boiler as an example, there are products that "marry" to older systems to increase their efficiency. And there are other products and maintenance methods that will extend the useful life of that boiler system. Any vendor who avoids these conversations is a vendor that should be passed over.

This method of questioning applies to product-based vendors as well. Supply salespeople may not know about boilers, but if they are selling products related to boilers, they have to possess some level of understanding to discern necessary information. One very important question to ask product-based vendors is: What type of technical support do they offer for the products they sell and their application to a particular system? It is not reasonable to believe the average salesperson is overtly knowledgeable, but the company should be.

From all the questions asked and from all the vendors interviewed, start forming a "vendor list" for ranking the vendors in each category. The list on any subject should not be limited to one vendor. There should be a first, second, and third choice listed. In property operations, sometimes breakdowns or failures occur and, depending on the situation, need to be fixed in a hurry. For example, the boiler system goes down in subzero weather. The number-one vendor may not be available and the system needs to be fixed immediately. This list should be created right away upon purchasing of the property. Over the years it will change, but a problem could occur right away, and the earlier a comprehensive list of vendors is constructed, the more likely you'll be prepared.

Simple keys to remember:

❏ Question the current vendor (the one inherited from the previous ownership) on specific aspects of a subject.

❏ Visit competitors' properties and ask them which vendors they use.

❏ Contact these vendors and have them review the same issue as the present contractor, asking the same questions.

❏ Ask each vendor for references in the business and outside the business of apartment management. Visit these references in person.

❏ When equipment is the issue, contact the manufacturer of the equipment and ask the same questions.

▪ Get the Right Product, for the Right Price, for the Right Reason

The list of vendors is now constructed. The property is operating. Let's say the maintenance supervisor calls one day to explain that the boiler system is leaking all over the freshly painted boiler room floor. There is obviously something wrong with the power plant and it is time to hire someone or call someone if a service contract exists. There are ways to determine who should perform the work and how to ensure that the dollars expensed are reasonable and customary. Are you getting the right product, for the right price, for the right reason?

Once that list of vendors has been established, it is important that some distinctions be made, too. What items should be maintained on a continual basis (i.e., reoccurring expenses)? What items are of a onetime cost nature? And, of the reoccurring cost items, what are products as opposed to services? All three areas carry with them different concerns in the process of bidding on and hiring vendors or service providers.

Important note: Any time a bidding process is undertaken with any vendor or provider, it is advisable to have at least three similar providers bid on the exact same specifications.

Service Vendors and Agreements

For some services a property will need to contract with a vendor on an ongoing basis, such as for landscaping, extermination services, pool maintenance, elevator repair, and depending on the sophistication and local license requirements, boiler maintenance. There may be others as well, depending on the building type and specifics and what functions the owner has chosen to perform in-house. When deciding on a vendor for such services, it is important that there is a written *service agreement.* Often the service provider has its own agreement that it will present an owner. If at all possible, create a specific service agreement for the particular property. If that's not possible, read the service contract provided thoroughly and be prepared to amend it. Do not accept all terms of a service provider's agreement unless you are absolutely comfortable with the agreement. If the agreement is difficult to understand, have it reviewed by an attorney.

Let's review some of the important provisions of a service agreement. All of the following items are *negotiable* and should be insisted upon if a service agreement is to be entered into:

❑ *Proper Names.* Name all parties, the provider and the property entity, correctly. This ensures proper recourse should the vendor not live up to the spirit of the agreement.

❑ *Itemized Licenses.* Itemize and produce all required licenses, including a license to operate in this business.

❑ *Certificates of Liability Insurance.* Always ask to see a certificate of liability insurance. Also require that the vendor name the property entity as additionally insured. Obtain a copy of this certificate. Make sure the monetary dollar limits of liability are sufficient for the type of provider and its service.

❑ *Workers Compensation Coverage.* Require proof of workmen's compensation coverage as well.

❑ *Itemized Services.* Itemize each expected regular service item and frequency of service. For instance, a boiler service contract should be specific about regular maintenance such as cleaning as opposed to repair. It should be understood when and how often that boiler is cleaned.

❑ *Itemized Events.* Itemize what "events" would not be covered by the service provider under normal agreement conditions and what would be considered an extraordinary event. It is equally important to make clear the process a provider has to go through to gain permission to perform such extraordinary work.

❑ *Itemized Rates.* Itemize all regular and extraordinary service rates as they relate to each type of work. What does the monthly service contract cost for all normal work? What does it cost should a provider have to perform work on nonoperating business hours? What does each type of laborer or skilled worker cost? What conditions require additional bidding before extraordinary work is commenced?

❑ *Payment Policy.* Agree to a payment policy of all invoicing, including fees and terms for late payment.

❑ *Length of Contract.* Clarify the length of term of this agreement and all parameters to cancel or renew such an agreement.

❑ *Applicable Jurisdiction.* Make sure any disputes in regard to a service agreement are governed by the jurisdiction where the property is located. Some vendors are regional or national in scope, so many of them install in an agreement a provision that says disputes are to be handled in the courts where their main operating office is located. Yet this could make recourse difficult should a dispute arise.

What are some typical examples of the difference between what normal service is and what is an extraordinary service?

Normal Services	Extraordinary Services
Cleaning and operating pool filters	Fixing a broken skimmer line
Weekly lawn cutting	Trimming of all shrubs
Picking up weekly garbage	Picking up bulk items
Cleaning a boiler	Fixing a broken pump
Painting an empty apartment for rental	Fixing large holes in walls
Scheduled extermination service	Specific request for unusual insect
Daily operations on management software	Loss of operating material

Simple keys to remember:

❑ Negotiate service contracts. Don't accept a service contract unless all details are discussed and agreed upon.
❑ Solicit at least three bids at all times.

Single-Issue Contract Agreements

Often an owner will need a contractor to perform one-time repairs or capital improvements. Because the items are unusual and don't occur all the time, there is a danger in not firmly understanding the cost of such items. This is where most unscrupulous contractors will seek to take advantage. Especially in the case of one-time repairs, there is often a need to repair as soon as possible and it's very easy to feel forced to pay whatever the service provider asks for. There will be times when there is no choice, but these should be the exceptions not the rule.

When bidding out onetime work, if at all possible create *bidding specifications*. That is, the property owner should be the one to determine the scope of work, not the contractor. Obviously, the expertise may not be present among staff members to construct a scope of work. In that case you must ask contractors their opinions and have them suggest options. Then make sure all contractors bid on exactly the same fix or fixes. The term used all the time for consistent bidding is "apples to apples." For example, if a concrete contractor bids a job by square feet, make sure all concrete contractors bid it by square feet, then it is easier to understand the bids.

It is helpful to understand basic measuring techniques and generally accepted labor costs. *The Blue Book of Building and Construction* is a guide to such costs and contractors; the book is set up by state and by year and can be accessed at www.the bluebook.com. It is also advisable over time to record what typical per unit and labor costs are from year to year and vendor to vendor. For example, concrete is usually measured for delivery by the yard; the average hourly rate for an electrician might be $65 an hour.

If vendor bids do not compare directly or price variances are wide, then don't settle for the three-bid rule. Get as many bids as it takes to have a comfort level with the scope of work and to agree to a reasonable cost. If there are unknown factors involved in a task—for instance, there seems to be an underground pipe leak—bid *labor costs standard* and *material costs standard*. In this example, get the charge for each laborer and skilled worker by the hour, get the cost of the machine digging the hole by the hour, and get the piping materials priced by the lineal feet. There may still be some unknown factors, but bidding in this way reduces that possibility, and if the vendor cannot give you answers, it is a contractor that shouldn't be used. Contractors set prices based on profit so they know all the costs before they start.

Here are some other considerations when setting up a onetime contract:

❏ Ask to see a similar job performed by the contractor. It is important to make sure the contractor is up to the task.

❏ Negotiate definitive start and finish dates. Contractors juggle work and unfinished jobs are unsightly and can be dangerous.

❏ Make sure the limits of liability insurance are adequate to match the scope of the job. This is always important but even more so on large jobs.

❏ Require that the contractor obtain all necessary permits, permissions, and approvals. You aren't the expert; the contractor should be.

❑ Agree on a schedule of payment.

❑ Agree on the job parameters and necessary approvals that ownership requires before additional uncontracted work is undertaken.

❑ Specify the authorized spokesperson for the ownership and for the contractor. This avoids an unauthorized or unqualified source giving direction.

Structuring the bidding process ensures the proper scope of work and refines the pricing game so the cost to the ownership is safely controlled as best it can be. There will be occasional emergencies, when work needs to get done without the bidding process. So, when interviewing contractors, obtain their emergency numbers and rates for labor and machinery. If a contractor won't supply such information then it should be an indication of the vendor's trustworthiness.

Simple keys to remember:

❑ Create bidding specifications for one-time work; the property owner should be the one to determine *the scope of work*, not the contractor.

❑ Require all contractors to bid on exactly the same fix or fixes.

❑ Obtain three bids, but if vendors' bids do not compare directly or price variances are wide, don't settle for the three-bid rule. Get as many bids as it takes to reach a comfort level with the scope of work and to get a reasonable cost.

Product Vendors

Depending on the size of the apartment community, there may be an inventory of common products on site. If this is the case, it becomes necessary to know what products are constantly used and what they are worth. Common categories of products are plumbing, electrical, cleaning, painting, cabinetry, and door and window. Periodically there may also be a need for appliances, carpet, and other flooring. There are general rules of thumb to understand when purchasing this material:

❑ Local hardware stores are convenient but usually expensive.

❑ "One-stop" shopping, such as a Home Depot, will have most everything needed, but price can be an issue. If you buy on store credit, pay the bills timely. There are serious late fees and service charges.

❑ There are apartment-specific vendors that will have the most abundant selection of products, and there are enough of them to warrant a bidding process for material. Often these larger "supply houses" have support staffs for advice. Make sure you use them.

❑ The cheapest product isn't always the best. Using knockoff or imitation materials might save money up front, but it will cost down the road.

❑ Confirm a vendor's return and credit policy before committing.

It is advisable to use a purchase order system when buying material in bulk and material that will be a recurring purchase. Purchase order forms, such as the one in Figure 9-1, can be bought at most office supply stores. It is also advisable to keep a log of pricing by unit and date. Periodically check this pricing because vendors won't always tell you of a price increase. Many apartment-specific vendors will supply reports that will review community purchases over the course of a given time period. This is all useful information as time goes on.

When buying products and supplies for a community, there are some marketing concerns that help rent apartments and are more economical in the end:

❑ Neutral paint colors, usually an off-white, are most desirable. They make an apartment brighter and are a good base for new renters regardless of the color of their furnishings.

❑ Flooring should also be neutral. With carpet the "heavier" the ounce of the carpet, the tighter the weave and the more durable (and expensive) the carpet. With tile, ceramic always is much more durable but much more expensive.

❑ Appliances should all be the same color. The larger the better (people try to visualize storage capacity).

❑ Standardizing fixtures gives an apartment a streamlined look and simplifies future repair options.

Keep minimal stock on hand. Apartment-specific vendors can be reached with a phone call and usually can deliver within a day or two.

Simple keys to remember:

❑ Know the different options for purchasing parts and equipment.

❑ Use a purchase order system.

❑ Keep a comparative price log and constantly review it.

Figure 9-1. Purchase order.

PURCHASE ORDER

PROPERTY NAME _____   # _____

DATE _____

VENDOR _____

CONTACT _____

PHONE NUMBER _____

DESCRIPTION OF MATERIAL	UNIT PRICE	QUANTITY	TOTAL
1.			
2.			
3.			
4.			
5.			
6.			

GRAND TOTAL _____

PICKUP OR DELIVERY _____

DELIVERY DATE _____

PAYMENT TERMS _____

AUTHORIZED SIGNATURE _____

Beta-Test New Products

If the community is of any appreciable size, or the office is using any technology products such as software or computerized control systems, it is always advisable to "test" new products on a small scale. New and improved technological break-throughs are presented all of the time by ambitious sales representatives. Some new products do have merit, but come at new product costs. Don't rush into retrofitting an entire complex with new technology. Instead, agree to purchase one of a new item (or a few) and test it first to ascertain its value. In the case of new community management software, such as products provided by Yardi and MRI, the manufac-turers are aware you'll need to "test" their programs for a period of time to ascertain whether they fit all your management needs.

Vendors are aware of this practice, and if they want the "big sale," there should be no issue in giving you the opportunity to *beta-test* the product to ascertain its utility for your specific site. Make suggestions for product improvement also. Ven-dors and manufacturers alike do listen to suggestions because often the observation from one owner or community is common in the industry. Finally, make sure any piece of new technology is applicable for the use the vendor is selling. An example is a new heat control system for a boiler. Does it conform to and can it be operated in conjunction with your boiler equipment's make, model, and specifications? New technology usually has very advantageous aspects, especially given the age of some apartment stock, but it has to apply to your environment or else it is wasting money, not saving money.

"Creating the Product You Buy"

Vendors are in the business of securing more business and permanent business. The best way they can accomplish this is by satisfying customer needs. You can push them to excel by making them compete for your dollar and by never assuming they already have the answer. The vendor sells, but you understand the apartment operation. Only you know your needs, and vendors seek to understand that.

The computer is an increasingly important tool used in the apartment business, and Web-based products made specifically for the industry are springing up each day. On a computer today you can organize all your office requirements, order supplies, perform credit and background checks, and advertise your apartments. Advertising apartments on the Internet is becoming a more prevalent way to market communities and will grow in importance as time goes by. Naturally enough, as more people use online services, more vendors offer some derivative of their products for the Web.

My organization has experience advertising on many of these new Internet sites. Compared to the average cost per lease of other advertising sources, Internet marketers are much cheaper and they reach an ever-larger potential market. As often happens, though, many of these sources have a "higher primary purpose," and in my own experience, some of them were better at selling themselves than selling our properties. The Internet advertising "pages" were becoming obscured with self-promotion and with additional advertisers appearing on the same pages with our communities.

One of the keys to renting is pointing out the unique aspects of your property over the competition. What was happening was all the Web "pages" of all the properties—both ours and the competition—were starting to look quite the same. And with all the self-promotion and additional advertising, it was getting harder to distinguish ourselves. When questioning the vendors about customizing pages to even a modest extent, they almost all claimed technological challenges to being able to distinguish our properties over others. With all the bells and whistles that these sites had, it didn't seem logical that this was the case. The customer wasn't pushing the vendor enough and the vendor was therefore dictating the product.

There was too much to gain by advertising on the Internet, so my organization couldn't eliminate these sites, but we had to move the collective vendor "thought process" along. In-house, we decided to hire someone to create our own home page to market and brand our organization. When the vendors we were using discovered this, they all tried to sell us on "linking" their advertisements to our home page, but they all wanted to maintain control over the pages of the individual communities. We had been experimenting with several advertisers and were using different vendors for different properties within our portfolio; no one vendor had the complete portfolio.

I decided to increase the competitive fervor. I told all the Internet vendors that I would offer them our complete portfolio if, in fact, each "page" with each individual community was "branded" specifically for our organization and we could have more direct control over editing these sites ourselves. Whereas most of the vendors claimed there were technological reasons why this wasn't totally possible, one ambitious vendor wanting to make a name for itself offered to "research the possibilities."

The company contacts came back to us and said they could no doubt brand our sites, as long as somewhere on the site their logo also appeared. And they could allow us editorial access to most of what we wanted, but not all. We agreed to consummate the business and still do business with this vendor today. The vendor has provided us further technological advances and freedoms ever since. The real story here, though, is that suddenly its competition has also found a way to provide branding and customer editorial control. Although their actual capabilities vary to some extent, they all now offer similar products.

The key is to know what you need and insist on getting what you need. Housing is one of the largest businesses in this country and there are a lot of competitors out for your dollar. This story seems to support the power of a large organization, but many vendors would rather try a new product on a small scale first, so ask and push. These same principles apply to the contractor who insists that there is only one way to fix or build something; in most cases it simply isn't the case.

That Internet vendor has become our partner in the apartment business, and all your vendors should want to strive to be your partner, too.

CHAPTER 10

The Future

Multiplying Your Portfolio—Going from Small to Big

If the initial foray into multifamily real estate has been a successful one, then your natural impulse will be to repeat the process. Most real estate transactions are determined by the economics of the times and the art of the deal struck. Therefore, property is bought in locations where the economics makes sense. Very rarely is each piece of property going to be located ten minutes from your home base. As you acquire more and more property, you must put more thought into the logistical and operational concerns of how you are going to effectively manage your holdings. If you (or any investor) purchase strictly because the property is a bargain, you may be creating problems down the line.

If you will remember the story in Chapter 1 of the far-off investment in Topeka from New Jersey, the horror story that occurred there is not unusual. It happens all the time. From the moment you make the decision to expand, you should be starting the process of marrying an investment plan with a management strategy.

■ Strategic Thinking Is a Necessity

There are several baseline issues that should be considered as expansion is anticipated:

❑ *Market Familiarity.* Becoming familiar with particular markets and concentrating on these markets makes for a savvier investor and builds management intelligence for that particular market and location.

❑ *Similar Properties.* Purchasing similar-type properties creates a better understanding of the investment and mitigates the "learning curve" of a new acquisition.

❑ *Pooled Resources.* The tighter the concentration of investments geographically, the easier (and more realistic) it will be to manage and to "pool" resources.

❑ *Procedural Standardization.* Thought has to be put into creating standard procedures. The more property you own, the less time you'll actually spend on each site and the more you'll have to rely on others. Create policies so your staff knows how to handle something in your absence.

❑ *Financing Options.* Investment and financing considerations could affect the sophistication and size of the support staff. For instance, let's say your first purchases were with conventional financing, but you are now considering a subsidized Section 8 property. Your present staff, and possibly even the person who reviews your accounting, may not understand the Section 8 programs at all. Buying a different kind of investment could expand your staffing and overhead much faster than you may be prepared for.

❑ *Business Partnerships.* This is the time to really be honest about your weaknesses as an investor. If you are adept at the financial review but don't understand the mechanics or vice versa, it's important to choose the right business partners or associates. Know what you understand and be brutally honest about what you don't.

❑ *Market Positioning.* Start thinking about how the ownership will be positioned and recognized in the marketplace. Most investors need financial partners, and reputations do travel. Both investors and prospective residents will start making decisions based on what they hear and what they perceive about you as a property owner.

❑ *Staff Building.* Attracting talented people to be part of the management will be contingent upon how the ownership positions itself and is perceived. This is a vital concern in this industry. There are very few professional, comprehensive training programs in multifamily housing. Many individuals come into the industry from other walks of life; a truly experienced property professional is a rare and valuable commodity. Any owner will have to compete for the services of such an individual.

❑ *Levels of Control.* Decisions will have to be made relative to how much work you want to perform on your own and how much you will contract to others. It is important to understand that there will be a balance between expanding operations and losing direct control. Thought has to be given to subcontracted services and your oversight and review capabilities as the property owner.

❏ *Procurement*. Developing strong vendor relationships is a must because with greater numbers comes increased purchasing power and, conversely, people who will look to take advantage. Knowing and maintaining relationships with vendors builds trust and confidence in your business transactions for products and services.

❏ *Information Software*. Gathering and organizing information that applies to your investments will become critical, so consider using automation and communication tools. Try to standardize on management and accounting software. Once an organization starts to expand in size, it becomes more difficult to change software because the staff grows to understand the operations through the tools they are given. Retraining a workforce is a daunting task.

❏ *Strategic Networking*. Networking is a way to stay in touch with what is happening in the industry and how events or trends will affect your investment. Investment opportunities will present themselves.

These baseline concerns are discussed in greater length later in this chapter. It is not always going to be possible to buy next door to the original investment, and it may not always be possible to find absolutely similar investments, but the strategic process of planning what a portfolio might look like in a year or two should start with the way you operate your first investment. A well-thought-out foundation should be constructed from that point. In the business of property management, a business day can be rather mundane if everything is organized and all involved understand the properties the same way. If organization hasn't been established or doesn't exist, then day by day you may be moving from one disaster to another.

Throughout this book I have tried to emphasize and reinforce the notion that proper planning and forethought, combined with consistent execution of the basics, will result in the multifamily experience being a positive and financially rewarding one. True to these principles, where it relates to any of the baseline concerns of expansion, any concept or process created should be simple, detailed, and easy to review. The operation of a portfolio should be structured so that you, as a property owner, can keep in touch on a daily basis with how your investments are performing. If the process becomes too cumbersome, keeping an eye on the ball becomes a difficult exercise. Once you become detached from the reality of an investment, it can become a problem both operationally and financially very quickly. Controlling a problem from a distance is much more difficult than being there; therefore, establishing standards of operation are very important while the organization is small.

Today is the time to start thinking about tomorrow. The best and most established management and investment organizations culture a "team" atmosphere. They communicate constantly and develop ways of interpreting what an investment is doing without necessarily having to be in physical touch with it on a daily basis. These organizations are usually populated with individuals who grew with the company and have helped establish the culture. If you have such employees, you want to be able to leverage them.

Now, let's examine each of the aforementioned basic concerns and find a way to visualize what you may need to do to effectively grow an organization.

■ Invest in Due Diligence

The process of performing due diligence is important when considering a single property, but it becomes even more important when expanding. Unless the town of the first investment is a hotbed of real estate activity (and if it is, values tend to increase rapidly, thereby evaporating the bargains), it's more than likely that your second and subsequent deals will be located in another municipality or another state. This means learning a completely new set of parameters in relation to operating the real estate for profit. The reasons might be many. For example:

❑ *A municipality may have instituted rent control or rent stabilization, which will affect the upper threshold for potential income.* Making a visit to the local government offices and obtaining a copy of such an ordinance is essential. Many rent control ordinances do allow for what is known as *vacancy decontrol,* meaning when an apartment is vacated the rents can be raised to what the market will bear. Many rent control ordinances are liberal on the rent increases, yet others are very restrictive.

This factor alone can very much change how a property is operated. Investigating the turnover rate of the residents, for instance, now becomes a key issue. If the rent control is restrictive and you discover (through the due diligence) a low turnover rate, then your ability to increase the income, even if the town allows vacancy decontrol, becomes a serious concern.

❑ *Costs for goods and services can vary tremendously, even within the same state.* Utilities are where this issue is most evident. Many water authorities even one town apart are under completely different jurisdictions and control.

The way water and sewer services are billed can drastically affect the costs to the ownership. Heating fuel costs vary geographically. If it is understood that the property owner will provide some or all of the utilities, then this becomes a very important operational concern. It may be a marketing concern as well. For example, let's say the heat is electric. This type of heat is very expensive to operate and at a particular property the residents pay for their electric. It becomes very important to factor this into income potential. Why? The competitive market rents of the surrounding properties may force the hand of an owner on how to set rent rates, and renters will very much notice that they have to pay for an expensive fuel cost.

The interesting thing is that in structuring rents, if the resident didn't have to pay for the utility but you factor in a rent increase to cover the cost, it won't normally register with the resident—at least not as much as when the cost is directly charged to the resident. Therefore, reviewing costs such as utilities and who will pay for them is something that differs from town to town and property to property, and it should be investigated.

❑ *The power plants that a property maintains can significantly affect operations.* Again, geography can play a big role in this regard. For instance, heating costs are a much bigger part of an annual operating budget in New York State than in Arizona, while cooling costs are obviously a much greater concern in Arizona.

The type of power plants and their condition is an issue that needs to be thoroughly investigated. In the example of cooling systems in mid-rise or high-rise buildings, one can see the possibilities. Many high-rises contain what are called chiller systems. These are central in nature. Two significantly different systems have two completely different cost structures because of the way they operate.

An *absorption chiller* uses a building's heating system to convert steam into cooling elements; therefore it uses a tremendous amount of whatever fossil fuel a building uses for heat. It also means that the building's heating systems operate virtually the whole year, and the cost for that fossil fuel is a much bigger portion of the operating budget. Maintaining the heating systems will also be more costly and the expected useful life of the heating system will be shorter.

There are, therefore, many additional costs in investing in a building with these systems. By contrast, a *centrifugal chiller* operates off of a building's electrical system, so the heating system can be shut down for the summer to be serviced and the fossil fuel costs are not part of the summertime operation. If you don't investigate these nuances, the bottom line could look much different than first anticipated.

Another example is a *steam heating system* as opposed to a *baseboard hot water system*. Steam systems have many more parts, including "traps" throughout the piping that collect foreign matter in the lines and water vapor. These traps often corrode or become clogged. They are not all visible to the eye. Many are in basements and behind walls. If there's a steam system and it hasn't been well maintained, the costs of replacing and retrofitting new lines can be tremendous. You don't want to find out a steam system is in a state of disrepair the first time you turn on the heat.

❑ *Real estate taxes vary from town to town and state to state.* The history of tax increases and tax rate changes should be investigated because this issue can have a very negative impact on the operating budget. New Jersey, for instance, has some of the highest tax rates in the nation. It is also a state with a history of financial struggles and it is a state with more than 500 municipalities whose tax rates vary tremendously. You need to investigate the history of the municipalities, including their finances and relationships with multifamily owners. This information will shed necessary light on the purchase.

❑ *Property history with natural occurrences is very important.* An example is flood-zone properties. There are many different definitions of what are considered flood-zone properties. A property may be in a zone but it hasn't been flooded itself. Or it may be in a flood zone once every several decades. Water is the biggest single enemy of any structure, and the frequency of flooding can affect the infrastructure of a building and therefore can cost you in major structural improvements over time.

Investigate the history of a property and look at the structural elements that would be affected, such as crawl spaces. Dry rot in wooden structures, especially main support structures, is very expensive to repair and replace. This is a hidden cost that may not be apparent from financial statements.

Another reason to thoroughly investigate natural occurrences such as flooding is to decide on appropriate insurance coverage. Remember flood insurance is a separate policy. If you finance and the area the prospective purchase is located in is considered a flood zone, flood insurance may be required. If it isn't required, many owners look at the cost and feel it isn't necessary. The risk of overlooking the cost can be enormous. Water does major damage and if you aren't covered, or don't know the history of the property, then the price tag for an event that was inevitable could put you out of business. It's nice to market a waterfront property. But know the downside and factor it into a purchase decision.

❑ *Local laws regarding rental property can affect how you operate and can determine success or failure.* Understanding the rental market fully is critical. If a community has a lot of very large apartment complexes, it is easy to see who the competition is and what they offer. However, every market does not have mammoth apartment communities that compete with each other. The State of California, for instance, has one of the largest numbers of rental units nationwide, yet the majority of owners own small complexes of very few units. If you were anticipating buying in a southern California town and weren't aware of this fact, then you might be buying into a market that is completely saturated with rental units and competition may be fierce for the rental customer.

Market norms are also important to understand. Although short-term leasing is on the rise in the northeastern United States, longer-term leasing is the norm. In a market such as Texas or Florida, where competition is on every street corner, short-term leasing is quite acceptable. The reason is basic but overlooked. Because many northeastern communities are older, the available land to build on has long since evaporated; therefore, the competition is (and has been for some time) limited. In states where the infrastructure build up and out is more recent, the number of rental communities dictates more competitive options. Operationally, you need to understand this to accurately forecast income and what to expect in turnover and turnover costs.

❏ *Labor structure and nuances need to be recognized as well.* Unions exist in the multifamily industry in regional pockets. Health and benefit costs as well as size of staff can vary greatly if a union is involved. This regional difference can exist within communities just a river apart. New York City, for example, has many union rental locations but when you cross the Hudson River five minutes away, the incidence of union shops reduces significantly. As a testament to how different the economics are just a river away, many rental owners who operate in New York City don't operate in New Jersey and vice versa.

In terms of due diligence, an owner should be prepared to make these observations, ask questions, and be careful not to make baseline assumptions based on past experience.

A Process for Due Diligence

Now that the decision has been made to expand to multiple markets, it isn't like opening a McDonald's that looks and operates the same virtually anywhere. Rental property is affected by the market, the town, the environment, the construction, and the previous ownership practices (or lack thereof), and very much by local economics. It is vitally important to be a detective when buying property and to be realistic about what you are purchasing. Talk to people who own in the location where you might buy and ask the tough questions. Whatever you think is necessary to know, it is important that the previous ownership be forthcoming about the issues presented to them.

As your employee base expands, it may be important to identify the analytical minds among your staffing, both in a financial sense and in a physical sense. Part of the purchase should be an independent look at each aspect and then a comparative assessment of each. For instance, an accountant may notice a per-unit fuel cost that seems high, but can't tell an owner why. If you allow one of your best repair staff to look at a potential new property, that person may be able to warn you about expenses you might not think of. Create an organized and standardized way to break down a property into categories that make sense to you and the staff you are starting to build. Over the years, this exercise will change as more is learned. But, like anything else in life, if structure is put to the process, then the review of a property becomes more mechanical over time. If the ownership expands to multiple properties, then the possibility exists that more than one possible investment will be reviewed at the same time. The owner may have to rely on a support team to perform the legwork necessary to complete a purchase decision.

My experience has been that many owners become removed from the process. Although it is true that as an organization grows the owners may not be able to investigate the property personally, they still need to be involved and, as owner, you should be familiar with all the details and the process of investigation. For this reason, if you are anticipating creating a portfolio, establish your parameters for due diligence and insist they are followed each time a prospective investment is introduced. There is no standard; in fact, developing a management entity has everything to do with the personality and the viewpoint of those in ownership. To organize a standard due diligence process, you might start by examining these factors:

❏ *Market.* The market assessment may include competition and their amenities, market regularities and irregularities, occupancy rates, and denseness of the rental market.

❏ *Local Laws, Regulations, and Politics.* What general viewpoint does a town have toward a rental property? What laws affect income or the ability to operate on a daily basis?

❏ *Environmental Conditions and Occurrences.* Floods, hurricanes, and earthquakes may be rare or they may be a real cost of doing business in a location. Property environmental issues are equally important. Radon, oil tanks, and mold are just a few items that need to be reviewed.

❏ *Property Construction and Previous Upkeep.* Wood structures not properly weatherized will cost a lot of money to maintain. How is a property constructed? What materials were used and have they been maintained over the years? What types of mechanical equipment exist and are they functioning properly?

❑ *Unit Condition.* Look at every unit and understand the general shape and condition of the unit and of its amenities, such as carpets and appliances.

❑ *Residency.* Review the records, review the actual residents, and know what you are up against in terms of a community's personality.

A constant theme repeated throughout this chapter is that as you expand, hands-on control will become more difficult. That makes it all the more critical that you create systems that you understand and start developing trust in people around you. Start identifying individuals who exhibit talent with certain aspects of the management. Start developing your specialists.

Simple keys to remember:

❑ Perform due diligence. It is essential to expanding in multiple markets, where it is harder to instantly associate what an owner has experienced and what an owner can expect to experience in a different market.

❑ Develop methods of identifying and selecting individuals to perform these critical tasks in an owner's absence.

Attract Financial Partners

As an expansion takes hold, the opportunities that will present themselves and/or need to be reviewed will be many. At some point the need for partners will most likely be a strategy you'll consider. Partners will bring in more of the up-front dollars that make for reasonably leveraged investments. How do you attract those would-be partners to your organization? The most obvious way is if you can consistently deliver as promised on quoted returns on the investment. Real estate investors know the reputations and will know who consistently performs. Over time, investors tend to gravitate toward a proven commodity, so the task of drawing investors to your company gets easier with success.

There are, though, things you can do to have the potential investor focus in your direction over another. Much of this chapter is about positioning a growing company in the competitive marketplace. The things that an owner or a managing partner can do are many of the same things the organization would do to attract renters. Presentation and philosophy have everything to do with attracting prospective partners to the organization.

❑ *Create a company brochure.* A brochure creates the appearance of long-term stability. Show your team players, saying something about those players, and describe your mission statement and existing portfolio.

❑ *Use brand signage, property brochures, and advertising.* Create a company logo and display that logo everywhere.

❑ *Create a professional corporate office environment.* There has to be a presentation place that strikes the investor as a well-oiled, stable, profitable machine.

❑ *Network in the industry.* Industry functions and trade shows are meeting places for people who look to invest and are looking for partners themselves. Social functions often become business platforms.

❑ *Look the part, and have your staff look the part.* Everyone concerned with your operation should know that a presentation may be necessary at all times.

❑ *Produce complete presentations for any investment you are trying to shop.* Different people process information in varied ways, so make sure a presentation allows for different thinkers to understand the proposed investment. Projected income and expenses, property pictures, improvement strategy, and terms of the investment—all should be included. The more complete a presentation, the more your potential investors will understand up front, and the fewer reservations they will have when contemplating an investment opportunity.

❑ *Be willing to show prospective investors whatever they need.* Hiding or shading the truth doesn't build confidence. Remember, too, that these potential investors could be partners for a long time.

❑ *Maintain relationships with brokers.* They know where the would-be investors are hiding.

Investors respond to the same stimuli we all do: stability, security, a good product, and a management team that appears to understand the product it is dealing with when anticipating a possible relationship. They will come back for future investments based on the return being as advertised.

▦ Engage in the Community ("Be Part of It, Not Apart from It")

As expansion takes hold, the more likely the investments will be spread into neighboring towns that you are unfamiliar with. And, of course, the powers that be won't be familiar with you, either. A term often associated with multifamily ownership is *absentee ownership*. Although this simple term should not have a negative connotation, it often does. Owners are often viewed as not only physically removed from a property and municipality, but emotionally removed as well. If an owner is not cognizant of this phenomenon, then the owner shouldn't be surprised when the local officials react in a harsh or impersonal way to an event or events that have taken place on a property. Are rental owners often misunderstood, or more likely, do owners allow themselves to be misunderstood?

In large part, owners view an investment for the deal and the future value of that deal. Yet if the real estate investment is to be long term, investing in the community where that property is located should be a factor in creating the value. Every town and hamlet in this country operates differently, structurally and politically, and these factors often have a direct cause and effect on owning and managing real estate. An owner who doesn't seek to understand the local environment risks becoming a victim of it rather than a power broker in shaping it.

Start the process of understanding a town from the day the decision is made to possibly buy in that town. Even before purchasing, visit the local municipal complex and introduce yourself. Day-to-day interaction with local officials is something that eventually will have to be ceded to other individuals in your organization, but as the owner, it is absolutely essential when buying in multiple markets to make yourself known. Engage the local officials, from the mayor or city manager to the code enforcement individuals to the local police departments. It is always important to project the image of wanting to sincerely understand the investment and the concerns the town may have about the property you are acquiring. If the local officials feel that you and your staff are sincere, they'll be more disposed to share with you a very clear picture of the history of the property and what you, as owner, might expect to encounter at the community level when it comes to handling issues occurring at a site.

There is another very important reason to make contact with a town and its officials while anticipating a purchase. Reputations linger longer than reality many times. A property may have a history of mismanagement, or violence, or poor resident relations. While any sale is a matter of public record, many officials are skeptical of real estate transactions. They don't trust that the ownership has truly changed simply by a title change.

If you are the new owner and you don't present yourself or a suitable company representative, a town and its officials may continue to view the property through the historic lenses and you may be left to fight old ghosts, so to speak. Town officials will want a recognizable new face to connect to the new situation; otherwise, they'll handle your real estate very impersonally. In Chapter 1, I described my firsthand experience with an investment in Topeka, Kansas. Although the strategic decision to purchase property that far away from anything else we operated was the main reason it failed, the problem was compounded because the town had identified absentee ownership as the source of many of the problems. When we reintroduced ourselves to the town and expressed our sincerest regrets for what had taken place, the town officials were very helpful in making an attempt to correct some of what was happening at the property. It helped that we had presented ourselves as concerned human beings for the community as a whole.

Once a property is purchased, staying engaged with the town is equally important because personal relationships build understanding, and understanding builds patience. No matter how good a management team may be, things will occur that have the possibility of reflecting poorly on the management and ownership of a property. How the town perceives such an ownership will directly influence how it chooses to handle a situation. Many local codes and ordinances provide latitude in enforcement of violations. An ownership that attempts to stay personally in touch with a town will often fare better than one that hasn't. You want to make sure you have a chance to discuss events related to your property and know how town officials will handle it. As a property owner, don't underestimate the importance of these relationships.

Public officials can affect your property directly or indirectly. I once had a very large fire at a property, an incident that played out on the local news live. Often there is a lot of misinformation when events like this happen live, and often the people who own and manage the property are kept away from the situation until local officials feel they understand it. When this fire occurred, I met my manager at the site as quickly as I could. We had long since established a very good rapport with the local fire and police officials. When I arrived at the site, it was overwhelmed by emergency vehicles and the press. Immediately we located the fire battalion chief and the police official. Rather than exclude us from the situation as it evolved, they welcomed our input and wanted us close by. In an indirect way they aided our cause, because the fire official asked us to review what he would give to the press before he spoke.

In the same municipality, local police officials once warned us of a possible situation on our property and let us know the press was already asking questions. This cooperative effort resulted in minimal publicity and allowed the police in the end to capture a suspect.

As you grow, what are some ways that you or your staff can get connected and stay connected in a town that is removed from the main office, so to speak?

- ❏ *Make personal visits.* Each level of the management chain should be compelled to personally visit specific officials in the municipality. That includes the owners, the regional staff (if the operation has grown large enough for this level), and the site management staff.

- ❏ *Join the chamber.* Join the local chamber of commerce, and assign someone to attend the meetings and sponsor portions of events.

- ❏ *Become a board member.* If a town allows representation on local boards or committees relative to property issues, a representative of yours should join. An example is a town with a rent control or stabilization board. These boards usually look for a representative from the apartment industry to sit on the board. It is always better to be viewed as part of the solution, not part of the problem.

- ❏ *Host community programs.* Sponsor local safety programs, such as the "night out" program usually hosted by local police, and volunteer to help coordinate the creation of neighborhood watch programs.

- ❏ *Attend town council meetings.* Assign someone to attend town council meetings to stay current with politics and actual changes in the local law.

- ❏ *Join local trade organizations.* Become a member of local chapters of the predominant trade organizations and participate in their meetings and functions. This topic will be talked about at greater length later in this chapter.

- ❏ *Contribute financially.* Contribute financially to local health and safety organizations. I have found that actual physical symbols of contribution work very effectively. For example, consider buying actual bulletproof vests for police officers rather than just contributing to a fund. The officers will put a face to the contribution and won't forget it.

- ❏ *Negotiate.* Always look to find a negotiated settlement to a dispute with a local municipality. If the issue is an absolute disagreement, then agree to disagree and find some common ground. If your position is to own long term, then the nature of the relationship with the local municipality should be long term, also.

❑ *Do business "in town."* Utilize local businesses wherever possible. Communities are often smaller in terms of relationships than their actual size, and word will travel that you are supporting the local community and its economy.

❑ *Be proactive.* Be proactive with a town when a problem arises and don't just wait for it to come to you. An example would be a property having a serious heating problem in the winter. The mechanics have told the staff this problem is no easy fix and the heat will be off for several hours. Staff should inform the town well before the residents do. Township officials don't like answering to angry people any more than you do, especially without being informed. If they have the information and the property has established a track record of being honest and diligent with a problem, the town itself will reinforce with possible residents that the property is working on the problem and will correct it as soon as possible.

❑ *Cooperate.* Always be cooperative with any investigations or police activity occurring on a site, whether a resident or a staff member is a subject of that investigation. Again, towns often are smaller in relationships than they are in actual size and an uncooperative property will receive reciprocal cooperation (or lack thereof).

Whether the perception is fair or not, real estate transactions are expensive and those that buy real estate are viewed as individuals of substantial wealth. It is very easy to view ownership as being able to afford whatever a town feels it should. It is just as easy for that town to perceive an ownership as insensitive as it relates to local issues. The only way to combat that perception is to insist that whoever represents ownership stay in touch with the town where the property is located.

Owners who move into a market they are not familiar with, and then operate in that market in a vacuum of sorts, won't know when issues relative to the investment are occurring until the effect hits the investment directly. At that point the ability to change the situation is long past. Learning about, becoming personal with, and participating in the town where the investment is located is absolutely necessary as your organization expands. Be part of a community, not apart from it.

Simple keys to remember:

❑ Start the process of understanding a town by visiting it when reviewing a possible purchase.

❑ Require all levels of management to engage town officials.

❑ Look to constantly be cooperative with all officials and situations.

❑ Join organizations and local committees and participate.

Engage the Residents (They Pay the Bills)

The best way to pay down the mortgage on an investment is by keeping the community occupied with paying residents. The residents are the lifeblood of the multifamily business, and often investors hone their investment and financing skills but not their people skills. Many times in this industry, not dealing with a resident's issue properly ends up being the reason a resident leaves. As expansion takes hold, creating standard procedures and policies when dealing with issues relative to residents becomes very important. It has been repeated many times but always remember: This is a resident's home and as such, ownership and management often end up having to handle situations laced with emotion.

The investment is a business to the owner, but it is much more personal to the renter. Renting an apartment may be the single largest monthly expense for individual residents, and it is where they carry on their private lives. Whatever takes place in a resident's life will eventually be brought back to the apartment and possibly the community. Residents' living habits, which may reflect the way they were raised, will follow them to the apartment living. Many a resident manager has been charged with the unenviable task of telling a resident that some of his or her private habits are not acceptable under the lease terms or in relation to the other residents of a community.

Truly effective ownership and management realizes these dynamics and integrates sensitivity into daily operations when communicating with residents and would-be residents. An astute manager will gain a situational awareness of what might occur (or is starting to occur) in the community with residents and can usually minimize a potentially stressful incident from mushrooming into a bigger problem. This process or "skill set" starts with prospective renters and how they are "coached" upon moving in. This process should never stop. Effective ownership continually communicates with residents and channels behavior. Resident managers have to possess a combination of good communication skills, steady emotional control, and conflict-resolution skills equal to that of an experienced politician.

While other chapters deal with the technical aspects of many residential issues such as marketing, selling, the lease, and nonpayment, this chapter deals with the actual customer and resident contact, which is central to many of those other issues. If the owner and staff learn to master communication and awareness skills, it will go a long way to reducing turnover, which reduces costs. The income and expense equation on any property always balances toward the positive when apartments stay occupied. This should be the constant goal of any ownership and management team.

Resident relations should also not be limited to the ownership and manager. Many of the line personnel that operate any community have more direct contact with residents than the owner, and depending on the size of the community, possibly the manager, too. Effective management strategy will include customer service training and awareness of all personnel. Any individual who is employed at a community becomes a reflection of ownership. Owners must keep that in mind when hiring personnel and reviewing the success or tribulations of the community they own. If just one person on your staff is not sensitive when communicating with residents, it could be costing you literally tens of thousands of dollars.

The process of communicating with an individual starts when seeking renters, continues through an individual's occupancy, and should not stop even when that person vacates. Remember that referrals are a key renting tool, so the feeling and opinion left on anybody the staff comes in contact with, positive or negative, will be repeated to other individuals.

Initial Contact: Making First Impressions Count

Resident relations begin with enticing the renting public to believe that your community is superior to the surrounding competition. Effective customer relations become resident relations through the marketing, screening, sales, and lease process. It is important to remember that communication is not limited to what a person says. Resident relations start with the message and perception sent through advertising and the way a property is kept. What is it that is unique about a particular community? What will draw a prospective renter's attention to one community over another?

Ownership should start by surveying a property and deciding what aspects draw positive attention and what aspects detract from a community's overall appearance and perception. The term most often used in this book is *curb appeal,* and it should be the mantra of any ownership and management team. If individuals are going to stop by or call to inquire about the community, it has to appeal to them. If it doesn't, there is no incentive to stop and look further.

A significant amount of time and care should be put into the way a community presents itself to the public. The signage, landscaping, garbage areas, resident storage areas, recreation facilities, building decor (e.g., shutters, doors, gutters), and rental office should be a focus of attention when purchasing and in daily operations. Owners and managers alike should review all aspects of property presentation each and every time they enter a community. If anything that can affect the public perception is compromised, it should be addressed immediately.

For example, if graffiti was sprayed overnight anywhere on or near the property, it should be removed promptly. Don't underestimate the value that residents attach to the surrounding community. They rent the four walls and usually adorn those walls to their liking, so the interior living environment is their own, yet residents are very sensitive to community as well. There's a reason that I like to use the word *community,* not complex or simply apartments. Residents invite family and friends to their home, and the community as a whole is a reflection of the lifestyle they have chosen. Prospective residents will very much take this into account when contemplating one community over another. And it all starts with how well the community is physically presented to the public.

How advertising is designed also affects public perception and is another communication tool that should be reviewed daily, depending on the advertising sources. Price relative to the competition always has a bearing on where someone decides to rent, too, but there are other aspects of a community that can have an enormous effect on people searching for a new home. What is it about a specific community that is unique and would entice a prospective renter? Some examples are:

❑ *Location and Setting.* Is the property located in a quiet country-like setting, or is it conveniently located central to all the larger community has to offer? Properties usually have some appealing aspects relative to location and setting. Make sure advertising highlights them.

❑ *Community Advantages.* School systems or public transportation (e.g., being near a train station that connects with an important commerce district) may be appealing to working families, while hospitals may be important to seniors. Point these community advantages out in advertising.

❑ *Apartment Community Amenities.* Pools, exercise facilities, clubhouses, parks, and business facilities are items many people will seek out in the renting process. It is not important whether the renters actually end up using these facilities, but advertising the availability of such amenities provides options.

❑ *Individual Apartment Amenities.* Square footage, appliance packages, Internet and satellite TV capabilities, storage capacity, and layout often can draw individuals.

❑ *Economic Issues.* Who pays for heat and up-front rental costs are money issues, over and above the rent, that can affect a person's decision to rent, so highlight these advantages, too.

When creating advertising, a review of the competition's advertising is essential. You have to know what to compare to know what is unique about your community. Pictures are very important. If pictures will be used in any advertising medium, they should be reviewed by ownership and approved before they end up in publications. Imagine having a beautiful lakeside property that in the fall presents a wonderful "picture" for advertising. The advertiser snaps off a beautiful color photograph of the lake, the autumn trees, and the community. He shows the ownership a photograph on the spot and rushes it to production. When the publication comes out it is in black and white and the beautiful autumn picture appears as a blob of different grays and blacks. The essence of what was supposed to be communicated was totally lost.

Many advertisers will provide *proofs* for owner and manager review, so they can check for quality before any advertisements are fully reproduced. Insist on receiving an advertising proof, and have a policy that no advertising reflecting your community can be run without an authorized representative's written approval for the advertisement.

One commonly made mistake is not reviewing contact information thoroughly. Imagine paying premium dollar to coordinate an event at a property with an ad in a very visible but expensive advertising medium such as the *New York Times*. The staff is all geared up at its desks waiting for the phone to ring off the hook, but the calls never come. Finally the phone does ring and at the other end is an irate individual asking why her phone is ringing off the hook with calls for the apartment complex—the phone number in the ad was incorrect.

These last two examples are not rhetorical; they both happened. Mistakes such as these affect the perception and the traffic a community receives with potential renters.

Phone contact is the predominant, first personal contact a property has with a potential renter. The first words uttered often establish a mind-set. It is imperative, then, that you train your staff on telephone procedures. A "greeting" should be established as a requirement. Any greeting should have pertinent information such as a salutation ("Good morning" or "Good afternoon"), followed by the name of the community. Staff members answering the phone should identify themselves by name and then ask how they can help the caller. One very important rule of verbal communication to remember is to always be a patient and attentive listener! Prospective residents will usually let people know exactly what their needs are; good listeners guide a caller to exactly what they desire.

Essential Phone Tactics for the Apartment Industry

- ❑ *Draft a script.* Always keep a script handy at the main desk that will provide a comprehensive overview to the caller of the essentials and advantages of the community.

- ❑ *Document contact information.* Document the caller's name, contact information, desires, and source for the rental contact. This information becomes essential for follow-up and for "normalizing" the conversation so it will be more personal.

- ❑ *Ask questions.* Constantly ask questions or query the caller so that it becomes clearer what a caller's goal and possible objections are.

- ❑ *Invite a visit.* The goal of any prospective renter's call should be for you to encourage the person to continue the process by visiting the property and possibly filling out an application. Make an attempt to set an appointment to show an apartment.

- ❑ *Know what not to say.* Be mindful of what kind of questions shouldn't be answered. An example would be if someone asks if the community is safe. This is a very subjective topic and should not be answered with absoluteness. Refer the individual to the local police department to obtain objective answers to such a question. Any question that seeks to ascertain a community's restriction should be answered in regard to the posted rental criteria that each office should possess.

- ❑ *Be positive.* Whether the call goes well or not, always end the call on an upbeat note, thanking individuals for calling and their time. Remember, a call that ends on a bad note will be repeated to other individuals who may have anticipated calling.

Fair housing laws apply to every aspect of the renting procedure, including phone conversations. All of these general categories of the phone presentation are subject to fair housing laws:

- ❑ Setting appointments
- ❑ Asking for personal information
- ❑ Describing the location and availability of properties

❑ Phone demeanor or courteousness

❑ Callbacks and follow-up

On occasion the phone call can turn negative no matter what tact you take. Invariably, sometimes people are just not happy with the answers they are being given. While the more tenuous phone calls can tend to be with existing residents (a topic covered later in this chapter), prospective renters can have an emotional response as well. For example, a caller who has a rather large family may try to "push" a renting situation by becoming combative or threatening. You and your staff should always maintain a calm demeanor and answer questions according to set policy, and don't editorialize. A possible tactic is to continue to ask questions of such callers so that they clearly understand for themselves that you've made an attempt to accommodate and clarify.

Questions about family composition should always be asked in terms of occupants. Don't make a distinction between children and adults. The key is to be consistent with community policy from caller to caller. An answer for one person should be the answer given to anyone who asks the identical questions.

The Internet has now become a first-contact source as well. There are some rules of the road that should be followed when receiving Internet inquiries.

Essential Rules for Handling Internet Contacts

❑ *Provide same-day response.* The word *virtual* is often associated with the Internet. How that applies to apartment renting is that those who view Internet ads are looking for quick responses to their queries. An Internet inquiry should be answered within hours of receiving it; and certainly no more than twenty-four hours should pass. Many Internet advertisers have an "automatic response" capability, which is a good feature, but it still requires personal follow-up in a relatively short period of time.

❑ *Answer an Internet inquiry in the method the individual requests.* Many people browsing the Internet enjoy the anonymity and would rather receive an e-mail response than a call. Ask about their preferred contact method and whether they'd like a follow-up phone call.

❑ *Be persistent.* Internet inquiries may come from a great geographical distance, so it may take more than one volley on the Internet to get a person to physically stop by and see the property. Follow up. Persistence is essential.

❑ *Make daily review of Internet sources a must.* Use the Internet advertiser's tracking technology to make sure all inquiries have been followed up.

❑ *Answer objections and questions in writing.* Handle them the same way phone inquiries are handled, and always be consistent with rental criteria and community policies.

Personal visits are the ultimate in first impressions. Phone calls make up the largest share of inquiries, and the predominant way most properties rent is by the prospective resident driving or walking by the building. This translates into a visit to the rental office or unit if the community is small. Everything leading up to an eventual rental (or failure to rent) tips the scale. Those first impressions may decide whether an individual decides when she walks in to just gather some information and leave or ask to see an apartment. Personal presentation has a tremendous amount to do with those decisions.

If customer contact will be a daily task, then it is imperative that individuals be aware of their presentation and the manner in which they greet prospective residents. First, pay attention to the professionalism your representative is presenting. Ask this fundamental question: If you walked into a community for the first time and the office was unkempt and the first individual you met was poorly dressed and groomed and didn't show enthusiasm, would you rent? The answer in most cases would be no.

Personal Presentation Rules for Customer Contact

❑ *Dress professionally and be well-groomed.* Business attire that properly fits should be the standard. If more than one person is located in an office, then uniforms or common dress themes are advisable. Name tags, too, are always helpful to visitors.

❑ *Stand and greet visitors with a welcoming handshake.* Of course, professionalism in dress also needs to extend to attitude. To work in the rental environment, everyone has to believe in what he is selling; if he doesn't, it will be apparent to everyone who enters the environment. When someone enters the rental area, go to that person; don't make him come to you. Introduce yourself, welcome him, and ask his name and how he can be helped.

❑ *Always remain enthusiastic.* Even when an answer to a question may not be what the person wants to hear, there are many ways to politely give an answer.

❑ *Question in a conversational manner.* Always try to form answers that accentuate the community and its positive assets relative to the question.

❑ *Always suggest alternatives.* If an answer is no, don't leave it at that. Try to approach the issue from another angle. Having visitors fill out an information card always makes for easy reference to their names and situations and leaves the door open to future contact.

The whole goal of the first in-person contact is to further the process along, assess the visitor's interest, proceed to prequalify the person, and finally have a visitor apply. This fact should never leave the mind of anyone who meets and greets prospective renters. However, cheerful and positive will win the day over harried and canned. It is okay to have a practiced presentation, but comfortable communication and conversation always disarms individuals.

Invariably, there will be times where more than one prospect shows up at the same time. Always acknowledge those who may have to wait. Use this time to have them fill out an information card and constantly acknowledge their presence if the first visitor is taking an inordinate amount of time. Occasionally another individual might be there for negative reasons, because she is unhappy or upset with something. If this is the case, be creative in trying to minimize the potential damage when a new visitor stops in. Keep the same outward presentation with the visitor and, when returning to the problem, maintain composure. If it is possible to relocate one of the individuals to another room or area within the environment, that is advisable. Always apologize for any inconvenience but otherwise do not comment further.

First impressions lead to furthering the process. Whether that first impression is the result of someone's driving by the property, an advertisement, Internet source, phone or personal contact, pay attention. "Community" is reflected not only in the brick and mortar, but in how people feel when in your community and how they perceive they are treated.

Simple keys to remember:

❑ Property presentation is a key ingredient in first impressions, for better or for worse.
❑ Advertising should be reviewed constantly to make sure content is consistent and representative.
❑ Phone and personal contact with prospective renters should be enthusiastic and conversational.
❑ Asking questions can help understand what a person's goal is.
❑ Internet responses should be same day.

The Rental Pitch: Closing the Deal

A key point in the relationship between a prospective resident and the community representative is the transition from visitor to applicant. If the goal is to have every visitor who comes in the door apply and qualify, what can be done to affect this process? The guest card can be used as a springboard for posing questions that determine if a visitor is qualified to rent and that more clearly explain a visitor's needs. If asked correctly, questions can lead to affirmations. For instance, if a person isn't sure what size unit she is looking for, a rental professional might clarify by asking if this person will be renting alone. If the answer is yes, a rental agent might then ask if the individual has particular furniture or computer equipment. What you are trying to discern is the need for possible extra space. Armed with a better understanding, a rental professional then can try to suggest available choices for the visitor.

This "feeling out" process also applies to *prequalifying* visitors. Prequalifying is essentially a querying process between a rental professional and visitor where the outcome should be a mutual agreement that if the community is appealing, then a person could qualify to rent according to the community's posted rental criteria. It's done by reviewing basic financial information as well as preferences for apartments and probable move-in target dates.

The rental professional can reach reasonable conclusions by taking information when the visitor enters the office and then asking questions that clarify the individual's ability to financially afford the apartment and the community's ability to provide the desired product. No assumptions should be made other than what applies to the posted rental criteria. An example would be an individual who wishes to rent a one-bedroom apartment but, when questioned further, indicates that five people will be occupying that apartment. The rental criteria have published standards on maximum occupancy of an apartment, and for a one bedroom it is less than five. The individual would not qualify. (It is important to repeat that when it comes to fair housing, there should be no distinction between children and adults.)

Another example would be if the criteria clearly state that one week's income must equal one month's rent. If the rent for the apartment is $1,000 a month and the individual clearly indicates that he earns $500 a week, then he clearly could not afford the apartment by the rental criteria. These standards have to be applied the exact same way at all times, though for now we're limiting the discussion to how the rental professional applies these criteria to the move-in process and qualifying process. Many of the legal concepts related to the renting process were discussed in Chapter 6 (on leasing).

The prequalifying process should not be forced; that is, it is only a tool that may be used. Some individuals may want to see an apartment. They want the full presentation, and that should take place. Rental professionals must keep in mind, though, that they won't please everyone and may encounter negative reactions from people they can't accommodate. Here are some ways to handle negative reactions:

❑ *Suggest alternatives.* If someone is looking for a unit that is clearly too small, suggest a larger unit; suggest that the person examine whether he can afford a larger rental. If an individual is not financially able to rent a certain-size unit, suggest a downgraded or less expensive unit. Always ask people if the choices being presented suit their needs. Never tell them what they want.

❑ *Clarify.* Do not assume that you understand what is upsetting someone. Ask questions to make the person respond explicitly, so you can determine if there is an alternative solution.

❑ *Offer an explanation.* Some visitors might attempt to "force" a situation or push the rental process. As long as you are clear on why they may not be qualified, then politely state the facts. Do not at any time end the rental process on pure opinion or assumption.

If prequalifying moves forward successfully, then the actual application process should take place. The application process is the time to completely verify all pertinent information. It may be an uneasy process because an applicant should be required to fill out all information and produce all pertinent documentation. There will be times when someone tries to convince a rental professional that this all the information available. A rental professional should be well versed in all alternative pieces of documentation and be wary of someone who's trying to convince him that anything less is adequate. This process of seeing the application through can become emotionally charged, too. By this time, visitors-turned-applicants may be convinced this is where they want to rent and eventually reside. They become more emotionally attached to the decisions they have made even though sometimes they've made that decision knowing full well they do not have the financial wherewithal to afford the apartment, but still they believe they can somehow get by. They will try to shade the truth or avoid what they know will not show well in the application process and seek to convince a community representative of their overall ability to afford the rental.

Stay diligent with the qualifying standards you've created and posted and insist politely on receiving all pertinent information. When confronted with this type of customer issue, suggest acceptable alternative sources of documentation and income. In other words, try to be a partner in making the rental work. If you can help make it work *by the rules,* you'll have solidified what could become a long-term relationship. And if through this process you cannot satisfy the applicant, then at least it should be apparent that you made a clear effort. Never avoid or procrastinate when it comes to the application process, even though it may not be comfortable at times. The individual who has decided to apply is anxious; making someone wait, even for negative news, only leads to greater frustration.

Money issues should be explained up front and in detail. For instance, if the policy is to have a nonrefundable application fee and a refundable deposit to secure an apartment, then make sure an applicant fully understands these terms—it will be important especially if the applicant fails to financially qualify. Many rental office arguments have occurred over what monies are refundable and which are not. If an issue regarding funds becomes overtly contentious, then the short-term gain in a few dollars might be canceled out or even trumped by ill will. When dealing with the renting public and fees, advise your staff to be flexible. Bad news travels fast and furious at times.

It is important to note that while the legal aspects of the rental application process have been discussed before, the customer service aspects are of equal importance. From the visitor stage through the applicant stage, if you want an individual to become a resident, learn to communicate properly. Even if it doesn't work out and the relationship seems to be coming to a premature end, individuals who go through the process will tell others how they were treated. Rental professionals must keep in mind that their actions and demeanor reflect on the community no matter what. Many prospective residents may have friends and relatives who already live at the community or may one day look to rent. The remainder of this chapter, however, deals specifically with the applicant-turned-resident.

Simple keys to remember:

❑ Prequalifying an individual is useful only as it relates to written rental criteria.

❑ Closing a rental deal requires some tough questions to be asked and answered. A rental professional needs to be thorough.

❑ Handling objections, no matter how sensitive, is the key to a successful rental professional.

220THE PROPERTY MANAGEMENT TOOL KIT

220 THE PROPERTY MANAGEMENT TOOL KIT

❑ Understanding the emotions that go into the decision to apply for an apartment, and being sensitive in your responses, are also valuable skills.

The Move-in: Securing the Future Renewal

Up to this point, the customer has been somewhat transient. If he is not handled correctly, he simply won't come back. If the property is in a market where there's high demand, management may not even register that bad customer contact is the cause. Once an individual comes to sign a lease and move in, though, his presence is more stable and permanent. If staff is not sensitive to the needs of the applicant-turned-resident, then an owner will soon discover that through high turnover.

Move-in day is possibly the most important day in a person's residency. How well this day goes forms the resident's opinion about the long-term relationship. Why? Through the rental process an applicant was marketed a concept and a lifestyle. An apartment is a means to that end, and once an applicant makes the conscious decision to rent at one place over another, the emotional process of "taking possession" already begins. The person is mentally invested in the process.

People also have a significant financial investment in that day, too. If they come with positive expectations, anything less than advertised can be devastating. A staff should therefore put maximum value on the move-in process. It can certify for new residents that the community they have chosen is backed with quality service. Of course, it can do quite the opposite, too, if the move-in is mishandled.

What should a staff do to make move-in day run smoothly?

❑ *Make sure, during the rental process, that applicants see what they will rent.* Don't show upgrades that will not exist in the person's eventual apartment, or if you do, be very clear to point out the differences.

❑ *Pick a realistic move-in date.* Don't put the make-ready staff in a position where they cannot deliver quality. One day longer for a perfect apartment might mean one year longer on the residency.

❑ *Explain the details thoroughly.* Newly approved future residents should know what they will need to have and do prior to the move-in day. Spend significant time explaining, verbally and in writing, all the necessary details about monies, documentation, and how to notify utilities, for example.

❑ *Prepare all move-in documents prior to a resident's arrival and make it easy for a new resident to review.* Spend time explaining all important portions of the lease that the resident will most likely deal with while living in the community, especially the rent policy and rules.

❑ *Physically inspect the apartment the resident will move into prior to her arrival.* And correct any problems, no matter how minor, before the resident takes possession.

In regard to the last item, customer service isn't limited to the rental or management team. Move-in day is when maintenance personnel become intimately involved with a resident, and most likely they will have more contact with a resident than the office staff does from this point forward. Maintenance personnel need to be sensitized to this fact and brought into the process. They need to understand how important their actions are to resident retention. One often-made mistake is overlooking a problem in a new make-ready as "minor." For example, let's say there's a burn in a countertop in the kitchen. Don't try to cosmetically "hide" it, because it won't look good. For what a countertop traditionally costs, it is better to replace it. Put yourself in the shoes of the new resident. This person is committing several thousand dollars in this apartment and the staff is trying to skimp on a $100 item expecting the new resident to live with it because it is minor.

Whenever new residents arrive for the move-in, greet them with a team approach, if the staff is large enough. A representative from management and maintenance should be present. Something that always softens up new residents is some type of "welcome gift." Make this gift something they might have forgotten or have packed, such as toiletries. Also, allow residents to thoroughly inspect their new home, and have maintenance personnel on hand to fix anything that causes concern, even if your staff thinks residents are just being picky. Of course they are; this is their new home, after all.

There will be times when something negative occurs that is unavoidable. An example is if an apartment was "pre-leased," meaning that the former resident had indicated a move-out date and a new move-in was scheduled based on that date, but the former resident moves out later than scheduled. As a result, the apartment isn't completely finished on the scheduled move-in day. It is best to inform a new resident prior to arrival that there may be a problem with the move-in. One of the biggest mistakes a staff can make is allowing a new resident to be surprised.

If a resident has a serious objection to something on move-in day, provide alternatives. If alternatives are not possible, then make whatever concessions will satisfy this new move-in. There shouldn't be any negativity involved on move-in day; even if the day doesn't start as planned, a quick recovery can make all the difference. The wrong answer on move-in day is that nothing can be done to address residents' concerns. New residents will feel like they've been taken, and quite possibly they'll begin revising their opinion about staying long term right at that moment.

If new residents cannot be satisfied, is it proper to allow them to back away from renting? Yes, absolutely it is. Forcing a completely dissatisfied individual to commit to living in the community simply won't work. The term of the lease will be miserable for the resident and the staff, and the ill will created will undoubtedly be transmitted to other existing and potential residents. It is always important for an owner or a manager to understand that every action leads to a reaction and short-term satisfaction may be sacrificing long-term stability.

A sincere ownership looks to build a reputation and a sense of community that carries itself. If you force people into a situation and don't treat them with care, that reputation will never be solidified—in fact, the opposite will occur. Make move-in day special and it may be the event that carries a resident into a long-term relationship with your community.

Simple keys to remember:

❑ Move-in day is the start of a long-term relationship or the beginning of the end, depending on how it is handled.

❑ Having all paperwork and the apartment prepared prior to move-in will make the day go smooth.

❑ Emotions can run high on this day, so be sensitive to this fact.

❑ Be prepared with alternatives in case you need to recover from a bad start.

Continuing the Customer Contact

Once the resident has moved in it is time to move on and forget she exists, right? Obviously this is not the case. Many staffs make the mistake of ending the contact at this point, but there are many opportunities and reasons to keep the resident contact constant and fresh.

❑ *Many individuals won't outwardly voice their dissatisfaction.* They may have had no choice but to accept the apartment as is, because they committed. If the staff doesn't continue to have contact with them, then you won't know about their dissatisfaction and there'll be no way to fix the problem. Too many individuals reach the end of their lease term and simply leave because of their dissatisfaction.

❑ *Building a sense of belonging to a community is important to many people.* They don't know their neighbors but they do know the staff, so the staff can become the bridge to welcoming them to the community.

❑ *Constantly informing residents of community activities transmits interest on behalf of the ownership or management.* This sends a signal to residents that their happiness is and will be a shared experience.

It should be the policy of your staff to continue the process of communicating and listening to residents. A constructive way to operate is to have the staff contact new residents the day after move-in and ask them if they have settled in and whether everything went satisfactorily. Ask them if they are happy with the condition of the apartment. This may sound redundant, but remember some people don't respond verbally. If you send a note or call on the phone the day after move-in, the resident has a chance to answer in a much less intimidating and pressured situation. If the resident has issues, deal with them immediately. Most people are forgiving if a staff reacts quickly.

Make a habit of reviewing with your staff how move-ins take place. It is good to discover if a common theme or pattern develops that points to flaws around move-in day. The more that this day and the ones immediately after can be handled efficiently and with care, the less likely a staff will have to deal with a perpetually unhappy resident.

There are many ways to continue this contact throughout a resident's lease period that indicate that ownership is truly concerned about residents' happiness, safety, and comfort. As mentioned in an earlier chapter, bad maintenance practices and customer service are the main reasons people tend not to renew. Maintenance, therefore, is an important customer satisfaction topic. It starts with an effective maintenance response to concerns raised by residents. Make sure staff understands how to handle a maintenance concern—how to take a call, document a call, and follow through on a call. It is vitally important when taking a maintenance call to discern whether a resident is giving the staff "permission to enter" to make repairs in the resident's absence. This at times becomes a problem; some residents do not feel comfortable with other individuals being in their apartment in their absence. It is best for a staff to honor whatever the resident requests; it will gain trust.

Many staffs make the mistake of trying to force the "permission to enter" option, disregarding the fact that a resident may have had a bad experience in the past.

Many times when a resident has a maintenance issue and an appointment needs to be set, the issue lingers for far too long and the resident becomes disenchanted. Having to set appointments does effect the workload of the staff, but more often than not if the first maintenance call goes well, most residents will drop their guard and begin to trust the staff and the "permission to enter" dilemma clears itself rather quickly.

How staff members handle themselves in a resident's apartment, which again is the person's home, is also important. Protecting a resident's personal belongings and keeping a clean workplace is essential. Whatever else happens, leaving a home the way it was found is of the utmost importance. If, for some reason, something personal to the resident is damaged or some features of the apartment are compromised, such as staining a carpet, there should be no good reason the management does not take responsibility. There may be a cost, but the cost of watching that resident leave at the end of the lease term is far greater.

It is advisable to consider leaving with residents some sort of feedback form to fill out to indicate whether the maintenance experience was a good one and whether they in fact were satisfied with the service. A "door hanger" form is shown in Figure 10-1. It not only informs the resident that staff was in the apartment to perform maintenance tasks, but asks the resident to rate the service and give comments. Make sure that whatever form you use allows residents to respond in writing or by a phone call. Remember that everyone does not choose to respond the same way and if options can be provided, the chances are greater that honest responses will get back to management. Honest responses breed an understanding, which improves the process, and ultimately that improves the relationship.

Another maintenance-related issue in regard to resident relations is the emergency call during nonoperating hours. This type of call typically occurs late at night or on the weekends, and it becomes a source of sensitivity with residents when issues are not handled correctly. The emergency call procedure must be clearly defined with a resident at move-in. Most important, from a customer service point of view, is that a resident must be able to reach and talk to a human being as quickly as possible when an emergency happens. The vast majority of "emergencies" are not that at all; they are inexperienced home dwellers not understanding how to handle a simple problem in their home, and a phone call usually solves the issue very quickly. Response time, once it is determined there is a truly serious situation, is imperative. The maintenance professional handling the call should always let an individual know exactly how long it will take to arrive on the scene.

Figure 10-1. "Door hanger" feedback form.

Community _____

Resident _____

Address _____

Work order _____
_____

Technician _____

Date _____ Time _____ am ❑ pm ❑

Maintenance
Was in Your Home Today

How Was Our Service?

Our goal is your 100% satisfaction with our service.

Your opinion is important to us. Your comments will help us serve you better.

Please feel free to drop in our comments box or call

our manager at _____

or e-mail us at _____

Yes ⭕	No ⭕	Was our staff considerate while taking your service order?
Yes ⭕	No ⭕	Did we take care of your service order promptly or when promised?
Yes ⭕	No ⭕	Were you satisfied with the completed service?
Yes ⭕	No ⭕	Was the service area left clean?

MAINTENANCE EMPLOYEE IS IN YOUR HOME NOW!

If the community is big enough, it is advisable to have a service, usually subcontracted, that records on a nightly basis any calls so that the management knows what has taken place the night before. If the staff isn't large enough, there should be a policy of debriefing a manager each morning on any issues that took place the night before. There should also be a "call" procedure whereby as an issue escalates, the management is advised and involved. If resident concerns are routinely handled well, the number of truly monumental events should be small. And if residents are handled correctly in a real emergency situation, their confidence level in the staff will increase significantly.

If an emergency occurs that will inconvenience residents for an extended period of time, such as a heating system being down or water supply being disrupted, communicate as honestly as possible with residents early on. If they are upset with the inconvenience, they'll become more upset about not knowing what is wrong and how long it will take to fix. Most people realize mechanical systems sometimes break through no fault of the staff; they can be patient. But if residents are uninformed, distrust starts to form and they start to doubt the staff's sincerity. It is always advisable to create some type of communiqué to the residents that provides them with basic information in the case of a major loss of utility or amenity.

One final note about maintenance and its net effect on customer satisfaction: If a staff prepares an apartment properly on move-in and maintains the physical plant on a daily basis, it lessens the chances that a problem will occur during a resident's lease term. It's then more likely that the apartment is satisfactory and the resident is happy with her or his home.

There are many other ways to maintain positive resident contact throughout the lease term that have nothing to do with paying rent or making maintenance calls. Prudent management learns that creating a sense of community is vital to resident retention. Some methods are relatively simple:

❏ Send birthday cards and holiday cards to residents. (Make sure holiday cards are generic. Never assume a person's religious orientation.)

❏ Create a monthly or quarterly community newsletter. Use it to inform and educate residents and provide tips on apartment living.

❏ Make periodic calls to residents with no precipitating event, simply to ask how they are doing and get feedback.

❏ Create resident events, such as serving coffee and doughnuts on a Friday morning, and annual "resident appreciation days." Make these events very special to the residents of the community.

❑ Sponsor larger community events on the property, such as blood drives and toy drives for the holidays.

❑ Sponsor resident contests such as flower contests to help beautify the property and engage residents in their own community.

❑ Volunteer to spearhead a neighborhood watch program.

All these events serve to remind residents that you in fact do value their residency and that they are all part of the community. Each resident contact becomes an event in a person's lease term that may determine whether he decides to renew and stay in the community. Each contact should therefore carry significance. Many staffs have the feeling that the only time they hear from some residents is when they are unhappy. Why is that? More than likely it is because the staff doesn't proactively reach out to these residents on their own; they wait for the bad news. If they really never get to know their residents, then of course when something negative occurs it becomes amplified. It is essential that your staff reach out constantly to residents during their lease term.

Simple keys to remember:

❑ Contact a resident the day after move-in because it sets a positive tone.

❑ Performing maintenance is a key customer service component. Be sensitive to this fact.

❑ Contact residents throughout the lease term. Think about using creative measures to engage residents.

Resolving Resident Conflicts

There are many different reasons that residents get into conflicts with other residents, with each other in one apartment, or with management over living habits. The reasons are as varied as the multitude of personalities that are on this earth. Multifamily living requires a respect for others and willingness to make adjustments to others. Some people settle in with that, yet others have problems. In management, the community staff are often put in the position of being the keeper of the guard, which they should be, but sometimes they are put plain in the middle. There is a tact and procedure that all multifamily professionals should gain and follow to successfully navigate these situations.

Typical Situations a Management Team Has to Handle

❏ *Internal Conflicts Between Roommates or Family Members.* The home is where personal business is taken care of, and unfortunately, it sometimes spills out into the community or becomes a financial issue between roommates who do not see the joint responsibility.

❏ *Conflicts Between Neighbors.* Everyone lives close and the walls in many apartments are not the thickest. People don't always appreciate the way others live.

❏ *Living Behaviors That Are Unsightly or Unhealthy to Neighbors.* Management has responsibility for the entire community; sometimes what one person does is not good for the community.

❏ *Residents Who Are a Danger to Themselves.* Unfortunately, some people are left in apartments who shouldn't be. You may think they may be someone else's responsibility, but if they are in a community, it becomes something the management has to address.

❏ *Issues of a Financial Nature.* These should be cut-and-dried but they aren't always that clear. Managers may be uncomfortable "chasing debt," but it is a very necessary part of the job.

The procedural aspect of dealing with these issues is very similar and to some extent has already been discussed. Every state and locale has its own indigenous paperwork and procedure that needs to be followed precisely or else issues will not come to the conclusion a manager hopes for. Basically, a written warning to any clear violation of the lease needs to be sent to a resident with a cure date. This is often known as a *cease order.* If the violation continues past the cure date, then a second notice is sent indicating legal action or eviction actions may be initiated. In many places this second notice is called a *quit order.* These names and procedures again are not absolute and vary across the country, but there is a similar procedure virtually everywhere.

The second commonality with these issues is that, with the exception of nonpayment of rent, showing cause to evict is usually far more difficult because proof is necessary and corroboration from other residents may be difficult. Courts therefore should be the avenue of last resort.

Managers should become adept at handling and solving conflicts without having to force the most serious form of action. Many of the issues that occur are in a gray area when it comes to lease violation. In this case, using the courts is not a possibility.

How, then, should a management team handle such issues? Let's work the aforementioned list backward and explore each scenario:

❑ *Financial Matters*. Nonpayment of rent is basic to living in an apartment and most jurisdictions have clear-cut procedures. The general rule of thumb is that if you have a policy on rent, stick to it. Require a late fee after the late date. Have a consistent legal filing date each month and follow the eviction procedure through on each case. What about negotiating payment plans? This is not advisable past small amounts because the rent accumulates each month and an individual with any size debt won't catch up.

Often a manager will be asked to remove late fees or legal fees. Use judgment here. If a resident can prove it was a mistake or a mishap, then removing fees is acceptable. If an individual has rarely been late, removing the fees is a courtesy gesture. Anyone else who has been there before is probably taking advantage of your good nature. If someone claims a check was lost, then suspend fees until the issue can be proved or cleared up. Put the onus on the resident to do the legwork. If the check or money order was truly lost, there will be remedies.

If the late payment was management's fault, always reverse the charges. When arguments ensue over fees, such as fines from lease violations and damage to an apartment, again use judgment. The aggravation may not be worth the money. Gauge the issue against the value of the resident involved and the severity of the issue.

❑ *Residents Who Are a Danger to Themselves*. Sometimes residents grow mentally or physically ill, or are left in an apartment long past the time they can care for themselves. This usually comes to the attention of the management by behavior patterns that manifest themselves in public, a neighbor complaint, or a visit to the apartment. Always approach these issues with understanding and care. Emergency contact information should have been obtained at move-in. If this information is available, contact a family member and discuss the issue with that person. If the family member is unavailable or unresponsive, then contact the local authorities. Again, each town is different, so the local police may intercede or they may direct you to another agency. This may be a painful and uncomfortable issue for a manager to confront, but owners and managers alike have to remember that an irrational human being can be a danger to the rest of the community if left unchecked. Imagine the example of a person who has over time been afflicted with Alzheimer's and does not remember to turn off the stove. That individual's neglect could hurt many innocent people.

❑ *Living Behaviors That Are Unsightly or Unhealthy for the Community.* Some people just live differently, but sometimes their way of living is unacceptable because it compromises the health and safety of the community. In addition, some living behaviors are not conducive to multifamily living, and although their presence may not be unhealthy, they disturb the "quiet enjoyment" of the other residents in the community.

Some examples are leaving garbage outside the front door of the apartment when there are clearly marked garbage receptacles, leaving a half-torn-apart car leaking oil in the parking lot, or not curbing a dog on the property. Most of these incidents can be considered lease violations or violations of the rules and regulations of the community.

An effective manager politely confronts the situation personally. People always react better to direct contact. Sometimes people don't perceive what they are doing as "wrong," so having a dialogue helps solve a situation with less animosity. It also creates a buffer for surrounding residents. If a resident were to receive a pure violation letter, he might assign blame to a neighbor. This is never a good thing.

When the management personally handles these situations, it shifts a resident's focus, and neighbors also see that. Managers who remain neutral and explain to residents this is a community for all, and therefore rules have to be followed, often get very good cooperation. If a resident refuses to comply after discussing and requesting his cooperation, follow through on the procedural requirements.

❑ *Conflicts Between Neighbors.* Playing referee wasn't supposed to be part of the job description, but it often is. An example of this type of conflict is a neighbor playing a stereo too loud in the opinion of another neighbor, but the neighbor playing the stereo believes it is reasonable. First of all, no matter who reports the issue, never reveal a complainant to a resident voluntarily. As a manager, you can inadvertently cause more harm this way. Always indicate it is your responsibility to investigate any claim objectively. Always investigate the claim in this manner, continually emphasizing that all sides of an issue will be reviewed.

If there is a clear guilty party, verbally reason a solution, but back it up in writing. On occasion the parties simply do not like each other, which makes the situation all the more sensitive to handle. Always handle it fairly. If it appears one party is being favored, World War Three could be inadvertently started. If the parties involved simply become uncooperative, then discuss equal adjudication for both parties.

Letting both parties know they will suffer equal punishment can often stop an issue dead in its tracks. Most individuals are looking to be a "victor" in these situations. It is not always advisable simply to offer a transfer to another apartment without first understanding if the individual you'll move cannot live around other people. It is more appropriate to try to make people understand they rented a particular apartment and will have to abide by the lease terms. If a resident-on-resident issue gets violent, stop being a referee and involve authorities.

❑ *Internal Roommate or Family Issues.* Domestic issues are those that carry the most emotion and are the most difficult with which to deal. A rule of thumb is to always treat roommates and spouses the same, even if you feel one is more at fault. They are renting the apartment jointly. Management deals with the residents and the occupancy. Drawing sides in domestic issues can be very dangerous.

If a manager feels there is a domestic situation that may be dangerous to a spouse, roommate, or child, then he should contact the proper authorities immediately. A manager has to confront these issues because more than likely other members of the community are disturbed by them. As a rule, though, a manager should limit involvement to tenancy issues only and leave the other issues to individuals trained to handle them. Don't ignore such situations, because it can drive other residents away and serious harm could occur, but don't overinvolve the staff.

Eventually some people will end up being evicted. The eviction procedure is available to regain possession of an apartment for the ownership when an issue has reached an impasse and the resident is clearly in violation of the lease terms. Each locale has a different procedure, but most jurisdictions require an officer of the court to affect the actual eviction. Make sure this procedure is followed; it is a clear violation of law to stage an eviction without proper procedure and professional support. When someone is forcibly removed from "her" home, it can be emotional and it could become dangerous. An owner or a manager can also expose himself to penalties and fines for attempting an independent eviction.

There are some creative ways to deal with residents who need to leave. Offer a resident out of the lease obligation and reduce financial penalties if he will leave on a prescribed date. The goal is to get the apartment back so the short-term financial loss will allow the apartment to become income producing again. There have been instances where a creative manager has offered money in return for a resident voluntarily moving.

When residents pay the bills, though, they still have to be communicated with on sensitive issues. Tact, fairness, and neutrality can usually bring these issues to a more reasonable solution. Management should always do what is best for the community and should constantly verbalize that this is what its role is. If property management handles issues correctly, respect will grow and most residents will appreciate the way issues are dealt with.

Simple keys to remember:

❑ Conflict can happen in multifamily housing because, by its nature, it puts individuals in very close proximity who don't all live the same way.

❑ Viewing issues objectively is a must for managers.

❑ Contacting people in person almost always produces the best results.

❑ Looking out for what is best for the community at large should always be a priority to a manager. Fairness is always respected.

■ Expand Your Team in Stages

When thinking about moving from one to many properties, the need to rely on others becomes an absolute. As a portfolio grows, the ability for the owner to keep pace with the activity grows too, and the need to have better control over the collection and movement of information becomes central to how an owner understands how multiple investments are performing.

Fee management is an option, but it has to be looked at as an absolute option because you are ceding day-to-day operational control over many (if not all) aspects of running your properties to an agent. There are many very good fee management organizations out there, but all fee managers have their own internal motives and goals. The first decision to make internally is how big and how fast do you intend on expanding? If the expansion will be rapid, then fee management may be a way to have established management practices in place right away and a workforce to maintain the real estate.

The next decision to be made is how much day-to-day control you need and want. Some investors want to grow real estate by creating investment portfolios with many investors such as *syndications*. This kind of investor looks more at the financial deal for the collective and is probably not adept at the actual operation of the individual pieces of real estate. Fee managers often operate in this relationship. If, however, you plan to expand through a strategy of long-term investing, with you as the key investor on each one of the deals, then fee management won't be the best option.

If you decide to manage in-house as opposed to hiring fee managers, then start giving thought to what pieces of the management puzzle are most important. If you want to keep pace with the evolution of the investments, you have to ask yourself the same key question you asked when purchasing that first property: What are your management weaknesses?

If your weakness is in daily management of the real estate, then concentrate on hiring a seasoned manager of multiple properties. If your weakness is in bookkeeping, then hiring someone with these skills is the first step. No matter how small the expansion first is, owners should know their weaknesses and augment the managerial function with an individual whose strengths best complement the owners' capabilities. Pick this individual carefully because this person may become your alter ego in regard to the dynamics of the properties and the management.

Multiple properties grow the management activity exponentially and therefore weaknesses will magnify very quickly. An individual who only owns one property can review and discuss at great length what is occurring on a property. When expanding, there may be multiple problems taking place simultaneously at separate locations. The ability to mull over decisions becomes a luxury, and single-handedly understanding the nuances of one town over another is difficult to mentally manage. An owner has to start the transformation. Being a "hands-on" manager is less important than being able to process information from other sources. Those other sources should be people with whom the owner communicates well and who understand how to manage the owner's real estate according to ownership goals.

Part of the decision-making process will be determined by the size of the properties. If the properties in general are small, they will carry with them small staffs that the owner will have to rely on heavily, but most likely won't have very broad skill sets. The owner will end up doing many of the more typical management functions until the number of properties justifies having a central management staff. If the first properties are a bit larger, then the sites themselves will probably have specialists and the collective units will allow support from a central place. If the first investments are located in a tight regional circle, then the support can almost grow within that group. This is why keeping the initial investments in close proximity to one another (as close as the economy and market will allow) is an important concept to keep in mind.

One strategy can be to augment your staff with subcontractors or vendors to cover certain tasks. Ownership could decide to have payroll done by outsourcers such as Automatic Data Processing, Inc. (ADP). The owner could hire a maintenance company to perform the repairs or unit turns. There are even companies that market and rent for an owner. One such company is CLASS, which stands for Certified Leasing and Sales Specialists. CLASS often is hired to rent apartments quickly when a property has many vacancies or an ill-suited rental staff. These services come at a cost, but the more repetitive aspects of the business, such as producing payroll, are usually logical choices for outsourcing.

If the portfolio has multiple properties, it is now also time to start getting to know the personnel. Even if the owner is more adept at the paperwork and not field operations, site visits are still essential so the owner can start identifying individuals who excel at one aspect of the business or another. As an owner realizes what works and what type of individual works in each position, the owner should start building a profile of the ideal candidate for each job class in the portfolio. Sooner or later the job of hiring individuals for each position will fall out of the hands of the owner and on to other employees. Establishing a job description and personality for each position will allow the owner to feel more confident that a good fit between employee and employer is being made.

Property management is a people business, and the initial group of people you, as the owner, surround yourself with is critical to the eventual operation and reputation of the organization as a whole. But once the property management task expands beyond that tight inner circle that was first formed, you may reach the point where there are enough employees to warrant a hiring procedure. Here are a few helpful thoughts for the hiring process:

❑ *Create a job description.* Make sure the goals of each position are clear in that job description. Be specific about tasks, functions, and expectations that signify success. Include all mental and physical requirements of a job.

❑ *Use the job description as a general boilerplate for recruiting for a position.* Use it in ads and in interviews to guide a job search. Obviously, different property duties may vary, so edit each one, but keep the general format.

❑ *Ask present performers for help.* The job description may have been created based on the performance of someone on your staff. If staff members helped "write" the job description, then ask them to review an open position and document their answers to questions.

❑ *Be mindful of a personality fit.* Having a cohesive team is critical in the multifamily business in a portfolio-type setting where there are many remote sites, most of them unique in their own right. Because staffs tend to be small and the corporate office is removed from the locations, communication and trust become very necessary attributes. You need a team where each person on the staff interacts well and understands each other. Likewise, if the employees don't mesh with the owner's personality to a certain extent, the message will get lost and the work won't get completed properly.

❏ *Make sure the job application is filled out.* Applications vary significantly, so consider gathering up many examples from other companies and decide which is best for your organization. Then make sure applicants provide all the information requested. A completely filled out job application will tell a story.

❏ *Perform a background check with a qualified company.* Background checks often finish the story by allowing you to verify what the applicant has told you verbally and in writing. Be careful to use services that legally can perform these functions and be mindful of labor laws. If you perform background checks on one potential employee, they need to be performed on all applicants.

Where do you find employees for the multihousing business? This is a question that is very hard to answer. There are very few breeding grounds for this business. Some sources are:

❏ *Universities.* Very few institutions of higher learning have programs for property management. The University of North Texas is one of the few with a degree program for residential property management. More universities are discovering property management is a viable degree path, but the number of individuals nationally who go through these programs remains small.

❏ *Vocational Schools.* Many of your maintenance technicians will go through specific programs to learn technical aspects of becoming an apartment professional.

❏ *Real Estate Licensing Schools.* Individuals who attain a broker's and agent's license usually are seeking careers in real estate.

❏ *Trade Publications.* Magazines that cater to the industry at every level of professional frequently post classified ads and websites in their publications. Some examples are *UNITS* magazine and *Multifamily Executive*. There are regional publications as well.

❏ *Career Websites.* These websites will post resumes and job offerings. The most well-known sites are www.monster.com and www.careeers.com. They are a good way to find someone especially if your office is removed from the property location at which a candidate is needed.

❏ *Search Firms.* Search firms are a source for more technically skilled positions; however, there is a fee attached to procuring an individual this way. Although there are search firms that specialize in property-type people, they tend to provide "temporary to permanent employment."

❏ *Trade Organizations.* This source will be discussed later in this chapter for other reasons; for now, suffice it to say that networking and knowing other professionals breeds relationships with people who understand the business.

Many people come into property management from another career. In fact, there are very few people who start in this business and stay in this field. Having multiple resources for searching is therefore vital.

Your next major decision when expanding your team is: How do you know what to pay?

Because property management is a very regionalized field, there is no set standard. There are many websites such as www.salary.com that can be used as reference guides. You should also contact the National Apartment Association's local affiliate in your area, because it may have that information. Review job advertisements and inquire as a prospective candidate for jobs in the area where your investments are located.

In the end, salary becomes an owner's decision. It is important to note that if benefits such as health insurance will be offered that the cost of an employee is likely 25 percent to 35 percent higher than the base salary. Owners sometimes lose sight of the fact that there are very few employees relative to the value of an investment. Yet just one or a few people can have a tremendous impact, both positive or negative, on how well your property does. To pay well is better than to pay little. Dissatisfaction grows quickly, and because you aren't there on a daily basis to see what is happening to your investment, you'll be highly dependent on the staff.

The most effective way to grow an organization from small to large is through a core group that has worked the properties from the time you purchased them, supplemented with whatever hired professionals you have brought on board. Build from within that team. If the talent base exists, these individuals will grow with the organization and develop a fundamental understanding of how you, the owner, view the real estate. The more the portfolio is understood through the owner's eyes in an operational sense, the more faith you'll have that the investments are operating as you envision. If the core group carries owner-influenced experience and has essential property management, leasing, maintenance, administration, and accounting skills, then they'll mature as the organization matures. In effect, they'll become the ambassadors for the message you want to spread to future personnel.

The more properties you own, the more professional and/or specialized personnel you'll need. Property managers who have been in the field for any length of time are very proud of the fact that they operate in more spheres of management than most anyone they know. A property manager has to be a marketer one day, a good judge of mechanical issues the next, a politician another day, and always a people person. Yet regulatory concerns, technical challenges, and varied occupancy issues, among many other issues, must sometimes require a more watchful eye.

It is important to know who in your core group has specialized skills. As the organization grows, assign professionals from this group to specific aspects of the business until such time as it is clear that even more experienced professionals may be needed in these categories. Some of these areas are:

- ❏ *Environmental.* Oil tanks, asbestos, lead-based paint, mold, and radon—all have specific regulatory concerns. Someone needs to watch them in more detail.

- ❏ *Personnel.* People left to their own devices many miles from the corporate office sometimes need counseling and owners need to limit their liability. There should also be safety in the workplace.

- ❏ *Mechanical.* Bigger properties have bigger problems; someone with a deep understanding of how to handle mechanical inspections and repairs may be necessary.

- ❏ *Technology.* Almost every company and staff uses computers daily to get work done. Managing and supporting that technology can become a full-time job; start assigning someone to understand it.

- ❏ *Leasing and Marketing.* It's what the business is about. A first-class experienced person may become a first-class instructor to others or, at the very least, a role model.

- ❏ *Government and Legal.* A property management organization needs to keep up with laws, codes, regulations, and statutes. Someone should be assigned to track these issues.

- ❏ *Accounting.* Accounting may be an absolute stand-alone function. Regardless, someone from an operations perspective should understand how the numbers work.

By assigning certain aspects of the business to the core group, an owner over time starts building mechanisms to understand changing dynamics as more property is acquired. It may someday be necessary to hire a personnel manager or an information technologies expert or an in-house attorney, but the business at hand is property management. Having property professionals understand these concepts marries them to the business.

You may not think you have the opportunity or luxury to build an organization in stages. Yet in my years of experience, the strongest management organizations I have seen started with a core group and the message stayed with them to success.

Simple keys to remember:

❑ Know your weaknesses.

❑ Look to complement those weaknesses when making all your staffing decisions.

❑ Identify achievers among your staff and use their performance for creating job descriptions.

❑ Make these achievers the inner core of a growing organization.

❑ Carry the ownership message with this group.

❑ Start to specialize.

Develop Corporate Communication Strategies

When expansion is on the horizon, the way a team communicates—and the effectiveness of that communication—becomes a lynchpin of success. The broader the geographic scope of the investments, the more critical communication becomes. As an owner, your ability to be in all places at all times diminishes the more and varied locations you own. If your goal is set to expand continuously, then obviously staff and complexity will grow proportionally. Thus, it is critical to understand how organizational communication can be most effective and how systems can be expanded.

Communication is generated "from and to" the corporate office. This location over time will become the nerve center from which the management operates. When operating those first small investments, it may suffice to run the "corporate office" out of the home. Sooner or later this is not possible and a place of business has to be created. When anticipating creating a corporate office, some thought should go into preparing for the future. What are your future needs and future expansion plans?

When negotiating for office space, most of the people or organizations that you'll be negotiating with will want you to commit to a long-term lease. You'll need expansion room, but if locked into a long-term lease, the space may fill up quickly and there might be an obligation or penalty clause to break that lease. The simple fact that the property management business requires a multitude of paper-work means that storage space for files will become a critical issue. You'll be refer-ring to old files often, so immediate access to these files will be necessary. Federal statutes on keeping and maintaining paperwork vary depending on the documents, but it suffices to say that most of the paper has to be kept.

The second reason to look at space with an eye for the future is specialization. As an organization grows, experience and necessity tell an owner what specialized tasks enhance a management team. Space will be necessary to accommodate these specialists.

If investment partners will be brought in, then the office becomes a meeting site and a reflection of what the ownership wants to communicate. So you have to think about the aesthetics of the office and office location. Obviously, lease rates will escalate with premier locations and you have to decide how much of the man-agement's operating budget will be consumed by the office space. But looking into the future, this office will be a presentation stage; therefore it should not be just a vanilla box.

When looking at space, make sure there is the possibility of setting up a wel-coming public reception area and a meeting room. It is very important if partners will be involved to get a feel for a professional organization. This is taking the "curb appeal" concept and applying it to the office space. First impressions do count. This concept also applies to other visitors such as public officials and residents (many will discover that a main office exists and whether you envisioned them visiting or not, they will).

Finally, the impression the office makes on prospective employment candidates is very important to an organization's growth. If the best people are to be drawn to the management team, then the way they view the organization becomes key to their decision to join the team. I once made the decision that I wanted to work for an organization within the first fifteen minutes I was in the offices. The welcoming atmosphere and the natural friendliness of everyone I came in contact with was so pronounced that it was clear to see these people liked working there.

Work environment has everything to do with work performance, so the office space becomes critical to the way an organization is perceived and perceives itself. Remember, every day will be filled with communication to residents who often have issues that need to be resolved. If the office staff does not feel comfortable and if the work environment is not conducive to keeping stress levels to a minimum, then that will be reflected in the behavior or attitude the staff projects to the public. Negative customer transactions and employee turnover can be directly related to work environment. When internal tensions surface, created by personnel who aren't happy where they are, they'll feed that unhappiness in large helpings to those with whom they come in contact—namely, the residents. Again, it cannot be over-emphasized that the way staff mentally operate once they hit the office doors in the morning becomes a personality that represents the business.

The space and how it is allotted should obviously be functional to the business. Property management realms of responsibility will differ from organization to organization, but in general most firms will have an accounting function, an administrative function, an operations function, and a public receiving area. Creating an office kitchen and sitting area is very functional, too, again because it benefits the staff's mental outlook on the office and the business. Most likely the staff will expand in the future in areas where ownership recognizes weaknesses, so allow room for potential future employees as well.

Make sure, too, that the space you'll eventually lease can technically handle all your communications equipment. Typically a management office will require copying machines, fax machines, postage equipment, phone equipment, and computer servers. As an organization grows, communications equipment becomes critical to daily business. This equipment will also need to be monitored and serviced and it will need to have expansion capability, so the space and location become especially important.

The farther a central office is located from the investments in your portfolio, the more communication will take place over the phone or by computer or fax machine, and the less often you'll actually visit the real estate. Even so, it is always important for ownership to stay physically connected with the real estate as much as possible. Location is important also to how employees operate. The farther away from the home office the real estate is located, the more time key personnel spend simply getting from location to location. Therefore, less time gets spent between site personnel and home office personnel on substantive work.

Picking Key Office Personnel

Now that you've expanded to a central office, you need to fill the key positions of:

❑ Receptionist
❑ Office manager
❑ Portfolio property manager or regional property manager

One of the most important individuals to consider is who will answer the phone. The receptionist, although not high up on the management structure totem pole, is the voice and the personality of the organization. The way the phone is answered and the way calls are passed and questions are answered is important. If a receptionist is cold and impersonal, the caller is now sensitized to that emotional mind-set, and the next person who takes the call is probably going to start a conversation with someone who is guarded and tense. Projecting the right image may seem like a skin-deep concept, but as they say, perception is reality. You want to smoothly transition people from being callers to happy consumers.

Many companies are substituting a human voice with voice mail. Voice mailboxes are great as a secondary connection, but systems that start with voice mail leave the individual calling with the feeling that the ownership will do all it can *not* to have personal contact. In the real estate management business, most of the calls from residents to this office are because of an issue that needs to be resolved. The quicker residents speak to someone who appears to be concerned and provides at least a preliminary answer or direction, the sooner they'll feel as though they are being serviced. (And remember, renters who think their concerns aren't handled properly will tell other renters about their experience.)

A good receptionist can take all the bite out of somebody before the call is transferred. When picking a receptionist, look for someone who has a positive disposition, likes to talk and listen, has patience, and is diplomatic. This person is the front line for the organization, so care needs to be taken in selecting someone for this position. When the wrong person is put in the chair, it also is a high-turnover position.

If voice mail is used, again it should be for secondary contact. Early in the evolution of an organization it is important to establish that phone calls are to be personally answered whenever possible and messages should be returned promptly. Human beings do not like to feel they are ignored or insignificant. Property professionals have to continually remember that they are always dealing with people for whom the apartments aren't an investment—rather, those apartments are their homes, and they spend a large share of their total income on this home.

Another individual your organization will rely on is the office manager. In the property management field, two things are certain: There will be a lot of paper and there will be a substantial amount of conversation about that paper and how it relates to the day-to-day management of apartments. Organization becomes critical to storing and retrieving information, and accurate information is a necessity to the property management function. A skilled office manager who understands these concepts will become ever more critical as an organization grows.

This individual will help create office communication systems and work flow, such as the routing of important documents and memos and the review of all documents such as leases and move-out rationales. This person will also help an owner refine the details of procedures—and the larger an organization gets, the more the procedures will be essential. The monthly management cycle will have scheduled tasks that generally fall in the same time period each month, and if systems aren't refined the detail will get missed.

An effective office manager will be detail oriented and disciplined when it comes to the repetitive tasks that take place in the property management business. The office manager will be someone who can understand how the different parts of an operation, such as management and accounting, need to integrate to a certain extent; the office manager is usually the facilitator to this end. The office manager often also becomes a conduit to the administrative functions that are performed at the site level and helps an owner maintain continuity from site to corporate office.

Owners may choose to immediately remove themselves from the daily operating of the investments to focus on the investment portion of the business. Alternatively, an owner may, over time, need to transition out of the day-to-day operations because of size and time constraints. Once either one of these possibilities takes place, the portfolio property manager or regional property manager becomes a necessary part of the puzzle.

This individual will serve as the owner's eyes and ears and will be the front-line communicator to site staffs. This individual will serve as the bridge between those defining company goals and those charged with actually carrying out those goals. It is essential that managers at this level have practical experience in managing a site because they will need to motivate and instruct others and they will also have to carry out ownership's wishes. This person will need to be a first-class communicator, a motivator, and a problem solver. This individual needs to have a grasp on all the aspects of a management team and needs to be able express the necessity and importance of each discipline to the others so that they all work as an integrated machine. Finally, this person needs to be able to handle multiple situations virtually simultaneously, even though they may be very different in scope. One property may have a mechanical issue to deal with, while another may have a legal concern and the main office may have an administrative issue about downfield work. A good portfolio manager is sensitive to all of these circumstances and many more.

When deciding on an individual to handle this important job, make sure that philosophically you and the portfolio manager view the investments (and how they are managed) the same way. This individual is carrying on your business in your physical absence; therefore the person in this position will be speaking and acting for you, for better or for worse. Picking an individual who does not mirror your philosophical mind-set is a recipe for disaster as an organization grows.

Other key office personnel may also be necessary as an organization becomes more sophisticated. A controller or chief financial officer will at some point be necessary. An information technology (IT) professional may become a necessity. A personnel, or human resources, function will become essential to manage the internal business of a property management organization. There will be others. My present organization is large enough that a separate payroll department exists, as well as insurance specialists and specialized management personnel such as a leasing director.

The main point I want to make, though, is that the core individuals you place on your original team at that new office will create the system that becomes the signature of your organization for years to come.

Communication Tools

It has never been easier to get a message to someone than it is in today's technology age, and it has never been more important to understand how to utilize all the communication tools at your disposal. Property management is a mix of two big essentials: paperwork and physical communication. When expanding, you need to know how to keep both these functions operational and efficient.

In the office, the copier and the fax machine are your workhorses. Choosing this equipment can be a chore in and of itself. The copying equipment will be used nonstop. Most likely you'll be leasing these machines because they are so technical and sensitive that buying is not economically advisable. So make sure a very good eye reviews the lease documents. These leases often have restrictions on included servicing, as opposed to premium servicing. These leasing agreements can run for lengths of time that far outlast the useful life of the equipment, and therefore contract length should be a negotiable item.

Be sensitive to functionality when adding this equipment to the office. You may need double-sided reports and collating features; you may need color copying and printing. The clarity and quality of your printed documents are always important when you are communicating information to residents and employees. Picking a copier with scanning and e-mailing capability may be invaluable. Original documents can be scanned and transmitted within seconds of a request.

Pick a phone system that is expandable. As you grow, reinventing the wheel with each major expansion becomes costly, so plan for the future. The phone system should have several key functions, including individual voice mail and remote re-trieval. It should have a directory for in-house and often-dialed individuals or sites. It should possess speaker phone and conferencing abilities and it should be sturdy because it will be heavily used.

The most significant office communication tool today is the computer, and if it wasn't a consideration when there were only one or two investments, it is an abso-lute must when expanding. The computer has become the ultimate weapon in the property management operation. Choosing computer equipment for a main office is both confusing and critical. These systems must serve as many functions that take place in an office as possible, although some disciplines, such as graphics design, require specialized machines. Make sure the machines you pick will serve all of your business functions properly. These questions are essential to ask when choosing computer equipment:

❑ *Speed.* Ask the computer dealer about memory and processing speed. If the com-puters cannot handle the volume of work a management office has on any given day, then you'll have unnecessary downtime.

❑ *Storage Space.* Information will be added every day. The more hard disk space, the longer the computer will be functional to the operation.

❑ *Port Compatibility.* Make sure all printers, scanners, and Internet cables can attach to the computer.

❑ *Software Compatibility.* Make certain all software chosen can be loaded and oper-ated on the machines chosen.

❑ *Speed and Storage Expandability.* Is the unit able to have these functions expanded to meet your changing (future) requirements? Expandability is important when assessing the overall cost, over time, of the equipment.

❑ *Connectivity.* Is this unit able to satisfy the ever-growing need that the computer serve as a communication tool connected to the Internet or an internal network?

As the number of computers in your office environment grows, eventually you'll want to expand to a central "server" type of system. The server houses all general files and manages the speed and efficiency of the integrated office system. When choosing a server, consider the number of possible users, not only today but in light of your *five-year plan* or your expansion plans. In terms of storage capacity or *archive capability,* you want a "future proof" system so that as the number of users grows the speed of daily backups will keep up. At some point the service agreements with suppliers is a critical decision, too, since computer hardware and software can be complicated and needs constant servicing.

There are operational concerns with computers as well:

❑ Form factor (i.e., the computer's size and shape) matters because computer "towers" all have to be located at the workspace.

❑ Aesthetics is important as well, both in how the equipment affects the office decorum and how the operator views the screens. Flat-screen monitors are more expensive, but they take up less space and look better because they produce a sharper image.

❑ Centrally located printing equipment is efficient, but these items will then be shared and that will sacrifice speed. So another decision point is whether each operator should have independent printing capability.

The Internet, Intranet, and Cell Phone

The computer runs your management software, accounting software, word processor and spreadsheets, as well as specialized management tasks. But the computer is also the primary vehicle for communicating downfield and in the office itself. This communication happens over the Internet and intranet.

What is the difference?

The Internet is public. It is accessible to everyone and anyone. If transmissions go out on the Internet, they are susceptible to individuals who look to use or take your information. Anything discussed on the Internet is in the public domain. The intranet exists only on what is called the local area network (LAN) and, therefore, it is internal to your organization; it isn't in or accessible to the public domain. Both networks provide a venue for instant communications of thoughts and documents, including pictures. Sales, marketing, management tools, and training can all be accessed by the Internet. Both communication sources are invaluable in property management to tie together the rental locations and the home office. However, both carry with them some concerns:

❑ *Security.* Security of organizational information passed on the Internet is essential. The "firewall" is the gatekeeper of your system. It prevents unauthorized access to your system by blocking transmissions that don't meet certain security criteria. The firewall, in combination with antivirus protection, stops people from "infecting" your computers.

❏ *Access.* If the employees at work have Internet access, they have the ability to "surf," and that potentially takes them from their work as well. If it becomes necessary, a technician can add software filters to control access time and restrict where a person can go online.

❏ *Shared Files.* Shared files mean shared access. Nothing is private about computer-generated communication. Designing an access security structure that limits access to certain files at certain levels may be necessary.

❏ *E-mail.* E-mail is a very important communication tool, but with it comes etiquette and misuse problems. An e-mail that includes a misunderstood comment can start an inner-office argument. Be sure to set a policy about allowed versus prohibited uses of company e-mail.

The cell phone and now the BlackBerry, which combines e-mail and phone capability, are tools that suit the portfolio property manager in particular. This manager often has to commute from site to site. With the advent of hands-free cell phones, the car has become a place for the business of business to continue. Site personnel often have to get answers quickly, such as approval to purchase expensive equipment or make an emergency repair. The cell phone allows instant access so the site can move these tasks along. It also makes up for commuting downtime because the manager can return calls while going from place to place. The calling plan is important, though, because minutes will be used up in bundles and a plan not appropriately purchased can become quite expensive very quickly.

In a business where people at the site level rely on information and communication, technology has far more positive aspects than negative ones, but it is a function that has to be managed. Decisions relative to technology become among the organization's most important because there is an intrinsic cost in managing and maintaining technology and training people to use it. As expansion takes hold, poor decisions will drive down productivity. Sooner or later the organization will want to consider bringing someone in-house to maintain and service all this technology.

Communication Philosophy

Once the central office is picked, the equipment delivered, and key personnel added to the team, establishing a communication philosophy now becomes essential. There are two facets to this philosophy: internal communications as it relates to passing of information and directives, and external communications that serves as a marketer of the organization.

Internal communications should be standardized. In property management *everything should be documented*. Each piece of documentation has significance to someone in the organization. For this reason, create a "routing policy" for the core group. Make it clear who needs to see what memos and documents and when. This policy will perpetuate itself down the chain. For example, I require thresholds on spending. The policy is that any project over X dollars and any invoice over X dollars has to be reviewed and approved. A threshold on delinquency has been established and upper management has to be made aware of anyone exceeding that threshold. Legal documents have to be routed to certain individuals and directives need to be routed to department heads.

Establishing these policies very early on structures communications and also establishes a collective intelligence about what is occurring in the organization. Establish a regular meeting with the core group and then later with other, specific groups so that as an owner you stay in touch with the issues of the day. Require these meetings to be consistent. One essential meeting would be with different department heads. Because they exist in different operational and philosophical environments, the need to keep them all on the same page is important.

You might also want to institute orientations to expose the downfield personnel to the home office operation and environment; otherwise these people may never get to see the main office. Having them understand who they work for carries with it a valuable message. Company newsletters are another internal communication tool for ownership and upper management to inform employees as an organization grows. If the organization is made up of smaller, geographically separated entities, companywide events can serve as a way to connect them. Require, too, that "like groups" such as site managers communicate. It is a way to create peer groups among staff that spend a lot of time on their own.

You should also establish communication standards when discussing any matters with the public. Some recommendations follow:

❑ The occupants of your apartments are not to be referred to as tenants; they should always be viewed and discussed as residents and guests.

❑ Residents dwell in their homes, not an apartment, and the property should be referred to as a community.

- Calls from residents should be returned in a required time frame.
- Presentation is part of communicating, so establish a dress code.
- Disagreeing with a resident should never be done in a personal manner or in a disrespectful way. Sometimes the resident needs to be counseled, but this should be done with the same respect that a resident is shown at all times.
- Residents should be communicated with regularly. The move-in day shouldn't be the end of that communication.
- Property newsletters are just as effective as company newsletters.
- Advertising should be reviewed and approved by senior-level management and ownership because it is a reflection of the organization.

As an owner, establish communication philosophy and procedures as early as possible to solidify the personality of the organization. Depending on how well communication is controlled, it will enhance (or damage) the reputation of an organization as it grows. The office environment, the tools, and the people are only as good as the philosophy that is imparted to them.

Simple keys to remember:

- Develop a corporate communication strategy; if there are remotes sites, it should be a priority.
- Sensitivity to office location and design is important when creating a corporate environment.
- Consider carefully the choices concerning key home office personnel when expanding.
- Pick the tools of communication carefully.
- Establish a philosophy for internal and external communications early in the corporate expansion.

Network in the Industry

Rental markets can vary significantly even when properties are located just a town or two apart. Owners who purchase or invest where the deal makes the most financial sense may end up in a locale they know little about. Local nuances to regulations, codes, or statutes can affect the way an ownership operates. Depending on the locale, for example, nonpayment cases may be handled by a magistrate, not a judge. A new owner to a market may not know how that market operates and whether the existing staff on a newly purchased property is up to the task.

To help navigate the marketplace there are several industry trade organizations that serve as a communication and support system for their members. Many of these organizations have local chapters as well as a national umbrella organization. The three most prevalent organizations are:

National Apartment Association (NAA)
201 N. Union Street, Suite 200
Alexandria, VA 22314
Phone: (703) 518-6141
Website: www.naahq.org

Institute of Real Estate Management (IREM)
430 North Michigan Avenue
Chicago, IL 60611
Phone: 1-800-837-0706
Website: www.irem.org

National Multi Housing Council (NMHC)
1850 M Street, NW, Suite 540
Washington, DC 20036-5843
Phone: 202-974-2300
Website: www.nmhc.org

Each group mentioned is renowned for different aspects of the business. Generally speaking, for example, the NAA is known for its vast affiliate network nationwide. IREM is known for its education and certification programs, and NMHC is widely respected for its ability to affect housing policy, both on a federal and state level.

There are also specialized groups such as the National Affordable Housing Management Association (NAHMA) and the Independent Rental Owners Council (IROC). Trade organizations can include the local chamber of commerce as well. Most of these organizations communicate with each other and on many issues form coalitions when the need arises.

What are the benefits to you of joining one or more of these organizations?

❑ They keep you informed of local, state, and federal legislation that will affect the industry and the investment.

❑ They lobby on owners' behalf at all levels in regard to legislation.

❑ They provide platforms for information exchange in the form of websites, publications (such as the NAA's *UNITS* magazine), and regularly scheduled meetings.

❑ They serve as think tanks and idea exchanges. Many of the individuals who belong to these organizations have been successful in the industry. Any meeting attended usually can teach the average owner something.

❑ They serve as networking and support groups. Each ownership and management organizations sometimes feels that it experiences unique problems. Join and stay active in one of these groups and you will find you are not alone.

❑ They are a source for possible future employees. By networking through these organizations, people meet people and form relationships, many of which go on to become business relationships that last through time.

❑ They serve as a collective marketing venue for the industry as a whole, one goal of which is to attract better people to the industry.

❑ They promote education. Industry-recognized certifications from trade industry programs are available in all disciplines, from management to maintenance to leasing. Many of these organizations offer periodic seminars on important issues of the day, whether it is environmental issues, legal issues, or new marketing techniques.

❑ They sponsor trade shows and expositions. Through product introduction, there is a chance to see all that the market offers and to become sensitized to products and services that assist and support the industry.

❑ They may have local affiliates through which an ownership can gain access to immediate resources to understand and operate in a new market.

Many of members of these trade organizations are competitors, yet when coming together they become partners of sorts working toward the same purpose of improving the industry and helping each other understand the ever-changing marketplace. If investing in a new market, inquire with these organizations about local affiliates near the property. If possible, contact them before purchasing. More than likely there will be individuals in these associations who are familiar with the market and the particular property and can provide invaluable background and insight into both. These organizations typically have a dues structure, but the dues are well worth the value returned for money.

As your organization grows, encourage team members to participate in these professional organizations, too. As the owner, you'll need to rely on these staff people to be your conduit to a changing multifamily environment. Trade organizations that sponsor seminars, education programs, and/or awards programs also become a source of enrichment and motivation to the employee base. It has been my experience that awards programs have a significant motivational benefit because many individuals who work in the multifamily industry have never been recognized for their efforts and to nominate someone for an industry award—and better still, to have them win an award—provides energy for these individuals to keep progressing. And you want them to be energized because remember, they are watching after your investment.

The business of owning and managing multifamily real estate involves keeping up-to-date with constant changes in regulation and an ever-evolving marketplace. Once an owner ventures into multiple locations and markets, it becomes increasingly more difficult to stay in touch with what is occurring in those markets. Trade associations are another way for an owner to stay in tune with the real estate as the ability to be physically present on a site diminishes.

Brand Your Company

Because there's an element of uncertainty about where the next real estate investment opportunity might be, you may think you don't need to create a corporate persona. Oftentimes, owners can have a large portfolio but none of the real estate is centrally located. Or the ownership entities are different from property to property, even if slightly, so the commonality is in the managing of the properties. This situation also leads to virtually anonymous ownership personas. Some would argue that keeping a low profile serves a purpose, but there are many reasons why creating a "brand" and a company persona can benefit an organization. If you are beginning to expand, you should be thinking about establishing a mind-set and an image. In fact, branding should be an intentional business strategy as an organization goes from few to many properties.

Think about traveling cross-country into towns never before visited. Your natural instinct would be to locate hotels and restaurants that are widely known because they provide a comfort zone for the traveler. People who are relocating to a new community will also gravitate toward a recognizable name and/or a regionally prevalent name. Your property management firm may not be as recognizable as Ramada Inn, but if it appears to offer stability, then prospective renters gain a comfort level with this, too.

There is another very important reason to brand that is more internal: attracting good talent in the industry. A respectable name resonates with industry professionals, and after all, this is a people business. The industry-average turnover rate among employees is 55 percent; therefore, attracting and keeping experienced, motivated talent is one the highest priorities within the industry. A respected name won't go unnoticed in the very small neighborhood that is the property management community.

Ways to Create and Broadcast a Brand for Your Organization

- ❑ Create a company logo and display this logo on all community ads and letterhead.
- ❑ Create a company motto or credo, display it in rental offices, and draw employees' attention to it.
- ❑ Consider creating a company website that contains company history, highlights team members, and clearly states the goals of the organization.
- ❑ Enforce business attire (uniform) policies and name tag policies; standardize as much as possible from property to property.
- ❑ Standardize signage by using similar colors and styles.
- ❑ Advertise in employment and trade journals, again being very conscious of your logos and design.
- ❑ Sponsor industry events and charity events, requesting only that your logo be displayed.
- ❑ Join industry associations such as the NAA or its local affiliate.
- ❑ Encourage officers and management to become active in industry associations; visibility in the industry attracts talented people.
- ❑ Make it policy that any advertisement or any signage be approved at the highest levels of management and ownership.
- ❑ Create community events at each one of your properties that promote a sense of community to all residents and prospective residents.
- ❑ Influence all locations to maintain a positive working relationship with local government officials.

Not unlike the company communication strategy, creating a brand and vehicles to market that brand are essential to the healthy growth of an organization. As time goes on, however, you will need to revisit your branding effort in order to see whether the organization is being consistent with supporting the brand perception the owner has created. If emphasis shifts away from the principles the ownership first espoused, branding can become a liability.

Remember two key concepts discussed in this book: 1) curb appeal and 2) resident referrals as a prime source of continued rentals. If branded material such as signage and uniforms are ignored or allowed to deteriorate, then it will affect how an organization is viewed. If employees do not reflect the company's motto or mission statement, then this too can become a significant problem in regard to your organization's public persona. As discussed earlier in this chapter, an owner's personality has everything to do with how an organization evolves and matures as it grows ever larger. Ownership has to stay diligent in making sure the organization remains true to that personality and reflects an image the ownership is comfortable with.

Branding will also attract financial partners and can influence the perception lenders and government officials have of an organization. This fact cannot be understated. If an organization is trusted and respected, its reputation can make it easier to get past a disagreement or a business problem. Many public officials communicate better with entities that have a public face; they are not as suspicious or guarded when confronting an ownership that they are familiar with. Issues frequently get resolved because these officials see the common ground and are willing to work with reputable firms.

Over time branding also can give your organization leverage with vendors and subcontractors. There is nothing wrong with promoting the fact that your organization is growing and is a reputable player. All suppliers to the multifamily business recognize the value in servicing larger, more successful organizations.

Simple keys to remember:

❑ Trade organizations are a source of education, information, and networking.
❑ Branding is essential to creating and maintaining a positive reputation in the market.
❑ As strategies, both trade organization activity and branding can attract professional talent to the organization.

■ "It's the People"

As your organization grows, the people you bring into the organization and the way that they are nurtured and cultured has everything to do with the continued success of your growing business. Owning and operating multifamily real estate becomes all about the individuals who manage the property on a daily basis. Unlike many other businesses, staffs are small compared to the value of each property, and these individuals spend an enormous amount of time on their own as your representatives. I have been in this industry for twenty years and I have been in other industries as well. I have operated at every management level. I have been fortunate to work with ownership and upper-level management that saw the value in the people who operated these communities each day. The sense of camaraderie and trust that I have been exposed to has become the overwhelming philosophical message I carry with me about operating in this industry.

If you create and maintain a consistent strategy of growing an organization, paying special attention to customer service and employee regard, the organization will have at its core a good foundation that can solidly be built upon over time. The investments have to be acquired with care, of course, but once they are, you as the owner have to operate under one of two mind-sets—calculated and nurtured trust or blind faith— because you cannot be at each property all the time. The prudent owner or manager will not trust blind faith.

Property management requires attention to detail, documentation, follow-up, customer service, mechanical acumen, discipline in regimented tasks, and communication skills, as well as many more talents discussed in this book. Every one of these traits collectively makes for an effective management strategy, but they can all be achieved through the building of a good team. This industry is best suited to growth from within, augmented by that occasional professional who is brought in to enhance a team. The real performers in this industry grow through the business and therefore understand its unique operating environment. For this reason, identifying individuals who possess the work ethic, mental toughness, organizational skills, and love of human interaction is a priority for any owner or manager. Once you have identified these people, keeping them in your organization is equally if not more important as finding them.

Make it a personal priority to continually visit sites and personally get to know each and every person that operates in the field and in your main office. Learn to understand what each of them does at their respective communities. If you are in ownership or upper management, respect the chain of command but don't become dogmatic. Each management and operational level can teach you something and each level has its surprises when it comes to an individual's capabilities.

I once managed a very small property, twenty-three units to be exact. As it goes in the business, the smaller the property the more dependent you are on the individual who manages it. This property was small enough and the income was minimal that it was difficult to find an individual at a reasonable pay rate who could work it with any skills. I was always in need of someone and couldn't keep anybody for any length of time whom I trusted.

One day while visiting the property, a clean-cut young gentleman knocked on the office door. He introduced himself and explained he had just moved to the area and was looking for something part-time because he watched his children after school. I wasn't sure if part-time would work, but given the alternatives I decided to take a chance. This property was a mess, it was broken, and it seemed to me to be somewhat of a lost cause. At the time the number and size of properties directly under my responsibility were enormous compared to this property; in fact, we already knew by now that this property did not fit our portfolio, so I gave this gentleman all the instruction I could and left him to his own devices.

When I returned about two weeks later, I was absolutely astounded by the effort and care this new employee had taken. He had gotten more work done in two weeks part-time than the previous five people combined had in months. The parking area and garbage locations were spotless, the hallways meticulous, and the boiler room spotless. Not only that, the boiler room was newly painted and a log was placed on the heating equipment to indicate operational benchmarks. This new employee had arranged all supplies and told me what he was lacking and what possibly was overstocked. He then proceeded to tell me his game plan for the empty apartments. This man did not have any experience in the business but clearly possessed many of the necessary attributes to manage in this industry. This man's hard work and attention to detail enhanced the value of this property from what its perceived value was only a few months before his arrival.

As I said, we knew this property did not fit our portfolio and we intended to sell it, but without a doubt I also knew this was an individual I had to somehow retain. In his present capacity the job was getting rather easy, so I asked him if he would take on another challenge and split the week between two locations. We had a community more than double the size that shouldn't have been floundering, but it was. It was about fifteen miles away from his original location, but it was across a state line and it was suburban as opposed to inner city. The second property had potential; it just never lived up to it. I saw a property that needed daily TLC and

I had found someone to give it. This property would also require this gentleman to concentrate more on the paperwork side of the business because it was much more active, and it had a difficult occupancy.

This man was now operating two very different properties in two different markets simultaneously, and he was operating them both better than any of his predecessors had before he arrived. When we sold the first property, we located our employee to the second suburban property where he achieved monumental success, so much so that I knew this challenge would also be conquered in short measure. I asked him if he wanted to attempt a quantum leap to a much larger property, but I also asked for his input about a replacement at his present site. And I told him that in his next position I wanted him to partner with one of my best site managers and learn the nuances of the business. That partnership would take place on a 300-plus-unit property that was one of our signature properties, but the maintenance was always lacking. Just one year after taking over the maintenance department and working with this manager, this property was named property of the year in the state association awards. The next year it won again and this gentleman won maintenance manager of the year.

We moved this person to a 700-unit apartment community, where he repeated both the awards and the financial success of the entity through his work ethic. We noticed in him many of the same motivational aspects that we, as an organization, looked to extol upon all our people. Nine years after walking into that small apartment complex office looking for part-time work, this phenomenal human being is one of our regional vice presidents in charge of a portfolio. And his performance is excellent at that level, just as it's been at every level.

If this were an isolated story it would make for a happy ending but wouldn't completely stress the point. People are what drive this industry, and investing in people who exhibit acumen for this industry should be a focus of every owner and top manager. If you can find or recognize someone who exhibits capability and a mental affinity for this business, you can grow an organization of people who all see the glass as half full. There was no mistake in partnering this gentleman with the seasoned manager who started with us as a leasing agent, went on to run our property very successfully, and is now our corporate director of leasing and marketing. If you will recall the story from Chapter 3, she's the former accounting person who now is responsible for our largest entity, real estate valued at more than $100 million. We have another gentleman who started at a forty-eight-unit apartment community who now designs and creates most of our marketing and branding materials, including building and managing our company website. Many of our office personnel have been with the organization for decades, not just a year or two.

Brick and mortar and wood and aluminum are what the buildings you invest in are made of. And you rent an apartment, the proverbial four walls. What keeps people in those apartments and what influences people to refer others to your community is the customer service and the care the people you have entrusted with your investments give them. The attitude and standards that you create and the people you pick and nurture are the vehicles for that customer service and for continuing to grow the type of communities you envisioned when you invested in your first property.

In real estate, more than any other industry I know, the trust necessary for your investments requires one thing over anything else: the right people. Repeat that as a daily operational mantra and spend as much time as you can realizing its significance. The way your staff maintains and markets the property you purchase will determine its ultimate value to the prospective renter and in the marketplace (unless the product you purchase is new construction, and even then it will have its own warts that will need ongoing attention). Real estate can be a very satisfying investment and career. I wake up every day thrilled with the relationships I have made and the accomplishments of those I have managed. The investments, by and large, have been very successful. My hope is that this book has made the basics of the business evident and the goals clear.

Property management is a customer service business that requires attention to detail, follow-up, and consistent systems. Most of all, it's the people—it's the good people—and it always will be.

Appendix A

NAA Lease Contract

This is a binding contract. Read carefully before signing.

Date of Lease Contract: _____
(when the Lease Contract is filled out)

Moving In—General Information

1. PARTIES. This Lease Contract is between *YOU*, the resident(s) *(list all people signing the Lease Contract):* _____

   _____ and the owner:

   (name of apartment community or title holder). You've agreed to rent
   Apartment No. _____, at _____ (street address) in _____ _____ (city), Louisiana, _____ (zip code) for use as a private residence only. The terms "you" and "your" refer to all residents listed above. The terms "we," "us," and "our" refer to the owner listed above (or any of owner's successors in interest or assigns). Written notice to or from our managers constitutes notice to or from us. If anyone else has guaranteed performance of this Lease Contract, a separate Lease Contract Guaranty for each guarantor is attached.

2. OCCUPANTS. The apartment will be occupied only by you and *(list all other occupants not signing the Lease Contract):*

3. LEASE TERM. The initial term of the Lease Contract begins on the _____ day of _____, _____ and ends at Midnight the _____ day of _____, _____. This Lease Contract will automatically renew month-to-month unless either party gives at least _____ days written notice of termination or intent to move-out as required by paragraph 37. *If the number of days isn't filled in, at least 30 days notice is required.*

4. SECURITY DEPOSIT. The total security deposit for all residents is $_____, due on or before the date this Lease Contract is signed. This amount *{check one}*: ❑ does or ❑ does not include an animal deposit. See paragraphs 41 and 42 for security deposit return information.

5. KEYS AND FURNITURE. You will be provided _____ apartment key(s), _____ mailbox key(s), and _____ other access devices for _____. Any resident, occupant, or spouse who, according to a remaining resident's affidavit, has permanently moved out or is under court order to not enter the apartment, is (at our option) no longer entitled to occupancy, keys, or other access devices. Your apartment will be {check one}: ❏ furnished or ❏ unfurnished.

6. RENT AND CHARGES. You will pay $_____ per month for rent, payable in advance and without demand {check one}:
   ❏ at the on-site manager's office, or
   ❏ at _____

   Prorated rent of $_____ is due for the remainder of {check one}:
   ❏ 1st month or ❏ 2nd month, on _____

   Otherwise, you must pay your rent on or before the 1st day of each month (due date) with no grace period. Cash is unacceptable without our prior written permission. You must *not withhold or offset rent unless authorized by statute.* We may, at our option, require at any time that you pay all rent and other sums in cash, certified or cashier's check, money order, or one monthly check rather than multiple checks. If you don't pay all rent on or before the _____ day of the month and we haven't given notice notice to vacate before that date, you'll pay an initial late charge of $_____ plus a late charge of $_____ per day after that date until paid in full. Daily late charges will not exceed 15 days for any single month's rent. You'll also pay a charge of $_____ for each returned check, plus initial and daily late charges from due date until we receive acceptable payment. If you don't pay rent on time, you'll be delinquent and all remedies under this Lease Contract will be authorized. If you violate the animal restrictions of paragraph 27 or other animal rules, you'll pay an initial charge of $_____ per animal (not to exceed $100 per animal) and a daily charge of $_____ per animal (not to exceed $10 per day per animal) from the date the animal was brought into your apartment until it is finally removed. We'll also have all other remedies for such violation.

7. UTILITIES. We'll pay for *the* following items, if checked:
   ❏ water ❏ gas ❏ electricity ❏ master antenna ❏ wastewater ❏ trash ❏ cable TV ❏ other _____
   You'll pay for all other utilities, related deposits, and any charges, fees, or services on such utilities. You must not

allow utilities to be disconnected for any reason—including disconnection for not paying your bills—until the lease term or renewal period ends. Cable channels that are provided may be changed during the Lease Contract term if the change applies to all residents. Utilities may only be used for normal household purposes and must not be wasted. If your electricity is ever interrupted, you must use only battery-powered lighting. If your utility charges are determined by an individual utility meter or an alternative formula, we will attach an addendum to this Lease Contract in compliance with state agency rules or city ordinance.

8. INSURANCE. We *urge you* to *get your own insurance for losses due to theft, fire, and water damage.* You intend to {check one}:

   ❏ not buy insurance to protect against such losses, or
   ❏ buy insurance from your own agent to cover such losses.

   If neither is checked, you acknowledge that you will not have insurance coverage.

9. SECURITY DEVICES. Keyed lock(s) will be rekeyed after the prior resident moves out. The rekeying will be done either before you move in or, if the apartment has a keyless deadbolt on each exterior door, within 10 days after you move in.

   You may at any time ask us to: (1) install one keyed deadbolt lock on an exterior door if it does not have one; (2) install a bar and/or sliding door pin lock on each sliding glass door; (3) install one keyless deadbolt on each exterior door; (4) install one doorviewer on each exterior door; and (5) change or rekey locks or latches during the lease term. We must comply ❏ doorviewer with those requests, but you ❏ sliding door pin lock must pay for them.

   What You Are Now Requesting. You now request the following to be installed at your expense (if one is not already installed), subject to any statutory restrictions on what you may request.

   ❏ keyed deadbolt
   ❏ keyless deadbolt ❏ sliding door bar

   Payment for Rekeying, Repairs, Etc. You must pay for all repairs or replacements arising from misuse or damage to devices by you or your family, occupants, or guests during your occupancy. You may be required to pay in advance if we notify you within a reasonable time after your request that you are more than 30 days delinquent in reimbursing us for repairing or replacing a device

Initials of all Residents: _____

which was misused or damaged by you, your guest, or an occupant; or if you have requested that we repair, install, change or rekey the same device during the 30 days pre-ceding your request and we have complied with your request.

Special Provisions and "What If" Clauses

10. SPECIAL PROVISIONS. The following special provisions and any addenda or written rules furnished to you at or before signing will become a part of this Lease Contract. These "Special Provisions" will override any sections of this lease in conflict with the Special Provisions. _____. See page 6 for any additional special provisions.

11. EARLY MOVE-OUT; RE-RENTING CHARGE. You'll be liable to us for a re-renting charge of $ _____ if you:

(1) fail to give written move-out notice as required in paragraphs 23 or 37; or
(2) move out without paying rent in full for the entire Lease Contract term or renewal period; or
(3) move out at our demand because of your default; or
(4) are judicially evicted.

The *re-renting charge is not a cancellation fee and does* not *release YOU from your obligations under this Lease Contract. See the next paragraph.*

Not a Release. The re-renting charge is not a Lease Contract cancellation fee or buyout fee. It is an agreed-to estimate covering only part of our damages, that is, our time, effort, and expense in finding and processing a replacement. These damages are uncertain and difficult to ascertain—particularly those relating to inconvenience, paperwork, advertising, showing apartments, utilities for showing, checking prospects, office overhead, marketing costs, and locator-service fees. You agree that the re-renting charge is a reasonable estimate of such damages and that the charge is due whether or not our re-renting attempts succeed. If no amount is written in this lease contract, you must pay our actual re-renting costs so far as they can be determined. The re-renting charge does not release you from continued liability for: future or past-due rent; charges for cleaning, repairing, repainting, or unreturned keys; or other sums due.

12. DAMAGES AND REIMBURSEMENT. You must promptly reimburse us for loss, damage, government fines, or cost of repairs or service in the apartment community due to a violation of the Lease Contract or rules, improper use, negligence, or intentional conduct by you or your invitees, guests or occupants. Unless the damage or wastewater stoppage is due to our negligence, we're not liable for—and you must pay for—repairs, replacement costs, and damage to the following if occurring during the Lease Contract term or renewal period: (1) damage to doors, windows, or screens; (2) damage from windows or doors left open; and (3) damage from waste-water stoppages caused by improper objects in lines exclusively serving your apartment We may require payment at any time, including advance payment of repairs for which you're liable. We have not waived our right to collect these payments from you if there is a delay in our demanding payment from you.

13. PROPERTY LEFT IN APARTMENT. "Apartment" excludes common areas but includes interior living areas and exterior patios, balconies, attached garages, and storerooms for your exclusive use.

Removal After Surrender, Abandonment, or Eviction. We or law officers may remove and/or store all property remaining in the apartment or in common areas (including any vehicles you or any occupant or guest owns or uses) if you are judicially evicted or if you surrender or abandon the apartment (see definitions in paragraph 42).

Storage. We may store, but have no duty to store, property removed after judicial eviction, surrender, or abandonment of the apartment. We're not liable for casualty loss, damage, or theft. You must pay reasonable charges for our packing, removing, or storing any property.

Redemption. If we've removed and stored property after surrender, abandonment, or judicial eviction, you may redeem only by paying packing, Removal, and storage charges. We may return redeemed property at the place of storage, the management office, or the apartment (at our option). We may require payment by cash, money order, or certified check.

Disposition or Sale. Except for animals and property removed after the death of a sole resident, we may throw-away or give to a charitable organization all items of personal property that are: (1) left in the apartment after surrender or abandonment; or (2) left outside more than 1 hour after eviction is completed. Animals removed after surrender, abandonment, or eviction may be kenneled or turned over to local authorities or humane societies.

14. FAILING TO PAY FIRST MONTH'S RENT. If you don't pay the first month's rent when or before the Lease

Initials of all Residents: _____

Contract begins, all future rent will be immediately due without notice. We also may end your right of occupancy and recover damages, future rent, re-renting charges, attorney's fees, court costs, and other lawful charges. Our rights and remedies under paragraphs 11 and 32 apply to acceleration of rent payments under this paragraph.

15. RENT INCREASES AND LEASE CONTRACT CHANGES. No rent increases or Lease Contract changes are allowed before the initial Lease Contract term ends, except for changes allowed by any special provisions in paragraph 10, by a written addendum or amendment signed by you and us, or by reasonable changes of apartment rules allowed under paragraph 18. If, at least 5 days before the advance notice period referred to in paragraph 3, we give you written notice of rent increases or Lease Contract changes effective when the Lease Contract term or renewal period ends, this Lease Contract will automatically continue month-to-month with the increased rent or Lease Contract changes. The new modified Lease Contract will begin on the date stated in the notice (without necessity of your signature) unless you give us written move-out notice under paragraph 37.

16. DELAY OF OCCUPANCY. If occupancy is or will be delayed for construction, repairs, cleaning, or a previous resident's holding over, we're not responsible for the delay. The Lease Contract will remain in force subject to: (1) reduction of rent on a daily basis during delay; and (2) your right to terminate as set forth below. Termination notice must be in writing. After termination, you are entitled only to refund of deposit(s) and any rent paid. Rent reduction or Lease Contract termination does not apply if delay is for cleaning or repairs that don't prevent you from occupying the apartment.

If there is a delay and we haven't given notice of delay as set forth immediately below, you may terminate up to the date when the apartment is ready for occupancy, but not later.

(1) If we give written notice to any of you when or after the Lease Contract begins—and the notice states that occupancy has been delayed because of construction or a previous resident's holding over, and that the apartment will be ready on a specific date—you may terminate the Lease Contract within 3 days of your receiving the notice, but not later.

(2) If we give written notice to any of you before the effective Lease Contract date and the notice states that construction delay is expected and that the apartment will be ready for you to occupy on a specific date, you may terminate the Lease Contract within 7 days after any of you receives written notice, but not later. The readiness date is considered the new effective Lease Contract date for all purposes. This new date may not be moved to an earlier date unless we and you agree.

17. DISCLOSURE RIGHTS. If someone requests information on you or your rental history for law enforcement, governmental, or business purposes, we may provide it.

While You're Living in the Apartment

18. COMMUNITY POLICIES OR RULES. You and all guests and occupants must comply with any written apartment rules and community policies, including instructions for care of our property. Our rules are considered part of this Lease Contract. We may make reasonable changes to written rules, effective immediately, if they are distributed and applicable to all units in the apartment community and do not change dollar amounts on page 1 of this Lease Contract.

19. LIMITATIONS ON CONDUCT. The apartment and other areas reserved for your private use must be kept clean. Trash must be disposed of at least weekly in appropriate receptacles in accordance with local ordinances. Passageways may be used only for entry or exit. Any swimming pools, saunas, spas, tanning beds, exercise rooms, store rooms, laundry rooms, and similar areas must be used with care in accordance with apartment rules and posted signs. Glass containers are prohibited in or near pools and all common areas. You, your occupants, or guests may not anywhere in the apartment community: use candles or use kerosene lamps without our prior written approval; cook on balconies or outside; or solicit business or contributions. Conducting any kind of business (including child care services) in your apartment or in the apartment community is prohibited—except that any lawful business conducted "at home" by computer, mail, or telephone is permissible if customers, clients, patients, or other business associates do not come to your apartment for business purposes. We may regulate: (1) the use of patios, balconies, and porches; (2) the conduct of furniture movers and delivery persons; and (3) recreational activities in common areas.

We may exclude from the apartment community, to the extent permitted by Louisiana statutes, guests or others who, in our judgment, have been violating the law, violating this Lease Contract or any apartment rules, or disturbing other residents, neighbors, visitors, or owner representatives. We may also exclude from any outside

Initials of all Residents: _____

area or common area to the extent permitted by Louisiana statutes, a person who refuses to show photo identification or refuses to identify himself or herself as a resident, occupant, or guest of a specific resident in the community.

20. PROHIBITED CONDUCT. You and your occupants or guests may not engage in the following activities: behaving in a loud or obnoxious manner; disturbing or threatening the rights, comfort, health, safety, or convenience of others (including our agents and employees) in or near the apartment community; disrupting our business operations; manufacturing, delivering, possessing with intent to deliver, or otherwise possessing a controlled substance or drug paraphernalia; engaging in or threatening violence; possessing a weapon prohibited by state law; discharging a firearm in the apartment community; displaying or possessing a gun, knife, or other weapon in the common area in a way that may alarm others; storing anything in closets having gas appliances; tampering with utilities or telecommunications; bringing hazardous materials into the apartment community; or injuring our reputation by making bad faith allegations against us to others.

21. PARKING. We may regulate the time, manner, and place of parking all cars, trucks, motorcycles, bicycles, boats, trailers, and recreational vehicles. Motorcycles or motorized bikes may not be parked inside an apartment unit or on sidewalks, under stairwells, or in handicapped parking areas. We may have unauthorized or illegally parked vehicles towed by following applicable state law procedures. A vehicle is unauthorized or illegally parked in the apartment community if it:

(1) has a flat tire or other condition rendering it inoperable; or
(2) is on jacks, blocks, or has wheel(s) missing; or
(3) has no current license or no current inspection sticker; or
(4) takes up more than one parking space; or
(5) belongs to a resident or occupant who has surrendered or abandoned the apartment; or
(6) is parked in a marked handicap space without the legally required handicap insignia; or
(7) is parked in a space marked for manager, staff, or guest at the office; or
(8) blocks another vehicle from exiting; or
(9) is parked in a fire lane or designated "no parking" area; or
(10) is parked in a space marked for other resident(s) or unit(s); or
(11) is parked on the grass, sidewalk, or patio; or
(12) blocks garbage trucks from access to a dumpster.

22. RELEASE OF RESIDENT. Unless you're entitled to terminate this Lease Contract under paragraphs 10, 16, 23, 31, or 37, you won't be released from this Lease Contract for any reason—including but not limited to voluntary or involuntary school withdrawal or transfer, voluntary or involuntary job transfer, marriage, separation, divorce, reconciliation, loss of co-residents, loss of employment, bad health, or death.

23. MILITARY PERSONNEL CLAUSE. You may terminate the Lease Contract if you enlist or are drafted or commissioned and are on active duty in the U.S. Armed Forces. You also may terminate the Lease Contract if:

(1) you are (i) a member of the U.S. Armed Forces or reserves on *active* duty or (ii) a member of the National Guard called to active duty for more than 30 days in response to a national emergency declared by the President; *and*
(2) you (i) receive orders for permanent change-of-station, (ii) receive orders to deploy with a military unit or as an individual in support of a military operation for 90 days or more, *or* (iii) are relieved or released from active duty.

After you deliver to us your written termination notice, the Lease Contract will be terminated under this military clause 30 days after the date on which your next rental payment is due. You must furnish us a copy of your military orders, such as permanent change-of-station orders, call-up orders, or deployment orders or written notification from your commanding officer. Military permission for base housing does not constitute change-of-station order. After you move out, we will return your security deposit, less lawful deductions. For the purposes of this Lease Contract, orders described in (2) above will only release the resident who qualifies under (1) and (2) above and receives the orders during the Lease Contract term and such resident's spouse or legal dependents living in the resident's household. A co-resident who is not your spouse or dependent cannot terminate under this military clause. Unless you state otherwise in paragraph 10, you represent when signing this Lease Contract that: (1) you do not already have deployment or change-of-station orders; (2) you will not be retiring from the military during the Lease Contract term; and (3) the term of your enlistment or obligation will not end before the Lease Contract term ends. Even if you are entitled to terminate this Lease Contract under this paragraph, liquidated damages for making a false representation of the above will be the amount of unpaid rent for the remainder of the lease term when and if you move out, less rents from others received in mitigation under paragraph 32. You must immediately notify us if you are called to active duty or receive deployment or permanent change-of-station orders.

Initials of all Residents: _____

24. RESIDENT SAFETY AND PROPERTY LOSS. You and all occupants and guests must exercise due care for your own and others' safety and security, especially in the use of smoke detectors, keyed deadbolt locks, keyless bolting devices, window latches, and other safety or security devices. You agree to make every effort to follow the Security Guidelines on page 5.

Smoke Detectors. We'll furnish smoke detectors as required by statute, and we'll test them and provide working batteries when you first take possession. After that, you must pay for and replace batteries as needed, unless the law provides otherwise. You must test automatic fire alarms at the beginning of your lease term and monthly thereafter. We may replace dead or missing batteries at your expense, without prior notice to you. You must immediately report smoke detector malfunctions to us. Neither you nor others may disable smoke detectors. If you damage or disable the smoke detector or remove a battery without replacing it with a working battery, you may be liable to us for $100 plus one month's rent, actual damages, and attorney's fees. If you disable or damage the smoke detector, or fail to replace a dead battery or report malfunctions to us, you will be liable to us and others for any loss, damage, or fines from fire, smoke, or water.

Casualty Loss. We're not liable to any resident, guest, or occupant for personal injury or damage or loss of personal property from fire, smoke, rain, flood, water leaks, hail, ice, snow, lightning, wind, explosions, interruption of utilities, theft, or vandalism unless otherwise required by law. We have no duty to remove any ice, sleet, or snow but may remove any amount with or without notice. Unless we instruct otherwise, you must—for 24 hours a day during freezing weather—(1) keep the apartment heated to at least 50 degrees; (2) keep cabinet and closet doors open; and (3) drip hot and cold water faucets. You'll be liable for damage to our and others' property if damage is caused by broken water pipes due to your violating these requirements. If you ask our representatives to perform services not contemplated in this Lease Contract, you will indemnify us and hold us harmless from a liability for these services.

Crime or Emergency. Dial 911 or immediately call local medical emergency, fire, or police personnel in case of accident, fire, smoke, or suspected criminal activity, or other emergency involving imminent harm. You should then contact our representative. You won't treat any of our security measures as an express or implied warranty of security, or as a guarantee against crime or of reduced risk of crime. Unless otherwise provided by law, we're not liable to you or any guests or occupants for injury, damage, or loss to person or property caused by criminal conduct of other persons, including theft, burglary, assault, vandalism, or other crimes. We're not obliged to furnish security personnel, security lighting, security gates or fences, or other forms of security unless required by statute. We're not responsible for obtaining criminal-history checks on any residents, occupants, guests, or contractors in the apartment community. If you or any occupant or guest is affected by a crime, you must make a written report to our representative and to the appropriate local law-enforcement agency. You also must furnish us with the law-enforcement agency's incident report number upon request.

25. CONDITION OF THE PREMISES AND ALTERATIONS. You accept the apartment, fixtures, and furniture as is, except for conditions materially affecting the health or safety of ordinary persons. We disclaim implied warranties except those required by Louisiana statutes. You'll be given an Inventory and Condition form on or before move-in. Within 48 hours after move-in, you must note on the form all defects or damage and return it to our representative. Otherwise, everything will be considered to be in a clean, safe, and good working condition.

You must use customary diligence in maintaining the apartment and not damaging or littering the common areas. Unless authorized by statute or by us in writing, you must not perform any repairs, painting, wallpapering, carpeting, electrical changes, or otherwise alter our property. No holes or stickers are allowed inside or outside the apartment. But we'll permit a reasonable number of small nail holes for hanging pictures on sheetrock walls and in grooves of wood-paneled walls, unless our rules state otherwise. No water furniture, washing machines, additional phone or TV-cable outlets, alarm systems, or *lock* changes, additions, or rekeying is permitted unless statutorily allowed or we've consented in writing. You may install a satellite dish or antenna provided you sign our satellite dish or antenna lease addendum which complies with reasonable restrictions allowed by federal law. You agree not to alter, damage, or remove our property, including alarm systems, smoke detectors, furniture, telephone and cable TV wiring, screens, locks, and security devices. When you move in, we'll supply lightbulbs for fixtures we furnish, including exterior fixtures operated from inside the apartment; after that, you will replace them at your expense with bulbs of the same type and wattage. Your improvements to the apartment (whether or not we consent) become ours unless we agree otherwise in writing.

26. REQUESTS, REPAIRS, AND MALFUNCTIONS. IF YOU OR ANY OCCUPANT NEEDS TO SEND A

Initials of all Residents: _____

NOTICE OR REQUEST—FOR EXAMPLE, FOR REPAIRS, INSTALLATIONS, SERVICES, OR SECURITY-RELATED MATTERS—IT MUST BE SIGNED AND IN WRITING TO OUR DESIGNATED REPRESENTATIVE (except in case of fire, smoke, gas, explosion, overflowing sewage, uncontrollable running water, electrical shorts, or crime in progress). Our written notes on your oral request do not constitute a written request from you.

Our complying with or responding to any oral request regarding security or nonsecurity matters doesn't waive the strict requirement for written notices under this Lease Contract. You must promptly notify us in writing of: water leaks; electrical problems; malfunctioning lights; broken or missing locks or latches; and other conditions that pose a hazard to property, health, or safety. We may change or install utility lines or equipment serving the apartment if the work is done reasonably without substantially increasing your utility costs. We may turn off equipment and interrupt utilities as needed to avoid property damage or to perform work. If utilities malfunction or are damaged by fire, water, or similar cause, you must notify our representative immediately. Air-conditioning problems are not emergencies. If air-conditioning or other equipment malfunctions, you must notify our representative as soon as possible on a business day. We'll act with customary diligence to make repairs and reconnections. Rent will not abate in whole or in part unless authorized under Louisiana law.

If we believe that fire or catastrophic damage is substantial, or that performance of needed repairs poses a danger to you, we may terminate this Lease Contract within a reasonable time by giving you written notice. If the Lease Contract is so terminated, we'll refund prorated rent and all deposits, less lawful deductions.

27. ANIMALS. No *animals (including mammals, reptiles, birds, fish, rodents, and insects) are allowed, even temporarily, anywhere in the apartment or apartment community unless we've so authorized in writing.* If we allow an animal, you must sign a separate animal addendum and pay an animal deposit. An animal deposit is considered a general security deposit. We will authorize a support animal for a disabled (handicapped) person. We may require a written statement from a qualified professional verifying the need for the support animal. You must not feed stray or wild animals.

If you or any guest or occupant violates animal restrictions (with or without your knowledge), you'll be subject to charges, damages, eviction, and other remedies provided in this Lease Contract. If an animal has been in the apartment at any time during your term of occupancy (with or without our consent), we'll charge you for de-fleaing, deodorizing, and shampooing. Initial and daily animal-violation charges and animal-removal charges are liquidated damages for our time, inconvenience, and overhead (except for attorney's fees and litigation costs) in enforcing animal restrictions and rules. We may remove an unauthorized animal by following the procedures of paragraph 32.

28. WHEN WE MAY ENTER. If you or any guest or occupant is present, then repairers, servicers, contractors, our representatives, or other persons listed in (2) below may peacefully enter the apartment at reasonable times for the purposes listed in (2) below. If nobody is in the apartment, then such persons may enter peacefully and at reasonable times by duplicate or master key (or by breaking a window or other means when necessary) if:

   (1) written notice of the entry is left in a conspicuous place in the apartment immediately after the entry; *and*

   (2) entry is for responding to your request; making repairs or replacements; estimating repair or refurbishing costs; performing pest control; doing preventive maintenance; changing filters; testing or replacing smoke-detector batteries; retrieving unreturned tools, equipment, or appliances; preventing waste of utilities; leaving notices; delivering, installing, reconnecting, or replacing appliances, furniture, equipment, or security devices; removing or rekeying unauthorized security devices; removing unauthorized window coverings; stopping excessive noise; removing health or safety hazards (including hazardous materials), or items prohibited under our rules; removing perishable foodstuffs if your electricity is disconnected; retrieving property owned or leased by former residents; inspecting when immediate danger to person or property is reasonably suspected; allowing persons to enter as you authorized in your rental application (if you die, are incarcerated, etc.); allowing entry by a law officer with a search or arrest warrant, or in hot pursuit; showing apartment to prospective residents (after move-out or vacate notice has been given); or showing apartment to government inspectors, fire marshals, lenders, appraisers, contractors, prospective buyers, or insurance agents.

29. MULTIPLE RESIDENTS OR OCCUPANTS. You are individually responsible for all Lease Contract obligations. You are also responsible for all other residents' Lease Contract obligations. If you or any guest or occupant violates the Lease Contract or rules, all residents are considered to have violated the Lease Contract. Our re-

Initials of all Residents: _____

quests and notices (including sale notices) to any resident constitute notice to all residents and occupants. Notices and requests from any resident or occupant (including notices of Lease Contract termination, repair requests, and entry permissions) constitute notice from all residents. In eviction suits, each resident is considered the agent of all other residents in the apartment for service of process. Security deposit refunds may be by one check jointly payable to all residents; the check and any deduction itemizations may be mailed to one resident only.

Replacements

30. **REPLACEMENTS AND SUBLETTING.** Replacing a resident, subletting, or assignment is allowed *only when we consent in writing.* If departing or remaining residents find a replacement resident acceptable to us before moving out and we expressly consent to the replacement, subletting, or assignment, then:

(1) a re-renting charge *will not* be due;
(2) an administrative (paperwork) fee *will* be due, and a rekeying fee *will* be due if rekeying is requested or required; and
(3) you *will* remain liable for all Lease Contract obligations for the rest of the original Lease Contract term.

Procedures for Replacement. If we approve a replacement resident, then, at our option: (1) the replacement resident must sign this Lease Contract with or without an increase in the total security deposit; *or* (2) the remaining and replacement residents must sign an entirely new Lease Contract. Unless we agree otherwise in writing, your security deposit will automatically transfer to the replacement resident as of the date we approve. The departing resident will no longer have a right to occupancy or a security deposit refund, but will remain liable for the remainder of the original Lease Contract term unless we agree otherwise in writing—even if a new Lease Contract is signed.

Default by Either Party

31. **DEFAULT BY OWNER.** We'll act with customary diligence to:

(1) keep common areas reasonably clean, subject to paragraph 25;
(2) maintain fixtures, furniture, hot water, heating, and A/C equipment;
(3) substantially comply with applicable federal, state, and local laws regarding safety, sanitation, and fair housing; and
(4) make all reasonable repairs, subject to your obligation to pay for damages for which you are liable.

If we violate any of the above, you may terminate this Lease Contract and exercise other remedies under state statute by following this procedure:

(a) you must make a written request for repair or remedy of the condition, and all rent must be current at the time;
(b) after receiving the request, we have a reasonable time to repair, considering the nature of the problem and the reasonable availability of materials, labor and utilities;
(c) if we haven't diligently tried to repair within a reasonable time, you must then give us written notice of intent to terminate the Lease Contract unless the repair is made within 7 days; and
(d) if repair hasn't been made within 7 days, you may terminate this Lease Contract and exercise other statutory remedies. Security deposits and prorated rent will be refunded as required by law.

32. **DEFAULT BY RESIDENT.** You'll be in default if you or any guest or occupant violates any terms of this Lease Contract including but not limited to the following violations: (1) you don't pay rent or other amounts that you owe when due; (2) you or any guest or occupant violates the apartment rules, or fire, safety, health, or criminal laws, regardless of whether arrest or conviction occurs; (3) you abandon the apartment; (4) you give incorrect or false answers in a rental application; (5) you or any occupant is arrested, convicted, or given deferred adjudication for a felony offense involving actual or potential physical harm to a person, or involving possession, manufacture, or delivery of a controlled substance, marijuana, or drug paraphernalia; (6) any illegal drugs or paraphernalia are found in your apartment; (7) you or any guest or occupant engages in any of the prohibited conduct described in Paragraph 20; or (8) you or any occupant, in bad faith, makes an invalid habitability complaint to an official or employee of a utility company or the government.

Eviction. If you default by not paying your rent on time, we may end your right of occupancy by giving you 10 days' written notice to vacate. If you default by breaching the lease in any other manner, we may end your right of occupancy by giving you 15 days' written notice to vacate or other notice as required by law. Notice may be by: (1) personal delivery to the adult resident(s); or (2) personal delivery al the apartment to any adult occupant in charge of the residence; or (3) any other method allowed by Louisiana law. Termination of your possession rights or subsequent re-renting doesn't release you from

Initials of all Residents: _____

liability for future rent or other Lease Contract obligations. After giving notice to vacate or filing an eviction suit, we may still accept rent or other sums due; the filing or acceptance doesn't waive or diminish our right of eviction, or any other contractual or statutory right. Accepting money at any time doesn't waive our right to damages; past or future rent or other sums; or to continue with eviction proceedings. However, we will accept past-due rent and costs at any time prior to eviction being completed as required by Louisiana statutes.

Acceleration. All monthly rent for the rest of the Lease Contract term or renewal period will be accelerated automatically without notice or demand (before or after acceleration) and will be immediately due and delinquent if, without our written consent: (1) you move out, remove property in preparing to move out, or give oral or written notice (by you or any occupant) of intent to move out before the Lease Contract term or renewal period ends; *and* (2) you've not paid all rent for the entire Lease Contract term or renewal period. Such conduct is considered a default for which we need not give you notice. Remaining rent also will be accelerated if you're judicially evicted or move out when we demand because you've defaulted. You will be refunded any future rent payments you have made because you defaulted on the lease as long as a new tenant is found. You will still be liable for rent for the period of time during which no tenant is living in the unit. We will attempt, to the extent required under Louisiana law, to find a new tenant to rent the unit.

Holdover. You or any occupant, invitee, or guest must not hold over beyond the date contained in your move-out notice or our notice to vacate (or beyond a different move-out date agreed to by the parties in writing). If a holdover occurs, then: (1) holdover rent is due in advance on a daily basis and may become delinquent without notice or demand; (2) rent for the holdover period will be increased by 25% over the then-existing rent, without notice; (3) you'll be liable to us for all rent for the full term of the previously signed Lease Contract of a new resident who can't occupy because of the holdover; and (4) at our option, we may extend the Lease Contract term—for up to one month from the date of notice of Lease Contract extension—by delivering written notice to you or your apartment while you continue to hold over.

Other Remedies. If your rent is delinquent and we give you prior written notice, we may terminate electricity that we've furnished at our expense, by following applicable Louisiana law, unless governmental regulations on submetering or utility proration provide otherwise. We may report unpaid amounts to credit agencies. If you default and move out early, you will pay us any amounts stated to be rental discounts in paragraph 10, in addition to other sums due. Upon your default, we have all other legal remedies, including Lease Contract termination. If allowed by Louisiana law, the prevailing party, in a lawsuit under this contract, may recover from the nonprevailing party attorney's fees and all other litigation costs. Late charges are liquidated damages for our time, inconvenience, and overhead in collecting late rent (but are not for attorney's fees and litigation costs). All unpaid amounts bear 18% interest per year from due date, compounded annually. You must pay all collection-agency fees if you fail to pay all sums due within 10 days after we mail you a letter demanding payment and stating that collection agency fees will be added if you don't pay all sums by that deadline.

Mitigation of Damages. If you move out early, you'll be subject to paragraph 11 and all other remedies. We'll exercise customary diligence to re-rent and minimize the amount you owe us. We will credit all subsequent rent that we actually receive from subsequent residents against your liability for past-due and future rent and other sums due.

General Clauses

33. MISCELLANEOUS. *Neither we nor any of our representatives have made any oral promises, representations, or agreements. This Lease Contract is the entire agreement between you and us. Our representatives (including management personnel, employees, and agents) have no authority to waive, amend, or terminate this Lease Contract or any part of it, unless in writing, and no authority to make promises, representations, or agreements that impose security duties or other obligations on us or our representatives unless in writing.* No action or omission of our representative will be considered a waiver of any subsequent violation, default, or time or place of performance. Our not enforcing or belatedly enforcing written-notice requirements, rental due dates, acceleration, liens, or other rights isn't a waiver under any circumstances. Except when notice or demand is required by statute, you waive any notice and demand for performance from us if you default. Written notice to or from our managers constitutes notice to or from us. Any person giving a notice under this Lease Contract should retain a copy of the memo, letter, or fax that was given. Fax signatures are binding. All notices must be signed. Notices may not be given by e-mal.

If we exercise one legal right against you, we still have all other legal rights available in any legal proceeding against you. Insurance subrogation is waived by all parties. No employee, agent, or management company is personally liable for any of our contractual, statutory, or other obligations merely by virtue of acting on our behalf. This Lease

Initials of all Residents: _____

Contract binds subsequent owners. Neither an invalid clause nor the omission of initials on any page invalidates this Lease Contract. All notices and documents may be in English and, at our option, in any language that you read or speak. All provisions regarding our non-liability and non-duty apply to our employees, agents, and management companies. This Lease Contract is subordinate or superior to existing and future recorded mortgages, at lender's option. All Lease Contract obligations must be performed in the county where the apartment is located.

Cable channels that are provided may be changed during the Lease Contract term if the change applies to all residents. Utilities may be used only for normal household purposes and must not be wasted. If your electricity is ever interrupted, you must use only battery-operated lighting.

NEW NOTICE LAW/REGISTERED SEX OFFENDERS—The Louisiana Bureau of Criminal Identification and Information maintains a State Sex Offender and Child Predator Registry, which is a public access database of the locations of individuals required to register pursuant to LA-R.S. 15:540 et seq. Sheriffs' Departments and Police Departments serving jurisdictions of 450,000 also maintain such information. The State Sex Offender and Child Predator Registry database can be accessed at: www.lasocpr.lsp.org/socpr/ and contains addresses, pictures, and conviction records for registered offenders. The database can be searched by zip code, city, parish, or by offender name. Information is also available by telephone at 1-800-858-0551 or 1-225-925-6100, or mail at Post Office Box 66614, Mail Slip #18, Baton Rouge, LA 70896, or e-mail State Services at: SOCPR@dps .state.la.us for more information.

WAIVER OF JURY TRIAL. To minimize legal expenses and, to the extent allowed by law, you and we agree that a trial of any lawsuit based on statute common law, and/or related to this Lease Contract shall be to a judge and not a jury.

34. PAYMENTS. You are required to pay rent whether or not we fulfill our lease obligations under this contract. At our option and without notice, we may apply money received (other than sale proceeds under paragraph 13 or utility payments subject to governmental regulations) first to any of your unpaid obligations, then to current rent—regardless of notations on checks or money orders and regardless of when the obligations arose. All sums other than rent are due upon our demand. After the due date, we do not have to accept the rent or any other payments.

35. NAA MEMBERSHIP. We represent that, at the time of signing this Lease Contract or a Lease Contract Renewal Form: (1) we; (2) the management company that represents us; or (3) any locator service that procured you is a member in good standing of both the National Apartment Association and the affiliated local apartment association for the area where the apartment is located. The member is either an owner/management company member or an associate member doing business as a locator service (whose name and address is disclosed on page 6). If not, the following applies: (1) this Lease Contract is voidable at your option and is unenforceable by us (except for property damages); and (2) we may not recover past or future rent or other charges. The above remedies also apply if both of the following occur: (1) the Lease Contract is automatically renewed on a month-to-month basis two or more times after membership in NAA and the local association has lapsed; and (2) neither the owner nor the management company is a member of NAA and the local association at the time of the third automatic renewal. Governmental entities may use NAA forms if NAA agrees in writing.

Security Guidelines for Residents

36. SECURITY GUIDELINES. In cooperation with the National Apartment Association, we'd like to give you some important safety guidelines. We recommend that you follow these guidelines and use common sense in practicing safe conduct. Inform all other occupants in your dwelling, including any children you may have, about these guidelines.

PERSONAL SECURITY—WHILE INSIDE YOUR APARTMENT
1. Lock your doors and windows—even while you're inside.
2. Engage the keyless deadbolts on all doors while you're inside.
3. When answering the door, see who is there by looking through a window or peephole. If you don't know the person, first talk with him or her without opening the door. *Don't open the door if you have any doubts.*
4. If children (who are old enough to take care of themselves) are left alone in your apartment, tell them to use the keyless deadbolt and refuse to let anyone inside while you are gone—regardless of whether the person is a stranger or an apartment maintenance or management employee.
5. Don't put your name, address, or phone number on your key ring.
6. If you're concerned because you've lost your key or because someone you distrust has a key, ask the management to rekey the locks. You have a statutory right to have that done, as long as you pay for the rekeying.

Initials of all Residents: _____

7. Dial 911 for emergencies. If the 911 number does not operate in your area, keep phone numbers handy for the police, fire, and emergency medical services. If an emergency arises, call the appropriate governmental authorities first, then call the management.

8. Check your smoke detector monthly to make sure it is working properly and the batteries are still okay.

9. Check your door locks, window latches, and other devices regularly to be sure they are working properly.

10. If your doors or windows are unsecure due to break-ins or malfunctioning locks or latches, stay with friends or neighbors until the problem is fixed.

11. Immediately report to management—in writing, dated and signed—any needed repairs of locks, latches, doors, windows, smoke detectors, and alarm systems.

12. Immediately report to management—in writing, dated and signed—any malfunction of other safety devices outside your apartment, such as broken gate locks, burned-out lights in stairwells and parking lots, blocked passages, broken railings, etc.

13. Close curtains, blinds, and window shades at night.

14. Mark or engrave your driver's license number or other identification on valuable personal property.

PERSONAL SECURITY—WHILE OUTSIDE YOUR APARTMENT

15. Lock your doors while you're gone. Lock any door handle lock, keyed deadbolt lock, sliding door pin lock, sliding door handle latch, and sliding door bar that you have.

16. Leave a radio or TV playing softly while you're gone.

17. Close and latch your windows while you're gone, particularly when you're on vacation.

18. Tell your roommate or spouse where you're going and when you will be back.

19. Don't walk alone at night. Don't allow your family to do so.

20. Don't hide a key under the doormat or a nearby flowerpot. These are the first places a burglar will look.

21. Don't give entry keys, codes, or electronic gate cards to anyone.

22. Use lamp timers when you go out in the evening or go away on vacation. They can be purchased at most hardware stores.

23. Let the manager and your friends know if you'll be gone for an extended time. Ask your neighbors to watch your apartment since the management cannot assume that responsibility.

24. While on vacation, temporarily stop your newspaper and mail delivery, or have your mail and newspaper picked up daily by a friend.

25. Carry your door key in your hand, whether it is daylight or dark, when walking to your entry door. You are more vulnerable when looking for your keys at the door.

PERSONAL SECURITY—WHILE USING YOUR CAR

26. Lock your car doors while driving. Lock your car doors and roll up the windows when leaving your car parked.

27. Don't leave exposed items in your car, such as cassette tapes, wrapped packages, briefcases, or purses.

28. Don't leave your keys in the car.

29. Carry your key ring in your hand whenever you are walking to your car—whether it is daylight or dark and whether you are at home, school, work, or on vacation.

30. Always park in a well-lighted area. If possible, try to park your car in an off-street parking area rather than on the street.

31. Check the backseat before getting into your car.

32. Be careful when stopping at gas stations or automatic-vendor machines at night or anytime when you suspect danger.

PERSONAL SECURITY AWARENESS

No *security system is failsafe. Even the best system can't prevent crime. Always act as if security systems don't exist since they are subject to malfunction, tampering, and human error. We disclaim any express or implied warranties of security. The best safety measures are the ones you perform as a matter of common sense and habit.*

When Moving Out

37. MOVE-OUT NOTICE. Before moving out, you must give our representative advance written move-out notice as provided below. Your move-out notice will not release you from liability for the full term of the Lease Contract or renewal term. You will still be liable for the entire Lease Contract term if you move out early (paragraph 22) except under the military clause (paragraph 23). YOUR MOVE-OUT NOTICE MUST COMPLY WITH EACH OF THE FOLLOWING:

We must receive advance written notice of your move-out date. The advance notice must be at least the number of days of notice required in paragraph 3. However, if a move-out notice is received on the first, it will suffice for move-out on the last day of the month of intended move-out, provided that all other requirements above are met.

The move-out date in your notice *(check one):* ❑ must be the last day of the month; or ❑ may be the exact day designated in your notice. *If neither is checked, the second applies.*

Your move-out notice must be in writing. Oral move-

Initials of all Residents: _____

out notice will not be accepted and will not terminate your Lease Contract.

Your move-out notice must not terminate the Lease Contract sooner than the end of the Lease Contract term or renewal period.

YOUR NOTICE IS NOT ACCEPTABLE IF IT DOES NOT COMPLY WITH ALL OF THE ABOVE. Please use our written move-out form. You must obtain from our representative written acknowledgment that we received your move-out notice. If we terminate the Lease Contract, we must give you the same advance notice—unless you are in default.

38. MOVE-OUT PROCEDURES. The move-out date can't be changed unless we and you both agree in writing. You won't move out before the Lease Contract term or renewal period ends unless all rent for the entire Lease Contract term or renewal period is paid in full. Early move-out may result in re-renting charges and acceleration of future rent under paragraphs 11 and 32. You're prohibited from applying any security deposit to rent. You won't stay beyond the date you are supposed to move out. All residents, guests, and occupants must abandon the apartment before the 30-day period for deposit refund begins. You must give us and the U.S. Postal Service, in writing, each resident's forwarding address.

39. CLEANING. You must thoroughly clean the apartment, including doors, windows, furniture, bathrooms, kitchen appliances, patios, balconies, garages, carports, and storage rooms. You must follow move-out cleaning instructions if they have been provided. If you don't clean adequately, you'll be liable for reasonable cleaning charges—including charges for cleaning carpets, draperies, furniture, walls, etc. that are soiled beyond normal wear (that is, wear or soiling that occurs without negligence, carelessness, accident, or abuse).

40. MOVE-OUT INSPECTION. You should meet with our representative for a move-out inspection. Our representative has no authority to bind or limit us regarding deductions for repairs, damages, or charges. Any statements or estimates by us or our representative are subject to our correction, modification, or disapproval before final refunding or accounting.

41. SECURITY DEPOSIT DEDUCTIONS AND OTHER CHARGES. You'll be liable for the following charges, if applicable: unpaid rent; unpaid utilities; unreimbursed service charges; repairs or damages caused by negligence, carelessness, accident, or abuse, including stickers, scratches, tears, burns, stains, or unapproved holes; replacement cost of our property that was in or attached to the apartment and is missing; replacing dead or missing smoke-detector batteries; utilities for repairs or cleaning; trips to let in company representatives to remove your telephone or TV cable services or rental items (if you so request or have moved out); trips to open the apartment when you or any guest or occupant is missing a key; unreturned keys; missing or burned-out lightbulbs; removing or rekeying unauthorized security devices or alarm systems; agreed re-renting charges; packing, removing, or storing property removed or stored under paragraph 13; removing illegally parked vehicles; special trips for trash removal caused by parked vehicles blocking dumpsters; false security-alarm charges unless due to our negligence; animal-related charges under paragraphs 6 and 27; government fees or fines against us for violation (by you, your occupants, or guests) of local ordinances relating to smoke detectors, false alarms, recycling, or other matters; late payment and returned-check charges; a charge (not to exceed $100) for our time and inconvenience in our lawful removal of an animal or in any valid eviction proceeding against you, plus attorney's fees, court costs, and filing fees actually paid; and other sums due under this Lease Contract.

You'll be liable to us for: (1) charges for replacing all keys and access devices referenced in paragraph 5 if you fail to return them on or before your actual move-out date; (2) accelerated rent if you have violated paragraph 32; and (3) a re-renting fee if you have violated paragraph II.

42. DEPOSIT RETURN, SURRENDER, AND ABANDONMENT. We'll mail you your security deposit refund (less lawful deductions) and an itemized accounting of any deductions no later than 30 days after surrender or abandonment, unless statutes provide otherwise.

You have *surrendered* the apartment when: (1) the move-out date has passed and no one is living in the apartment in our reasonable judgment; or (2) all apartment keys and access devices listed in paragraph 5 have been turned in where rent is paid—whichever date occurs first.

You have *abandoned* the apartment when all of the following have occurred: (1) everyone appears to have moved out in our reasonable judgment; (2) clothes, furniture, and personal belongings have been substantially removed in our reasonable judgment; (3) you've been in default for non-payment of rent for 5 consecutive days, or water, gas, or electric service for the apartment not connected in our name has been terminated; and (4) you've not responded for 2 days to our notice left on the inside of the main entry door, stating that we consider the apartment abandoned. An apartment is also "abandoned" 10 days after the death of a sale resident.

Surrender, abandonment, and judicial eviction ends your right of possession for all purposes and gives us the immediate right to: clean up, make repairs in, and re-let the apartment; determine any security deposit deductions; and remove property left in the apartment. Surrender, abandonment, and judicial eviction affect your rights to property left in the apartment (paragraph 13), but do not affect our mitigation obligations (paragraph 32).

Signatures, Originals and Attachments

43. ORIGINALS AND ATTACHMENTS. This Lease Contract has been executed in multiple originals, each with original signatures—one for you and one or more for us. Our rules and community policies, if any, will be attached to the Lease Contract and given to you at signing. When an Inventory and Condition form is completed, both you and we should retain a copy. The items checked below are attached to this Lease Contract and are binding even if not initialed or signed.

- ○ Animal Addendum
- ○ Inventory and Condition Form
- ○ Mold Addendum
- ○ Enclosed Garage Addendum, dated
- ○ Community Policies Addendum, dated _____
- ○ Lease Contract Guaranty (___ guaranties, if more than one)
- ○ Notice of Intent to Move Out Form
- ○ Parking Permit or Sticker (quantity: ___)
- ○ Satellite Dish or Antenna Addendum
- ○ Asbestos Addendum (if asbestos is present)
- ○ Lead Hazard Information and Disclosure Addendum (federal)
- ○ Utility Addendum
- ○ Card Access Addendum, dated _____
- ○ Code Access Addendum, dated _____
- ○ Early Termination Addendum
- ○ Intrusion Alarm Addendum, dated _____
- ○ Other
- ○ Other

Name and address of locator service (if applicable)

Resident or Residents (all sign below)

Owner or Owner's Representative (signing on behalf of owner)

Address and phone number of owner's representative for notice purposes

Date form is filled out (same as on top of page 1)

You are legally bound by this document. Please read it carefully.

Before submitting a rental application or signing a Lease Contract, you may take a copy of these documents to review and/or consult an attorney.

Additional provisions or changes may be made in the Lease Contract if agreed to in writing by all parties.

You are entitled to receive an original of this Lease Contract after it is fully signed. Keep it in a safe place.

SPECIAL PROVISIONS (CONTINUED FROM PAGE 1).

Louisiana/National Apartment Association Official Form A-Os (Sheets 1, 2, and 3), May 2005

Rental Application for Residents and Occupants

Each co-applicant and each occupant over 18 years old must submit a separate application.
Spouses may submit a single application.

Date when filled out: _____

NATIONAL APARTMENT ASSOCIATION

ABOUT YOU Full name *(exactly as on driver's license or govt. ID card)*: _____

Your street address *(as shown on your driver's license or government ID card)*: _____

Driver's license # and state: _____
 OR govt. photo ID card #: _____
Former last names (maiden and married): _____
Your Social Security #: _____
Birthdate: _____ Height: _____ Weight: _____
Sex: _____ Eye color: _____ Hair color: _____
Marital Status: ❑ single ❑ married ❑ divorced ❑ widowed ❑ separated
Are you a U.S. citizen? ❑ Yes ❑ No
Do you or any occupant smoke?   ❑ Yes ❑ No
Will you or any occupant have an animal? ❑ Yes ❑ No
Kind, weight, breed, age: _____

Current home address (where you now live): _____
City/State/Zip: _____
Home/cell phone: (_____) _____ Current rent: $_____
E-mail address: _____
Name of apartment where you now live: _____
Current owner or manager's name: _____
Their phone: _____ Date moved in: _____
Why are you leaving your current residence? _____

Your previous home address: _____
City/State/Zip: _____
Apartment name: _____
Name of above owner or manager: _____
Their phone: _____ Previous monthly rent: $_____
Date you moved in: _____ Date you moved out: _____

YOUR WORK Present employer: _____
Address: _____
City/State/Zip: _____
Work phone: (_____) _____
Position: _____
Your gross monthly income is over: $_____
Date you began this job: _____
Supervisor's name and phone: _____

Previous employer: _____
Address: _____
City/State/Zip: _____
Work phone: (_____) _____
Position: _____
Gross monthly income was over: $_____
Dates you began and ended this job: _____
Previous supervisor's name and phone: _____

YOUR CREDIT HISTORY Your bank's name, city, state: _____

List major credit cards: _____
Other nonwork income you want considered. Please explain: _____

Past credit problems you want to explain. *(Use separate page.)*
_____

YOUR RENTAL/CRIMINAL HISTORY *Check only if applicable.* Have you, your spouse, or any occupant listed in this Application ever: ❑ been evicted or asked to move out? ❑ moved out of a dwelling before the end of the lease term without the owner's consent? ❑ declared bankruptcy? ❑ been sued *for* rent? ❑ been sued for property damage? ❑ been charged, detained, or arrested for a felony or sex crime that was resolved by conviction, probation, deferred adjudication, court-ordered community supervision, or pretrial diversion? ❑ been charged, detained, or arrested for a felony or sex-related crime that has not been resolved by any method? Please indicate the year, location, and type of each felony and sex crime other than those resolved by dismissal or acquittal. We may need to discuss more facts before making a decision. *You represent the answer is "no" to any item not checked above.*
_____

YOUR SPOUSE Full name: _____
Former last names (maiden and married): _____
Spouse's Social Security #: _____
Driver's license # and state: _____
 OR govt. photo ID card #: _____
Birthdate: _____ Height: _____ Weight: _____
Sex: _____ Eye color: _____ Hair color: _____
Are you a U.S. citizen? ❑ Yes ❑ No
Present employer: _____
Address: _____
City/State/Zip: _____
Work phone: (_____) _____
Position: _____
Date began job: _____ Gross monthly income is over: $_____
Supervisor's name and phone: _____

OTHER OCCUPANTS *Names of all persons under 18 and other adults who will occupy the unit without signing the lease. Continue on separate page if more than three.*
Name: _____ Relationship: _____
 Sex: _____ DL or govt. ID card # and state: _____
 Birthdate: _____ Social Security #: _____
Name: _____ Relationship: _____
 Sex: _____ DL or govt. ID card # and state: _____
 Birthdate: _____ Social Security #: _____
Name: _____ Relationship: _____
 Sex: _____ DL or govt. ID card # and state: _____
 Birthdate: _____ Social Security #: _____

YOUR VEHICLES *List all vehicles owned or operated by you, your spouse, or any occupants (including cars, trucks, motorcycles, trailers, etc.). Continue on separate page if more than three.*
Make and color of vehicle: _____
Year: _____ License #: _____ State: _____
Make and color of vehicle: _____
Year: _____ License #: _____ State: _____
Make and color of vehicle: _____
Year: _____ License #: _____ State: _____

WHY YOU RENTED HERE Were you referred: ❑ Yes ❑ No. *If yes, by whom:*
Name of locator or rental agency: _____
Name of individual locator or agent: _____
Name of friend or other person: _____
Did you find us on your own? ❑ Yes ❑ No *If yes, fill in information below:*
❑ On the Internet ❑ Stopped by ❑ Newspaper (name): _____
❑ Rental publication: _____
❑ Other: _____

EMERGENCY *Emergency contact person over 18, who will not be living with you:*
Name: _____
Address: _____
City/State/Zip: _____
Work phone: (_____) _____ Home phone: (_____) _____
Relationship: _____
If you die or are seriously ill, missing, or in a jail or penitentiary according to an affidavit of *(check one or more)* ❑ the above person, ❑ your spouse, or ❑ your parent or child, we may allow such person(s) to enter your dwelling to remove all contents, as well as your property in the mailbox, store rooms, and common areas. If no box is checked, any of the above are authorized at our option. If you are seriously ill or injured, you authorize us to call EMS or send for an ambulance at your expense. We're not legally obligated to do so.

AUTHORIZATION I or we authorize *(owner's name)* _____
_____
to obtain reports from consumer reporting agencies before, during, and after tenancy on matters relating to a lease by the above owner to me and to verify, by all available means, the information in this application, including income history and other information reported by employer(s) to any state employment security agency. Work history information may be used only for this Rental Application. Authority to obtain work history information expires 365 days from the date of this Application.
Applicant's signature _____
Spouse's signature _____

Contemplated Lease Contract Information
To be filled in only if the Lease Contract is not signed by resident(s) at time of application for rental.

The NAA Lease Contract to be used must be the latest version published by the association unless an earlier version is initialed by resident(s) and attached to this Application. The blanks in the Lease Contract will contain the following information:

- Names of all residents who will sign Lease Contract _____

- Name of Owner/Lessor _____

- Property name and type of dwelling *(bedrooms and baths)* _____

- Complete street address _____
  City/State/Zip _____
  - Names of all other occupants not signing Lease Contract *(persons under age 18, relatives, friends, etc.)* _____

- Total number of residents and occupants _____
- Consent necessary for guests staying longer than _____ days;
- Beginning date and ending date of Lease Contract. _____
- Number of days notice for termination _____
- Total security deposit $_____; Animal deposit $_____
- # of keys/access devices for ____ unit, ____ mailbox, ____ other
- Total monthly rent for dwelling unit $_____
  - Rent to be paid at *(check one)* ❑ on-site manager's office or ❑ other

- Prorated rent for: ❑ first month or ❑ second month $_____
- Monthly rental due date _____
- Late charges due if rent is not paid on or before the: _____
- Initial late charge $_____; Daily late charge $_____
- Returned-check charge $_____
- Animal violation charges: Initial $_____; Daily $_____
- ❑ Check if the dwelling is to be furnished;
- Utilities paid by owner *(check all that apply)*: ❑ electricity, ❑ gas, ❑ water, ❑ wastewater, ❑ trash, ❑ cable TV, ❑ master antenna;
- You will *(check one)*: ❑ not buy insurance or ❑ buy insurance;
- Agreed re-letting charge $_____
- Your move-out notice will terminate Lease Contract on *(check one)*: ❑ last day of month, or ❑ exact day designated in move-out notice;
- If dwelling unit is house or duplex, owner will be responsible under paragraph 26 of the Lease Contract for ❑ lawn/plant maintenance, ❑ lawn/plant watering, ❑ picking up trash from grounds, ❑ lawn/ plant fertilization, ❑ trash receptacles. If not checked, applicant will be responsible. The applicant will be responsible for the first $_____ of each repair.
- Special provisions regarding parking, storage, etc. (see attached page, if necessary): _____

Application Agreement

1. <u>Lease Contract Information.</u> The Lease Contract contemplated by the parties is attached—or, if no Lease Contract is attached, the Lease Contract will be the current NAA Lease Contract noted above. Special Information and conditions must be explicitly noted on an attached Lease Contract or in the Contemplated Lease Information above.

2. <u>Application Fee</u> (nonrefundable). You have delivered to our representative an application fee in the amount indicated below, and this payment partially defrays the cost of administrative paperwork. *It is nonrefundable.*

3. <u>Application Deposit</u> (may or may not be refundable). In addition to any application fee, you have delivered to our representative an application deposit in the amount indicated in paragraph 14. *The application deposit is not a security deposit.* However, it will be credited toward the required security deposit when the Lease Contract has been signed by all parties; OR it will be refunded under paragraph 10 if you are not approved; OR it will be retained by us as liquidated damages if you fail to sign or attempt to withdraw under paragraph 6 or 7.

4. <u>Approval When Lease Contract Is Signed in Advance.</u> If you and all co-applicants have already signed the Lease Contract when we approve the application, our representative will notify you (or one of you if there are co-applicants) of our approval, sign the Lease Contract, and then credit the application deposit of all applicants toward the required security deposit.

5. <u>Approval When Lease Contract Isn't Yet Signed.</u> If you and all co-applicants have not signed the Lease Contract when we approve the Application, our representative will notify you (or one of you if there are co-applicants) of the approval, sign the Lease Contract when you and all co-applicants have signed, and then credit the application deposit of all applicants toward the required security deposit.

6. <u>If You Fail to Sign Lease After Approval.</u> Unless we authorize otherwise in writing, you and all co-applicants must Sign the Lease Contract within 3 days after we give you our approval in person or by telephone, or within 5 days after we mail you our approval. *If you or any co-applicant fails to sign as required, we may keep the application deposit as liquidated damages, and terminate all further obligations under this Agreement.*

7. <u>If You Withdraw Before Approval.</u> You and any co-applicants may not withdraw your Application or the application deposit. *If, before signing the Lease Contract, you or any co-applicant withdraws application or notifies us that you've changed your mind about renting the dwelling unit, we will be entitled to retain all application deposits as liquidated damages, and the parties will then have no further obligation to each other.*

8. <u>Completed Application.</u> An Application will not be considered "completed" and will not be processed until all of the following have been provided to us *(unless checked)*: ❑ a separate application has been fully filled out and signed by you and each co-applicant; ❑ an application fee has been paid to us; ❑ an application deposit has been paid to us. *If no item is checked, all are necessary for the Application to be considered completed.*

9. <u>Nonapproval in Seven Days.</u> We will notify you whether you've been approved within seven days after the date we receive a completed Application. Your Application will be considered "disapproved" if we fail to notify you of your approval within seven days after we have received a completed Application. Notification may be in person or by mail or telephone unless you have requested that notification be by mail. You must not assume approval until you receive actual notice of approval.

10. <u>Refund After Nonapproval.</u> If you or any co-applicant is disapproved or deemed disapproved under paragraph 9, we will refund all application deposits within _____ days (not to exceed 30 days; 30 days if left blank) of such disapproval. Refund checks may be made payable to all co-applicants and mailed to one applicant.

11. <u>Extension of Deadlines.</u> If the deadline for signing, approving, or refunding under paragraphs 6, 9, or 10 falls on a Saturday, Sunday, or a state or federal holiday, the deadline will be extended to the end of the next day.

12. <u>Notice to Co-applicants.</u> Any notice we give you or your co-applicant is considered notice to all co-applicants, and any notice from you or your co-applicant is considered notice from all co-applicants.

13. <u>Keys or Access Devices.</u> We'll furnish keys and/or access devices only after: (1) all parties have signed the contemplated Lease Contract and other rental documents; and (2) all applicable rents and security deposits have been paid in full.

14. Application Fee (nonrefundable): $_____

    Application Deposit (may or may not be refundable): $_____

    Total of above application fee and application deposit: $_____

Total amount of money we've received to this date: $_____

15. Signature. *Our representative's signature is consent only to the above application agreement. It does not bind us to accept applicant or to sign the proposed Lease Contract.*

Acknowledgment. You declare that all your statements on the first page of this Application are true and complete. You authorize us to verify same through any means, including consumer reporting agencies and other rental housing owners. If you fail to answer any question or give false information, we may reject the application, retain all application fees and deposits as liquidated damages for our time and expense, and terminate your right of occupancy. Giving false information is a serious criminal offense. In lawsuits relating to the application or Lease Contract, the prevailing party may recover all attorney's fees and litigation costs from the losing party. We may at any time furnish information to consumer reporting agencies and other rental housing owners regarding your performance of your legal obligations, including both favorable and unfavorable information about your compliance with the Lease Contract, the rules, and financial obligations.

If you are seriously ill or injured, what donor may we notify? *(We are not responsible for providing medical information to doctors or emergency personnel.)*

Name: _____ Phone: (_____) _____

Important medical information in emergency:

    This Rental Application and the Lease Contract are binding legal documents when signed. Please read them carefully. Before submitting a Rental Application or signing a Lease Contract, you may take a copy of these documents to review and/or consult an attorney. Additional provisions or changes may be made in the Lease Contract if agreed to in writing by all parties. You are entitled to an original of the Lease Contract after it is fully signed.

Applicant's Signature: _____ Date: _____

Signature of Spouse: _____ Date: _____

Signature of Owner's Representative: _____ Date: _____

FOR OFFICE USE ONLY

1. Applicant's name or dwelling address (street, city): _____ Unit # or type: _____
2. Person accepting application: _____ Phone: _____
3. Person processing application: _____ Phone: _____
4. Date that applicant or co-applicant was notified by ❑ telephone, ❑ letter, or ❑ in person of ❑ acceptance or ❑ nonacceptance: _____
    (Deadline for applicant and all co-applicants to sign lease is three days after notification of acceptance in person or by telephone, five days if by mail)
5. Name of person(s) who were notified (at least one applicant must be notified if multiple applicants): _____
6. Name of owner's representative who notified above person(s): _____

© 2004, National Apartment Association, Inc.

Louisiana/National Apartment Association Official Form B·04, 2004

Animal Addendum

NATIONAL
APARTMENT
ASSOCIATION

Date: _____
(when this Addendum is filled out)

Please note: We consider animals a serious responsibility and a risk to each resident in the dwelling. If you do not properly control and care for an animal you'll be held liable if it causes any damage or disturbs other residents.

1. DWELLING UNIT DESCRIPTION.
   _____, at _____
   _____ *(street address)* in _____ *(city)*,
   Louisiana, _____ *(zip code)*.

2. LEASE CONTRACT DESCRIPTION.
   Lease Contract date: _____
   Owner's name: _____

   Residents *(list all residents)*: _____

   The Lease Contract is referred to in this Addendum as the "Lease Contract."

3. CONDITIONAL AUTHORIZATION FOR ANIMAL.
   You may keep the animal that is described below in the dwelling until the Lease Contract expires. But we may terminate this authorization sooner if your right of occupancy is lawfully terminated or if in our judgment you and your animal, your guests, or any occupant violate any of the rules in this Addendum.

4. ANIMAL DEPOSIT. An animal deposit of $ _____
   will be charged. This animal deposit will increase the total security deposit under the Lease Contract. We will consider this additional security deposit a general security deposit for all purposes. Refund of the security deposit will be subject to the terms and conditions set forth in the Lease Contract. The additional security deposit is not refundable before all residents surrender the premises, even if the animal has been removed. It is our policy to not charge a deposit for support animals.

5. ADDITIONAL MONTHLY RENT. Your total monthly rent (as stated in the Lease Contract) will be increased by $ _____

6. ADDITIONAL FEE. You must also pay a one-time nonrefundable fee of $ _____ for having the animal in the dwelling unit. It is our policy to not charge a deposit for support animals.

7. LIABILITY NOT LIMITED. The additional monthly rent and additional security deposit under this Animal Addendum do not limit residents' liability for property damages, cleaning, deodorization, defleaing, replacements, or personal injuries.

8. DESCRIPTION OF ANIMAL. You may keep only the animal described below. You may not substitute any other animal for this one. Neither you nor your guests or occupants may bring any other animal—mammal, reptile, bird, fish, rodent, or insect— into the dwelling or apartment community.

Animal's name: _____
Type: _____
Breed: _____
Color: _____
Weight: _____ Age: _____
City of license: _____
License no.: _____
Date of last rabies shot: _____
Housebroken? _____
Animal owner's name: _____

9. SPECIAL PROVISIONS. The following special provisions control over conflicting provisions of this printed form:

10. EMERGENCY. In an emergency involving an accident or injury to your animal, we have the right, but not a duty, to take the animal to the following veterinarian for treatment, at your expense.
    Doctor: _____
    Address: _____
    City/State/Zip: _____
    Phone: _____

11. ANIMAL RULES. You are responsible for the animal's actions at all times. You agree to abide by these rules:

    The animal must not disturb the neighbors or other residents, regardless of whether the animal is inside or outside the dwelling.

    Dogs, cats, and support animals must be housebroken. All other animals must be caged at all times. No animal offspring are allowed.

    Inside, the animal may urinate or defecate *only* in these designated areas:

    Outside, the animal may urinate or defecate *only* in these designated areas: _____

- Animals may not be tied to any fixed object anywhere outside the dwelling units, except in fenced yards (if any) for your exclusive use.

    You must not let an animal other than support into swimming-pool areas, laundry rooms, clubrooms, other recreational facilities, or dwelling units.

    Your animal must be fed and watered inside the dwelling unit. Don't leave animal food or water outside the dwelling unit at any time, except in fenced yards (if any) for your exclusive use.

You must keep the animal on a leash and under your supervision when outside the dwelling or any private fenced area. We or our representative may pick up unleashed animals and/or report them to the proper authorities. We'll impose reasonable charges for picking up and/or keeping unleashed animals.

Unless we have designated a particular area in your dwelling unit or on the grounds for animal defecation and urination, you are prohibited from letting an animal defecate or urinate *anywhere* on our property. You must take the animal off our property for that purpose. If we allow animal defecation inside the dwelling unit in this Addendum, you must ensure that it's done in a litter box with a kitty litter-type mix. If the animal defecates anywhere on our property (including in a fenced yard for your exclusive use), you will be responsible for immediately removing the waste and repairing any damage. Despite anything this Addendum says, you must comply with all local ordinances regarding animal defecation.

12. ADDITIONAL RULES. We have the right to make reasonable changes to the animal rules from time to time if we distribute a written copy of any changes to every resident who is allowed to have animals.

13. VIOLATION OF RULES. If you, your guest, or any occupant violates any rule or provision of this Animal Addendum (based upon our judgment) and we give you written notice, you must remove the animal immediately and permanently from the premises. We also have all other rights and remedies set forth in paragraph 27 of the Lease Contract, including damages, eviction, and attorney's fees.

14. COMPLAINTS ABOUT ANIMAL. You must immediately and permanently remove the animal from the premises if we receive a reasonable complaint from a neighbor or other resident or if we, in our sole discretion, determine that the animal has disturbed neighbors or other residents.

15. REMOVAL OF ANIMAL. In some circumstances, we may allow an animal control officer or humane society representative to enter the dwelling unit and remove the animal if, in our sole judgment, you have:

- abandoned the animal;

- left the animal in the dwelling unit for an extended period of time without food or water; or

- failed to care for a sick animal.

If you have violated our animal rules or let the animal defecate or urinate where it's not supposed to you will be subject to eviction and other remedies under paragraphs 27, 28 or 32 of the Lease Contract.

16. LIABILITY FOR DAMAGES, INJURIES, CLEANING, ETC. You and all co-residents will be jointly and sever ally liable for the entire amount of all damages caused by the animal, including all cleaning, defleaing, and deodorizing. This provision applies to all parts of the dwelling unit, including carpets, doors, walls, drapes, wallpaper, windows, screens, furniture, appliances, as well as landscaping and other outside improvements. If items cannot be satisfactorily cleaned or repaired, you must pay for us to replace them completely. Payment for damages, repairs, cleaning, replacements, etc. are due immediately upon demand.

As owner of the animal, you're strictly liable for the entire amount of any injury that the animal causes to a person or anyone's property. You will indemnify us for all costs of litigation and attorney's fees resulting from any such damage.

17. MOVE-OUT. When you move out, you will pay for defleaing, deodorizing, and shampooing to protect future residents from possible health hazards, regardless of how long the animal was there. We—not you—will arrange for these services.

18. MULTIPLE RESIDENTS. Each resident who signed the Lease Contract must sign this Animal Addendum. You, your guests, and any occupants must follow all animal rules. Each resident is jointly and severally liable for damages and all other obligations set forth in this Animal Addendum, even if the resident does not own the animal.

19. GENERAL. You acknowledge that no other oral or written agreement exists regarding animals. Except for special provisions noted in paragraph 9 above, our representative has no authority to modify this Animal Addendum or the animal rules except in writing, as described under paragraph 12. This Animal Addendum and the animal rules are considered part of the Lease Contract described above. It has been executed in multiple originals, one for you and one or more for us.

You are legally bound by this document. Please read it carefully.

Resident or Residents
(All residents must sign)

Owner or Owner's Representative
(Signs below)

You are entitled to receive an original of this Animal Addendum after it is fully signed. Keep it in a safe place.

Louisiana/National Apartment Association Official Form C-04,2004 1S)
© 2004, National Apartment Association, Inc.

Inventory and Condition Form

Resident's Name: _____ Home Phone: (____)_____ Work Phone: (____)_____
Resident's Name: _____ Home Phone: (____)_____ Work Phone: (____)_____
Resident's Name: _____ Home Phone: (____)_____ Work Phone: (____)_____
Resident's Name: _____ Home Phone: (____)_____ Work Phone: (____)_____
Apartment Community Name: _____

or Street Address *(if house, duplex, etc.)*: _____ Apt. # _____

Within 48 hours after move-in, you must note on this form all defects or damage and return it to our representative. Otherwise, everything will be considered to be in a clean, safe, and good working condition. Please mark through items listed below if they don't exist. This form protects both you (the resident) and us (the owner). We'll use it in determining what should and should not be considered your responsibility upon move-out. You are entitled to a copy of this form after it is filled out and signed by you and us.

☐ Move-In or ☐ Move-Out Condition *(Check one)*

Living Room
Walls _____
Wallpaper _____
Plugs, Switches, A/C Vents _____
Woodwork/Baseboards _____
Ceiling _____
Light Fixtures, Bulbs _____
Floor/Carpet _____

Doors, Stops, Locks _____
Windows, Latches, Screens _____
Window Coverings _____
Closets, Rods, Shelves _____
Closet Lights, Fixtures _____
Lamps, Bulbs _____
Water Stains on Walls or Ceilings _____
Other _____

Kitchen
Walls _____
Wallpaper _____
Plugs, Switches, A/C Vents _____
Woodwork/Baseboards _____
Ceiling _____
Light Fixtures, Bulbs _____
Floor/Carpet _____

Doors, Stops, Locks _____
Windows, Latches, Screens _____
Window Coverings _____
Cabinets, Drawers, Handles _____
Countertops _____
Stove/Oven, Trays, Pans, Shelves _____
Vent Hood _____
Refrigerator, Trays, Shelves _____
Refrigerator Light, Crisper _____
Dishwasher, Dispensers, Racks _____
Sink/Disposal _____
Microwave _____
Plumbing Leaks or Water Stains on Walls or Ceilings _____

Other _____

General Items
Thermostat _____
Cable TV or Master Antenna _____
A/C Filter _____
Washer/Dryer _____
Garage Door _____
Ceiling Fans _____
Exterior Doors, Screens/Screen Doors, Doorbell _____

Fireplace _____
Other _____

Dining Room
Walls _____
Wallpaper _____
Plugs, Switches, A/C Vents _____
Woodwork/Baseboards _____
Ceiling _____
Light Fixtures, Bulbs _____
Floor/Carpet _____

Doors, Stops, Locks _____
Windows, Latches, Screens _____
Window Coverings _____
Closets, Rods, Shelves _____
Closet Lights, Fixtures _____
Water Stains on Walls or Ceilings _____
Other _____

Halls
Walls _____
Wallpaper _____
Plugs, Switches, A/C Vents _____
Woodwork/Baseboards _____
Ceiling _____
Light Fixtures, Bulbs _____
Floor/Carpet _____

Doors, Stops, Locks _____
Closets, Rods, Shelves _____
Closet Lights, Fixtures _____
Water Stains on Walls or Ceilings _____
Other _____

Exterior (if applicable)
Patio/Yard _____
Fences/Gates _____
Faucets _____
Balconies _____
Other _____

Bedroom *(describe which one)*: _____
Walls _____
Wallpaper _____
Plugs, Switches, A/C Vents _____
Woodwork/Baseboards _____
Ceiling _____
Light Fixtures, Bulbs _____
Floor/Carpet _____

Doors, Stops, Locks _____
Windows, Latches, Screens _____
Window Coverings _____
Closets, Rods, Shelves _____
Closet Lights, Fixtures _____
Water Stains on Walls or Ceilings _____
Other _____

Bedroom *(describe which one):* _____
Walls _____
_____
Wallpaper _____
Plugs, Switches, A/C Vents _____
Woodwork/Baseboards _____
Ceiling _____
Light Fixtures, Bulbs _____
Floor/Carpet _____
_____
Doors, Stops, Locks _____
Windows, Latches, Screens _____
Window Coverings _____
Closets, Rods, Shelves _____
Closet Lights, Fixtures _____
Water Stains on Walls or Ceilings _____
Other _____

Bath *(describe which one):* _____
Walls _____
_____
Wallpaper _____
Plugs, Switches, A/C Vents _____
Woodwork/Baseboards _____
Ceiling _____
Light Fixtures, Bulbs _____
Exhaust Fan/Heater _____
Floor/Carpet _____
_____
Doors, Stops, Locks _____
Windows, Latches, Screens _____
Window Coverings _____
Sink, Faucet, Handles, Stopper _____
Countertops _____
Mirror _____
Cabinets, Drawers, Handles _____
Toilet, Paper Holder _____
Bathtub, Enclosure, Stopper _____
Shower, Doors, Rods _____
Tile _____
Plumbing Leaks or Water Stains on Walls or Ceilings _____
_____
Other _____

Half Bath
Walls _____
_____
Wallpaper _____
Plugs, Switches, A/C Vents _____
Woodwork/Baseboards _____
Ceiling _____
Light Fixtures, Bulbs _____
Exhaust Fan/Heater _____
Floor/Carpet _____
_____
Doors, Stops, Locks _____
Windows, Latches, Screens _____
Window Coverings _____
Sink, Faucet, Handles, Stopper _____
Countertops _____
Mirror _____
Cabinets, Drawers, Handles _____
Toilet, Paper Holder _____
Tile _____
Plumbing Leaks or Water Stains on Walls or Ceilings _____
_____
Other _____

Bedroom *(describe which one):* _____
Walls _____
_____
Wallpaper _____
Plugs, Switches, A/C Vents _____
Woodwork/Baseboards _____
Ceiling _____
Light Fixtures, Bulbs _____
Floor/Carpet _____
_____
Doors, Stops, Locks _____
Windows, Latches, Screens _____
Window Coverings _____
Closets, Rods, Shelves _____
Closet Lights, Fixtures _____
Water Stains on Walls or Ceilings _____
Other _____

Bath *(describe which one):* _____
Walls _____
_____
Wallpaper _____
Plugs, Switches, A/C Vents _____
Woodwork/Baseboards _____
Ceiling _____
Light Fixtures, Bulbs _____
Exhaust Fan/Heater _____
Floor/Carpet _____
_____
Doors, Stops, Locks _____
Windows, Latches, Screens _____
Window Coverings _____
Sink, Faucet, Handles, Stopper _____
Countertops _____
Mirror _____
Cabinets, Drawers, Handles _____
Toilet, Paper Holder _____
Bathtub, Enclosure, Stopper _____
Shower, Doors, Rods _____
Tile _____
Plumbing Leaks or Water Stains on Walls or Ceilings _____
_____
Other _____

Safety-Related Items *(Put "none" if item does not exist)*
Door Knob Locks _____
Keyed Deadbolt Locks _____
Keyless Deadbolts _____
Keyless Bolting Devices _____
Sliding Door Latches _____
Sliding Door Security Bars _____
Sliding Door Pin Locks _____
Doorviewers _____
Window Latches _____
Porch and Patio Lights _____
Smoke Detectors (push button to test) _____
Alarm System _____
Fire Extinguishers (look at charge level—BUT DON'T TEST!) _____
Garage Door Opener _____
Gate Access Card(s) _____
Other _____
_____

Date of Move-In: _____
or Date of Move-Out: _____

Acknowledgment. You acknowledge that you have inspected and tested all of the safety-related items (if in the dwelling) and that they are working, except as noted above. All items will be assumed to be in good condition unless otherwise noted on this form. You acknowledge receiving written operating instructions on the alarm system and gate access entry systems (if there are any). You acknowledge testing the smoke detector(s) and verify they are operating correctly.

In signing below, you accept this inventory as part of the Lease Contract and agree that it accurately reflects the condition of the premises for purposes of determining any refund due to you when you move out.

Resident or Resident's Agent: _____   Date of Signing: _____

Owner or Owner's Representative: _____   Date of Signing: _____

     Louisiana/National Apartment Association Official Form D.

Federally Required Lead Hazard Information and Disclosure Addendum

IMPORTANT NOTICE TO RESIDENTS: The following information is taken from a brochure entitled "Protect Your Family from Lead in Your Home" prepared by the U.S. Environmental Protection Agency, the U.S. Consumer Product Safety Commission and the U.S. Department of Housing and Urban Development. While the information must be distributed to residents before they become obligated under the lease for most types of housing built before 1978, it does not mean that the dwelling contains lead-based paint (LBP). The brochure was written in general terms and applies to both home purchasers and renters. The information outlines action that can be taken to test for, remove or abate LBP in a dwelling. The NAA Lease Contract specifically prohibits a resident from performing this type of work—only the dwelling owner may do so under the lease contract. If you have any questions about the presence of LBP in your dwelling, please contact the owner or management company before taking any action to test, abate or remove LBP. NOTE: Page references in the content of this form are to pages in the EPA brochure.

Lead from Paint, Dust, and Soil Can
Be Dangerous If Not Managed Properly

FACT: Lead exposure can harm young children and babies even before they are born.

FACT: Even children that seem healthy can have high levels of lead in their bodies.

FACT: People can get lead in their bodies by breathing or swallowing lead dust, or by eating soil or paint chips containing lead.

FACT: People have many options for reducing lead hazards. In most cases, lead-based paint that is in good condition is not a hazard.

FACT: Removing lead-based paint improperly can increase the danger to your family.

© 2004, National Apartment Association, Inc.
0622

If you think your home might have lead hazards, read this pamphlet to learn some simple steps to protect your family.

Are You Planning To Buy, Rent, or Renovate a Home Built Before 1978?

Many houses and apartments built before 1978 have paint that contains high levels of lead (called lead-based paint). Lead from paint, chips, and dust can pose serious health hazards if not taken care of properly.

OWNERS, BUYERS, and RENTERS are encouraged to check for lead (see page 6) before renting, buying, or renovating pre-1978 housing.

Federal law requires that individuals receive certain information before renting, buying, or renovating pre-1978 housing:

LANDLORDS have to disclose known information on lead-based paint and lead-based paint hazards before leases take effect. Leases must include a disclosure about lead-based paint.

SELLERS have to disclose known information on lead-based paint and lead-based paint hazards before selling a house. Sales contracts must include a disclosure form

about lead-based paint. Buyers have up to 10 days to check
for lead.

RENOVATORS disturbing more than 2 square feet of
painted surfaces have to give you this pamphlet before
starting work.

IMPORTANT!
Lead Gets in the Body in Many Ways

Childhood lead poisoning remains a major environmental
health problem in the U.S.

Even children who appear healthy can have dangerous levels
of lead in their bodies. People can get lead in their body if
they:

- Breathe in lead dust (especially during renovations that
  disturb painted surfaces).
- Put their hands or other objects covered with lead dust in
  their mouths.
- Eat paint chips or soil that contains lead.

Lead is even more dangerous to children under the age of 6:

- At this age children's brains and nervous systems are more
  sensitive to the damaging effects of lead.
- Children's growing bodies absorb more lead.
- Babies and young children often put their hands and other
  objects in their mouths. These objects can have lead dust
  on them.

Lead is also dangerous to women of childbearing age:

- Women with a high lead level in their system prior to
  pregnancy would expose a fetus to lead through the
  placenta during fetal development.

Lead's Effects

It is important to know that even exposure to low levels of
lead can severely harm children.

In children, lead can cause:

- Nervous system and kidney damage.
- Learning disabilities, attention deficit disorder, and
  decreased intelligence.
- Speech, language, and behavior problems.
- Poor muscle coordination.
- Decreased muscle and bone growth.
- Hearing damage.

While low-lead exposure is most common, exposure to high
levels of lead can have devastating effects on children,
including seizures, unconsciousness, and, in some cases,
death.

Although children are especially susceptible to lead exposure,
lead can be dangerous for adults too.

In adults, lead can cause:

- Increased chance of illness during pregnancy.
- Harm to a fetus, including brain damage or death.
- Fertility problems (in men and women).
- High blood pressure.
- Digestive problems.
- Nerve disorders.
- Memory and concentration problems.
- Muscle and joint pain.

Lead affects the body in **many ways.**

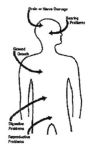

Where Lead-
Based Paint Is
Found

In general, the older your home, the
more likely it has lead-based paint.

Get your children and home tested if
you think your home has high levels of
lead.

Many homes built before 1978 have
lead-based paint. The federal
government banned lead-based paint
from housing in 1978. Some states
stopped its use even earlier. Lead can be
found:

- In homes in the city, country, or
  suburbs.
- In apartments, single-family homes,
  and both private and public housing.
- Inside and outside of the house.
- In soil around a home. (Soil can pick up lead from exterior
  paint or other sources such as past use of leaded gas in cars.)

Checking Your Family for Lead

To reduce your child's exposure to lead, get your child
checked, have your home tested (especially if your home
has paint in poor condition and was built before 1978) and
fix any hazards you may have. Children's blood lead levels
tend to increase rapidly from 6 to 12 months of age, and
tend to peak at 18 to 24 months of age.

Consult your doctor for advice on testing your children. A
simple blood test can detect high levels of lead. Blood tests
are usually recommended for:

- Children at ages 1 and 2.
- Children or other family members who have been exposed
  to high levels of lead.
- Children who should be tested under your state or local
  health screening plan.

Your doctor can explain what the test results mean and if
more testing will be needed.

Identifying Lead Hazards

Lead-based paint is usually not a hazard if it **is in good
condition, and it is not on an** impact or friction surface,
like a window. It is defined by the federal government as

paint with lead levels greater than or equal to 1.0 **milligram per square centimeter, or more** than 0.5% by weight.

Deteriorating lead-based paint (peeling, chipping, chalking, cracking, or damaged) is a hazard and needs immediate attention. It may also be a hazard when found on surfaces that children can chew or that get a lot of wear-and-tear, such as:

• Windows and window sills.
• Doors and door frames.
• Stairs, railings, banisters, and porches.

Lead dust can form when lead-based paint is scraped, sanded, or heated. Dust also forms when painted surfaces bump or rub together. Lead chips and dust can get on surfaces and objects that people touch. Settled lead dust can re-enter the air when people vacuum, sweep, or walk through it. The following two federal standards have been set for lead hazards in dust:

• 40 micrograms per square foot (pg/ft²) and higher for floors, including carpeted floors.
• 250 pg/ft and higher for interior window sills.

Lead in soil can be a hazard when children play in bare soil or when people bring soil into the house on their shoes. The following two federal standards have been set for lead hazards in residential soil:

• 400 parts per million (ppm) and higher in play areas of base soil.
• 1,200 ppm (average) and higher in bare soil in the remainder of the yard.

The only way to find out if paint, dust, and soil lead hazards exist is to test for them. The next page describes the most common methods used.

Checking Your Home for Lead

Lead from paint chips, which you **can see, and** lead dust, which you can't always see, can both be serious hazards

Just knowing that a home has lead-based paint may not tell you if there is a hazard.

You can get your home checked for lead in several different ways:

• A paint inspection tells you whether your home has lead-based paint and where it is located. It won't tell you whether or not your home currently has lead hazards.

• A risk assessment tells you if your home currently has any lead hazards from lead in paint, dust, or soil. It also tells you what actions to take to address any hazards.

• A combination risk assessment and inspection tells you if your home has any lead hazards and if your home has any lead-based paint, and where the lead-based paint is located.

Hire a trained and certified testing professional who will use a range of reliable methods when testing your home.

• Visual inspection of paint condition and location.
• A portable x-ray fluorescence (XRF) machine.
• Lab tests of paint, dust, and soil samples.

There are state and federal programs in place to ensure that testing is done safely, reliably, and effectively. Contact your state or local agency for more information, or call 1-800-424-LEAD (5323) for a list of contacts in your area.

Home test kits for lead are available, but may not always be accurate. Consumers should not rely on these tests before doing **renovations or to assure safety.**

What You Can Do Now to Protect Your Family

If you suspect that your house has lead **hazards, you can take some immediate** steps to reduce your family's risk:

• If you rent, notify your landlord of peeling or chipping paint.
• Clean up paint chips immediately.
• **Clean floors, window frames, window** sills, and other surfaces weekly. Use a mop or sponge with warm water and a general all-purpose cleaner or a cleaner made specifically for lead. REMEMBER: NEVER MIX AMMONIA AND BLEACH PRODUCTS TOGETHER SINCE THEY CAN FORM A DANGEROUS GAS.
• Thoroughly rinse sponges and mop heads after cleaning dirty or dusty **areas.**
• Wash children's hands often, especially before they eat and before nap time and bed time.
• Keep play areas clean. Wash bottles, pacifiers, toys, and stuffed animals regularly.
• Keep children from chewing window sills or other painted surfaces.
• Clean or remove shoes before entering your home to avoid tracking in lead from soil.
• Make sure children eat nutritious, low-fat meals high **in iron and calcium, such as** spinach and dairy products. Children with good diets absorb less lead.

Reducing Lead Hazards In The Home

Removing lead improperly **can increase** the hazard to your family by spreading **even more** lead dust around the house.

Always use a professional who is trained to remove lead hazards safely.

In addition to day-to-day cleaning and good nutrition:

- You can temporarily reduce lead hazards by taking actions such as repairing damaged painted surfaces and planting grass to cover soil with high lead levels. These actions (called "interim controls") are not permanent solutions and will need ongoing attention.
- To permanently remove lead hazards, you should hire a certified lead "abatement" contractor. Abatement (or permanent hazard elimination) methods include removing, sealing, or enclosing lead-based paint with special materials. Just painting over the hazard with regular paint is not permanent removal.

Always hire a person with special training for correcting lead problems—someone who knows how to do this work safely and has the proper equipment to clean up thoroughly. Certified contractors will employ qualified workers and follow strict safety rules as set by their state or by the federal **government.**

Once the work is completed, dust cleanup activities must be repeated until testing indicates that dust leaf levels are below the following:

- 40 micrograms per square foot (pg/ft²) for floors, including carpeted floors;
- 250 /pg/ ft2 for interior window sills; and 400 pg/ft² for window troughs.

Call your state or local agency for help with locating certified professionals in your area and to see if financial assistance is available.

Remodeling or Renovating a Home with Lead-Based Paint

Take precautions before your contractor or you begin remodeling or renovating anything that disturbs painted surfaces (such as scraping off paint or tearing out walls):

- Have the area tested for lead-based paint.
- Do not use a belt-sander, propane torch, high temperature heat gun, dry **scraper, or dry** sandpaper to **remove** lead-based paint. These actions create large amounts of lead dust and fumes. Lead dust can remain in your home long after the work is done.
- Temporarily move your family (especially children and pregnant women) out of the apartment or house until the

work is done and the area is properly cleaned. If you can't move your family, at least completely seal off the **work area.**

- Follow other safety measures to reduce lead hazards. You can find out about other safety measures by calling 1-800-424-LEAD. Ask for the brochure "Reducing Lead Hazards When Remodeling Your Home." This brochure explains what to do before, during, **and after renovations.**

If you have already completed renovations or remodeling that could have released lead-based paint or dust, get your young children tested and follow the steps outlined on page 7 of this brochure.

Other Sources of Lead

If not conducted properly, certain types of renovations can release lead from paint and dust into the air.

While paint, dust, **and soil are the most common sources of lead, other lead sources** also exist:

- Drinking water. Your home might have plumbing with lead or lead solder. Call your local health department or water supplier to find out about testing your **water. You cannot see, smell, or taste** lead, and boiling your water will not get rid of lead. If you think your plumbing might have lead in it
- Use only cold water for drinking and cooking.
- Run water for 15 to 30 seconds before drinking it, especially if you have not used your water for a few hours.
- The job. If you work with lead, you could bring it home on your hands or clothes. Shower and change clothes before coming home. Launder your work clothes separately from the rest of your family's clothes.
- Old painted toys and furniture.

- Food and liquids stored in lead crystal or lead-glazed pottery or porcelain.
- Lead smelters or other industries that release lead into the air.
- Hobbies that use lead, such as making pottery or stained glass, or refinishing furniture.
- Folk remedies that contain lead, such as "greta" and "azarcon" used to treat an upset stomach.

For More Information

The National Lead Information Center
Call 1-800-424-LEAD (424-5323) to learn how to protect children from lead poisoning and for other information on lead hazards. To access lead information via the Web, visit www.epa.gov/lead www.hud.gov/offices/Iead/.

EPA's Safe Drinking Water Hotline

Call 1-800-426-4791 for information about lead in drinking water.

Consumer Product Safety Commission (CPSC) Hotline

To request information on lead in consumer products, or to report an unsafe consumer product or a product-related injury call 1-800-638-2772, or visit CPSC's Web site at: www.@:psc.gov.

State Health and Environmental Agencies

Some cities, states, and tribes have their own rules for lead-based paint activities. Check with your local agency to see which laws apply to you. Most agencies can also provide information on finding a lead abatement firm in your area, and on possible sources of financial aid for reducing lead hazards. Receive up-to-date address and phone information for your local contacts on the Internet at www.epa.gov/lead or contact the National Lead Information Center at 1-800-424-LEAD.

For the hearing impaired, call the Federal Information Relay Service at 1-800-..&77-8339 to access any of the phone numbers in this brochure.

Simple Steps to Protect Your Family from Lead Hazards

If you think your home has high levels of lead:

- Get your young children tested for lead, even if they seem healthy.
- Wash children's hands, bottles, pacifiers, and toys often.
- Make sure children eat healthy, low-fat foods.
- Get your home checked for lead hazards.
- Regularly clean floors, window sills, and other surfaces.
- Wipe soil off shoes before entering house.
- Talk to your landlord about fixing surfaces with peeling or chipping paint.
- Take precautions to avoid exposure to lead dust when remodeling or renovating (call 1-800-424-LEAD for guidelines).
- Don't use a belt-sander, propane torch, high temperature heat gun, scraper, or sandpaper on painted surfaces that may contain lead.
- Don't try to remove lead-based paint yourself.

Louisiana Department of Environmental Quality (504) 765-0219

CPSC Regional Office *(includes Louisiana)* 1-800-638-2m

EPA Region 6 Office *(includes Louisiana)* (214) 665-7244

FEDERALLY REQUIRED LESSOR DISCLOSURE, AGENT STATEMENT, AND LESSEE ACKNOWLEDGMENT OF INFORMATION ON LEAD-BASED PAINT AND LEAD-BASED PAINT HAZARDS

LEAD WARNING STATEMENT. Housing built before 1978 may contain lead-based paint. Lead from paint, paint chips, and dust can pose health hazards if not managed properly. Lead exposure is especially harmful to young children and pregnant women. Before renting pre-1978 housing, lessors (owners) must disclose the presence of lead-based paint and/or lead-based paint hazards in the dwelling. Lessees (residents) must also receive a federally approved pamphlet on lead poisoning prevention. (This addendum is a "pamphlet" within the meaning of federal regulations. The term "in the housing" means either inside or outside the housing unit.)

LEAD-FREE HOUSING. If the housing unit has been certified as "lead free" according to 24 CFR Section 35.82, the lead-based paint and lead-based paint hazard regulations do not apply, and it is not necessary to provide this addendum, or a lead-based paint warning pamphlet and lead-based paint disclosure statement, to the lessee (resident).
LESSOR'S DISCLOSURE
    Presence of lead-based paint and/or lead-based paint hazards *(check only one box)*
    ❏ Lessor (owner) has no knowledge of lead-based paint and/or lead-based paint hazards in the housing.
    ❏ Lessor (owner) knows that lead-based paint and/or lead-based paint hazards are present in the housing *(explain)*.

    Records and reports available to lessor *(check only one box)*
    ❏ Lessor (owner) has no reports or records pertaining to lead-based paint and/or lead-based hazards in the housing.
    ❏ Lessor (owner) has reports or records indicating the presence of some lead-based paint and/or lead-based paint hazards in the housing, and has provided the lessees (residents) with all such records and reports that are available to lessor *(list documents)*.

AGENT'S STATEMENT. If another person or entity is involved in leasing the dwelling as an agent of the lessor (i.e., as a management company, real estate agent, or locator service acting for the owner), such agent represents that (1) agent has informed the lessor of the lessor's obligations under 42 U.S.C.4582(d); and (2) agent is aware of agent's responsibility to ensure that lessor complies with such disclosure laws. Such compliance may be through lessor himself or herself, or through lessor's employees, officers or agents. Lessor's obligations include those in 24 CFR Sections 35.88 and 35.92 and 40 CPR Sections 745.107 and 745.113. Agent's obligations include those in 24 CPR Section 35.94 and 40 CPR Section 745.115.

ACCURACY CERTIFICATIONS AND RESIDENT'S ACKNOWLEDGMENT. Lessor and any agent named below certify that to the best of their knowledge the above information and statements made or provided by them, respectively, are true and accurate. The person who signs for the LESSOR may be: (1) the owner himself or herself; (2) an employee, officer, or partner of the owner; or (3) a representative of the owner's management company, real estate agent, or locator service if such person is authorized to sign for the lessor. The person who signs for the AGENT may be: (1) the agent himself or herself; or (2) an employee, officer, or partner of the agent if such person is authorized to sign for the agent. The lessees (residents) signing below acknowledge that they have received a copy of this lease addendum before becoming obligated under the lease and have been informed that it contains the disclosure form and pamphlet information required by federal law regarding lead poisoning prevention.

Apartment name & unit number OR street address of dwelling

Lessee   Date   Lessee   Date
(Resident)   (Resident)
Lessee   Date   Lessee   Date
(Resident)   (Resident)

Printed name of LESSOR (owner) of the dwelling   Printed name of any AGENT of lessor, i.e., management
Signature of person signing on behalf of   company, real estate agent, or locator service involved in
above LESSOR   Date   leasing the dwelling.
                                                           Signature of person signing on behalf of above
                                                           AGENT, if any   Date

You are entitled to receive an original of page 4 of this Lead Hazard Addendum after it is fully signed. Keep it in a safe place.

Mold Information and Prevention Addendum

NATIONAL
APARTMENT
ASSOCIATION

Please note: It is our goal to maintain a quality living environment for our residents. To help achieve this goal, it is important to work together to minimize any mold growth in your dwelling. That is why this addendum contains important information for you, and responsibilities for both you and us.

1. ADDENDUM. This is an addendum to the Lease Contract executed by you, the resident(s), on the dwelling you have agreed to rent. That dwelling is:

   Apt. # _____ at

   (name of apartments)

   or other dwelling located at _____

   (street address of house, duplex, etc.)

   City/State where dwelling is located _____

2. ABOUT MOLD. Mold is found virtually everywhere in our environment—both indoors and outdoors and in both new and old structures. Molds are naturally occurring microscopic organisms which reproduce by spores and have existed practically from the beginning of time. All of us have lived with mold spores all our lives. Without molds we would all be struggling with large amounts of dead organic matter.

   Mold breaks down organic matter in the environment and uses the end product for its food. Mold spores (like plant pollen) spread through the air and are commonly transported by shoes, clothing and other materials. When excess moisture is present inside a dwelling, mold can grow. There is conflicting scientific evidence as to what constitutes a sufficient accumulation of mold which could lead to adverse health effects. Nonetheless, appropriate precautions need to be taken.

3. PREVENTING MOLD BEGINS WITH YOU. In order to minimize the potential for mold growth in your dwelling, you must do the following:

   Keep your dwelling clean—particularly the kitchen, the bathroom(s), carpets and floors. Regular vacuuming, mopping and using a household cleaner to clean hard surfaces is important to remove the household dirt and debris that harbor mold or food for mold. Immediately throw away moldy food.

   Remove visible moisture accumulation on windows, walls, ceilings, floors and other surfaces as soon as reasonably possible. Look for leaks in washing machine hoses and discharge lines—especially if the leak is large enough for water to infiltrate nearby walls. Turn on any exhaust fans in the bathroom and kitchen *before* you start showering or cooking with open pots. When showering, be sure to keep the shower curtain *inside* the tub or fully close the shower doors. Also, the experts recommend that after taking a shower or bath, you: (1) wipe moisture off of shower walls, shower doors, the bathtub and the bathroom floor; (2) leave the bathroom door open until all moisture on the mirrors and bathroom walls and tile surfaces has dissipated; and (3) hang up your towels and bath mats so they will completely dry out.

   Promptly notify us in writing about any air conditioning or heating system problems you discover. Follow our rules, if any, regarding replacement of air filters. Also, it is recommended that you periodically open windows and doors on days when the outdoor weather is dry (i.e., humidity is below 50 percent) to help humid areas of your dwelling dry out.

   Promptly notify us in writing about any signs of water leaks, water infiltration or mold. We will respond in accordance with state law and the Lease Contract to repair or remedy the situation, as necessary.

4. IN ORDER TO AVOID MOLD GROWTH, it is important to prevent excessive moisture buildup in your dwelling. Failure to promptly pay attention to leaks and moisture that might accumulate on dwelling surfaces or that might get inside walls or ceilings can encourage mold growth. Prolonged moisture can result from a wide variety of sources, such as:

   rainwater leaking from roofs, windows, doors, and outside walls, as well as flood waters rising above floor level;

   overflows from showers, bathtubs, toilets, lavatories, sinks, washing machines, dehumidifiers, refrigerator, or A/C drip pans or clogged up A/C condensation lines;

   leaks from plumbing lines or fixtures, and leaks into walls from bad or missing grouting/caulking around showers, tubs, or sinks;

   washing machine hose leaks, plant watering overflows, pet urine, cooking spills, beverage spills, and steam from excessive open-pot cooking;

   leaks from clothes dryer discharge vents (which can put lots of moisture into the air); and

   insufficient drying of carpets, carpet pads, shower walls, and bathroom floors.

5. IF SMALL AREAS OF MOLD HAVE ALREADY OCCURRED ON *NON-POROUS* SURFACES (such as ceramic tile, Formica, vinyl flooring, metal, wood, or plastic), the federal Environmental Protection Agency (EPA) recommends that you first clean the areas with soap (or detergent) and water, let the surface dry, and then within 24 hours apply a premixed, spray-on-type household biocide, such as Lysol Disinfectant®, Pine-Sol Disinfectant® (original pine-scented), Tilex Mildew Remover®, or Clorox Cleanup®. (Note: Only a few of the common household cleaners will actually kill mold). Tilex® and Clorox® contain bleach which can discolor or stain. Be sure to follow the instructions on the container. Applying biocides without first cleaning away the dirt and oils from the surface is like painting over old paint without first cleaning and preparing the surface.

   Always clean and apply a biocide to an area 5 or 6 times larger than any visible mold because mold may be adjacent in quantities not yet visible to the naked eye. A vacuum cleaner with a high-efficiency particulate air (HEPA) filter can be used to help remove nonvisible mold products from *porous* items, such as fibers in sofas, chairs, drapes, and carpets—provided the fibers are completely dry. Machine washing or dry cleaning will remove mold from clothes.

6. DO NOT CLEAN OR APPLY BIOCIDES TO: (1) visible mold on *porous surfaces,* such as sheetrock walls or ceilings, or (2) *large areas* of visible mold on *non-porous* surfaces. Instead, notify us in writing, and we will take appropriate action.

7. COMPLIANCE. Complying with this addendum will help prevent mold growth in your dwelling, and both you and we will be able to respond correctly if problems develop that could lead to mold growth. If you have questions regarding this addendum, please contact us at the management office or at the phone number shown in your Lease Contract.

   If you fail to comply with this Addendum, you can be held responsible for property damage to the dwelling and any health problems that may result. We can't fix problems in your dwelling unless we know about them.

   Resident or Residents
   (All residents must sign here)

   Owner or Owner's Representative
   (Signs here)

   Date of Lease Contract

You are entitled to receive an original of this Mold Information and Prevention Addendum after it is fully signed. Keep it in a safe place.

Louisiana/National Apartment Association Official Form F-04, 2004
© 2004, National Apartment Association, Inc.

LEASE ADDENDUM FOR
CARD ACCESS GATE

1. Addendum. This is an addendum to the NAA Lease Contract for Apt. No. _____ in the _____ Apartments in _____ **Louisiana.**

2. Cards for gate access. Each person who is 18 years of age or older and listed as a resident on the lease will be given a card at no cost to use during his or her residency. Each additional card for you or your children or other occupants will require a **$_____** nonrefundable fee.

3. Damaged, lost or unreturned cards. If a card is lost, stolen, or damaged, a **$_____** fee will be charged for a replacement card. If a card is not returned or is returned damaged when you move out, there will be a **$_____** deduction from the security deposit.

4. Report damage or malfunctions. Please immediately report to the office any malfunction or damage to gates, fencing, locks, or related equipment.

5. Follow written instructions. We ask that you and all other occupants read the written instructions that have been furnished to you regarding the access gates. This is important because if the gates are damaged by you or your family, guest, or invitee through negligence or misuse, you are liable for the damages under your lease, and collection of damage amounts will be pursued.

6. Personal injury and/or personal property damage. Anything mechanical or electronic is subject to malfunction. Fencing, gates or other devices will not prevent all crime. No security system or device is foolproof or 100 percent successful in deterring crime. Crime can still occur. Protecting residents, the families, occupants, guests and invitees from crime is the sole responsibility of residents, occupants, and law enforcement agencies. You should first call 911 or other appropriate emergency police numbers if a crime occurs or is suspected. We are not liable to any resident, family member, guest, occupant, or invitee for personal injury, death, damage, or loss of personal property from incidents related to perimeter fencing, automobile access gates, and/or pedestrian access gates. We reserve the right to modify or eliminate security systems other than those statutorily required.

7. Precautions in using vehicle gates.

Always approach entry and exit gates with caution and at a very slow rate of speed.

Never stop your car where the gate can hit your vehicle as the gate opens or closes.

Never follow another vehicle into an open gate. Always use your card to gain entry.

Never force the gate open with your car.

Never get out of your vehicle while the gates are opening or closing.

If you are using the gates with a boat or trailer, please contact management for assistance. The length and width of the trailer may cause recognition problems with the safety loop detector and could cause damage.

Do not operate the gate if there are small children nearby who might get caught in it as it opens or closes.

If you lose your card, please contact the management office immediately.

Do not give your card to anyone else.

Resident or Residents
[All residents must sign here]

Owner or Owner's Representative *[signs here]*

Date of Lease Contract

LEASE ADDENDUM FOR
CODE ACCESS GATE

1. **Addendum.** This is an addendum to the NAA Lease Contract for Apt. No _____ in the _____ Apartments in _____ **Louisiana.**

2. **Code for gate access.** Each resident will be given, at no cost, an access code (keypad number) for the pedestrian or vehicular access gates. It is to be used only during your residency.

3. **Code changes.** We may change the code(s) at any time and notify you accordingly.

4. **Report damage or malfunctions.** Please immediately report to the office any malfunction or damage to gates, fencing, locks or related equipment.

5. **Follow written instructions.** We ask that you and all other occupants read the written instructions that have been furnished to you regarding the access gates. This is important because if the gates are damaged by you or your family, guest or invitee through negligence or misuse, you are liable for the damages under your lease, and collection of damage amounts will be pursued.

6. **Personal injury and/or personal property damage.** Anything mechanical or electronic is subject to malfunction. Fencing, gates or other devices will not prevent all crime. No security system or device is foolproof or 100 percent successful in deterring crime. Crime can still occur. Protecting residents, their families, occupants, guests and invitees from crime is the sole responsibility of residents, occupants and law enforcement agencies. You should first call 911 or other appropriate emergency police numbers if a crime occurs or is suspected. We are not liable to any resident, family member, guest, occupant or invitee for personal injury, death, damage, or loss of personal property from incidents related to perimeter fencing, automobile access gates and/or pedestrian access gates. We reserve the right to modify or eliminate security systems other than those statutorily required.

7. **Rules in using vehicle gates.**

   Always approach entry and exit gates with caution and at a very slow rate of speed.

   Never stop your car where the gate can hit your vehicle as the gate opens or closes.

   Never follow another vehicle into an open gate. Always use the keypad to gain entry.

   Never force the gate open with your car.

   Never get out of your vehicle while the gates are opening or closing.

   If you are using the gates with a boat or trailer, please contact management for assistance. The length and width of the trailer may cause recognition problems with the safety loop detector and could cause damage.

   Do not operate the gate if there are small children nearby who might get caught in it as it opens or closes.

   If you forget your code, please contact the management office immediately.

   Do not give your code to anyone else.

   Do not tamper with gate or allow your occupants or guests to tamper or play with gates.

Resident or Residents
[All residents must sign here]

Owner or Owner's Representative
[signs here]

Date of Lease Contract

LEASE ADDENDUM
FOR INTRUSION ALARM

1. Addendum. This is an addendum to the NAA Lease Contract for Apt. No. ———————— in the ———————— Apartments in ———————————————— Louisiana.

2. Intrusion alarm. Your dwelling is equipped with an intrusion alarm. It must not be considered a guaranty of safety or security. You should at all times take precautions as if the intrusion alarm were malfunctioning. You acknowledge that the security of you and your family, occupants, and guests are your responsibility alone. Your use of the alarm system is *(check one)* ❑ required or ❑ optional. You are responsible for all false alarm charges for your dwelling.

3. Permit from city. You *(check one)* ❑ do or ❑ do not have to obtain a city permit for activation and use of the intrusion alarm. If you do, the phone number to call is ———————————— and it is your responsibility to obtain the permit. You also will be responsible for any fines due to excessive false alarms.

4. Follow instructions. You agree to use reasonable care in operating the alarm and to follow the written instructions, rules, and procedures furnished to you by us. Instructions ❑ are attached or ❑ will be provided to you when you move in.

5. Alarm company. You *(check one)* ❑ will or ❑ will not have to make arrangements with an independent alarm company to activate and maintain the alarm system. You *(check one)* ❑ may choose your own alarm company or ❑ are required to use ———————————— as your alarm company. The alarm system is repaired and maintained by ————————————————

6. Entry by owner. Upon activation of the alarm system, you must immediately provide us (management) with your security code and any special alarm system instructions for lawful entry into the unit when no one is there, as authorized in paragraph 28 (when we may enter) of your NAA Lease Contract. You must **reimburse us for any expenses we incur in entering your** dwelling, when those expenses are due to your failure to provide the foregoing information.

7. Repairs or malfunctions. If the intrusion alarm malfunctions, you agree to *(check one)* ❑ contact your intrusion alarm company immediately for repair or ❑ contact us immediately for repair. The cost of repair will be paid by *(check one)* ❑ you or ❑ us.

8. No warranty. We make no guarantees or warranties, ex- press or implied, concerning the alarm system. All guarantees and warranties are expressly disclaimed. Crime can and does occur despite the best security measures. Anything electronic or mechanical in nature will malfunction from time to time. We are absolutely not responsible for malfunction of the alarm.

9. Liability. We are not liable to you, your guests or other occupants for any injury, damage or loss resulting from the alarm or any malfunction of the alarm. It is recommended that you purchase insurance to cover casualty loss of your property, including loss by theft.

10. Emergencies. Always call 911 or law enforcement authorities or emergency medical services in the event of a crime or emergency. Then contact us. We are not required to answer the alarm, but we do have the right to enter and cut off the alarm to minimize annoyance to neighbors when it malfunctions or is not timely cut off.

11. Entire agreement. We've made no promises or representations regarding the alarm system except those in this addendum.

Resident or Residents
[All residents must sign here]

Owner or Owner's Representative
[signs here]

Date of Lease Contract

Asbestos Addendum

NATIONAL
APARTMENT
ASSOCIATION.

Date: _____

(when this Addendum is filled out)

1. ADDENDUM. This is an addendum to the Lease Contract executed by you, the resident(s), on the dwelling you have agreed to rent. That dwelling is:

Apt. # _____ at _____ (name of apartments) located at _____

City/State where dwelling is located _____

2. ASBESTOS. In most dwellings which were built prior to 1981, asbestos was commonly used as a construction material. In various parts of your dwelling, asbestos materials may have been used in the original construction or in renovations prior to the enactment of federal laws which limit asbestos in certain construction materials.

3. FEDERAL RECOMMENDATIONS. The United States Environmental Protection Agency (EPA) has determined that the mere presence of asbestos materials does not pose a health risk to residents and that such materials are safe so long as they are not dislodged or disturbed in a manner that causes the asbestos fibers to be released. Disturbances include sanding, scraping, pounding, or other techniques that produce dust and cause the asbestos particles to become airborne. The EPA does not require that intact asbestos materials be removed. Instead, the law simply requires that we take reasonable precau-

tions to minimize the chance of damage or disturbance of those materials.

4. COMMUNITY POLICIES AND RULES. You, your families, other occupants, and guests must not disturb or attach anything to the walls, ceilings, floor tiles, or insulation behind the walls or ceilings in your dwelling unless specifically allowed in owner's rules or community policies that are separately attached to this Lease Contract. The foregoing prevails over other provisions of the Lease Contract to the contrary. Please report any ceiling leaks to management promptly so that pieces of acoustical ceiling material or ceiling tiles do not fall to the floor and get disturbed by people walking on the fallen material.

Resident(s)
(All residents must sign)

Date of Signing Addendum

Owner or Owner's Representative

Date of Signing Addendum

You are entitled to receive an original of this Asbestos Addendum after it is fully signed. Keep it in a safe place.

Lease Contract Guaranty

Each guarantor must submit a separate guaranty form, unless guarantors are husband and wife.

Lease Contract Information

ABOUT LEASE: Date of Lease Contract *(top left hand corner of Lease Contract):*

Owner's name *(or name of apartments):*

Resident names *(list all residents on Lease Contract):*
ABOUT GUARANTOR: Full name *(exactly as on driver's license or govt. ID card)*

Unit No. of Apartment
City/State/Zip of above
dwelling:
Monthly rent for dwelling
unit: $
Beginning date of Lease
Contract:

Contract:
Driver's license # and state:
OR govt. photo ID card #:
Birthdate:
and street address of dwelling being leased:
Sex

Guarantor Information
Use for one guarantor only (can include spouse of guarantor)

Current address where you live:
Phone: (_____)
(Please check one) Do you ❑ own or ❑ rent your home? If renting, name of apartments:
Manager's name: Phone:
Your Social Security #:

YOUR WORK: Present employer:
Employer's address:

Work phone: (_____)

YOUR SPOUSE: Full name *(exactly as on driver's license or govt. ID card):*

Driver's license # and state:
OR govt. photo ID card #:
Birthdate:
How long? Position:
Your gross monthly income is over: $ Supervisor's name:
Social Security #:

YOUR CREDIT HISTORY:
Your bank's name:
City/State:
List major credit cards:

To your knowledge, have you, your spouse, or any resident listed in this Guaranty ever: ❑ been asked to move out? ❑ broken a rental agreement? ❑ declared bankruptcy? or ❑ been sued for rent? To your knowledge, has any resident listed in this Guaranty ever: ❑ been sued for property damage? ❑ been charged, detained, or arrested for a felony or sex-related crime that was resolved by conviction, probation, deferred adjudication, court-ordered community supervision, or pretrial diversion? or ❑ been charged, detained, or arrested for a felony or sex-related crime that has not been resolved by any method? Please explain:

You, as guarantor and surety signing this Lease Contract Guaranty, guarantee and become a surety for all obligations of resident(s) under the above Lease Contract, including but not limited to rent, late fees, property damage, repair costs, animal violation charges, re-letting charges, utility payments, and all other sums which may become due under the Lease Contract.

You agree that your obligations as guarantor will continue and will not be affected by amendments, modifications, roommate changes or deletions, unit changes, or renewals in the Lease Contract which may be agreed to from time to time between resident(s) and us. If we, as owner of the dwelling, delay or fail to exercise lease rights, pursue remedies, give notices to you, or make demands to you, as guarantor you will not consider it as a waiver of our rights as owner against you as guarantor. All of our remedies against the resident(s) apply to guarantor as well. All residents, guarantors, and guarantor's spouse are jointly and severally liable. It is unnecessary for us to sue or exhaust remedies against residents in order for you to be liable. This Guaranty is part of the Lease Contract and shall be performed in the county where the apartment unit is located.

You represent that all information submitted by you on this Guaranty is true and complete. You authorize verification of such information via consumer reports, rental history reports, and other means. A facsimile signature by you on this Guaranty will be just as binding as an original signature. It is not necessary for you, as guarantor, to sign the Lease Contract itself or to be named in the Lease Contract. This Guaranty does not have to be referred to in the Lease Contract. It is not legally necessary for this Guaranty to be notarized. Payments under this Guaranty must be mailed to or made in the county where the dwelling unit is located. We recommend that you obtain a copy of the Lease Contract and read it. This Guaranty applies even if you don't do so. We will furnish you a copy of the Lease upon written request.

Ending date of Lease:
Marital Status: ❑ single ❑ married ❑ divorced ❑ widowed ❑ separated
Total number of dependents under the age of 18 or in college:
What relationship are you to the residents(s)? ❑ parent ❑ brother or sister ❑ employer ❑ other
Are you or your spouse a guarantor for any other lease? ❑ Yes ❑ No If so, how many?

Present employer:
How long?
Work phone: (_____)   Position:
Monthly gross income is over : $

Phone:

FOR OFFICE USE ONLY
Guarantor(s) signature(s) was (were) verified by owner's representative.
    Verification was by ❑ phone or ❑ face-to-face meeting.
    Telephone numbers called (if applicable)
    Name(s) of Guarantor(s) who was (were) contacted
    Name of Owner's Representative who talked to Guarantor(s)

Date of signing Guaranty

Signature of Guarantor

Signature of Guarantor's Spouse
    After signing, please return the signed original of this Guaranty to

    at *(street address or P.O. Box)*

    or *(optional)* fax it to us at _____
    Our telephone number _____
You are entitled to receive a copy of this Lease Contract Guaranty when it is fully signed.
Keep it in a safe place.

Date(s) of verification _____

UTILITY ADDENDUM FOR WATER, SEWER, GAS,
TRASH, AND ELECTRIC SERVICE

**NATIONAL
APARTMENT
ASSOCIATION.**

This Utility Addendum is incorporated into the Lease dated _____ between _____
("We") and _____ ("You") of Apt. No. _____
and is in addition to all terms and conditions in the Lease. To the extent that the terms of this Utility Addendum conflict with those of the Lease, this Utility Addendum shall control.

1. Responsibility for payment of utilities, and the method of metering or otherwise measuring the cost of the utility, will be as indicated below.
    a) Water service to your apartment will be paid by you either:
        ❑ directly to the utility service provider; or
        ❑ water bills will be billed by the service provider to us and then allocated to you based on the following formula:
    b) Sewer service to your apartment will be paid by you either:
        ❑ directly to the utility service provider; or
        ❑ sewer bills will be billed by the service provider to us and then allocated to you based on the following formula:
    c) Gas service to your apartment will be paid by you either:
        ❑ directly to the utility service provider; or
        ❑ gas bills will be billed by the service provider to us and then allocated to you based on the following formula:
    d) Trash service to your apartment will be paid by you either:
        ❑ directly to the service provider; or
        ❑ trash bills will be billed by the service provider to us and then allocated to you based on the following formula:
    e) Electric service to your apartment will be paid by you either:
        ❑ directly to the utility service provider; or
        ❑ electric bills will be billed by the service provider to us and then allocated to you based on the following formula:

METERING/ALLOCATION METHOD KEY
"1" Submetering of all of your water/gas/electric use
"2" Calculation of your total water use based on submetering of hot water
"3" Calculation of your total water use based on submetering of cold water
"4" Flat rate of $_____ per month
"5" Allocation based on the number of persons residing in your apartment unit
"6" Allocation based on the number of persons residing in your apartment unit using a ratio occupancy formula
"7" Allocation based on square footage of your apartment unit
"8" Allocation based on a combination of square footage of your apartment unit and the number of persons residing in your apartment unit
"9" Allocation based on the number of bedrooms in your apartment unit
"10" Allocation based on a lawful formula not listed here
        (Note: if method "10" is selected, a separate sheet will be attached describing the formula used)

2. If an allocation formula above is used, we or our billing company will calculate your allocated share of the utility services in accordance with state and local laws. If allowed by state law, we at our sole discretion may change the above methods of determining your allocated share of the utility services, by written notice to you.

3. When billed by us directly or through our billing company, you must pay utility bills within _____ days of the date when the utility bill is issued at the place indicated on your bill, or the payment will be late. If a payment is late, you will be responsible for a late fee in the amount of $_____ The late payment of a bill or failure to pay any utility bill is a material and substantial breach of the Lease and we will exercise all remedies available under the Lease, up to and including eviction for nonpayment. To the extent there is a billing fee for the production of any utility bill or a set-up charge or initiation fee by our billing company, you shall pay such fees in the amount of $_____.

4. You will be charged for the full period of time that you were living in, occupying, or responsible for payment of rent or utility charges on the apartment. If you breach the Lease, you will be responsible for utility charges for the time period you were obligated to pay the charges under the Lease, subject to our mitigation of damages. In the event you fail to timely establish utility services, we may charge you for any utility service billed to us for your apartment and may charge a reasonable administration fee for billing for the utility service in the amount of $_____.

5. When you move out, you will receive a final bill which may be estimated based on your prior utility usage. This bill must be paid at the time you move out or it will be deducted from the security deposit.

6. We are not liable for any losses or damages you incur as a result of outages, interruptions, or fluctuations in utility services provided to the apartment unless such loss or damage was the direct result of negligence by us or our employees. You release us from any and all such claims and waive any claims for offset or reduction of rent or diminished rental value of the apartment due to such outages, interruptions, or fluctuations.

7. You agree not to tamper with, adjust, or disconnect any utility submetering system or device. Violation of this provision is a material breach of your Lease and may subject you to eviction or other remedies available to us under your Lease and this Utility Addendum.

8. The following special provisions and any addenda or written rules furnished to you at or before signing will become a part of this Utility Addendum and will supersede any conflicting provisions of this printed Utility Addendum and/or the Apartment Lease Contract.

Resident Signature _____   Date _____

Resident Signature _____   Date _____

Resident Signature _____   Date _____

Resident Signature _____   Date _____

Management _____   Date _____

© 2004, National Apartment Association, Inc.

LEASE ADDENDUM
FOR SATELLITE DISH OR ANTENNA

Under a Federal Communications Commission (FCC) order, you as our resident have a right to install a transmitting or receiving satellite dish or antenna on the leased premises, subject to FCC limitations. We as a rental housing owner are allowed to impose reasonable restrictions relating to such installation. You are required to comply with these restrictions as a condition of installing such equipment. This addendum contains the restrictions that you and we agree to follow.

1. Addendum. This is an addendum to the NAA Lease Contract for
   Apt. No. _____ in the _____
   Apartments in _____
   Louisiana.

2. Number and size. You may install _____ satellite dish(es) or antenna(s) on the leased premises. A satellite dish may not exceed one meter (3.3 feet) in diameter. Antennas that only transmit signals or that are not covered by 47 CFR § 1.4000 are prohibited.

3. Location. Your satellite dish or antenna must be located: (1) inside your dwelling; or (2) in an area outside your dwelling such as a balcony, patio, yard, etc. of which you have exclusive use under your lease. Installation is not permitted on any parking area, roof, exterior wall, window, window sill, fence, or common area, or in an area that other residents are allowed to use. A satellite dish or antenna may not protrude beyond the vertical and horizontal space that is leased to you for your exclusive use.

4. Safety and non-interference. Your installation: (1) must comply with all applicable ordinances and laws and all reasonable safety standards; (2) may not interfere with our cable, telephone, or electrical systems or those of neighboring properties; (3) may not be connected to our telecommunication systems; and (4) may not be connected to our electrical system except by plugging into a 110-volt duplex receptacle. If the satellite dish or antenna is placed in a permitted outside area, it must be safely secured by one of three methods: (1) securely attaching it to a portable, heavy object such as a small slab of concrete (cinder block); (2) clamping it to a part of the building's exterior that is within your leased premises (such as a balcony or patio railing); or (3) any other method approved by us in writing. No other methods are allowed. We may require reasonable screening of the satellite dish or antenna by plants, etc., so long as it does not impair reception.

5. Signal transmission from exterior dish or antenna to interior of dwelling. You may not damage or alter the leased premises and may not drill holes through outside walls, door jams, window sills. etc. If your satellite dish or antenna is installed outside your dwelling (on a balcony, patio, etc.), the signals received by it may be transmitted to the interior of your dwelling only by the following methods: (1) running a "flat" cable under a door jam or window sill in a manner that does not physically alter the premises and does not interfere with proper operation of the door or window; (2) running a traditional or flat cable through a pre-existing hole in the wall (that will not need to be enlarged to accommodate the cable); (3) connecting cables through a window pane, similar to how an external car antenna for a cellular phone can be connected to inside wiring by a device glued to either side of the window—without drilling a hole through the window; (4) wireless transmission of the signal from the satellite dish or antenna to a device inside the dwelling; or (5) any other method approved by us in writing.

   Safety in installation. In order to assure safety, the strength and type of materials used for installation must be approved by us. Installation must be done by a qualified person or company approved by us. Our approval will not be unreasonably withheld. An installer provided by the seller of the satellite dish or antenna is presumed to be qualified.

7. Maintenance. You will have the sole responsibility for maintaining your satellite dish, antenna and all related equipment.

8. Removal and damages. You must remove the satellite dish or antenna and all related equipment when you move out of the dwelling. In accordance with the NAA Lease Contract, you must pay for any damages and for the cost of repairs or repainting caused by negligence, carelessness, accident or abuse which may be reasonably necessary to restore the leased premises to its condition prior to the installation of your satellite dish, antenna or related equipment. You will not be responsible for normal wear.

9. Liability insurance and indemnity. You must take full responsibility for the satellite dish, antenna, and related equipment. If the dish or antenna is installed at a height that could result in injury to others and if it becomes unattached and falls, you must provide us with evidence of liability insurance (if available) to protect us against claims of personal injury and property damage to others, related to your satellite dish, antenna and related equipment. The insurance coverage must be $_____, which is an amount reasonably determined by us to accomplish that purpose. Factors affecting the amount of insurance include height of installation above ground level, potential wind velocities, risk of the dish/antenna becoming unattached and falling on someone, etc. You agree to hold us harmless and indemnify us against any of the above claims by others.

10. Security deposit. Your security deposit (in paragraph 4 of your Lease Contract) is increased by an additional reasonable sum of $_____ to help protect us against possible repair costs damages, or failure to remove the satellite dish, antenna and related equipment at time of move-out. Factors affecting any security deposit may vary, depending on: (1) how the dish or antenna is attached (nails, screws, jag bolts drilled into walls); (2) whether holes were permitted to be drilled through walls for the cable between the satellite dish and the TV; and (3) the difficulty and cost of repair or restoration after removal, etc.

11. When you may begin installation. You may start installation of your satellite dish, antenna or related equipment only after you have: (1) signed this addendum; (2) provided us with written evidence of the liability insurance referred to in paragraph 9 (Liability Insurance and Indemnity) of this addendum; (3) paid us the additional security deposit, if applicable, in paragraph 10 (security deposit); and (4) received our written approval of the installation materials and the person or company that will do the installation, which approval may not be unreasonably withheld.

12. Miscellaneous. If additional satellite dishes or antennas are desired, an additional lease addendum must be executed.

Resident or Residents
[All residents must sign here)

Owner or Owner's Representative
[signs here]

Date of Lease Contract

Supplemental Rental Application for Non–U.S. Citizens

Each co-resident and each occupant over 18 who is not a U.S. citizen must submit a separate application.
Spouses may submit a joint application.

NATIONAL
APARTMENT
ASSOCIATION.

We are requesting you to fill out this Supplemental Rental Application because you have indicated that you are not a U.S. citizen. We are asking all applicants who are not U.S. citizens to fill out this form. We are committed to compliance with fair housing laws and do not discriminate based on race, color, religion, sex, national origin, handicap, or familial status. The purpose of this form is:
1. to give you the option to furnish information about an emergency contact person for you in your home country;
2. to verify that you are lawfully in the United Slates;
3. to determine whether your right to be in the U.S. expires during your Lease Contract term; and
4. to enable us to better cooperate with government officials in the performance of their duties, when requested.
We don't anticipate sharing this Supplemental Application with anyone except government officials who might inquire about you.

ABOUT YOU   Your full name *(exactly as on any card or document issued by U.S. Immigration and Naturalization Service):*

Your place of birth. *Please indicate the city, state (region, province, etc.) and country:*

Country or countries of which you are a citizen *(list all):*

Approximately how long have you been in the United States?

Years: Months:

Visa expiration date:

Have you ever been asked or ordered by a representative of any government to leave the U.S. or any other country? ❏ Yes ❏ No If yes, please state when and what country or countries *(list all):*

Person in your home country whom we may contact in event of an emergency *(optional).*
Name:
Relationship:
Mailing address:
E-mail address:
Phone:
Please check the U.S. Immigration and Naturalization Service (INS) document that entitles you to be in the United States:
     ❏ Form 1-551 Permanent Resident Card [Alien Registration Receipt Card] (form includes photo and fingerprint).
     Card number:
     ❏ Form 1-688 Temporary Resident Card (form includes photo and fingerprint).
     Expiration date:
     Card number:
     ❏ Form 1-688A Employment Authorization Card (form includes photo and fingerprint).
     Expiration date:
     Card number:
     ❏ Form 1-94 Arrival-Departure Record (form does not include photo or fingerprint).
     Expiration date:
     Form number:
     ❏ INS receipt for replacement of one of the above documents, with verification by INS of your entitlement to the above.

If you are relying on Form 1-94, we will ask to see your passport and visa, and you will need to answer the questions below.

Country issuing your passport:
     Your passport number:
     Expiration date:
Do you have a visa? ❏ Yes ❏ No
     If yes, what type? ❏ student ❏ work ❏ visitor ❏ other *(specify):*
     Visa expiration date:

YOUR SPOUSE   Your full name *(exactly as on any card or document issued by U.S. Immigration and Naturalization Service):*

Your place of birth. *Please indicate the city, state, (region, province, etc.) and country:*

Country or countries of which you are a citizen *(list all):*

Approximately how long have you been in the United States?

Years: Months:

Visa expiration date:

Have you ever been asked or ordered by a representative of any government to leave the U.S. or any other country? ❏ Yes ❏ No If yes, please state when and what country or countries *(list all):*

Person in your home country whom we may contact in event of an emergency *(optional).*
Name:
Relationship:
Mailing address:
E-mail address:
Phone:
Please check the U.S. Immigration and Naturalization Service (INS) document that entitles you to be in the United States:
     ❏ Form 1-551 Permanent Resident Card [Alien Registration Receipt Card] (form includes photo and fingerprint).
     Card number:
     ❏ Form 1-688 Temporary Resident Card (form includes photo and fingerprint).
     Expiration date:
     Card number:
     ❏ Form 1-688A Employment Authorization Card (form includes photo and fingerprint).
     Expiration date:
     Card number:
     ❏ Form 1-94 Arrival-Departure Record (form does not include photo or fingerprint).
     Expiration date:
     Form number:
     ❏ INS receipt for replacement of one of the above documents, with verification by INS of your entitlement to the above.

If you are relying on Form 1-94, we will ask to see your passport and visa, and you will need to answer the questions below.

Country issuing your passport:
     Your passport number:
     Expiration date:
Do you have a visa? ❏ Yes ❏ No
     If yes, what type? ❏ student ❏ work ❏ visitor ❏ other *(specify):*
     Visa expiration date:

Applicant's signature _____

Spouse's signature_____

Date _____

We may ask to make a photocopy of any of the INS documents checked above and, if needed, your passport and visa.

Louisiana/National Apartment Association Official Form 04oGG, 2004
© 2004, National Apartment Association, Inc.

LEASE ADDENDUM FOR
ENCLOSED GARAGE, CARPORT, OR STORAGE UNIT

1. **Addendum.** This is an addendum to the lease between you and us for Apt. No. _____ in the _____ Apartments in _____ **Louisiana.**

2. **Garage, carport, or storage unit.** You are entitled to exclusive possession of: *(check as applicable)*
   ❑ garage or carport attached to the dwelling;
   ❑ garage space number(s) _____
   ❑ carport space number(s) _____; and/or
   ❑ storage unit number(s) _____
   The monthly rent in paragraph 6 of the lease covers both the dwelling and the checked area(s) above. All terms and conditions of the lease apply to the above areas unless modified by this addendum.

3. **Use restrictions.** Garage or carport may be used only for storage of operable motor vehicles unless otherwise stated in our rules or community policies. Storage units may be used only for storage of personal property. No one may sleep, cook, barbecue, or live in a garage, carport, or storage unit. Persons not listed as a resident or occupant in the lease may not use the areas covered by this addendum. No plants may be grown in such areas.

4. **No dangerous items.** Items that pose an environmental hazard or a risk to the safety or health of other residents, occupants, or neighbors in our sole judgment or that violate any government regulation may not be stored. Prohibited items include fuel (other than in a properly capped fuel tank of a vehicle or a closed briquette lighter fluid container), fireworks, rags, piles of paper, or other material that may create a fire or environmental hazard. We **may remove from such areas, without prior notice, items that we** believe might constitute a fire or environmental hazard. Because of carbon monoxide risks, you may not run the motor of a vehicle inside a garage unless the garage door is open to allow fumes to escape.

5. **No smoke, fire, or carbon monoxide detectors.** No smoke, fire, or carbon monoxide detectors will be furnished by us unless required by law.

6. **Garage door opener.** If an enclosed garage is furnished, you ❑ will ❑ will not be provided with a ❑ garage door opener and/or ❑ garage key. You will be responsible for maintenance of any garage door opener, including battery replacement. Transmitter frequency settings may not be changed on the garage door or opener without our prior written consent.

7. **Security.** We will not have any security responsibilities for areas covered by this addendum. Always remember to lock any door of a garage or storage unit and any door between a garage and the dwelling. When leaving, be sure to lock all keyed deadbolt locks.

8. **Insurance and loss/damage to your property.** Any area covered by this addendum is accepted by you "as is." You will maintain liability and comprehensive insurance coverage for any vehicle parked or stored. We will have no responsibility for loss or damage to vehicles or other property parked or stored in a garage, carport, or storage unit, whether caused by accident, fire, theft, water, vandalism, pests, mysterious disappearance, **or** otherwise. We are not responsible for pest control in such areas.

9. **Compliance.** We may periodically open and enter garages and storerooms to ensure compliance with this addendum. In that event, written notice of such opening and entry will be left inside the main entry door of your dwelling or inside the door between the garage and your dwelling.

10. **No lock changes, alterations, or improvements.** Without our prior written consent, locks on doors of garages and storage units may not be rekeyed, added, or changed, and improvements, alterations, or electrical extensions or changes to the interior or exterior of such areas are not allowed. You may not place nails, screws, bolts, or hooks into walls, ceilings, floors, or doors. Any damage not caused by us or our representatives to areas covered by this addendum will be paid for by you.

11. **Move-out and remedies.** Any items remaining after you have vacated the dwelling will be removed, sold, or otherwise disposed of according to paragraph 13 of the lease, which addresses disposition or sale of property left in an abandoned or surrendered dwelling. All remedies in the lease apply to areas covered by this addendum.

Resident or Residents
[All residents must sign here]

Owner or Owner's Representative
[signs here]

Date of Lease Contract

LEASE ADDENDUM
FOR EARLY TERMINATION OF LEASE CONTRACT

1. **Addendum.** This is an addendum to the NAA Lease Contract for Apartment No. _____ in the _____ Apartments in _____ **Louisiana.**

2. **Right of early termination.** We understand that circumstances may arise in the future that pose a need for you to terminate this Lease Contract prior to the end of the lease term. The purpose of this addendum is to give you the right to do so—subject to any special provisions in paragraph 8 below. In order to terminate early, your notice must be signed by all residents listed in paragraph 1 of the Lease Contract and you must comply with all provisions of this addendum.

3. **Procedures.** You may terminate the Lease Contract prior to the end of the lease term and cut off all liability for paying rent for the remainder of the lease term *if all of the following occur:*
   (a) you give us written notice of early termination at least _____
   days prior to your early termination date (i.e., your early move-out date), which *(check one):* ❑ must be the last day of a month or ❑ may be during a month;
   (b) you specify the early termination date in the notice, i.e., the date by which you'll move out;
   (c) you are not in default under the Lease Contract on the date you give us the notice of early termination;
   (d) you are not in default under the Lease Contract on the early termination date (move-out date);
   (e) you move out on or before the early termination date and do not hold over;
   (f) you pay us a $_____ early termination fee;
   (g) you pay us the amount of any concessions you received when signing the Lease Contract; and
   (h) you comply with any special provisions in paragraph 8 below.

4. **When payable.** The early termination fee in paragraph 3(f) is due and payable no later than _____ days after you give us your early termination notice. The total dollar amount of any concessions regarding rent or other monetary lease obligations for the entire lease term is $_____ and is due and payable on the same day as the early termination fee, subject to any special provisions in paragraph 8 regarding the amount, calculation method, or payment date.

5. **Showing unit to prospective residents.** After you give us notice of early lease termination, paragraph 28 (when we may enter) of the Lease Contract gives us the right to begin showing your unit to prospective residents and tell-ing them it will be available immediately after your early termination date.

6. **Compliance essential.** Our deposit of all amounts due under paragraphs 3(f) and 3(g) constitutes our approval of the move-out date Stated in your notice of early termination. If you fail to comply with any of the procedures or requirements in this addendum after we deposit such monies, your early termination right and this addendum will be voided automatically; and (1) any amounts you have paid under this addendum will become part of your security deposit, and (2) the lease will continue without early termination. Then, if you move out early, you are subject to all lease remedies, including re-letting fees and liability for all rents for the remainder of the original lease term.

7. **Miscellaneous.** If moving out by the early termination date becomes a problem for you, contact us. An extension may be possible if we have not already re-let the dwelling unit to others. We and any successor residents who may be leasing your unit will be relying on your moving out on or before the early termination date. Therefore, you may not hold over beyond such date without our written consent—even if it means you have to make plans for temporary lodging elsewhere. "Default" as used in paragraphs 3(c) and 3(d) of this addendum means default as defined in paragraph 32 of the Lease Contract. You will continue to be liable for any damages and any sums accruing and unpaid prior to the early **termination date.**

8. **Special provisions.** Your right of early termination *(check one):* ❑ is or ❑ is not limited to a particular fact situation. If limited, early termination may be exercised only if the following facts occur and the described documents are furnished to us (for example, a letter verifying your job transfer to another city at least 30 miles away, or a letter from a title insurance company verifying your contract to purchase a home and the scheduled closing date). Any special provisions below will supersede any conflicting provision of this printed form. Any false statements or documents presented to us regarding early termination will automatically void your early termination right and this addendum. The special **provisions are:**

Resident or Residents
[All residents must sign]

Owner or Owner's Representative
[signs below]

Date of Lease Contract

©2004, National Apartment Association, Inc.

COMMUNITY POLICIES, RULES AND REGULATIONS
ADDENDUM

This addendum is incorporated into the Lease Contract (the "Lease") identified below and is in addition to all the terms and conditions contained in the Lease. If any terms of this Addendum conflict with the Lease, the terms of this Addendum shall be call/rolling:

Property Owner:

Resident(s):
Apartment Community:
Apartment No: *Address:*
Lease Date:

I.   GENERAL CONDITIONS FOR USE OF APARTMENT PROPERTY AND RECREATIONAL FACILITIES.

Resident(s) permission for use of all common areas, Resident amenities, and recreational facilities (together, "Amenities") located at the Apartment Community is a privilege and license granted by Owner, and not a contractual right except as otherwise provided for in the Lease. Such permission is expressly conditioned upon Resident's adherence to the terms of the Lease, this Addendum, and the Community rules and regulations ("Rules") in effect at any given time, and such permission may be revoked by Owner at any time for any lawful reason. In all cases, the most strict terms of either the Lease, this Addendum, or the Community Rules shall take precedence. Owner reserves the right to set the days and hours of use for all Amenities and to change the character of or close any Amenity based upon the needs of Owner and in Owner's sale and absolute discretion, without notice, obligation or recompense of any nature to Resident. Owner and management may make changes to the Rules for use of any Amenity at any time.

Additionally, Resident(s) expressly agrees to assume all risks of every type, including but not limited to risks of personal injury or property damage, of whatever nature or severity, related to Resident's use of the amenities at the Community. Resident(s) agrees to hold Owner harmless and release and waive any and all claims, allegations, actions, damages, losses, or liabilities of every type, whether or not foreseeable, that Resident(s) may have against Owner and that are in any way related to or arise from such use. This provision shall be enforceable to the fullest extent of the law.

THE TERMS OF THIS ADDENDUM SHALL ALSO APPLY TO RESIDENT(S)' OCCUPANTS, AGENTS AND INVITEES, TOGETHER WITH THE HEIRS, ASSIGNS, ESTATES AND LEGAL REPRESENTATIVES OF THEM ALL, AND RESIDENT(S) SHALL BE SOLELY RESPONSIBLE FOR THE COMPLIANCE OF SUCH PERSONS WITH THE LEASE, THIS ADDENDUM, AND COMMUNITY RULES AND REGULATIONS, AND RESIDENT(S) INTEND TO AND SHALL INDEMNIFY AND HOLD OWNER HARMLESS FROM ALL CLAIMS OF SUCH PERSONS AS DESCRIBED IN THE PRECEDING PARAGRAPH. The term "Owner" shall include the Management, officers, partners, employees, agents, assigns, Owners, subsidiaries and affiliates of Owner.

II. POOL. This Community ❑ DOES; ❑ DOES NOT have a pool. When using the pool, Resident(s) agrees to the following:

Residents and guests will adhere to the rules and regulations posted in the pool area and Management policies.

All Swimmers swim at their own risk. Owner is not responsible for accidents or injuries.
For their safety, Residents should not swim alone.
Pool hours are posted at the pool.
Children under the minimum age (posted at the pool) must be accompanied at all times by a parent or legal guardian.
No glass, pets, or alcoholic beverages are permitted in the pool area. Use paper or plastic containers only.
Proper swimming attire is required at all times and a swimsuit "cover up" should be worn to and from the pool.
No running or rough activities are allowed in the pool area. Respect others by minimizing noise, covering pool furniture with a towel when using suntan oils, leaving pool furniture in pool areas, disposing of trash, and keeping pool gates closed.
Resident(s) must accompany their guests.
Resident(s) must notify Owner any time there is a problem or safety hazard at the pool.

IN CASE OF EMERGENCY DIAL 911

III. FITNESS CENTER. This Community ❑ DOES; ❑ DOES NOT have a fitness center. When using the fitness center, Resident agrees to the following:

Residents and guests will adhere to the rules and regulations posted in the fitness center and Management policies.

The Fitness Center is not supervised. Resident(s) are solely responsible for their own appropriate use of equipment.
Resident(s) shall carefully inspect each piece of equipment prior to Resident's use and shall refrain from using any equipment that may be functioning improperly or that may be damaged or dangerous.
Resident(s) shall immediately report to Management any equipment that is not functioning properly, is damaged or appears dangerous, as well any other person's use that appears to be dangerous or in violation of Management Rules and Policies.
Resident(s) shall consult a physician before using any equipment in the Fitness Center and before participating in any aerobics or exercise class, and will refrain from such use or participation unless approved by Resident's physician.
Resident(s) will keep Fitness Center locked at all times during Resident's visit to the Fitness Center.
Resident(s) will not admit any person to the Fitness Center who has not registered with the Management Office.
Children under the minimum age (posted at the fitness center) must be accompanied at all times by a parent or legal guardian.
Resident(s) must accompany guests, and no glass, smoking, eating, alcoholic beverages, pets, or black sole shoes are permitted in the Fitness Center.

Card # issued: (1) _____ (2) _____ (3) _____ (4) _____

IV. PACKAGE RELEASE. This Community ❑ DOES; ❑ DOES NOT accept packages on behalf of Residents.

For communities that do accept packages on behalf of Residents:
Resident(s) gives Owner permission to sign and accept any parcels or letters sent to Resident(s) through UPS, Federal Express, Airborne, United States Postal Service, or the like. Resident agrees that Owner does not accept responsibility or liability for any lost, damaged, or unordered deliveries, and agrees to hold Owner harmless for the same.

V.   BUSINESS CENTER. This Community ❑ DOES; ❑ DOES NOT have a business center.

Resident(s) agrees to use the business center at Resident(s) sole risk and according to the Community Rules. Owner is not responsible for data, files, programs or any other information lost or damaged on Business Center computers or in the Business Center for any reason. No software may be loaded on Business Center computers without the written approval of Community Management. No inappropriate, offensive, or pornographic images or files (in the sale judgment of Owner) will be viewed or loaded onto the Business Center computers at any time. Residents will limit time on computers to minutes if others are waiting to use them. Smoking, eating, alcoholic beverages, pets, and any disturbing behavior are prohibited in the business center. Children under the age of _____ must be accompanied by a Resident who is that child's parent or legal guardian.

VI.   AUTOMOBILES/BOATS/RECREATIONAL VEHICLES. The following policies are in addition to those in the Lease, and may be modified by the additional rules in effect at the Community at any given time:

Only _____ vehicle per licensed Resident is allowed.
All vehicles must be registered at the Management office.
Any vehicle(s) not registered, considered abandoned, or violating the Lease, this Addendum, or the Community Rules, in the sole judgment of Management, will be towed at the vehicle owner's expense after a _____ hour notice is placed on the vehicle.
Notwithstanding this, any vehicle illegally parked in a fire lane, designated no parking space or handicapped space, or blocking an entrance, exit, driveway, dumpster, or parked illegally in a designated parking space, will immediately be towed, without notice, at the vehicle owner's expense.
The washing of vehicles is not permitted on the property unless specifically allowed in designated area.
Any property repairs and/or maintenance of any vehicle must be with the prior written permission of the Management.
Recreational vehicles, boats or trailers may only be parked on the property with Management's permission (in Management's sole discretion), and must be registered with the Management Office and parked in the area(s) designated by Management.

VII. FIRE HAZARDS. In order to minimize fire hazards and comply with city ordinances, Resident shall comply with the following:

Residents and guests will adhere to the Community rules and regulations other Management policies concerning fire hazards, which may be revised from time to time.
No person shall knowingly maintain a fire hazard.
Grills, barbecues, and any other outdoor cooking or open-flame devices will be used only on the ground level and will be placed a minimum of _____ feet from any building. Such devices will not be used close to combustible materials, tall grass or weeds, on exterior walls or on roofs, indoors, on balconies or patios, or in other locations which may cause fires.
Fireplaces: Only firewood is permitted in the fireplace. No artificial substances, such as DuraFlame® logs are permitted. Ashes must be disposed of in metal containers, after ensuring the ashes are cold.
Flammable or combustible liquids and fuels shall not be used or stored (including stock for sale) in apartments, near exits, stairways, breezeways, or areas normally used for the ingress and egress of people. This includes motorcycles and any apparatus or engine using flammable or combustible liquid as fuel.
No person shall block or obstruct any exit, aisle, passageway, hallway or stairway leading to or from any structure.
Resident(s) are solely responsible for fines or penalties caused by their actions in violation of local fire protection codes.

VIII. EXTERMINATING. Unless prohibited by statute or otherwise stated in the Lease, Owner may conduct extermination operations in Residents' apartment several times a year and as needed to prevent insect infestation. Owner will notify Residents in advance of extermination in Residents' Apartment, and give Resident instructions for the preparation of the Apartment and safe contact with insecticides. Residents will be responsible to prepare the Apartment for extermination in accordance with Owner's instructions. If Residents are unprepared for a scheduled treatment date Owner will prepare Residents' apartment and charge Residents accordingly. Residents must request extermination treatments in addition to those regularly provided by Owner in writing. Residents are to perform the tasks required by Owner on the day of interior extermination to ensure the safety and effectiveness of the extermination. These tasks will include, but are not limited to, the following:

Clean in all cabinets, drawers and closets in kitchen and pantry
If roaches have been seen in closets, remove contents from shelves and floor.
Remove infants and young children from the apartment.

Remove pets or place them in bedrooms, and notify Owner of such placement.
Remove chain locks or other types of obstruction on day of service.
Cover fish tanks and turn off their air pumps.
Do not wipe out cabinets after treatment.

RESIDENTS ARE SOLELY RESPONSIBLE TO NOTIFY OWNER IN WRITING PRIOR TO EXTERMINATION OF ANY ANTICIPATED HEALTH OR SAFETY CONCERNS RELATED TO EXTERMINATION AND THE USE OF INSECTICIDES

IX.   DRAPES AND SHADES. Drapes or shades installed by Resident, when allowed, must be lined in white and present a uniform exterior appearance.

X.   WATER BEDS. Resident shall not have water beds or furniture in the apartment without prior written permission of Owner.

XI.   BALCONY or PATIO. Balconies and patios shall be kept neat and clean at all times. No rugs, towels, laundry, clothing, appliances, or other items shall be stored, hung, or draped on railings or other portions of balconies or patios.

XII. SIGNS. Resident shall not display any signs, exterior lights, or markings on apartment. No awnings or other projections shall be attached to the outside of the building of which apartment is a part.

XII. SATELLITE DISHES/ANTENNAS. You must complete a satellite addendum and abide by its terms prior to installation or use.

XIV. WAIVER/SEVERABILITY CLAUSE. No waiver of any provision herein, or in any Community rules and regulations, shall be effective unless granted by the Owner in a signed and dated writing. If any court of competent jurisdiction finds that any clause, phrase, or provision of this Part is invalid for any reason whatsoever, this finding shall not affect the validity of the remaining portions of this addendum, the Apartment Lease Contract or any other addenda to the Apartment Lease Contract.

I have read, understand, and agree to comply with the preceding provisions.

Resident
Date

Resident
Date

Owner Representative
Date

LEASE ADDENDUM REGARDING
LIMITED WAIVER AND MODIFICATION OF RIGHTS UNDER U.S.
SERVICEMEMBERS CIVIL RELIEF ACT

1. Addendum. This is an addendum to the NAA Lease Contract for Apt. No. _____ in the _____, Apartments in _____ Louisiana.

   For purposes of this addendum, "you" means a servicemember as defined by the "U.S. Servicemembers Civil Relief Act" (SCRA).

2. Reason for addendum. Congress has enacted into law the "U.S. Servicemembers Civil Relief Act" (SCRA). This law, among other things, modifies the rights of military personnel to terminate a lease in certain cases and provides that military personnel may waive their rights under the SCRA in certain circumstances. There are different interpretations of how the SCRA affects dependents' and occupants' rights to terminate a lease in the event of a deployment. This addendum clarifies your rights and our obligations in the event of a deployment. This addendum provides for a limited waiver of the terms of the SCRA. However, we agree to grant individuals covered by the SCRA and their spouses all of the rights described in this addendum.

3. Waiver and modification of paragraph 23. The language of paragraph 23 of the NAA Lease Contract is entirely replaced by the language of this addendum. A resident who is a servicemember on active military duty at the time of signing this Lease Contract and such resident's spouse waive for the purposes of this Lease Contract all rights under the SCRA, and shall instead have the rights and obligations set forth below.

4. Military personnel right to terminate. Except as provided in paragraphs 5 or 11 below, you or your spouse may terminate the Lease Contract if you enlist or are drafted or commissioned in the U.S. Armed Forces during the original or renewal Lease Contract term. You or your spouse also may terminate the Lease Contract if:

   (1) you are (i) a member of the U.S. Armed Forces or reserves on active duty *or* (ii) a member of the National Guard called to active duty for more than 30 days in response to a national emergency declared by the President; *and*

   (2) you (i) receive orders for permanent change-of-station, (ii) receive orders to deploy with a military unit or as an individual in support of a military operation for 90 days or more, *or* (iii) are relieved or released from active duty.

   If you or your spouse terminates under this addendum, we must be furnished with a copy of your military orders, such as permanent change-of-station orders, call-up orders, or deployment orders or letter. Military permission for base housing does not constitute permanent change-of-station orders.

5. Exception for termination upon deployment orders. If you or your spouse are terminating the Lease Contract due to deployment orders, you or your spouse may terminate the Lease Contract only on the condition that during the remainder of the original or renewal Lease Contract term neither you nor your spouse will accept an assignment for or move into base housing,

or move into other housing located within 45 miles of the dwelling unit described above.

If you or your spouse terminate the Lease Contract and violate this paragraph, the Lease Contract shall be deemed to have not been legally terminated and you and your spouse shall be in default under the Lease Contract. In that event, we will have all legal remedies, including those described in the Lease Contract, such as charging a re-renting fee under paragraph 11 and accelerating rent under paragraph 32.

6. Effect of housing allowance continuation. The fact that the servicemember continues to receive a housing allowance for the servicemember's spouse and/or dependents after deployment does not affect the right of the servicemember or the servicemember's spouse to terminate unless otherwise stated in paragraph 11 of this addendum.

7. Other co-residents. A co-resident who is not a spouse of a servicemember may not terminate under this addendum. Your and your spouse's right to terminate the Lease Contract under this addendum only affects the Lease Contract as it applies to you and your spouse—other residents' rights and obligations under the Lease Contract remain unchanged.

8. Termination date. If you or your spouse terminates under this addendum, all rights and obligations of you and your spouse under the Lease Contract will be terminated 30 days after the date on which the next rental payment is due, with the exception of obligations arising before the termination date and lawful security deposit deductions.

9. Representations. Unless you state otherwise in paragraph 11 of this addendum, you represent when signing this addendum that: (1) you have not already received deployment or change-of-station orders; (2) you will not be retiring from the military during the Lease Contract term; and (3) the term of your enlistment or obligation will not end before the Lease Contract term ends. Liquidated damages for making a false representation of the above will be the amount of unpaid rent for the remainder of the lease term when and if you move out, less rents from others received in mitigation under paragraph 32 of the lease. You must immediately notify us if you are called to active duty or receive deployment or permanent change of station orders.

10. Other rights unchanged. All other contractual rights and duties of both you and us under the Lease Contract remain unchanged.

11. Additional Provisions. The following provisions will supersede any conflicting provisions of the Lease Contract and this addendum.

Resident or Residents
[All residents must sign here]

Owner or Owner's Representative
[signs here]

Date of Lease Contract

Appendix B:

Did You Know? . . .

- ❑ If you use boiler controls that work off of outside temperature, the probes to detect temperature should be on the north side of a building.
- ❑ Silver chain link fences can look rusty and old after a time and become unsightly looking. Rather than replace them, paint the chain link with an emerald or dark green paint. It makes the fence look like new. Don't spray paint it, though; everything will be green!
- ❑ Although beige or light tan carpet always looks brighter, don't use it on common hallways, because it stains very easily. Use blues and grays in common hallways.
- ❑ Never take a personal check for move-in day and then hand over the keys. Rubber checks and occupied apartments don't mix!
- ❑ Squirrels in attics can be lured into cages with peanut butter, then transported off the property.
- ❑ Although post office "gang boxes" for mail delivery may seem like an inconvenience at first, they centralize the circulars and keep the overall community looking cleaner. Always have a garbage can next to these mail locations.
- ❑ If you have oil-fired heating equipment and you see a puff of thick black smoke, it is time to service your burner before you have operating problems.
- ❑ You should always have carpet installed in closets so that if a portion of the carpet in the main living space is damaged, there are places from which to take matching pieces.

❑ Black is a stately color for an entrance door until it gets nicked and scratched; then black shows all imperfections.

❑ Deep blue pool paints accentuate the water better than light blue paints.

❑ Freshly baked cookies make a rental office smell like home, and visitors love to snack on them!

❑ If you do a mailing to market your units, put a trinket in the envelope. "Lumpy mail" always draws more attention.

❑ If your maintenance technician claims to know all about plumbing and proceeds to solder a pipe joint without "fluxing" it . . . get out the water buckets.

❑ If you clean the air-conditioner intake fins once a year before turning the unit on, it will last much longer and cool much more efficiently.

❑ Advertisements offering "rent specials" increase the phone traffic, but they don't ensure more financially qualified renters.

❑ Clean storm drains and gutters can save roofs and structures; always keep them free of debris.

❑ If you are repaving, don't schedule the work during weather that is less than 55 degrees.

❑ If you are putting concrete sidewalks in, start the process on a weekday after kids are in school and finish in time to let it set before they get home!

❑ Gray floors in heating rooms show leaks and stains immediately, so you'll know of a small problem before it is a big one.

❑ Kale and winter pansies are "color" you can add to the property in cold weather.

❑ Residents to your community should always be welcomed in signage and in person.

❑ If you have decks or enclosures made of pressure-treated wood, it darkens if left unprotected. Semitransparent stains can hide discoloration and won't peel like paint.

❑ If people are cutting around the building's grounds to get to parking areas, place a post-and-rail fence diagonally from the corner of the building to the corner of the sidewalk. You can adorn it with small bushes and the grass will grow without the footpath.

❑ Changing flags as they dull or fray is an instant eye-catcher.

❑ If you leave the blinds open on an empty unit, people then know the unit is empty and may get a little more than curious.

❑ If you leave the heat on in vacant units in the winter, it will keep pipes from freezing and bursting.

❑ Roommates never understand why paying "their half" of the rent is not okay.

❑ Motorcycles don't belong parked in the living room (yes, I've seen it several times).

❑ Steel wool placed in openings in walls and floors impedes the progress of rodents entering the apartments.

❑ Dryer vents, even if located high on a wall, should be affixed with screening; otherwise, rodents will sense the heat, and mice can climb walls.

❑ If bedbugs are found in an apartment, cushion-type furniture should be discarded; otherwise you will not rid the unit of the bugs.

❑ Residents are famous for pulling batteries out of smoke alarms because they are set off when cooking.

❑ Leaving crawl space doors and windows open in the winter will lead to broken or frozen pipes.

❑ One good way to determine a problem with piping in a heating room is to color code the pipes. Paint the cold pipes one color, the hot pipes another color, gas lines a third, and oil lines a fourth. Then label the lines directionally so you know the flow. Presto, finding a problem becomes much easier.

❑ The last task that should be undertaken in any apartment make-ready is floor finishing. Too often the mistake is made to do the floors first. If improperly coordinated, the new flooring will be damaged before the resident ever gets to move in.

Glossary

Absorption chiller   Cooling system used mostly in high-rise buildings that utilizes steam from the heating system and compresses it.

Accredited Residential Manager   Professional designation given to an individual who completes the Institute of Real Estate Management's training program; also known as ARM.

Actual cash value   Insurance term for a pay out on a loss that pays the insured replacement cost minus depreciation.

Ad valorem tax   Property tax that is based on the value of the property.

Apartments   Residential units that are offered for rent or lease.

Apartments.com   Internet advertising organization whose fee is based on a monthly advertising fee.

Archive capability   Term applied to a computer's ability to store old information.

Arrears   Back rent owed by a resident to the owner.

Assignment   Provision in a lease whereby the leaseholder has the right, with restrictions, to assign responsibility for the lease to a third party, usually with review and acceptance by the landlord.

Baseboard heating system   Heating system that uses hot water that travels to the apartments through radiation pipes or coils located in the baseboard or floor of the apartment rooms.

Beta test   New technology tested under real circumstances by property owners, either for a vendor (before the technology's commercial release) or on a small scale for themselves (to ascertain the tool's utility before purchase).

Binder   Insurance term referring to a document that "binds" the insurer to coverage for the insured.

Capital reserve account Account, usually established at time of purchase and generally equivalent to one month's mortgage payment, that is maintained and meant to be used for large onetime expenses or improvements.

Cash flow Income minus expenses, including financing costs such as interest and principal.

Centrifugal chiller Central cooling system, used mostly in high-rises, that operates independent of the building's heating system and does not need to utilize steam.

Certificate of occupancy Document issued by a locally governing authority that certifies an apartment is properly prepared for occupancy.

Certified Apartment Manager Professional designation given to an individual who successfully completes the National Apartment Association's training program; also known as CAM.

Certified Apartment Property Supervisor Professional designation given to an individual who successfully completes the National Apartment Association's training program; also known as CAPS.

Certified Property Manager Professional designation given to an individual who successfully completes the Institute of Real Estate Management's training program; also known as CPM.

Cheat sheet Synopsis of an apartment community that is usually left by the phone for a rental agent to use when receiving an inquiry for rental.

Closing rate Ratio of total applicants who end up renting an apartment.

Common area Any area defined in a home owner's association arrangement as being owned and maintained in common by all owners. This term can also apply to commercial real estate.

Common area maintenance In commercial real estate, when leaseholders are responsible for a calculated, proportional share of expenses incurred in regard to space and functions that all leaseholders benefit from. Also referred to as CAM charges.

Condominiums Real estate for sale in an arrangement whereby property and building elements are owned in "common" by all unit owners and common area expenses are shared equally by all owners. The managing of such an entity is usually accomplished through a board of directors made up of owners.

Cosigner Individual who agrees to sign a lease with an applicant and become equally responsible for all debt and damages; the cosigner is often viewed as a financial backer.

Cost approach Appraisal practice and term whereby the appraiser values a property by what the replacement cost of a property would be minus depreciation.

Cost per lease What a particular form of advertising costs per lease executed from that advertising source.

Curb appeal Term used to explain how a property presents itself to the public who walks and drives by.

Depreciation   Accounting practice that recognizes a property suffers wear and tear over time, so owners can deduct a specific portion of the value of the property from their taxes.

Display ad   Print advertisement that includes some type of graphics.

Drive-by and walk-by traffic   Term used to describe how many prospective renters first inquire about a property; they simply walk or drive onto the property to make an actual visit to the rental office.

Due diligence   Contractually agreed period of time, once an offer for sale has been accepted, during which a potential purchaser can thoroughly investigate, financially and physically, all aspects of the intended purchase.

Equal Credit Opportunity Act   Federal legislation requiring that if applicants are denied rental for bad credit, they must be given an adverse action letter indicating why they were denied.

Equity   Amount equal to the value of the property minus the balance owed on loans secured by the property.

Fee management   Arrangement where an owner of multifamily real estate chooses to hire a management company for a fee to manage all or certain aspects of the owner's property.

Flipping   Buying a property for the purpose of a short-term resale, presumably at a higher value.

Gross potential income   Maximum income that can be realized from a rental property based on full occupancy and receipt of 100 percent of expected rents.

Home owner's association   Real estate entity that manages the business of a shared ownership situation, given its authority by laws constructed at the origin of the community; this is accomplished through an elected board of directors.

HUD   U.S. Department of Housing and Urban Development.

Income approach   Appraisal practice and term whereby the appraiser values a property based on income derived from it.

IREM   Institute of Real Estate Management.

Lead   Any contact with an individual who seems interested in renting, whether it is a phone lead, an Internet lead, advertisement, or in-person referral.

Leverage   Buying into an investment with a mortgage and minimal personal cash.

Line item budget   Process of identifying very specific aspects of an operation by creating a separate "line" for each selected item in a budget, as opposed to grouping common expense items together.

Loan to value   Ratio of how much a lender will allow to be borrowed, as opposed to the appraised value of a property; usually used in a refinance.

Lockbox   Third-party rent acceptance system that is usually administered by financial institutions; rent is paid not to the ownership but to the third party.

Make-readies   Vacant units being prepared for rental.

Month to month   Lease terms that exist only for the period of the present month, which can be mutually extended for a subsequent month by the leaseholder and the landlord.

Move-in checklist   Report used to allow a new resident to inspect an apartment prior to renting and check off any issues that need to be addressed.

Multiple listing service   Central clearinghouse that realtors collectively use to list properties for sale; also known as MLS.

NAA   National Apartment Association.

Net operating income   Calculation of income and expenses before debt service without regard for cash invested; also known as NOI.

Nonrenew   Indication to a resident of the owner's intent not to renew a lease that is about to expire.

Operating budget   Tool constructed and used in management to predict and review income and expenses.

Operations and maintenance program   Required environmental programs that property ownership must adhere to; if terms were agreed upon in securing financing, the financier is the party requiring the programs. Also known as O&M.

OSHA   Occupational Safety and Health Administration.

Pass-through charges   Fees that are charged to a resident or applicant that cover the exact cost of the service rendered; these fees are simply passed through from the management or ownership to the resident or applicant.

Portfolio   Either an owner's group of properties or a manager's assigned group of properties under his or her responsibility.

Proofs   Sample advertisements for review before they appear in publication.

Purchase order   Form used to allow a vendor/supplier to fill an order based on a written request; this request usually itemizes the purchases.

Quiet enjoyment   Lease term to describe the overall living right a resident can expect, relative to other residents' behavior.

Ready to show   Describes an apartment that is prepared to the point that it can be shown to a prospective resident.

Rental criteria   Posted requirements in rental offices in regard to qualifying for a rental; this posting is required per fair housing regulations.

Rent.com   Internet advertising organization that charges fees based on actual rentals approved.

Rent control and rent stabilization   Ordinances established by municipalities that restrict or control the level of rents and rent increases an ownership that operates a rental property can charge leaseholders.

Rent roll   List that shows occupant, apartment number, rent, type of unit, and security deposit; ownership can augment the list to include other information.

Replacement cost   Insurance term whereby the insurer pays the insured on a loss an amount equal to the actual replacement cost(s), not accounting for depreciation.

Reservation fee   Fee taken upon acceptance of an application for an apartment that is usually applied to the move-in security deposit; it essentially reserves a particular apartment and is nonrefundable should the applicant decide not to rent the apartment.

Resident referrals   When a current or former resident recommends the community in question to another possible resident.

Return on investment   The financial return to investors based on their original cash investment; also known as ROI.

Run with the land   Obligations that contractually and legally pass from owner to owner when a property is sold; the new owner has the responsibility to fulfill all responsibilities.

Sales or market approach   Appraisal practice and term whereby the appraiser values the property by comparing one property to similar properties in the same market.

Schedule of estimated repairs   List of costs for replacement or repair of damaged items, usually given at move-in, so that residents know what damaged items will cost them.

Scope of work   Delineating, in writing, the exact details of a proposed repair or construction project.

SCRA   U.S. Servicemembers Civil Relief Act; this law protects military members from being held to lease terms if the government redeploys the individuals.

Seasonal color   Flowers and bushes that are changed out as the seasons change to maintain bright color in strategic locations on a property.

Section 8 programs   Federal, state, and local housing assistance programs governed and administrated through the Department of Housing and Urban Development. A recipient applies for and receives rental assistance based on income and family composition.

Security deposit   Funds used to secure an apartment for rental and safeguard the ownership should rent go unpaid or damage occur to the apartment. Amount of deposit is regulated by the state or municipality and is usually refundable.

Service agreement   Document used to set the terms between a service provider and an owner or a management company.

Site visit   Ownership or management regularly visiting and inspecting a property site that is separate from the home office.

Steam heating system   Central heating system that heats water to steam; then the steam is circulated throughout the building through heat registers and coils.

Stems, seats, and O-rings   Plumbing parts used in faucets.

Syndication   Type of investment group that has many investors and a large property portfolio.

Tax-deferred exchanges   Real estate transaction where an investor trades up to a larger property, thereby avoiding having to immediately pay capital gains taxes.

Traffic log   Report used to chart how people contact and find out about a community; used correctly, a traffic log can determine the best advertising source.

Turnover rate   Percentage of total apartment units that vacate residents in a given time period.

Useful life   Term in years given to certain building infrastructure or machinery to describe its functional life or anticipated life span.

Vacancy decontrol   Term that applies to rent control ordinances, whereby a newly vacated apartment is exempt from the restrictions under rent control.

Vacancy report   Report that varies from company to company that gives basic information about vacant apartments and upcoming vacancies in a prescribed period of time.

Walk-through inspection   Either the management or a resident literally walking through the apartment or complex and reviewing specific aspects of each.

Warrant of removal   Court order served on a resident who has been issued a judgment by the ruling court to vacate an apartment and return possession to the owner.

Index

absentee ownership/management, 23–25, 50–53, 62–63, 205–209
accredited resident manager (ARM), 10, 60
acquisition of property, *see* takeover process
addenda, to lease, 171–173
adult communities, 107
adverse action letter, 126
advertising
  in branding process, 252
  contact information and, 212
  effective forms of, 123–124
  for employees, 234, 236
  fair housing regulations and, 107–110, 114, 115, 213–214
  importance of, 204, 211–212, 248
  Internet, 80, 122–123, 124, 192–194, 214–215
  proofs in, 212
  traffic logs and, 118–120, 123, 124, 132–133, 213
aftermarketing, 131
age, of property, 55
air conditioning, *see* HVAC systems
alarm systems, 75
amenities, 30, 72–75, 211–212
Apartment Condition Report, 17–18
apartments (units)
  due diligence process and, 15–18, 22, 203

  as term, 22, 211
  in value creation, 73
  see also community
application-qualifying process
  application fees, 93, 219
  denials, 126
  federal fair housing laws concerning, 105, 106–111, 114, 115, 213–214
  initiating, 125–126
  Rental Application, 111, 112, 120–122
  rental criteria in, 36–39, 93, 106–113, 120, 125–126, 161, 165, 217–220
  standardizing, 95, 126
appraisals
  property tax, 48–49
  refinancing, 82–85
arrears, 34, 38–39
asbestos hazard, 6, 172–173

background checks
  on potential employees, 235
  on potential residents, 111, 125, 126
back rent agreements, 38–39
bankruptcy, 39
baseboard hot water systems, 199–200
baseline income budget, 29–31
bathrooms, 168
beta-testing, 192

About the Author

MIKE BEIRNE is a veteran of twenty years in the multifamily industry and has experienced all levels of operations and management. Presently, he is the executive vice president of The Kamson Corporation, one of the largest privately held real estate investment and management organizations in the United States. The Kamson Corporation consists of more than seventy-five separate entities and approximately 650 employees. It has been named by market industry professionals as the "Best Management Company" in their market.

Beirne holds a New Jersey and California real estate license. His experience is unique in that he has managed real estate in all four corners of the country. He has also managed at all levels in many industry disciplines, including multifamily rental, commercial, homeowner's association management, new construction, and master planned communities. In addition to operations and management, he has been a consumer of multifamily housing as the director of housing of a nationwide firm where he engaged with multiple properties across the United States.

Beirne serves on the National Apartment Association's board of directors as a regional vice president, as well as on the legislative and curriculum development committees. He also sits on the board of directors of the New Jersey Apartment Association and is currently the chair of its legislative committee.

A strong advocate for the industry, Beirne has written for *UNITS* magazine, *Multifamily Executive, AIM* magazine, and *The APTS Magazine,* and he is a frequent presenter at local and national conferences, sought after for his experience and expertise in people management, innovation, and strategic thinking. A graduate of Temple University and a native Californian, he believes that people are *any* industry's greatest asset. Beirne can be reached at his website www.mikebeirne.net.

Look for These Exciting Real Estate Titles at
www.amacombooks.org/realestate

A Survival Guide for Buying a Home by Sid Davis $17.95

A Survival Guide for Selling a Home by Sid Davis $15.00

Are You Dumb Enough to Be Rich? by G. William Barnett II $18.95

Everything You Need to Know Before Buying a Co-op, Condo, or Townhouse by Ken Roth $18.95

Make Millions Selling Real Estate by Jim Remley $18.95

Mortgages 101 by David Reed $16.95

Real Estate Investing Made Simple by M. Anthony Carr $17.95

The Complete Guide to Investing in Foreclosures by Steve Berges $17.95

The Consultative Real Estate Agent by Kelle Sparta $17.95

The Home Buyer's Question and Answer Book by Bridget McCrea $16.95

The Landlord's Financial Tool Kit by Michael C. Thomsett $18.95

The Property Management Tool Kit by Mike Beirne $19.95

The Real Estate Agent's Business Planner by Bridget McCrea $19.95

The Real Estate Agent's Field Guide by Bridget McCrea $19.95

The Real Estate Investor's Pocket Calculator by Michael C. Thomsett $17.95

The Successful Landlord by Ken Roth $19.95

Who Says You Can't Buy a Home! by David Reed $17.95

Your Successful Real Estate Career, Fourth Edition, by Kenneth W. Edwards $18.95

Available at your local bookstore, online, or call 800–250–5308

Savings Start at 35% on Bulk Orders of 5 Copies or More!
Save up to 55%!
For details, contact AMACOM Special Sales
Phone: 212-903-8316. E-mail: SpecialSls@amanet.org